# BROADWAY MUSICALS

GUYS & DOLLS

ROBERT MARTHA
ALDA STEWART

SAM
LEVENE

BIGLEY

# BEN BRANTLEY

# BROADWAY MUSICALS

FROM THE PAGES OF

**The New York Times**

ABRAMS, NEW YORK

# CONTENTS

MAJESTIC
MARY EZIO
MARTIN PINZA
IN SOUTH PACIFIC
N.Y. DRAMA CRITICS CIRCLE
"A masterpiece. One of the greatest musical plays in the history of the American theatre. Mary Martin is delightful and utterly darling. Pinza is superb."

BIALYSTOC PRE

KATZ

A STREETCAR NAMED MURRAY

HIGH BUTTON JEWS

47TH STREET

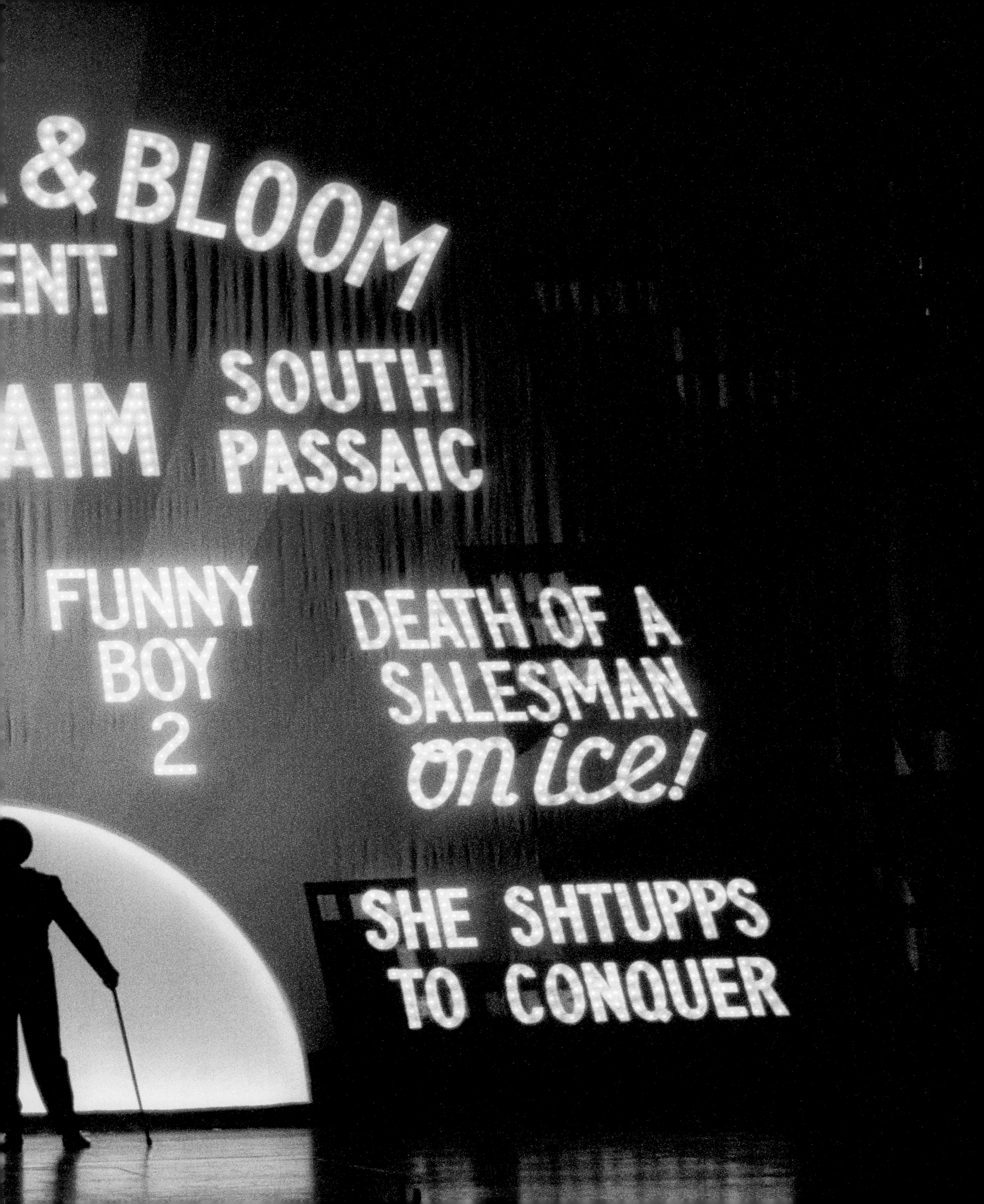

& BLOOM
ENT
AIM
SOUTH
PASSAIC
FUNNY
BOY
2
DEATH OF A
SALESMAN
on ice!
SHE SHTUPPS
TO CONQUER

# INTRODUCTION

## BEN BRANTLEY

The pieces assembled here—culled from more than a century of reviews and features from the *New York Times*—follow the winding journey of a mongrel art form in search of its own identity. I mean the musical, which is alternately classified in these pages as the musical comedy (when it's feeling giddy, which is much of the time) and the musical play or even the musical drama (for the more rare occasions when it's sober and thoughtful). While today there are many who would passionately argue that the musical is the United States's most original contribution to world theater, for much of its young life this shifting, hybrid genre had trouble getting even a little respect.

Part of the fascination for me in putting together this collection (with the invaluable oversight of editors Susan Homer and Caitlin Kenney, and designer Sarah Gifford) was in observing the changing tone of reviews over a century, as they bounce off and sometimes echo their very mutable subject. These scribes—who include two men who would go on to become formidable American cultural pundits (Alexander Woollcott and Frank Rich) and two who would have Broadway theaters named after them (Brooks Atkinson and Walter Kerr)—not only chronicled the musical. They also teased, chastised, fretted over, smiled upon, and (on occasion) worshipped it.

Sometimes—especially if you're familiar with the shows being talked about—you may imagine you hear the other side of that dialogue in the scores of composers like Jerome Kern, Richard Rodgers, and Stephen Sondheim, and in the words of Lorenz Hart, Oscar Hammerstein II, or Cole Porter. If you listen, you'll realize there's a lot of very lively conversation going on in these pages. And like the story of its ever-evolving subject, that conversation twists, circles, doubles back, pounces, and contradicts itself.

Certainly, describing the musical as an "art form" would have occasioned eye-rolling and hoots from many of the *Times* writers who show up early in these pages. The musical entertainments of the opening years of the twentieth century existed to divert, to comfort, and to titillate, a form of escapism from the fatiguing big-city burdens of getting and spending. They were, in other words, meant for that enduring archetype among theatergoers, the tired businessman (or as Woollcott, the fabled Algonquin-table phrasemaker, called him, "the exhausted commercial gentleman").

The gold standard for these frolics were the revues of Florenz Ziegfeld, the producer whose *Follies* (an essential part of the hedonist's cityscape from 1907 to 1931) gave burlesque a luxurious shimmer of glamour and respectability, while vaudeville acts (Fanny Brice! W. C. Fields! Will Rogers!) were presented as if they were visiting royalty. These productions were accorded a winking deference by *Times* writers, who paid sincere tribute to Ziegfeld's entrepreneurial genius and chutzpah.

But from the turn of the twentieth century into the Jazz Age and the Great Depression, whenever American musical shows pretended to be something more than excuses for serving corn and cheesecake and (at the high end) gilded spectacle, *Times* critics were quick to call their bluff. Operettas, imported from Europe and written by the likes of Sigmund Romberg and Victor Herbert, were another matter. They had the class conferred by their continental pedigrees and close kinship to opera itself, which qualified as Art with a capital A. An unsigned review of Franz Lehár's *The Merry Widow*, which arrived in New York in 1907, ended a breathless paean to the production's civilized virtues with the assertion that, in addition to being jolly and amusing and charming, it offered "the greatest kind of a relief from the American musical comedy."

But what exactly was this clumsy, lowbrow, native-born entertainment that was dismissed so flippantly and so regularly by those who wrote of it? No one seemed to be quite sure. Reviewing a 1914 show called *Watch Your Step*, the *Times* said, with the world-weary tone it affected for the consideration of frivolous matters, "So many things have been called musical comedies that *Watch Your Step* might as well be called one."

That show, by the way, featured the first complete score from a young composer named Irving Berlin (whose tunes, it was conceded, were most hummable), and its stars included the famous husband-and-wife dance team Vernon and Irene Castle. But finally, wrote the reviewer, *Watch Your Step* was really "vaudeville done handsomely." The show's

**OPPOSITE, CLOCKWISE FROM TOP LEFT:** Irene and Vernon Castle in *Watch Your Step*, 1914; Helen Barnes in Florenz Ziegfeld's *Midnight Frolic* at the New Amsterdam Theatre, New York, c. 1915; Donald Brian and an unidentified actress in *The Merry Widow*, 1911.

Copyright 1911
Charles Frohman

book writer, Harry B. Smith, was damned with an amiable aside: "He was in good form when he did his part, and he was careful not to get in anybody's way."

Five years later, Alexander Woollcott would note with deadpan astonishment of a new show called *Irene*, which promised to be a hit, "It has a plot. You never can tell what you are going to find in a musical comedy these days." Still, plots, it seemed, mostly existed merely to string together (to quote Woollcott in the same review) "girls and music and jokes and dances and scenery." And well on into the 1930s, *Times* critics continued to discuss musicals as if they were madcap, flighty young relatives, the kind you might spend a pleasant evening or two with and then send on their way with a pat on their tousled heads. "Crackbrained" was a common description for them, and it was meant kindly.

Flash forward to Howard Taubman, writing in the *Times* in 1964 of a show about a Yiddish milkman on a Russian shtetl that would occupy the Imperial Theatre for much of the next decade: "It has been prophesied that the Broadway musical theater would take up the mantle of meaningfulness worn so carelessly by the American drama in recent years. *Fiddler on the Roof* does its bit to make good on this prophecy." What's this? A little old musical being discussed in such highfalutin terms and with such solemn expectations? Could it be that in the four decades since Woollcott reviewed *Irene*, the crackbrained little brother of Broadway had grown up to the point that it could wear "the mantle of meaningfulness"?

By then New York had experienced the sentimental masterworks of Richard Rodgers and Oscar Hammerstein II—"integrated" shows that wove song into stories like *Oklahoma!* and *Carousel* and *South Pacific*. Now, according to Taubman, with *Fiddler on the Roof*, the musical had achieved such heights that it might well rank with, or even replace, on Olympus

the probing, socially earnest American drama, the form of O'Neill and Williams and Miller.

Ah, would that we could stop at such a lofty pinnacle and let an art form stand tall in its hard-won maturity, surveying all it has accomplished. But this book still has another forty-some years to cover. And there will be much lamentation over the state of the musical during those next decades. It will even be suggested that, for all intents and purposes, the musical is if not dead then an elderly anachronism, given either to coasting on the vestigial glow of its glory years or desperately dressing up and pretending to be one of those rock 'n' roll–loving youngsters. The moment for reverence for the musical was, it would appear, short-lived.

Of course it's hardly that simple. Art never progresses in a straight line, or never for long, anyway. It would be satisfying to read the history of musicals according to, say, the principles of Thomas Kuhn's theories of scientific revolutions—as a series of increasingly sophisticated paradigms that individually set the shape and tone for what followed until the older version was replaced by a new one.

To some extent, that theory has been applied to musicals, in a hazy and mythologizing way. According to this point of view, there were musicals before and after *Oklahoma!*, the 1943 Rodgers and Hammerstein hit about farmers, cowhands, and love in wide-open spaces. Before, musicals were silly and scattershot; after, they were far more likely to be (to quote Lewis Nichols about *On the Town* in 1944) a "well-knit fusion of the respectable arts."

But this theory doesn't account for another, much earlier musical, which also featured a book and lyrics by Hammerstein, working with another composer, Jerome Kern: *Show Boat*, which opened in 1927 to the same kind of appreciative amazement that would later greet *Oklahoma!*

"To recount in any detail the plot of a musical comedy is usually a silly and banal business," wrote Brooks Atkinson, the *Times*'s longest-running critic, in his opening night review. But the way in which Hammerstein's adaptation brought the characters to life from the Edna Ferber novel of the same title, Atkinson said, "is something else again."

Then again, in 1941, two years before *Oklahoma!* opened, Atkinson applauded *Lady in the Dark*—a show about (gulp!) psychoanalysis by the composer Kurt Weill and the playwright Moss Hart—for calling itself "a musical play" as opposed to "a musical comedy." What that means, Atkinson explained, "is a drama in which the music and the splendors of the production rise spontaneously out of the heart of the drama, evoking rather than embellishing the main theme." When Lewis Nichols reviewed *Oklahoma!* (which also called itself a "musical play"), he made fewer grand claims for it, though he suggested in his final sentence that perhaps *Oklahoma!* should be called a "folk operetta," adding, "whatever it is, it's very good."

So *Oklahoma!* didn't immediately register the revolutionary shock waves we now like to attribute to it. (Readers who enjoy the haughty wisdom of hindsight will have many opportunities to play Monday morning quarterback to *Times* reviewers. Just remember, they were usually writing from first impressions on the very night that they saw the show.) Only afterward would *Oklahoma!* be described as the show that changed everything. Writing about *Bells Are Ringing* in 1956, Atkinson said, "There have not been so many surprised hellos, inept song cues and dance signals since *Oklahoma!* drove hackneyed musical comedy out of business."

That admonitory note is heard often in the reviews of the 1940s and '50s. If musicals became more thoughtful in those decades, so too did the sound of *Times*' criticism. The jauntiness that characterized the reviews from the beginning of the century through the Great Depression is replaced by a stricter and more measured tone of appraisal. The idea seems to be that if musicals are asking to be taken seriously, they should

expect to be judged by sterner standards. *Times* critics were now watching the musical as if it were a reformed alcoholic in danger of backsliding. In 1959, Atkinson, reviewing Rodgers and Hammerstein's *The Sound of Music*, can be found taking to task the creators of *Oklahoma!* themselves. "It is disappointing to see the American musical stage succumbing to the clichés of operetta," he writes. "The revolution of the Forties and Fifties has lost its fire."

But had it really? The same year that gave us *The Sound of Music* also provided *Gypsy*—a "musical fable" about the last days of vaudeville (featuring a psychologically devastating portrait of the ultimate stage mother, played by Ethel Merman)—and a show that many critics consider the greatest American musical ever. And two years earlier had seen the opening of *West Side Story*, a tragedy of love on the mean streets of New York that ventured into unexpected social terrain while taking character-defining dance to unprecedented levels of complexity.

From reading the *Times*, you wouldn't have thought that these shows (both, as it happens, directed by Jerome Robbins) were watershed works. Yet *Gypsy*, in particular, is greeted with new claims for its depth and significance every time it is revived on Broadway (that's four times and counting). Frank Rich, reviewing a production starring Tyne Daly in 1989, felicitously called the show Broadway's "own brassy, unlikely answer to *King Lear*. It speaks to you in one way when you are a child, then chases after you to say something else when you've grown up." (That "you" might be said to embrace the theatergoing public in general, and we've included reviews of revivals that reflect such changes of perspective.)

Yet despite Taubman's claims for the enhanced stature of musicals with the arrival of *Fiddler on the Roof*, Atkinson wasn't wrong to sense,

OPPOSITE: A scene from *Oklahoma!*, 1943. **ABOVE, LEFT:** Clockwise from top left, Mary Martin, Joseph Stewart, Kathy Dunn, William Snowden, Lauri Peters, Mary Susan Locke, Evanna Lien, and Marilyn Rogers in *The Sound of Music*, 1959. **ABOVE, RIGHT:** Karen Moore, Ethel Merman, and Jacqueline Mayro in *Gypsy*, 1959.

INTRODUCTION

as he neared the end of his four-decade career (which had begun under the byline of "J. Brooks Atkinson"), that the musical that had grown and blossomed during his tenure was showing signs of atrophy. The 1960s had their share of Broadway hits that were built according to the now long-standard template for so-called "organic" musicals: *Camelot, Oliver, Funny Girl*, and (most enduringly) *Hello, Dolly!*, among others.

But there is also an increasing and uneasy awareness that the Rodgers and Hammerstein model for storytelling through song was becoming obsolete. For one thing, the musical's relationship to what America sings had shifted. For half a century, Broadway composers wrote many of the melodies that Americans danced to, whistled, and listened to on their phonographs. (It's a bit jolting to recall that matronly standards like "Some Enchanted Evening" were once the equivalent of Top 40 pop hits.)

Now the recording industry—and American culture in general—was moving to a more wayward beat and at a higher decibel level. Even as late as the early 1950s, what you heard on a Broadway stage was much like (if not identical to) what you heard on the radio. Ten years later, Broadway seemed hopelessly disconnected from a generation that listened to Elvis Presley and the Beatles. (True, the 1960 musical *Bye Bye Birdie* featured an Elvis-like character at its center, but only to make fun of him and send him packing.)

Rock 'n' roll—and its more neatly groomed, turtleneck-wearing cousins—was capturing the rhythms of broader changes in a fast-moving, fragmenting culture, in which traditional racial and sexual boundaries were called into question and, by some at least, freely crossed. *Hello, Dolly!* might be a hit, but it definitely wasn't hip. While American youth was doing the twist (and its freeform descendants), the American musical was still tap dancing.

Broadway did its best to get its groove back. It snapped its fingers to the swinging sounds of Burt Bacharach in *Promises, Promises*, a show about promiscuity in the workplace. It struck dark, cynical, socially conscious poses with musicals like *Cabaret* and *Chicago*. It even imported the hippies of *Hair* (which had invented a whole new self-defining category for itself: the "love-rock musical") from the Public Theater in Greenwich Village.

Most of these shows found an audience, sometimes an immense one. But the success of one kind of musical didn't guarantee that others in the same mold would succeed. There was no reliable form or formula to follow. From the 1970s to the present, you can detect a new buzz of anxious expectation in the *Times* reviews, which implicitly asks, *Is this the new* Oklahoma!*? Is this the show on which all others may be modeled for years to come?*

Such claims were made, more or less, for a dizzying diversity of shows: the confessional, navel-gazing *Chorus Line* (the perfect musical for the "Me Decade") in 1975; the cinematically fluid, Motown-inspired *Dreamgirls* in 1981; the spectacle-laden poperettas *Phantom of the Opera* and *Les Misérables* in the late 1980s; intimate psychological musicals like *March of the Falsettos* (1992) and *Next to Normal* (2009); and (oh, boy!) the musical as rock operetta with *Rent* (1996) and *American Idiot* (2010).

Many of us (this critic included) succumbed to the immediate visceral impact of such shows by writing something along the lines of "After this, the Broadway musical will never be the same again." Which I guess, looked at generously, was sort of true, since the Broadway musical continued to exist in a state of churning flux. But none of these musicals paved a safe and solid road for future productions to travel. The most reliable "new" kinds of musicals were those that recycled old material, like Disney's reinventions of its song-studded animated cartoons (*Beauty and the Beast* and *The Lion King*) or jukebox musicals, which strung together hits by one or more pop group, like *Mamma Mia!* (which used the songs of ABBA) and *Jersey Boys* (The Four Seasons).

**OPPOSITE, LEFT:** A scene from *Follies*, 1971. **OPPOSITE, RIGHT:** Joel Grey and a member of the cast in a scene from *Cabaret*, 1966. **LEFT:** Nathan Lane and Matthew Broderick in *The Producers*, 2001.

In creative terms, there was only one kind of musical that seemed to bear exciting fruit again and again. The problem was that all its incarnations bore the signature of one artist. As a composer and lyricist, Stephen Sondheim (a protégé of Oscar Hammerstein II) created his own unmistakable voice, which seemed to take apart and reassemble the traditional musical with an obsessive, loving, but brooding intelligence. Collaborating with writers and directors like Hugh Wheeler, George Furth, James Lapine, and Harold Prince, Sondheim turned the musical into a work of introspection, both for its psychologically fraught characters and for the form itself. Even if *Times* critics didn't always love him, they realized that a singular sensibility, unlike any before, was at work.

Probably the most obviously influential of Sondheim's shows was *Company*, the 1970 portrait of marital discontents in Manhattan, on which he collaborated with Furth (the librettist) and Prince (the director) and which established the nonlinear, so-called "concept musical" as a solid commercial proposition. Generally, though, his work is as difficult to categorize as it is to imitate, variations on genres as different as Viennese operetta (*A Little Night Music*), Victorian broadsheet ballads (*Sweeney Todd*), French pointillism (*Sunday in the Park with George*), and Japanese formalism (*Pacific Overtures*).

For me, *Follies* is the Sondheim work that resonates most penetratingly today. First staged in 1971 (and revived in 2001 and 2011), this collaboration with the playwright James Goldman assembles a group of one-time singers and dancers from a Ziegfeld-style revue. And their reunion becomes an occasion for them both to perform some of their old numbers and to look at their present lives through the prism of a musical past. Sondheim's pastiche songs here are tributes to and elegies for an earlier generation of Broadway shows. With its layering of sensibilities and use of quotes from another time, *Follies* might be called the first great post-modernist musical.

That makes the show sound chillier than it is, though. (Sondheim's reputation as an icy intellectual misses the deep love for the old-fashioned musical—and the role it played in so many lives—that saturates all of his work.) Let's say instead that *Follies* is the first great American musical to engage in a dialogue with its predecessors. There were pastiche musicals before, including *The Boy Friend* (1954), the British import that looked at the frothy 1920s boy-meets-girl frolic with a pencil-drawn arched eyebrow in the 1950s, or *Grease* (1972), which in turn made fun of the naiveté of the Elvis-loving 1950s.

Those shows, though, were spoofs and saturated in knowing irony. Another breed of self-conscious, retrospective musicals has emerged since then, which, if lacking the depth of *Follies*, shares much of its wit and affection in remembering musicals past. The best (and, as it happens, most commercially successful) of these shows are the work of men best known as satirists. And you'd expect them to skewer, slice, and roast the conventions of the classical storybook musical. Yet both *The Producers* (2001)—adapted by the comedian and filmmaker Mel Brooks from his own 1967 movie—and *The Book of Mormon*—conceived by the creators of the sacred cow–bashing animated series *South Park*—are valentines to the musical as the great American art form. They're ruder and cruder than anything Rodgers and Hammerstein might have come up with, but they look at what is generally perceived as an outmoded kind of entertainment not with a wink but with wide-eyed, ecstatic wonder.

These shows aren't parodies. Well, they are, but they're also celebrations, and they have it both ways. They send up *and* make love to the good old-fashioned musical and in the process rejuvenate it. They constitute two of the happier examples of a civilization whose culture at the moment—no matter how advanced its technology—seems to consist largely of quoting and recycling and respinning. No, neither is the next *Oklahoma!* But while we wait for the real thing, it's reassuring to know that a show like *The Book of Mormon*—the last of the musicals reviewed here— can still send crowds into ecstasy with a song, a dance, and a story.

# I. THE EARLY YEARS

"New York is the greatest of the country's Summer resorts," wrote the *New York Times*, its tongue probing its gentlemanly cheek, in 1915. Though hot months in the city were presumably even more unbearable in the early twentieth century than they are in the early twenty-first, there was an excellent reason to visit—or stick around in—Manhattan come late June. That was when Florenz (Flo, to his friends, who evidently included *Times* writers) Ziegfeld brought the latest edition of his *Follies* to town.

From 1907 into the early years of the Great Depression, *The Ziegfeld Follies* was the ne plus ultra of Broadway musical entertainments, the deluxe model to which all others aspired. Combining extravagantly (if skimpily) attired girls in extravagant settings, comedians, novelty dancers and vocalists, and the latest from Tin Pan Alley songwriters, the *Follies* turned vaudeville and dirty old burlesque into something grand. "The niche filled by the annual Ziegfeld production has become one so prominent and definite that an account of the entertainment calls for a description of its contents rather than an appraisal thereof," wrote the *Times* in 1920.

Those contents included names that would become legendary if they weren't already: Fanny Brice, a juggler named W. C. Fields, Billie Burke (aka Mrs. Florenz Ziegfeld), and Will Rogers, America's favorite cracker-barrel philosopher, of whom one *Times* critic observed memorably (anticipating generations of stand-up comics to come) that his "extemporaneous style of delivery needs the audiences; when practiced upon another actor the results are not happy." But the main event was always the glorified American girl. Describing one member of that breed in 1918, the *Times* drolly summed up the raison d'être of her species: "Miss Laurell opens the entertainment by posing atop the revolving globe, and later astonishes all by undertaking a regular part, with lines."

The *Follies* formula of feminine pulchritude plus songs and laughs was repeated in revues like *Earl Carroll's Vanities* and *George White's Scandals*. (The names speak volumes.) But the same elements also dominated what were beginning to be called book musicals, although as *Times* critics pointed out, plot was merely an excuse for all the other eye-popping, rib-tickling stuff. Some of the most popular works in the genre—which tended to involve mistaken identities in fashionable drawing rooms or on college campuses—were written for the Princess Theatre by P. G. Wodehouse (who became famous as the creator of Jeeves, the ultimate gentleman's gentleman), Guy Bolton, and a composer named Jerome Kern, who would assume immortal importance in the story of the American musical. The characters found in such shows were likely to be "not so much human beings as illustrated comics" from the funny papers, as the *Times* said. Alexander Woollcott, with typically grave flippancy, summed up the average book musical in these terms: "There was no plot and it was the fashion to call attention to the fact. 'Of course,' you would say, 'there isn't any plot to the darned thing, but it's amusing.' You never said: 'Of course there isn't any plot to the darned thing, so it's very amusing.'"

The (comparatively) highbrow theater patron might prefer the frothy, European-style operettas of Victor Herbert or Sigmund Romberg, which featured real singers (as opposed to singing actors, a distinction that was made in the *Times*) and production values to rival Ziegfeld's. When Franz Lehár's *The Merry Widow* arrived in New York in 1907, the *Times* reassured its readers, regarding the onstage presentation of a famous Parisian restaurant, "the Maxim's on view at the New Amsterdam will disappoint nobody, because it is more exciting than the real Maxim's." The same review noted of the show's signature waltz, "which everybody has talked about and which everybody will whistle and sing for the next few months," that it would surely now "be played in all restaurants and at all balls as it is in Europe."

Homegrown musicals, too, were generating songs that would be heard over all the country. And for those early years of the century, Broadway was America's hit factory, with composers like Kern, Irving Berlin, Cole Porter, and Rodgers and Hart contributing songs that (as the *Times* wrote of Berlin's score for *Watch Your Step* in 1914), were "born to be caught up and whistled at every street corner, and warranted to set any roomful a-dancing."

Then as now, it often took a star to sell a song. Fanny Brice would forever be associated with "My Man," and George M. Cohan owned "Yankee Doodle Dandy." When Marilyn Miller, a Ziegfeld protégée, appeared in the title role of *Sally*, the *Times* observed, she "seemed to feel that her elevation to stardom called for a greater show of effort. Whereupon, for this occasion, she appears to have gone searching about and returned with a voice." The description of singers' voices becomes increasingly particular and vivid in *Times* reviews. In 1920, it was noted that Eddie Cantor, appearing in a *Follies*, "sang a pair of characteristic songs characteristically." But in 1929, in a review of *The Little Show*, the paper remarked, simply but evocatively, on "the dark purple menace of Libby Holman in the blues."

By that time, a show had opened in New York that not only had the whole town talking but would in retrospect be regarded as the first great breakthrough American musical for its melding of songs and story. The critic Brooks Atkinson, who would rule as the *Times*' chief theater critic for the next several decades, had only accolades for the production, which was based on Edna Ferber's best-selling novel about riverboat entertainers, and adapted by a team that included the familiar names of Wodehouse, Bolton, and Kern. But it was the producer who was accorded the largest share of the credit: "*Show Boat* is, with a few reservations in favor of some of the earlier *Follies* and possibly *Sally*, just about the best musical piece ever to arrive under Mr. Ziegfeld's silken gonfalon." As is often the case, no one quite realized at the time what had been accomplished.

**OPPOSITE:** Fanny Brice, 1911.

# THE MERRY WIDOW

It was nearly 10:30 o'clock last night when the strains of the celebrated "Merry Widow" waltz floated over the footlights of the New Amsterdam Theatre, but it was not necessary to wait until then to know that this operetta was to become as popular in America as it has been in Europe since it was produced in Vienna in January, 1905.

The theatre was packed and all the available standing room was taken. It was one of the most brilliant audiences which has attended a New York first night in recent years. For the fame of this "widow" had preceded her, and very many persons in the audience had seen her in Europe and wished to know if she had lost any of her gayety in crossing the ocean. It should be stated at once that she had not, nor any of her melody either, as the audience quickly realized. The applause was almost terrifying in its intensity at times, and there were as many shouts of "Bravo!" as at a performance of *Pagliacci* when Caruso sings.

Every provincial capital in Europe has seen this operetta, which has just been introduced to us in the English version produced in London by George Edwardes at Daly's Theatre last Summer. The English version is practically a translation of the original libretto, with perhaps a few of the suggestive lines and situations accepted in Munich or Vienna eliminated. It is the story of a Marsovian widow's attraction for a Marsovian Prince, and the scenes are laid in Paris, commencing demurely enough in the Marsovian Embassy and ending in Maxim's, and the Maxim's on view at the New Amsterdam will disappoint nobody, because it is more exciting than the real Maxim's.

But it is on its music that *The Merry Widow* depends for its chief success, and which carries it into a class which compels one to remember *Fledermaus* and *La Grande Duchesse* to find anything to compare it with. There is the charming waltz, the "bal sirenen," which everybody has talked about and which everybody will whistle and sing for the next few months. And it will be played in all restaurants and at all balls as it is in Europe. Then there are the Maxim's song, the song of the Cavalier, "Villa," "A Dutiful Wife," and an amusing comic ditty called "The Women." Everything was encored last evening and pretty nearly everything deserved to be. It is all very jolly and amusing and charming, and the greatest kind of a relief from the American musical comedy.

Mr. Savage has provided a magnificent scenic and sartorial environment for the piece. The gowns in the first act were smart, in the second picturesque, and in the third dazzling. In fact, the scene in Maxim's was almost too exhilarating in its color scheme and gayety. When Eva Bennett entered, kicked a waiter's tray out of his hand and proceeded to kick all sorts of imaginary objects in the air there was nobody present who was unhappy.

Ethel Jackson was assigned to the title role. It was natural that she should be nervous at a performance of so much importance, and it is certain that she will play the part very much better to-night. Lilly Elsie, who played Sonia in London, was a demure widow, and that Sonia never was. Miss Jackson plays along truer lines. She comprehends the verve and joy of the part, as well as its seductiveness. She makes the waltz the dramatic moment in the action, as it should be, but she was always "the Merry Widow."

Donald Brian as Prince Danilo perhaps made the success of the evening. He was a complete surprise to those who had seen him in other parts. Lois Ewell was a very blonde Nathalie, R. E. Graham was an amusing Popoff, and Fred Frear a capital Nish. Eva Bennett and her last-act dance have already been mentioned.

The orchestra, under the direction of Louis F. Gottschalk, played with spirit, and a harp in the score provided a surprise for musical comedy goers.

Altogether it is very likely that *The Merry Widow* will remain on Forty-second Street for a very long time, and if Mr. Savage is serious in his announced intention to open another theatre in New York with another company in the same piece he must be considered a wise man.

**RIGHT:** A scene from *The Merry Widow*, c. 1907.

# WATCH YOUR STEP

Charles Dillingham has done it again. Not content to stage *Chin Chin* and call it a season's work, he went down from the Globe to the New Amsterdam Theatre last evening and there presented as gay, extravagant, and festive an offering as this city could possibly hope to see. For no particular reason this new piece is called *Watch Your Step*. It is one which the London dailies would describe in accents of horror as a "big, noisy, typically American entertainment," and which the London public would witness clamorously and with every evidence of high approval. As large a portion of the New York public as could be packed into the New Amsterdam last evening seemed uncommonly pleased, and with reason. *Watch Your Step* is no end of fun.

So many things have been called musical comedies that *Watch Your Step* might as well be called one. The programme sees fit to describe it as "a syncopated musical show." It is really vaudeville done handsomely. It is a large and expensive variety show, with Mr. Dillingham doing the booking in a prodigal mood and Irving Berlin called upon to do his best for all the acts. Mr. Berlin did his best and the result is highly entertaining. Also Mr. Dillingham did his best. Most of the chiefs of the assembled company could command the choicest position on a vaudeville bill and many of them have.

More than to anyone else, *Watch Your Step* belongs to Irving Berlin. He is the young master of syncopation, the gifted and industrious writer of words and music for songs that have made him rich and envied. This is the first time that the author of "Alexander's Ragtime Band" and the like has turned his attention to providing the music for an entire evening's entertainment. For it, he has written a score of his mad melodies, nearly all of them of the tickling sort, born to be caught up and whistled at every street corner, and warranted to set any roomful a-dancing.

Berlin has always enjoyed capturing a strain of fine, operatic music and twisting it to suit his own ragtime measures, and so in this,

his first musical comedy, it is altogether fitting and proper that he should escort the rest of the entertainers to the Metropolitan, where the ghost of Verdi might chant a protest against an irreverent chorus of syncopated classics, and where, as part of the fun, a mock Caruso can be seen singing against the unmannerly patter chorus in the boxes.

*Watch Your Step* affords this songwriter a rare opportunity. He has availed himself of it. In this new attack Berlin has found New York defenseless and captured it.

Of the entertainers, the happiest is surely Frank Tinney, one of the funniest men treading the boards today. He has come back from Europe with all his tricks and his manners unimpaired. Most of his jokes are new and all of them are funny.

Then there are the Castles, appearing largely as themselves in that cheerfully

personal way that is part of the vaudeville touch.

Mr. Castle is so variously competent that besides taking a stage fall that would make even Maude Eburne pale, he plays the traps and generally adds to the impression that *Watch Your Step* is not only as rapid, but just about as noisy as the *Twentieth Century Limited*. He dances several numbers with Mrs. Castle whose work is a delight.

These three entertain in their own fashion, and probably with many inventions of their own. The programme has it that the plot (if any) is by Harry B. Smith. He was in good form when he did his part, and he was careful not to get in anybody's way.

OPPOSITE: Irene and Vernon Castle, c. 1910. **ABOVE:** Sheet music for "Watch Your Step," 1915. Cover illustration by Al Barbelle.

# Leave It to Jane

The unmusical plays of George Ade had always a leaning toward musical comedy, which was his native genre; and now the best of them, having leaned a long time, has fallen. Or rather, Guy Bolton and P. G. Wodehouse have pushed it over, to music by Jerome Kern.

The plot, which always was a trifle light, falls easily within the scope of the sketchier stage; and the characters, which used to seem not so much human beings as illustrated comics from a college funny paper, are well within the range of song-and-dance acting. In a word, the new show at the Longacre has kept most of the quality of the original and added a very welcome investiture of melodic song and dance, gay costumes that are yet in excellent taste, and—last but not least in pulchritude, a chorus. Pulchritude has long been the word for choruses, as camouflage has become the moniker of curtain speeches.

Ah, the chorus: Learning rests lightly on the massive intellect of co-eds at this fresh water college. Digging Greek roots has not sullied the fair white symmetry of their hands, and abnormal psychology has left their hearts unclouded by any Freudian emotional complex. And how they do manage to dress on an undergraduate income! Radcliffe and Barnard have much to learn in the matter of Domestic Economy from this fresh water Atwater out in Indiana. One of them, unnamed in the program, but enshrined in the eye where fancy breeds, danced in a way that is rare, even upon dance-mad Broadway.

Jane, the college widow, who lured the star half back from the rival college, to the ruin of his affections and hers, was very capably played by Edith Hallor. Her Junonian smile invited, and her double-barreled searchlights swept the utmost depths of the ungraduate soul. When it came to siren stuff the whole college knew they could "leave it to Jane."

**ABOVE:** Cast of *Leave It to Jane*, c. 1917. **OPPOSITE:** Edith Hallor as Jane.

**ABOVE:** From left, W. C. Fields, Will Rogers, Lillian Lorraine, Eddie Cantor, and Harry Kelly in Florenz Ziegfeld Jr.'s *Follies* of 1918. **OPPOSITE:** Sheet music for "Any Old Time At All."

# FOLLIES *OF 1918*

The annual *Follies* of Florenz Ziegfeld, Jr., twelfth of the celebrated series, was given its premiere performance in these parts before an expectant and overflowing house last night at the New Amsterdam. It is a brave, bountiful, and beautiful show this season, possessed of all the gorgeousness which has distinguished its predecessors, and perhaps even a little bit more. The ever lavish Ziegfeld, mindful of the many fine scenes of the *Follies* of yesteryear, has seen to it that the new entertainment goes just a little further, as new entertainments always must, and the result is a succession of splendid vistas, smart drop curtains, and beautiful costumes. Beyond the shadow of a doubt, it will delight the soul of every *Follies* lover.

Apparently all of those who made up the first-night audience of notables were of this class, for the evening was a succession of receptions for the scenery and the performers. Lest the impression be conveyed that it is the greatest show of the world, let it be added that the new show has the weaknesses of preceding *Follies* as well as their points of strength. The comedy scenes contain no more than the legal amount of humor, and, as customary with the *Follies*, the biggest laughs are those brought into the show by its vaudevillians.

But with the *Follies* those matters generally take care of themselves before many weeks have passed. As played last night the show was a better entertainment than have been any of the recent *Follies* on the nights of their metropolitan premieres, and if the proportion of improvement is the same, there is reason to believe that the best *Follies* of them all will eventually grow out of the present show.

The scenic artist, of course, has been Joseph Urban, and he has managed to contribute at least half a dozen pictures which are remembered after the performance. Probably the best of these was a Japanese scene which came late in the evening, when the eye, all but satiated, could not appreciate it to the full. A patriotic finale to the first act was also splendidly mounted, thanks largely to Mr. Urban and in part to Ben Ali Haggin, one of whose tableaux brought down the curtain.

As for the list of entertainers, it is long, and fairly bristles with the names of the well known, most of whom have done their bits in the *Follies* before this. There were many favorites with the first-night crowd. Ann Pennington never danced quite so well as she did last night, and was rewarded with receptions which held up the entertainment each time she appeared. Marilyn Miller, making her first appearance as a *Follies* girl, was another who was wildly applauded. Miss Miller, possibly with recent triumphs in mind, carried a trifle too much assurance into her earlier numbers, but as the evening wore on she appeared at her best. In a Billie Burke costume, à la *Marriage of Convenience*, she captivated the house.

Lillian Lorraine, looking particularly pert in a feminine paraphrase of the garb of the French Blue Devils, was also among the principals, for the new *Follies* is nothing if not generous. Miss Lorraine also took part in a well-staged mirror scene, in which the delectable Fairbanks Twins reflected each other in an imaginary mirror and Miss Lorraine played opposite a very scared chorus girl named Marie Wallace. Another of the *Follies* girls is Kay Laurell, whom all early devotees of the series are certain to remember. Miss Laurell opens the entertainment by posing atop the revolving globe, and later astonishes all by undertaking a regular part, with lines.

The leaders among the men are Will Rogers, Eddie Cantor, W. C. Fields, Frank Carter, Harry Kelly, Savoy and Brennan, and Frisco. Rogers was at his best when he twirled the rope and chatted, particularly when he remarked that "England should give Ireland home rule, but reserve the motion picture rights." In addition to his role of rope twirler, Rogers was impressed into service at three or four other points along the line, with varying results.

A burlesque of Rogers's authorship, played with Harry Kelly, will go better when

the comedians learn where the laughs are, and Rogers's appearance in the role of the devil, in a scene in hell, was anything but a histrionic masterpiece. Rogers's extemporaneous style of delivery needs the audience; when practiced upon another actor the results are not happy.

W. C. Fields plays golf in the new show. Trick clubs and strange noises supply the major share of the humor of this scene; the comedian's extraordinary talent for juggling is taken advantage of not at all. Eddie Cantor runs through the entertainment this season, and is at his funniest in a scene in which he takes the aviator's test. His blackface bit before the curtain was funny here and there, but suffered a trifle from the need of a pencil, blue or otherwise. Savoy and Brennan amused the house vastly with one of their duologues, and the eccentric Frisco, brought downstairs from Mr. Ziegfeld's roof revue, also won applause.

The music is by Louis A. Hirsch and Dave Stamper, with an added patriotic number by Irving Berlin and a Victor Jacobi waltz. The best of the numbers is "In Old Versailles," sung by Allyn King. Otherwise the score touches no high spots, but is at all times sufficient to the purpose and the voices of the company.

# FOLLIES OF 1920

The unfolding of Mr. Ziegfeld's annual contribution to the gayety of the summer season took place last night at the New Amsterdam Theatre amid the scenes which have come to be associated with that momentous happening. The *Follies* of 1920 is a huge and fast-moving revue, somewhat less characteristically Ziegfeldian than some of its predecessors—several of the earlier entertainments have excelled it from the standpoint of beauty—but well stocked with talented performers and holding its own bravely until the final eleven-forty curtain. It is a good *Follies*, with all the traditions which are associated therewith.

The niche filled by the annual Ziegfeld production has become one so permanent and definite that an account of the entertainment calls for a description of its contents rather than an appraisal thereof. As a producer of revues of this kind Mr. Ziegfeld stands alone, and his ability to hit the popular mark has been so long a matter of record that it is no longer even to be marvelled at. Mr. Ziegfeld not only keeps pace with but anticipates the trend of the times in revues. The new show follows the prevailing mode in inclining more and more to drapes and away from mere scenery, it departs a bit from the Ziegfeldian tradition in offering a minimum of fine vistas, and—though it be heresy—it seemed last night to make a bit less of the Ziegfeld girls than has been the custom of the past.

It is in its principals that the new show is strongest. Of "book" there is comparatively none this year—James Montgomery had been expected to provide that feature, but the exigencies of *Follies* construction demanded that most of that be cast aside at the last moment—but there are some good scenes for all that. The talented Ray Dooley, for example, is hilariously funny in a skit which depends entirely upon her own gifts as a comedienne. Fanny Brice, working harder

and more often than she ever did before in her life, is quite at her most comical—which, it must be admitted, is hilarious enough. Charles Winninger, shamefully treated in the matter of material, extracts much from little, and Carl Randall, Jack Donahue, W. C. Fields, Van and Schenck, Mary Eaton (a *Follies* newcomer), and John Steel are among the others who contrive to make the revue what it is.

It begins with the chorus boys this year, but gets rapidly to a scene called "Creation" in which a girl posed in mid-air provides a striking figure. Later, in a Ben Ali Haggin picture, the unadorned feminine form came in for still further attention. Between these episodes there were paraded the succession of scenes which make up the *Follies*—many of them quite good to look at, and all filled with the things which are Ziegfeld.

It was Mr. Ziegfeld himself who led forth Eddie Cantor at a late hour, the comedian having been unprogrammed. The Cantor-Ziegfeld ovation was perhaps the greatest of the evening. Mr. Cantor sang a pair of characteristic songs characteristically. Miss Brice, among other things, offered variants of her vampire and ballet numbers,

as well as a "Florodora" number, and figured amusingly in a reminiscent automobile skit headed by W. C. Fields.

A youth named Jack Donahue contributed some eccentric dancing which met deserved approval, and Carl Randall danced both eccentrically and otherwise with vast success. The Messrs. Van and Schenck, appearing in various disguises, offered the harmony which has brought them fame, and Ray Dooley, as aforesaid, swept all before her in a skit in which she impersonated a squalling infant. John Steel, whose voice was one of the hits of last year's show, again won the vocal honors, even though he did not sing so well as a year ago. And there is also Bernard Granville, whom some people care for and others do not.

A theatre scene, with audience facing audience, is perhaps the outstanding novelty of the production.

. . . . . . . . . . . . . . . . . . . . . . . . .

**ABOVE:** Sheet music for "The Syncopated Vamp," from Florenz Ziegfeld Jr.'s *Follies* of 1920. **OPPOSITE:** The Cameron Sisters perform in a Florenz Ziegfeld production, c. 1920.

# FOLLIES *OF 1936*

If the 1936 edition offered nothing but Fannie Brice, most of us would feel sufficiently grateful. Fannie has been such a good sport for so many years that it is difficult as well as superfluous to attempt to separate the affection she has bred from the downright, wholesome enjoyment she supplies. Here you will see her up to all sorts of flamboyant, Bricean mischief—stretching her mobile mouth a hundred different ways to draw comedy out of her material, rolling those eloquent eyes, fairly engulfing the whole show. The coarse elegance she contrives for the upper-class English of Ira Gershwin's "Fancy Fancy," the infuriating temperament she puts into "Baby Snooks Goes Hollywood" and the grotesqueness of her burlesque of revolutionary dancing ("Rewolt," she screams with her wicked eyes crossed)—are Fannie in top form.

She has a capital partner in Bob Hope, who is gentleman enough to be a comrade and comedian enough to be funny on his own responsibility. In fact, most of the principals are well met in the current *Follies*. Hugh O'Connell is one of our most expansive merry-andrews and Eve Arden has an alert sense of humor. Here and there throughout the show the clowns satirize government spending, the grandiose promotion of super-specials from Hollywood, and amateur night on the radio. Without being devastatingly funny, the sketches are neatly written and they are acted in the highest good humor.

One major disappointment must be bluntly chronicled. After her cyclonic career abroad Josephine Baker has become a celebrity who offers her presence instead of her talent. They have given her ravishing settings, effulgent gowns or practically no costume at all, which is an improvement, but her singing voice is only a squeak in the dark and her dancing is only the pain of an artist. Miss Baker has refined her art until there is nothing left in it. When the two Nicholas Brothers follow her with some excellent Harlem hoofing out of the Bill Robinson curriculum they restore your faith in dusky revelry.

**OPPOSITE:** Fanny Brice and Bob Hope in Florenz Ziegfeld Jr.'s *Follies* of 1936. **BELOW:** The marquee for *The New 1936 Edition of Ziegfeld Follies*, Winter Garden Theatre, New York.

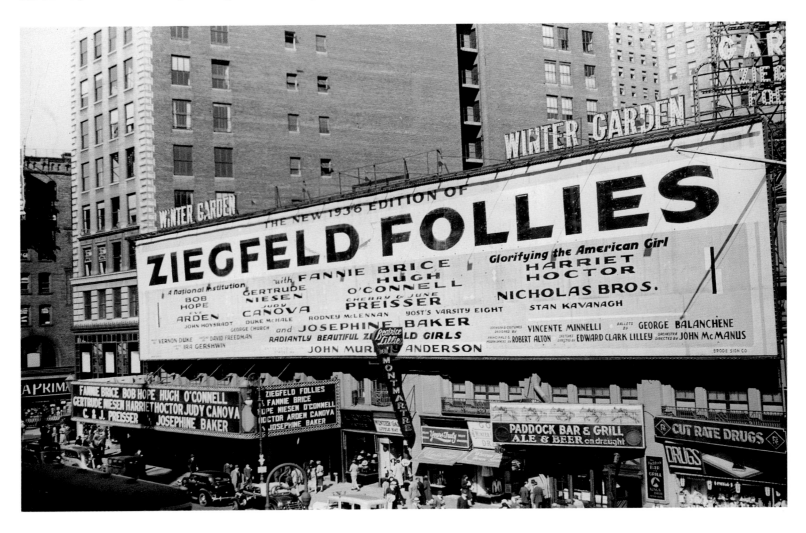

November 19, 1919

# *IRENE*

By ALEXANDER WOOLLCOTT

Broadway's desperate plight, with only seventeen or eighteen musical comedies on view, was magnificently relieved last evening when a new one called *Irene* was rushed into the breach at the Vanderbilt Theatre. This proved to be a brisk and pleasing piece, as moral as *Daddy Long Legs* and yet apparently full of things calculated to entrance the exhausted commercial gentleman. It has no prohibition joke, no Ford joke. It has no shimmy in word or deed. But it has a lot of catchy music. Also it has Edith Day and a comic fellow named Bobbie Watson. Also it has a plot. You never can tell what you are going to find in a musical comedy these days.

Not so very long ago, it was the way of these things to consist entirely of girls and music and jokes and dances and scenery. There was no plot and it was the fashion to call attention to the fact. "Of course," you would say, "there isn't any plot to the darned thing, but it's amusing." You never said: "Of course there isn't any plot to the darned thing, so it's very amusing." And the producers, stung to the quick, have taken to putting all sorts of things into their musical shows—plots and Julia Deans and everything.

The way now is to take a comedy that for some reason has not gone well, or that has not even been tried, diminish and elaborate the costumes, add twelve songs, stir passionately, and serve.

So it happened that a comedy called *Irene O'Dare*, and written some seasons ago by James Montgomery, author of *Ready Money*, was tried out on the road by a theatrical firm of bygone days known as Cohan & Harris, found wanting, shelved, and then taken down at last, renamed *Irene*, and hurried into New York to fill one of the vacant theatres.

*Irene* not only has a plot. It also has a sociological import. It is concerned with the adventures of three poor little shop girls who are taken up by a modiste, dressed perfectly elegantly, and introduced to society, where

they are actually taken for ladies. How shocking to think that the foundations of our society are as shaky as that! It fairly gives one the vapors just to contemplate the idea.

Of course the producers of this particular transformation had to go and spoil the moral by having Irene look eleven times as pretty in her plain little suit as she does when she emerges as a butterfly. She is brought out dressed like a showgirl on parade and the audience is expected to leap rapturously and say: "Why, she looks just like a lady!" when, as a matter of fact, she does not. It is all very confusing.

Irene is pleasantly embodied by Edith Day, who is pretty to behold, who sings passably, and who dances rather better than that. Indeed, everybody in the company dances a little bit better than they do anything else. Of course, as an actress Miss Day is handicapped by the fact that she is supposed to come wandering forlornly on in a drab

little dress and talk just a touch of a brogue. Whereupon every one thinks of *Peg o' My Heart* and Laurette Taylor. This makes them reminiscent, and that is enough to cramp any actress' style.

But if there is one thing the American theatre can be counted on to play to the Queen's taste, it is a male dressmaker. The male dressmakers in our shows are always good and the one in *Irene* is a perfect scream. His name is Bobbie Watson.

Dorothy Walters as Mrs. O'Hare and Walter Regan as a gentleman also acquit themselves creditably. They add good touches to a musical show that extracted from last night's audience the kind of audible approval which cannot be hired for the occasion.

. . . . . . . . . . . . . . . . . . . . . . . . .

**OPPOSITE:** Edith Day, c. 1920. **ABOVE:** Sheet music for "Alice Blue Gown" from *Irene,* 1919.

## REVIVAL

March 14, 1973

# IRENE *BUSTLES* MERRILY AND RELENTLESSLY

## 'THEY DON'T EVEN TAKE THEIR CLOTHES OFF'

By CLIVE BARNES

There is probably a market for *Irene*, the almost-new musical comedy that opened the completely new Minskoff Theatre last night, and I sincerely hope it finds it. One can only admire so much energy and effort.

The theater itself is large, spartan and yet not unattractive. The lack of a center aisle (a procedure called Continental seating but virtually unknown outside the United States) is a pity, but the sightlines are good, and the stage seems a decent size. So let us welcome the Minskoff Theatre, and may it be with us for many years.

The welcome for *Irene* must be a little more guarded, although doubtless many people will enjoy it. The elegant lady sitting next to me remarked to her husband halfway through the first act: "It is all so refreshing, and they don't take their clothes off." Well, I didn't stay for all of the curtain calls, but up until the time I left they hadn't.

*Irene* was a very considerable Broadway hit immediately after World War I in 1919, and perhaps it was felt appropriate to bring it back in triumph at the conclusion of the longest war in American history. However, tastes—and wars—have changed a little since 1919, and therefore naturally enough a few changes had to be made.

The project was masterminded by Harry Rigby, who won fame for first having the idea to resuscitate *No, No, Nanette*, and he adapted the original play by the late James Montgomery. From this adaptation a book has been devised by Hugh Wheeler and Joseph Stein. So one imagines that most of the book is of contemporary provenance.

The music—that is, the original music— is by Harry Tierney, and the lyrics are by Joseph McCarthy. But then there are additional music and lyrics by Charles Gaynor and Otis Clements (both of whom are alive and well). There are 13 numbers in the show; only 5 of them came from the original *Irene* and only 2 of them from Mr. Gaynor and Mr. Clements. So the music and lyrics are somewhat mixed up.

This would not matter very much if some kind of style had been imposed on the complete work, but often it seems to find its only common denominator in its almost relentless pulse. Too many cooks have in the past been known to have difficulty in the preparation of something even as simple as broth.

**LEFT:** A scene from the 1973 revival of *Irene*. In front, from left, Debbie Reynolds, George S. Irving, Carmen Alvarez, and Monte Markham. Carrie Fisher is visible between Alvarez and Markham.

December 22, 1920

# SALLY

By ALEXANDER WOOLLCOTT

By processes of their own, which are made up partly of secret service and partly of premonition, the connoisseurs of musical comedy seemed to know in advance that *Sally*, the new Ziegfeld production, would be worth going a long way to see. At least five or six times as many of them as could be housed at the New Amsterdam made a valiant effort to get into that theatre last evening for the New York premiere, and only those who were left outside were in any way disappointed. It is an amusing and tuneful diversion, this *Sally*. It unleashes Leon Errol in his most comical mood, and the spirited and beguiling Marilyn Miller is like a jewel in its lovely setting. But above all it bears witness to the fact that the annual production of the *Follies* does not exhaust the energy and talent of a producer who knows a little more than any of his competitors the secret of bringing beauty to his stage.

It can be imagined that with his own namesake launched on its tour of the richer cities Mr. Ziegfeld, on turning his attention to this provision of an occasion for Miss Miller, sent for the tireless Guy Bolton and that fount of melody, Jerome Kern, and bade them put together a pretty little piece after the pattern and in the modest manner of *Irene*. Then, from sheer force of habit, he began to enroll comedians and dancers as for some pretentious revue, told Professor Urban to spare no pains and so gather about him such a splendor of curtains and settings and costumes as few theatres in the world dare dream of. The result is the gay frolic which was romped last evening on the New Amsterdam's stage.

Also, to judge from the result, he must have told his song writers and comedians that a little vulgarity would not be amiss, for *Sally* is one of these pieces wherein, amid all the profusion of beauty and incongruous daintiness, you keep coming on an occasional jest that belongs in a lower grade of burlesque show.

Mr. Errol is at his best. It was, if memory serves, the hero of *The Egoist* of whom the neighbors said: "He has a leg." So has Leon Errol. It is the right one and all last evening it kept refusing to support him in the manner to which he had been accustomed. Naturally it hampers him in his earnest effort to dance a Russian ballet all by himself. The pitchings and tossings of this zany, the antics of him are beyond description, but they are of no common order. They have style and charm and whimsicality.

So has Marilyn Miller, whose sprightly dancing and tonic freshness have enchanted us all before this, but who seemed to feel that her elevation to stardom called for a greater show of effort. Whereupon, for this occasion, she appears to have gone searching about and returned with a voice. She is singing now as never before.

Then there is the stately Dolores and the captivating Mary Hay (who is a treat to the eye in her Russian costume) and one Walter Catlett, very fresh from his London triumphs. He is like a curious blend of Ed Wynn and Eddie Cantor. To say that he reminds you of each and creates a nostalgia for both would be an unfair thrust and yet the truth lies somewhere within it.

But strangely enough, it is of none of these, not of Urban nor Jerome Kern, not of Leon Errol, not even of Marilyn Miller that you think first as you rush for the subway at ten minutes to midnight. You think of Mr. Ziegfeld. He is that kind of producer. There are not many of them in the world.

. . . . . . . . . . . . . . . . . . . . . . . . . . . . . . . . . . .

**LEFT:** Marilyn Miller (center) and the Butterfly Chorus in *Sally*.

# ANDRE CHARLOT'S REVUE OF 1924

With three of the most popular London revue comedians as its stars, an English troupe came bravely to Forty-second Street last night and presented *Andre Charlot's Revue of 1924* at the Times Square. Mr. Charlot, so far as America has been permitted to learn, is the foremost of the English revue producers—London's Mr. Ziegfeld, in other words. The entertainment that he brought to New York last night is frequently brilliant in idea, less rich than American revue, and yet sufficiently attractive to the eye and particularly fortunate in having Beatrice Lillie and Gertrude Lawrence in its cast.

For Miss Lillie and Miss Lawrence are the mainstays of this English revue—comediennes in two distinct and separate fields, and each excellent. Something of their fame had already been brought to this shore by returning travelers, but no amount of advance description can take the edge off the enjoyment that is to be had from seeing and hearing Miss Lillie sing "March With Me," for example, or Miss Lawrence in the rendition of "I Don't Know."

There is no one in New York quite comparable to Beatrice Lillie. In appearance she is an exaggerated Lynn Fontanne, and it is in burlesque that she shines. The opening of the second act found her as a fifty-year-old soubrette, still bent upon singing the giddy ballades of her youth. And in "March With Me," a bit of patriotism near the finish, she rose to superb heights.

As for Miss Lawrence, she is invaluable in Mr. Charlot's comedy skits, and she can do wonders with a fair-to-middling song. The third of the leading players, Jack Buchanan, is a lengthy gentleman with an amiable stage presence and first-rate dancing ability, but hardly remarkable otherwise.

Mr. Charlot has probably had the advantage of being able to select his numbers from the numerous revues that he has produced in London, and thus the piece assays high. It is a far more literate entertainment than any

American revue—perhaps (terrible thought) it is a bit too literate for the general public.

A skit entitled "Inaudibility" turned out to be much funnier than any description of it would indicate, and there are three or four others equally entertaining. There are also, of course, a few dull ones. But, at least, it is English almost through and through—now and then someone woos a laugh by mentioning "Town Topics" or something else of the sort, but there is precious little concession to Times Square.

The music is swinging and the production moves rapidly, with nary an encore. The chorus, like the principals, is all English, and a little below the Ziegfeld–Music Box standard in appearance.

**OPPOSITE:** Gertrude Lawrence in *Andre Charlot's Revue of 1924*. **ABOVE:** Andre Charlot attending a theatrical garden party at Kew, 1916.

December 2, 1924

# Lady, Be Good

There is good news to spread among the mourners for Miss Beatrice Lillie's recent untimely departure from these parts. She returned last night, with an added freshness and a previously unrevealed dancing talent, in the piece called *Lady, Be Good* that came to the Liberty Theatre. But this time she calls herself Adele Astaire.

It should be explained, probably hastily, that it is a known fact that the Misses Lillie and Astaire are two different persons and that Miss Astaire is not exactly a newcomer. But Miss Astaire, in the opinion of at least one deponent, is as hilarious a comedienne as the gorgeous Miss Lillie. As recently as November, 1922, Miss Astaire was seen in the unlamented *Bunch and Judy*, to set sail soon thereafter for London. And ever since then the penny posts have been full of the details of her two-year triumph abroad in, of all things, *Goodness Knows*, with the title changed to *Stop Flirting* for no known reason.

But it is a different Adele Astaire whom last night's audience was privileged to see. When she left she was a graceful dancer—and she has returned, not only with all her glorious grace, but as a first-rate comedienne in her own right. Miss Astaire, in the new piece, is as charming and entertaining a musical comedy actress as the town has seen on display in many a moon.

Fred Astaire, too, gives a good account of himself in *Lady, Be Good*, participates enthusiastically and successfully in most of Miss Astaire's dance offerings, and is allowed to win the hand in marriage of Miss Kathlene Martyn for the final curtain. A second hero, destined, the librettist intimates, to be Miss Astaire's lifelong mate, is Alan Edwards, recently of *Poppy*, who again proves that he is one of the musical comedy stage's very best in one of its very worst assignments.

Walter Catlett, the leading comedian, manages to be consistently amusing almost all of the time, and Gerald Oliver Smith is allowed to deliver several attractive nifties in a pleasant manner. And there is further in the cast Cliff Edwards, who plays a ukulele.

George Gershwin's score is excellent. It contains, as might have been expected, many happy hints for wise orchestra leaders of the dancing Winter that lies ahead and a number of tunes that the unmusical and serious-minded will find it hard to get rid of. The lyrics, by Ira Gershwin, are capable throughout and at moments excellent.

*Lady, Be Good* has exceptionally handsome settings by Norman Bel Geddes. And there is an energetic chorus that dances excitedly and rhythmically under the direction of Sammy Lee.

The book of the piece contains just enough story to call Miss Astaire on stage at frequent intervals, which thus makes it an excellent book. But it could have had a little more humor.

**LEFT:** Fred and Adele Astaire in *Lady, Be Good.*
**OPPOSITE:** Fred Astaire surrounded by members of the *Lady, Be Good* chorus.

September 17, 1925

# NO, NO, NANETTE

It was not difficult last night at the Globe Theatre to understand why *No, No, Nanette*, for the last twelve and more months, has proved so popular with the natives of Chicago and points West, East, North, South. For the New York premiere of that merry musical comedy, imported practically intact after its many successful months in Chicago, showed that it is a highly meritorious paradigm of its kind.

There is to *No, No, Nanette*, let it be stated for the benefit of those who assemble such statistical material, a plot, in which for the final curtain Nanette, the heroine, embraces Tom, the hero. There is a score, with more familiar quotations from itself—one refers to "I Want to Be Happy" and "Tea for Two"—than even *Hamlet*. And there is an energetic cast of well selected comedians.

First honors among last night's participants should go to Charles Winninger. Mr. Winninger is no stranger hereabouts in any form of the popular theatre that could be named. To last night's audience, however, without a dissenting shout that was audible, Mr. Winninger gave the best performance of his career in the not entirely unfamiliar musical comedy role of the husband who has some incidents in his life that are not exactly firesidish. Mr. Winninger was extremely mirth-provoking and it was a more than hardened theatregoer who was not moved to near hysterics by his every appearance.

Louise Groody, the featured player, appeared to better advantage than has been her lot in an unfortunate number of recent years. She was lithe, tuneful and personable, and the attendants at last night's opening were in sympathy with the hero's desire to lead her to lawful wedlock, though they were unconcerned with the details of the plot leading to that consummation.

Georgia O'Ramey, as ever, was funny but unsupplied with sufficient material for her great comedy gifts. Wellington Cross was well received as Mr. Winninger's associate in the career of duplicity. Josephine Whittell was handsomely statuesque and sang well an interesting "blues" number in the last act. And a young woman named Mary Lawlor was loudly, if a bit too enthusiastically, welcomed on her contribution of acrobatic dancing to the piece.

It is full of much vigorous merriment and many agreeable tunes, this *No, No, Nanette*. And of Charles Winninger, who contributes to it whole quarter hours as pleasing as any that recent musical shows have had.

. . . . . . . . . . . . . . . . . . . . . . . . . . . . . . .

**RIGHT:** Louise Groody and Wellington Cross in *No, No, Nanette*.

41

# REVIVAL

January 20, 1971

# NO, NO, NANETTE
## *IS BACK ALIVE*
## REVIVED MUSICAL FITS HAPPILY INTO TODAY

By CLIVE BARNES

Nostalgia may prove to be the overriding emotion of the seventies, with remembrance of things past far more comfortable than the realization of things present. For everyone who wishes the world were 50 years younger—and particularly, I suspect, for those who remember it when it was 50 years younger—the revival of the 1925 musical *No, No, Nanette* should provide a delightful, care-free evening. It also has a certain amount of taste and imagination.

The resuscitation of operettas and musical comedies is a tricky operation, and the producers here have gone about their task with skill. It is described as adapted by Burt Shevelove, who is also the director, and although I do not know the original book by Otto Harbach and Frank Mandel, I would take a fair-sized bet that Mr. Shevelove's adaptation has been fairly extensive.

What emerges at the 46th Street Theatre is something like one of the new modish put-ons, such as *Dames at Sea* or *Curley McDimple*, but with the original music and lyrics, and of course, much more of the original spirit. This is far closer to a musical of the twenties than anything New York has seen since the twenties, but it is seen through a contemporary sensibility.

Time-travelers of all ages will revel in the simplicity of Vincent Youman's music. It is music to hum, and particularly music to dance to. Its rhythms suggest their own dancing feet, and the melodies are light, cheerful and exuberant, so that even the blues are not too blue.

There are a number of standards, and near-standards in the score, most notably "I Want to Be Happy" and "Tea for Two," and they emerge fresh but with reverberations of the past. They have also been cleverly arranged and orchestrated, so that while they sound familiar, they don't sound quite familiar enough to be impertinent.

Note also the lyrics by Irving Caesar and Mr. Harbach. These are as neat as a playful kitten, and on occasion as daring as a trapeze star. Youmans specialized in short musical phrases, which set his lyricists special technical problems. Those are sur-mounted with a dexterity that deserves a place in any museum of American musical comedy, and yet live wonderfully today. I doubt whether we will encounter any clev-erer or more purely musical lyrics than these all this season.

It seems that the books of most musi-cals in the twenties were not especially important. The boy met the girl, lost her and found her in time for the finale. At the drop of a hat, or the click of a cane, the stage would be invaded by a horde of happy dancing boys and girls, who would sing and tap in the background. There were also comedy scenes, but dream ballets were to come later.

In *No, No, Nanette* the story is of Jimmy Smith, a manufacturer of Bibles who wants a belt. He philanders in a gentlemanly way with three young ladies (he does not lay a hand on them, it says) and has to pay them off, in an intrigue that involves his young lawyer, who, in the way of young lawyers of

the day, would obviously do anything for money. How times have changed. Such nostalgia!

Nanette is the little girl to whom every-one says "No," until she escapes to an Atlantic City not yet made famous by Monopoly. There, of course, she gets engaged to Mr. Right. It all ends happily.

One of the show's many charms is the amount of dancing—not unexpected, when it is remembered that the production has been supervised by the great Busby Berkeley, who once made Hollywood a world fit for tap dancers, and stars Ruby Keeler, who, way back when, was sent on that stage by Warner Baxter, an unknown, and came back a star. Ruby still is a star.

Admittedly Miss Keeler is making acting into one of the arts of conversation, but she dances like a trouper and wears indomitability shyly like a badge of service. She is just enormously likable. Jack Gilford is also enormously likable, even though he has fewer opportunities to be liked, and Patsy Kelly, a formidable lady who special-izes in maids who have not only given notice but also taken notice, sucks up every scene she is in with the impressive suction of the vacuum cleaner she herself wields with such masterly expertise.

In this kind of show juveniles are juve-niles; Susan Watson (a really pretty girl) and Roger Rathburn were less juvenile than most. But for my money the best performances came from Bobby Van as the suave, debonair dancing lawyer (the man is a superb tap dancer—the program says he has never had a lesson; where would he be now with lessons?) and the adorable Helen Gallagher as his short-suffering wife. When Miss Gallagher sings the blues of a lovelorn wife with a piece of chiffon and a chorus of prop-erly epicene tailor's dummies, she makes the good old days come alive once more.

The staging by Mr. Shevelove and the supervision by Mr. Berkeley seemed attrac-tively tongue-in-cheek (where else, by the way, do people put tongues?) and the chore-ography by Donald Saddler was creatively the most important new element in the show. This choreography dazzled—I had forgotten tap-dancing could be so much fun.

**OPPOSITE:** Ruby Keeler in the 1971 revival of *No, No, Nanette.*

# The Cocoanuts

Perhaps for the first time in their rough-and-tumble lives, the four Marx brothers kept respectable company last evening at the Lyric Theatre, where George S. Kaufman's new musical comedy, *The Cocoanuts*, was put on. In a broad and spacious Florida hotel, decorated with the most exquisite taste, and in an airy patio, these low comedians associated on equal terms with people of refinement. For the new comedy is splendidly decked out with costumes of such brilliance that the eye fairly waters; with melodies by Irving Berlin; with Antonio and Nina de Marco for dancers; with Jack Barker and Mabel Witlee for singers; with clog-steppers; in sum, with the sublime beauty of a musical comedy set in Florida. Amid this opulent array the Marx brothers go through their antics as before.

In the first act they seem rather thin against the splendor of the general comedy scheme, and only occasionally do they enact the rapid, organized buffoonery that was so painfully funny in these parts last season. In the second act, however, they rise to the surface. Groucho Marx keeps up a steady rattle of patter; Harpo goes through his lazy chicaneries and Chico performs once again at the piano.

At the same time that Florida is developing its land, to the annoyance of the rest of the civilized world, it is apparently developing a restful, colorful type of architecture and decoration. The first scene of *The Cocoanuts* represents the lobby of the hotel where all these revelries occur, on generous, restful lines. And for the first moments of the comedy, ladies and gentlemen of the chorus dance and sing here. Then the earnest, thin, not unkindly face of Groucho Marx, bearing the inevitable cigar, appears tentatively on the stairs, and the fun begins. Through the rest of the comedy the Marx brothers retain their familiar roles—Groucho in the shabby cutaway, with the inadequate spectacles; Chico with the loud clothes and immigrant's accent; Harpo with the flaring wig, and the vulgar leers and grimaces far more effective than words; and Zeppo representing by contrast the decent young man.

And, as formerly, the voluble Groucho keeps up a heavy musketry of puns and gibes, twisting everything into the vulgar, unimaginative jargon of the shopkeeper. To him the eyes of his love "shine like the pants of a blue serge suit." When he steps down to the local jail to bail out a $2,000 prisoner, he finds a sale in progress and captures his prey for $1,900. And to him "jail is no place for a young man. There is no advancement." There are puns on a "poultry" $1,000, and a request to the lovers that they transfer their caresses to the "mushroom." Nothing is more amusing than the rapidity with which Groucho reduces everything to the stale bromides of the serious-minded merchant; and the speed with which he twists a burlesque probe for a missing shirt into a tailoring shop where he is measuring the victim for a suit of clothes and trying to sell him a pair of socks. All this with the seriousness of the instinctive man of business, bent upon doing his job well, and with such baffling twists in allusion that the audience is frequently three jumps behind him.

For the organized low comedy in which these brothers specialize, the current skit affords only one or two numbers, fewer than in their last appearance. Harpo shaking down his victims for watches and purses, stealing the detective's shirt from his chest and a guest's vest and coat from his back, or taking dictation on the cash register and calmly tearing the guest's mail into pieces and ripping up the telegrams as fast as they come—all these broad antics are particularly funny. In the first act the comedy is slow in starting, and is less loud and less funny than an expectant audience had hoped it to be. Throughout the second act the comedians are frequently on the stage and in good form. And yet the blatancy and fury of which they are capable do not reach the familiar extremes.

But *The Cocoanuts* surrounds them with better entertainment. Mr. Berlin's music is always pleasing. The number entitled "A Little Bungalow," sung by Miss Witlee and Mr. Barker, is especially melodious. The chorus number entitled "Five O'Clock Tea" runs swiftly with a charming theme. Most of the dance numbers, moreover, have an imaginative and elusive grace that are uncommon to the run of musical comedy. And Frances Williams sings the blues and shivers through a Charleston number.

According to the fashion of musical comedy, *The Cocoanuts* occasionally merges into ensemble numbers. At the close of the first act Groucho Marx, on the auctioneer's stand, conducts with all the enthusiasm of the development man and the sly candor of the comedian a sale of Florida real estate lots, some of them in the most exclusive residential district where no one lives at all. The second act resolves a probe into an old-time burlesque minstrel show with incidental clowneries and concludes with a garden fête with the skipjack comedians in ill-becoming Spanish vestments, with Chico "shooting" the piano keys and Harpo fooling languorously with the harp. One must not forget the brilliance of the patter and joking; it is never commonplace. Nor, as a matter of form, must one neglect to mention the existence of a plot.

. . . . . . . . . . . . . . . . . . . . . . . . . . . . . . . . . .

**OPPOSITE:** Clockwise from left, Groucho, Harpo, Chico, and Zeppo Marx in *The Cocoanuts*.

FLORENCE VANDAMM
NEW YORK

THE EARLY YEARS

November 9, 1926

# OH, KAY!

By J. BROOKS ATKINSON

Musical comedy seldom proves more intensely delightful than *Oh, Kay!* the new piece at the Imperial with a serviceable book by Guy Bolton and P. G. Wodehouse, specialists in collaboration, and a rich score by George Gershwin. Usually it is sufficient to credit as sponsors only the authors and the composer. But the distinction of *Oh, Kay!* is its excellent blending of all the creative arts of musical entertainment—the arts of staging no less than those of composing and designing. For half the enjoyment of the new musical play comes from the dancing, the comic pantomime and the drilling of a large company. Mr. Lee and Mr. Harwood have matched the authors at every turning with inventive and imaginative directing.

After two appearances in America as co-star in the English *Charlot Revues*, Gertrude Lawrence now appears as a principal in this new comedy. And the plot being what it is, she comes as the sister of a titled English bootlegger whose yacht hovers off our arid shores amid the excursions and alarums of Federal inspectors. ("The difference between a bootlegger and a Federal inspector," says the incriminating Victor Moore, "is that one of them wears a badge.") Most of us have heard Miss Lawrence singing various musical-hall tunes in good voice and excellent taste, with a wanton twinkle of comedy in her eyes.

In her present role she gives expression to that mimic quality more than ever with a versatility barely indicated in the *Charlot Revues* in which Beatrice Lillie cut such uproarious capers. Miss Lillie, by the way, was among those present last evening. So obliging is the book of *Oh, Kay!* that Miss Lawrence may play not only the love-sick English lady but also the Cockney serving-maid who performs tricks on a long roll of French bread and affects a domestic slouch in her walk. As a low comedian she does not paint the Lillie, but she keeps the enjoyment varied and broad.

Most of this entertainment has to do with a cargo of forbidden liquor and as scurvy a lot of bad puns as ever scuttled a rum-runner. The supercilious duke, with the dapper Gerald Smith "up" on that part, and "Shorty" McGee, buffooned by Victor Moore, have concealed a shipment in the capacious cellar of Jimmy Winter, represented engagingly by Oscar Shaw.

As the extemporaneous butler, battler or bottler (to speak from the book) Mr. Moore totters languidly through a long roulade of indiscriminate comedy, unseemly impertinence and a constant rattle of amusing "gags." Nothing since the Marx Brothers has been more hilarious than the offhand luncheon served clumsily by Miss Lawrence and Mr. Moore.

Mr. Gershwin's score is woven closely into the fun of the comedy. Sometimes it is purely rhythmic, as in "Clap Yo' Hands" and "Fidgety Feet"; sometimes it is capricious, as in "Do-Do-Do." Mr. Gershwin also composes in the familiar romantic vein of "Someone to Watch Over Me." In this plaintive number Miss Lawrence embellishes the song with expressive turns on the stage; she employs none of the artful rhetoric of musical comedy singing. For *Oh, Kay!* is the work of no individual. It is a group production to which every one has brought some appropriate decoration. When dramatic organizations pool their talents in this fashion, we prattle with smug satisfaction about the universal development of the stage. Revue and musical comedy producers excel in such organized handicraft as a matter of course.

**ABOVE:** Gertrude Lawrence as Kay. **OPPOSITE:** Oscar Shaw, Gertrude Lawrence, and Harry Shannon in *Oh, Kay!*

# FUNNY FACE

By J. BROOKS ATKINSON

If there were not two or three good musical plays already in town one might be reckless enough to dub *Funny Face*, at the Alvin last evening, as the best of them all. With Fred and Adele Astaire, Victor Moore and William Kent in the cast, with music by George Gershwin and lyrics by his brother, Ira, and with excellent dancing throughout, *Funny Face* makes for uncommonly rollicking entertainment. It opens the new Alvin Theatre auspiciously.

By this time it is no secret that Fred and Adele Astaire have a niche in musical comedy quite to themselves. They have not only humor but intelligence; not only spirit but good taste; not only poise but modesty; and they are not only expert eccentric dancers but they never make an ungraceful movement. Twice last evening Fred Astaire took the audience's breath away with his rapid footing and his intelligibility in a brand of clog-dance pantomime. In a particularly refreshing male chorus number, to the tune of "High Hat," he gave every indication of proceeding in two directions at once. As a gauche and prevaricating young lady, his sister also dances beautifully, meanwhile making the faces celebrated in the title of the comedy. Within their very individual field the Astaires appear to have things very much their own way.

Fred Thompson and Paul Gerard Smith, collaborating bookmakers for this racy diversion, propose Fred Astaire as the likable guardian of three young ladies and Adele as a harum-scarum ward. For some reason, which need not upset us in our critical orisons, two friendly gentlemen crack the family safe just before two professional safe experts appear on the scene. Now, as good fortune would have it in the modern theatrical world, the diminutive, wobbly William Kent and the comically thick-witted Victor Moore find themselves involved in this unlawful proceeding.

Forget all that. All that matters here is that Kent and Moore, as friendly enemies, put on one of the funniest shooting numbers seen during any Republican Administration. Those who remember Victor Moore from past musical shows know how full of sobs his voice can be. "Was you going anywheres in particular?" he pleads, trying to find a convenient time for shooting Kent. In spite of Kent's blue eyes, which remind him compassionately of three kittens he drowned in his youth, Moore deferentially squares off to murder Kent when the question of a shooting license comes up. Well, after all, it is not the business of the act that matters: it is Moore's slow, ponderous motions, the absurd shape of his bulging head and his sobbing voice. "Did it hit you?" he inquires hopefully after the first shot. No, one must not attempt to describe it.

Mr. Kent with his fluttering comedy makes a good deal more than he ought of "symtoms I'm happy; symtoms I'm sad," and other devastating comic rot. Who is it, by the way, who says he has "turned in his Chivalry for a Cadillac"? One cannot remember all the jokes.

Mr. Gershwin, maker of tunes, has composed several good songs for *Funny Face*, the

best of which naturally bears the same title as the play. "'S Wonderful, 's Marvelous," "Let's Kiss and Make Up," and "The Babbitt and the Bromide" manage successfully to avoid the old song banalities. The cast includes Betty Compton and Gertrude McDonald, and Allen Kearns, who makes a musical comedy vocalist less trying than usual. In directing the chorus Bobby Connolly has contrived to keep dancing vivacity from seeming ugly. In all its grimaces, *Funny Face* gives full entertainment measure.

The new Alvin Theatre, set defiantly across the street from the scholarly Theatre Guild, seems to have all the best features of the modern playhouse—even an old English lounge where refreshments may be had. The auditorium is decorated in pastel shades of blue and gray, with ivory and old gold decorations. The Alvin can serve 1,400 drama gluttons at one sitting. If *Funny Face* had been less engrossing, the audience might have had more time to appreciate the new theatre.

Scenes from *Funny Face*. **ABOVE:** Fred Astaire and members of the *Funny Face* chorus. **OPPOSITE:** From left, Betty Compton, Adele Astaire, Gertrude McDonald, and Fred Astaire.

December 28, 1927

# Show Boat

### By J. BROOKS ATKINSON

The worlds of Broadway and Park Avenue and their respective wives put on their best bibs and tuckers last night and converged at Mr. Ziegfeld's handsome new playhouse on Sixth Avenue. There they milled about elegantly in the lobby, were pictured by flashlight photographers and finally got to their seats and to the business in hand. That was the inspection of the newest offering from the workshops of the maestro, the much-heralded musical adaptation of Edna Ferber's novel, *Show Boat*.

From such remote centres of theatrical omniscience as Pittsburgh, Washington and Philadelphia had come the advance word that it was better than good—some reports even extravagantly had it that here was Mr. Ziegfeld's superlative achievement. It would be difficult to quarrel with such tidings, for last night's performance came perilously near to realizing the most fulsome of them.

All right, there you have it: *Show Boat* is, with a few reservations in favor of some of the earlier *Follies* and possibly *Sally*, just about the best musical piece ever to arrive under Mr. Ziegfeld's silken gonfalon. It has, barring perhaps a slight lack of one kind of comedy, and an overabundance of another, and a little slowness in getting under way—this last due to the fact that it is crammed with plot which simply must be explained—about every ingredient that the perfect song-and-dance concoction should have.

In its adherence to its story it is positively slavish. The adaptation of the novel has been intelligently made, and such liberties as the demands of musical comedy necessitate do not twist the tale nor distort its values. For this, and for the far better than the average lyrics with which it is endowed, credit Oscar Hammerstein II, who is rapidly monopolizing the function of author for the town's musical entertainments.

Then, too, *Show Boat* has an exceptionally tuneful score—the most lilting and

satisfactory that the wily Jerome Kern has contrived in several seasons. Potential song hits were as common last night as top hats. Such musical recordings of amorous reaction as "You Are in Love," "I Can't Help Lovin' That Man," "Why Do I Love You?" are sufficient for any show—to say nothing of "Old Man River," which Jules Bledsoe and a negro chorus make remarkably effective.

If these three contributions—book, lyrics and score—call for a string of laudatory adjectives, the production compels that they be repeated again—and with a short tiger. The colorful scenes on and around the showboat, plying its course along the Mississippi, that comprise the first act lend themselves well to a variety of effects and have been achieved with Mr. Ziegfeld's unimpeachable skill and taste.

In the second act the nine interludes carry the spectator from the gaudy Midway Plaisance of the World's Fair to the sombre quiet of St. Agatha's Convent and then back to the new and modernized floating theatre, 1927 variety. The settings are all atmospherically perfect; the costumes are in the style of each of the periods and there is a finish and polish about the completed entity that caused even a first performance to move with unusual smoothness.

To recount in any detail the plot of a musical comedy usually is a silly and banal business; to tell Miss Ferber's large and clamorous public what happens to Magnolia and Gaylord Ravenal is unnecessary. But to tell them of the manner in which these characters and the many others of the best seller have been brought to life is something else again.

As Magnolia, Norma Terris appeared to be a revelation, even to the first nighters who had watched her work in previous dance-and-tune saturnalias. Her realization of Captain Andy's daughter seemed complete, even when she got around to imitating Ted Lewis and Ethel Barrymore in the final, or 11:45 P.M., scene. Howard Marsh, one of the more facial tenors, made a handsome and satisfactory

Ravenal. Helen Morgan, who is among the town's most adept song saleswomen, was Julie, and purveyed two numbers in her distinctive style. As the dour and formidable New England mother, Partby Ann Hawks, Edna May Oliver played with requisite austerity, although she did forget herself long enough to engage in a dance.

But the outstanding hit of the evening seemed to be reserved for Charles Winninger, who cut capers to his heart's content as Captain Andy.

He is in top form, and when Mr. Winninger is in top form he is an extremely waggish fellow. And in a moment during the "Show Boat's" performance when through the defection of an affrighted villain he is compelled to seize the stage and act out the remainder of the play himself, he is extraordinarily persuasive and convincing. Then there are the

reliable Puck and White, presenting the low comedy specialties, and others too numerous to mention.

   *Show Boat*, as it should not be too difficult for the reader to ascertain by now, is an excellent musical comedy; one that comes perilously close to being the best the town has seen in several seasons. It must have afforded its producer, who has poured dollars into it by the thousands, a certain ironic satisfaction to hear the play's Chicago cabaret manager say with an air of finality, "No, I can't afford to take chances with amateurs with a $2,000 production on my hands." Mr. Ziegfeld can't afford to, either.

· · · · · · · · · · · · · · · · · · · · · · · ·

**OPPOSITE:** Cover of the *Show Boat* "Make Believe" songbook, 1927. **ABOVE:** A scene from *Show Boat*. From left, Francis X. Mahoney, Charles Ellis, Helen Morgan, Norma Terris (kneeling), Eva Puck, Charles Winninger, and Edna May Oliver.

**LEFT:** A scene from the original Broadway production of *Show Boat*, 1927.

May 1, 1929

# THE LITTLE SHOW

By J. BROOKS ATKINSON

Most of the wit, humor and intelligence that somehow escape the musical stage has settled down pleasantly into *The Little Show*, which rambled along in conversational tones at the Music Box last evening. It is unfailingly diverting. If that formal phrase appears to lack enthusiasm, be warned at the outset that the collectors of this pocket-edition revue have not sought to pain you with abdominal laughter or stimulate your gastric juices with wanton display. Having assembled several of the neatest entertainers in town, and put them to fooling with light and subtle materials, they have merely set about amusing you, and they have succeeded. Of course, that frenzied "Song of the Riveter" does seem to be intended seriously, although it lies close to travesty, and the humor has something more than a mere penchant for Anatole France's "la volupté." Otherwise, it is gay, sardonic, trifling and remarkably good fun.

Being completely off the beaten path, it turns up with novel ideas. You have no sooner recovered from the maudlin, sentimental theme song of our foremost hardware merchants ("Hammacher, Schlemmer, I love you—Always remember, Hammacher, Schlemmer")

than you are witnessing the ingenious tragedy of deaf-mutes, cursing under their whiskers or talking low—which is at the height of the knees—or you are hearing about the hot-cross-bun designer who naturally works only one day a year. Most of these glib humors Fred Allen delivers in a flat voice like the wit of the senior dormitories. He is not merely an ingratiating comedian, but a deft one, with an extraordinary talent for making his points at a skimming pace. But *The Little Show* is not reduced to one mountebank. Clifton Webb is there with mincing steps and a nice touch of comedy, and the clownish Romney Brent radiates good humor as far as the eye can reach.

In fact, these three comedians have at their disposal the keenest sketch in the revue, "The Still Alarm," by George S. Kaufman, who can draw without smudging a line. It is the story of a horrible hotel fire as viewed from the eleventh floor by perfect gentlemen whose breeding remains with them to the end. While the two guests are bending over a series of house plans in the well-appointed apartment, the alert call-boy comes with a well-phrased message of alarm

from the desk. There is no vulgar display of terror, rude haste, or selfishness. The deportment is flawless, at every point. In fact, when the floor grows hot and the smoke begins to roll in at the windows, good manners have triumphed so completely that the two guests are sitting down courteously, while the more artistic of the firemen starts to play on his violin, the "little thing" he played so brilliantly at the Equitable holocaust.

Although *The Little Show* is most notable for its humors, it can dance and pipe as brightly as the rest. The dances staged by Danny Dare tap an amiable tattoo. For the more conventional balladry Joan Carter-Waddell is engaging and John McCauley pleasant, though too persistently winsome. There is the flaxen-haired Helen Lynd for gauche pranks to tunes, and there is the dark purple menace of Libby Holman in the blues. Being a small-gauged affair, *The Little Show* keeps all its people uncommonly busy. By providing them with excellent material, all in one light key, it keeps the intimacies always agreeable.

. . . . . . . . . . . . . . . . . . . . . . . . . . . . . .

**OPPOSITE:** A scene from *The Little Show*.

November 6, 1929

# BITTER SWEET

By J. BROOKS ATKINSON

Mr. Coward is the master of little things, and the virtuosity of his talents amounts to genius. For what he describes as his operette, *Bitter Sweet*, which was put on at the Ziegfeld last evening, he has written the book and the lyrics, composed the music, staged the production, and stopped just this side of acting all the parts. Although considerable showmanship has gone into the staging and the organization of the story, it is not a musical show in the rapid, flamboyant style to which we have become accustomed. But it is sheerly delightful by reason of the delicate perfection of the workmanship and the radiant splendor of Evelyn Laye, who has the principal rôle. It is a production composed of miniatures, each one neatly turned. It is charming; it is subtle and witty. By his mastery of little things Mr. Coward has mastered the artistry of musical entertainment in a refreshingly civilized style.

Although the plot of his costume romance is not highly inventive, Mr. Coward

has managed to inform it with sufficient dramatic quality to carry the burden of his theme. When, in the first scene, the elderly Marchioness of Shayne surprises one of her party guests embracing the pianist, the story of her own high-spirited career begins. How, as a young lady of quality in 1875, she fell in love with her music teacher and ran off with him on the eve of the date set for her wedding to a gentleman of vast importance; how the music teacher became bandmaster in a Viennese café and she one of the hired dancing partners; how the bandmaster was slain in a duel with an officer who had kissed her; and how at length she returned to society as a famous singer and became the betrothed of the Marquis of Shayne—this is the burden of Mr. Coward's evening of song.

Although it is no great shakes as a story, it has more continuity than most books for musical productions, and it serves Mr. Coward's purpose admirably. For, again, his interest is in the style of romance. What

you enjoy in *Bitter Sweet* is the skill with which he has turned out the usual set-pieces—investing the usual ceremonies ball with a native gayety and a compelling caprice, and enlivening Herr Schlick's café with a revelry that does not travesty its setting. Meanwhile, he introduces divertissements that have an air of reticent originality—a nice-mannered frolic amid the prospective bridesmaids, a droll, piquant song for the shameless ladies of the town in Vienna, and a wry caricature of the Oscar Wildettes. It is decorous entertainment, reveling in the billowing costumes of a grandiose age of style, and courting humor in the bouncing bustle.

Really, the details hardly matter. All that matters is the unity of style in the sundry materials of musical romance. What makes Evelyn Laye so rare a presence in the leading part is not merely her fragile beauty but the daintiness with which she acts and sings in the precise spirit of the play. As an actress she catches the ardor of the romantic love scenes of the first act; she trips through the dramatic episodes with a skill equal to Mr. Coward's composition. She has, moreover, a voice sweet in quality and full in tone—as competent for the warmth of such a piece as "Tell Me What Is Love" as it is for the girlishness of "The Last Dance" and the folk rhythms of the concluding "Zigeuner."

The cast of English players assembled for the American production includes many others of unusual skill—Gerald Nodin as the music teacher, Mireille as a saucy French café singer ("Life is very rough-and-tumble for the humble diseuse"), Sylvia Leslie, Zoe Gordon, Nancy Barnett and Dorothy Debenham as the audacious ladies of the town, Desmond Jeans as an imposing military captain, and a host of credible ladies and gentlemen of fashion.

**ABOVE:** A scene from *Bitter Sweet*. **OPPOSITE:** Evelyn Laye as Sarah.

"Nothing so gutsy as this has come along for a week," wrote Brooks Atkinson in 1938. "Nothing so original has come along for a much longer period than that." The show was *The Boys from Syracuse*, a winking (and occasionally leering) musical adaptation of Shakespeare's *Comedy of Errors*. It featured a swell roster of songs from Richard Rodgers and Lorenz Hart (including "Sing for Your Supper," "He and She," and "Falling in Love With Love") that combined romantic wistfulness with snappy cynicism, and hopeful exuberance with a survivalist's eye for the main chance.

A similar crackle seems to infuse Atkinson's words of praise for *The Boys*. There had been nothing so gutsy in all of a week? What a season it must have been for Broadway musicals. You start to imagine a lineup of scrappy, feisty, smart-mouthed shows, running in place, boxing the air with their fists, impatient to show the original stuff they're made of.

That's not a bad way to look at the part of Broadway that sang and danced through the 1930s, the musicals that Americans went to while their nation's economy remained in the sick ward. Plots for these shows—including the one borrowed from Shakespeare—were still silly, often as not. But they seemed to have a newly focused and defiant vitality that didn't exclude a social conscience. And whether the show was a dizzy, demented lark like *The Boys from Syracuse* or an up-front satire of the presidency like *Of Thee I Sing*, the musical seemed to be thumbing its nose at hard times and the politicians who got us there.

The title *Anything Goes*, which opened in 1934, captured a what-the-heck, seat-of-the-pants spirit that informed many of these shows. (That spirit also, by contemporary accounts, informed the haphazard assembly of *Anything Goes* by a team that included Cole Porter and four different book writers, including P. G. Wodehouse.) An ultimately unparseable story of gangsters, stowaways, an heiress, an English lord, and a sassy nightclub evangelist, *Anything Goes* was all about making it up as you go along.

So was *Girl Crazy*, a way-out-West musical that had opened in 1930, with a score by George and Ira Gershwin and a featured player who would go on to star in *Anything Goes* and a whole lot of other hits. That was Ethel Merman, a former stenographer from Queens, "whose peculiar song style was brought from the night clubs to the stage to the vast delight . . . of the people who go places and watch things being done," wrote the *Times*. Merman's brass—vocal and otherwise—became a highly prized metal on Broadway. The way she sang Cole Porter's "You're the Top," it sounded like a trumpet-driven hymn to American competitiveness and inexhaustibility.

There were plenty of giddy shows that celebrated chutzpah and enterprising ingenuity in the 1930s: Rodgers and Hart's *Babes in Arms* (1937), the archetypal "let's put on a show" show, of which Atkinson wrote amiably, "Pardon the performers for the atrocious crime of being young." (Three years later the *Times* had fewer kind words for another Rodgers and Hart show, *Pal Joey*, a portrait of a womanizing heel, about which Atkinson wrote: "Can you draw sweet water from a foul well?")

Other shows faced the nation and its problems more directly. *Of Thee I Sing*, which featured a book by George S. Kaufman and Morrie Ryskind and songs by George and Ira Gershwin, made a mockery of the darnedest things folks do to get an American president elected, prompting Atkinson to write, "What little dignity there may have been in politics and government has been laughed out of court by *Of Thee I Sing*." (George Gershwin took a more somber and more musically ambitious approach for *Porgy and Bess*, his great opera about African Americans living hand-to mouth on Catfish Row.) There was even a second musical about the presidency, *I'd Rather Be President*, in which the first man of Broadway, George M. Cohan, played the first man of the nation, Franklin D. Roosevelt. The *Times* found these White House revels rather tame after *Of Thee I Sing*.

*As Thousands Cheer*, a revue with music by Irving Berlin and a book by Moss Hart, tied each number to a topical headline. The songs and sketches ranged from the impious (for vignettes about the Herbert Hoovers and the Rockefellers) to the solemn (Ethel Waters singing "Suppertime," about a lynching in the South). Another satiric revue, *Pins and Needles* had the distinction of being the first (and only) Broadway hit to be created and performed by the members of the International Ladies Garment Workers' Union. Then there was Marc Blitzstein's *The Cradle Will Rock*, the Mercury Theatre musical whose birth pains became legend after it was shut down by its sponsor, the Federal Theatre Project, and restaged with an almost illegal inventiveness that became its own testimony to American pluck. (The story behind the show is included in this section.) The *Times*, saluting this musical tale of corporate greed and dishonesty, wrote, "At last the comrades of the insurgent theatre can feel sure that they have a fully awakened artist on their side. What *Waiting for Lefty* was to the dramatic stage, *The Cradle Will Rock* is to the stage of the labor battle song." Despite the flippancy, that description suggested that there might actually be musicals that have to be taken seriously. After all, this was the same decade in which a mere musical, *Of Thee I Sing*, took the Pulitzer Prize for drama.

**OPPOSITE:** Todd Duncan and Anne Wiggins Brown in the original Broadway production of *Porgy and Bess*, 1935.

**ABOVE:** Ethel Merman with members of the *Girl Crazy* chorus. **OPPOSITE:** Ginger Rogers and Allen Kearns as Molly Gray and Danny Churchill.

# GIRL CRAZY

When the first curtain arose on last night's antics at the Alvin, a large sign on the stage informed the audience that it was looking at Custerville, Ariz., a happy community which feminine wiles had not penetrated for more than fifty years. But since this was a musical comedy, that womanless state obviously could not long endure. Before ten minutes had elapsed the personable Ginger Rogers had made her entrance, and from then on the young women principals and jazz coryphees came in droves. And, what with one thing and another, it all helped to make *Girl Crazy* what Broadway would call a lively and expert show. There is, then, fairly consoling news from Fifty-second Street this morning.

Not the least important item in these tidings is the part played by the brothers Gershwin. George has written some good tunes, while Ira has provided tricky and ingratiating lyrics that should stimulate any ear surfeited with the usual rhyming insipidities of musical comedy. In one number, "Bidin' My Time," he has poked fun at the theme song school in verse; in all he has been fresh and amusing. And his brother has provided melody in "Embraceable You" and "But Not for Me," travestied the imperishable "Frankie and Johnnie" in "Sam and Delilah," and turned out several excellent rhythmic numbers, one of which, "I Got Rhythm," induces a veritable frenzy of dancing.

The book is serviceable, rather than distinguished. It gets its characters in and out of the proper entanglements and tears its hero and heroine apart at the end of the first act as every orthodox musical show libretto should. Set in the Southwest, *Girl Crazy* concentrates on affairs in a dude ranch. The ranch is run by a New York playboy who falls in love with an Arizona girl. Around the premises lurk a hardbitten pair of villains, who are alternately after somebody's $6,000 and the scalp of Willie Howard, who impersonates Gieber Goldfarb, a Broadway taxicab driver forced by the

exigencies of the story to become a sheriff addicted to impersonations of Maurice Chevalier, Eddie Cantor and George Jessel. That is not all, but you get the idea. What is important is that, with the music, dancing and some of the comedy, it does not matter more than it should.

The dancing combines intricacy and speed in the manner of the day, and is definitely one of the assets. Another is Ethel Merman, whose peculiar song style was brought from the night clubs to the stage to the vast delight last evening of the people who go places and watch things being done. Willie Howard is, as usual, Willie Howard; in several instances, particularly at the start of the show, he is funnier than he has been lately. He is, it may be recalled, in the rôle

first intended for Bert Lahr, who was kept from joining the show by a previous contract. Assisting him in the comicalities of the evening is that gadfly merry-andrew, William Kent, who is permitted to be only moderately successful. The ingenue, Miss Rogers, is an oncoming young person of the type whom, at her first appearance, half of the audience immediately classifies as "cute."

The première performance was conducted by George Gershwin, and he got as much applause as anyone on the stage. Under his baton were a pit-full of experts in syncopation, who contributed their share to making *Girl Crazy* an agreeable diversion which seems destined to find a profitable place among the luxuries of Times Square, if not the necessities.

December 28, 1931

# Of Thee I Sing

## By J. BROOKS ATKINSON

What little dignity there may have been in politics and government has been laughed out of court by *Of Thee I Sing*, a brisk musical comedy staged at the Music Box Saturday evening. It is the work of George S. Kaufman and Morrie Ryskind, as neat a pair of satirists as ever scuttled a national tradition; and it has George Gershwin's most brilliant score to sharpen the humor and fantasticate the ideas. For this loud and blaring circus is no jerry-built musical comedy, although occasionally it subsides into the musical comedy formula. And it is no idle bit of buffoonery, although occasionally it degenerates into the specious cleverness of Broadway. The authors have transposed the charlatanry of national politics into a hurly-burly of riotous campaign slogans, political knavery, comic national dilemmas and general burlesque. They have fitted the dunce's cap to politics and government, and crowded an evening with laughter.

For half the evening they are blatantly attempting to elect John P. Wintergreen President of the United States on a maudlin platform of "Love." When the curtain goes up, after Mr. Gershwin's restless and echoing overture, you see a torchlight procession carrying illuminated sign-boards: "Vote for Wintergreen, A Man's Man's Man"; "Wintergreen, I Love You"; "Vote For Prosperity and See What You Get"; "Even Your Dog Likes Wintergreen"; "Wintergreen, The Flavor Lasts." Having a particularly bad political record, the Republican party wants a platform of popular generalities, and having an attractive bachelor as its candidate it seizes upon "Love" as the magic watchword. It holds a bathing-beauty contest at Atlantic City to choose the President's bride.

The campaign is vulgar and furious. Campaign speeches are roared out in Madison Square Garden amid a caterwauling of prize-fight announcements while a comic wrestling match goes on in the foreground. The election results are flashed on an excited screen. There is heavy voting in the South

for Jefferson Davis; heavy voting in California for Mickey Mouse, scattering votes here and there for light wines and beer, straight whisky, Walter Hampden and Mae West. America votes for what it likes best. After a good deal of such trumpery the President is elected; he is inaugurated and married at the same instant by a gymnastic Chief Justice; and as a climax to the second act he is saved from impeachment when the President's wife announces with pride that she is in a delicate condition. The Vice President proudly declares: "The United States has never impeached an expectant President." Whereupon the chorus sings "Posterity is just around the corner."

The book is long and complicated, heavily freighted with slanders and gibes; and before the evening is over you feel that it is becoming synthetic and unwieldy.

Being all in one strident key, it grows tiresome, for the authors are better satirists than story-tellers. They are also undiscriminating with their humors; they open their festivities with that unsavory bathroom joke. After developing a fantastic idea with the aid of Mr. Gershwin's full-bodied music, neither are they above destroying it with a hard or shallow gag. And, at least to this commentator, the obstetrical horseplay that concludes the evening is a craftsman's device for rescuing a faltering story rather than a spontaneous comic idea. When the satire slides from politics to generalities—the second act of *Of Thee I Sing* loses most of its distinction.

But one detail of the story is pure inspiration. Treating the Vice President as a common nuisance is a source of constant hilarity. As Alexander Throttlebottom, Vice President of the United States, Victor Moore is pathetic and futile and vastly enjoyable in a satire that wants emotion generally. Even after they have nominated him, the campaign managers cannot remember his name. They mistake him for a waiter when he stumbles hopefully into the campaign headquarters

and ask him to serve the pickles. Not knowing what to do with him, they finally ask him to keep out of sight until after the election. He is forgotten at the inaugural. The new government takes office without him. Finally he worms his frightened way into the White House in a crowd of nondescript tourists; and, talking with a White House lackey, he learns for the first time that the Vice President presides over the Senate. *Of Thee I Sing* is richest and ruddiest when Mr. Moore, full of good-will and bewildered innocence, teeters through the halls of statesmanship and tries to discover what place a Vice President has in the scheme of national affairs.

As the President, William Gaxton is dynamic and engaging, and very amusing in his parodies of Mayor Walker, although he itches to play snappy musical comedy. Lois Moran is a charming President's bride. Grace Brinkley is refulgent as an avaricious bathing beauty. As the French Ambassador, Florenz Ames has a subtlety that most of his colleagues lack.

There is dancing, both routine and inventive. There are lyrics done in Ira Gershwin's neatest style. There are settings by Jo Mielziner that adroitly convey the shoddiness of the political environment. Best of all, there is Mr. Gershwin's score. Whether it is satire, wit, doggerel or fantasy, Mr. Gershwin pours music out in full measure, and in many voices. Although the book is lively, Mr. Gershwin is exuberant. He has not only ideas but enthusiasm. He amplifies the show. Satire in the sharp, chill, biting vein of today needs the warmth of Victor Moore's fooling and the virtuosity of Mr. Gershwin's music. Without them *Of Thee I Sing* would be the best topical travesty our musical stage has created. With them it has the depth of artistry and the glow and pathos of comedy that are needed in the book.

........................................................

**OPPOSITE:** William Gaxton (third from right) as John P. Wintergreen and Lois Moran as his bride-to-be.

November 30, 1932

# GAY DIVORCE

By BROOKS ATKINSON

All the entrepreneurs of *Gay Divorce*, which was mounted at the Ethel Barrymore last evening, have gone to considerable pains to produce a clever musical comedy. In the stellar role they have cast Fred Astaire, who can dance the crisp idioms of the modish toe-and-heel fandango. The music and the lyrics are the work of Cole Porter, whose facetious grace is already familiar. Look down the long catalogue of credits on the title page: Book by Dwight Taylor, musical adaptation by Kenneth Webb and Samuel Hoffenstein, dances by Carl Randall and Barbara Newberry, settings by Jo Mielziner, costumes under the supervision of Raymond Sovey. Or look to the stage, where the colors and girls moving at high speed make a gay phantasmagoria. Certainly the audience recruited from the more luxurious quarters of this city last evening enjoyed

itself enormously and saluted the performers with gusto. Perhaps this column is alone in regarding *Gay Divorce* as flat and mirthless entertainment beneath a highly polished exterior.

The book chronicles the polite confusions of a young married person of London who has gone to a seaside hotel to establish grounds for a divorce. Through some artful misunderstanding she mistakes the young man whom she loves for the professional corespondent with whom she is supposed to be audaciously discovered. It is neither a brilliant plot nor an elaborate one. Before the evening is over it employs most of the hotel and bedroom fiddle-faddle that went out with risqué farces. And although the lines are glib, they cultivate the flat endings of genteel small talk which becomes singularly tiresome after the first five minutes.

Mr. Astaire can dance smartly. Here he makes his first appearance without that impudent gamin, Adele. Something vitally refreshing has gone with her to England. In the refulgent Claire Luce, Mr. Astaire has found a partner who can match him step for step and who flies over the furniture in his company without missing a beat. As a solo dancer Mr. Astaire stamps out his accents with that lean, nervous agility that distinguishes his craftsmanship, and he has invented turns that abound in graphic portraiture. But some of us cannot help feeling that the joyousness of the Astaire team is missing now that the team has parted.

Mr. Porter's tunes and lyrics have the proper dash and breeding. For the amusingly venomous Luella Gear he has written a sardonic number entitled "I Still Love the Red, White and Blue," and a politely coarse ballad mischievously entitled "Mr. and Mrs. Fitch." "You're in Love" and "Night and Day" pay their gentlemanly respects to romance. One might be more fervent about Mr. Porter's score if he had good voices to sing it. But Mr. Astaire and Miss Luce, being singers only by necessity, make the chief song numbers of *Gay Divorce* perfunctory items.

Among the other performers there are Betty Starbuck, who is candid and forthright in what little she has to do; Eric Blore, who struggles amiably with singularly labored humor, and G. P. Huntley Jr., who impersonates the stage Englishman willingly. An unusually attractive chorus dances with more spirit than you would think possible on so encumbered a stage. Last night's audience found *Gay Divorce* much to its liking. But to this censorious column the performance seemed always to be simulating a cleverness that it did not contain.

Scenes from *Gay Divorce*. **OPPOSITE:** Fred Astaire and Claire Luce. **ABOVE:** Fred Astaire, Erik Rhodes, and Claire Luce.

# AS THOUSANDS CHEER

### By BROOKS ATKINSON

No doubt someone will be able to suggest how *As Thousands Cheer* could be improved. But on the evidence disclosed Saturday evening at the Music Box, where the revue had its New York première, this column can only give its meek approval to every item on the program. Irving Berlin and Moss Hart, who wrote it in collaboration; Sam H. Harris, who has produced it in the pink of modern taste, and all the craftsmen who have contributed to it, have created a superb panorama of entertainment. By being topical it is a revue in the genuine meaning of that word. By being excellent in quality it is enormously exhilarating. Among the thousands who cheer, count this column as one of the noisiest. Let us all toss our sweaty nightcaps in the air.

In form it is a newspaper revue with columns of type streaming up and down the curtains and headlines introducing the various numbers. Under the banner line of "Franklin D. Roosevelt Inaugurated Tomorrow," for instance, you will discover what Mr. and Mrs. Hoover really think of Dolly Gann, Mellon, Stimson and their dynamic successors. "World's Wealthiest Man Celebrates 94th Birthday" reveals John D. Rockefeller Jr. trying to present Radio City to his father as a birthday gift, and running for his life as the curtains sweep together. There is a note on the baleful effect Noel Coward has upon hotel servants after they have been exposed to his mannerisms and macabre literary moods; and there is a domestic scene in Buckingham Palace to which the British object—possibly because it is the revue's only lapse from sententious brilliance. There is a great deal more of

general current significance, and it is all crisply written, adroitly presented and wittily acted.

For the performers are off the show-shop's top shelf. Helen Broderick never misses a chance to put poison in the soup, nor does she waste a drop of acid. Whether she is Mrs. Hoover writhing with contempt or the Statue of Liberty thumbing her nose at foreign statesmen or Aimee Semple MacPherson teaming up with Mahatma Gandhi, Miss Broderick is the perfect stage wit. Ethel Waters takes full control of the audience and the show whenever she appears. Her abandon to the ruddy tune of "Heat Wave Hits New York," her rowdy comedy as the wife of a stage-struck *Green Pastures* actor and her pathos in a deep-toned song about a lynching give some notion of the broad range she can encompass in musical shows.

Clifton Webb, king of the decadent pants, sings and dances with a master's dexterity, and puts a keen point to all his sardonic sketches. His John D. Rockefeller Sr. and Mahatma Gandhi are masterpieces in

miniature of topical parody. Marilyn Miller brings to the show not only the effulgence of her personality but a sense of humor as Joan Crawford and a chambermaid with literary delusions of grandeur. Among the secondary performers Leslie Adams has great relish of the humor involved in travestying Herbert Hoover and the King of England, and Hal Forde does a Ramsay MacDonald that is the subtlest caricature of the evening.

Nor does this exhaust the rich and bristling coffers of *As Thousands Cheer*. Charles Weidman's dance arrangements are revelations of the comment this art can make on current affairs. The costumes designed by Varady and Irene Sharaff have meaning as well as beauty. Albert Johnson's settings testify to one of the keenest minds in that business, and Hassard Short's lighting and staging are among his best works. As for Mr. Berlin, he has never written better tunes or more sparkling lyrics; and Mr. Hart has never turned his wit with such economical precision. In these circumstances there is nothing a reviewer can do except cheer. Bravo and huzzas!

PAGE 66: Helen Broderick as the Statue of Liberty.

PAGE 67, CLOCKWISE FROM TOP LEFT: Ethel Waters; Clifton Webb; and from left, Ethel Waters, Marilyn Miller, Helen Broderick, and Clifton Webb.

LEFT: Marilyn Miller and Clifton Webb in a scene from the original Broadway production of *As Thousands Cheer*, 1933.

November 22, 1934

# ANYTHING GOES

By BROOKS ATKINSON

By keeping their sense of humor uppermost, they have made a thundering good musical show out of *Anything Goes*, which was put on at the Alvin last evening. They are Guy Bolton and P. G. Wodehouse, whose humor is completely unhackneyed; Cole Porter, who has written a dashing score with impish lyrics, and Howard Lindsay and Russel Crouse, who have been revising the jokes in person. After all, these supermen must have had a good deal to do with the skylarking that makes *Anything Goes* such hilarious and dynamic entertainment. But when a show is off the top shelf of the pantry cupboard it is hard to remember that the comics have not written all those jokes and the singers have not composed all those exultant tunes. If Ethel Merman did not write "I Get a Kick Out of You" and also the title song of the show, she has made them hers now by the swinging gusto of her platform style.

Do you remember a pathetic, unsteady little man who answers to the name of Alexander Throttlebottom? Masquerading in the program as Victor Moore, he is the first clown of this festival, and he is tremendously funny. For it has occurred to the wastrels who wrote the book to represent him as a gangster disguised as a parson and to place him on a liner bound for Europe. Among the other passengers are a nightclub enchantress, who sings with the swaggering authority of Ethel Merman, and a roistering man about town who enjoys the infectious exuberance of William Gaxton. There is also a lady of considerable breeding who can sing the soprano of Bettina Hall.

What a voyage! Last year Howard Lindsay staged a memorable comedy entitled *She Loves Me Not*. What he learned there in the vein of theatre versatility he has generously applied to *Anything Goes*, and the product is a rag, tag and bobtail of comic situations and of music sung in the spots when it is most exhilarating. Throttle-

bottom looks mighty absurd in those prelate's vestments. When his gangster blood comes through his disguise and his bewildered personality, comedy is the most satisfying invention of the human race. He calls his portable machine gun "My little pal putt-putt-putt" with a dying inflection. He muses on the advisability of bumping off an annoying passenger as if he were composing a wistful sonnet. Whatever he does, Mr. Throttle bottom, who is just as sweet under any other name, is the quintessence of musical comedy humor, and the authors of *Anything Goes* have given him the sort of thing he can do best.

As far as that goes, it suits William Gaxton, too. Following the lead of a madcap book, he is in and out of all sorts of disguises—a sailor, a Spanish nobleman with false whiskers just clipped off a Pomeranian, a fabulous public enemy. Through the show

he fairly dances with enjoyment and high spirits, making every song sound good on his old Gaxiolaphone. When he sings with Miss Merman the composer ought to be very grateful for a pair of performers who can make every note burst with vitality and every line sound like a masterpiece of wit. "You're the Top" is one of the most congenial songs Mr. Porter has written. Mr. Gaxton and Miss Merman put their toes as well as their voices into it.

Although Miss Hall has a nicer talent, she plays the part of a girl of exalted station with winning good humor and she sings "All Through the Night" with the thrilling beauty of a trained artist. For minor diversion there is a foursome of dry-humored sailors for whom Mr. Porter has written a droll chanty. Count as items worth sober consideration a platoon of chorus girls whose dancing is also well-planned; a suite of Oenslager settings; a wardrobe of gowns by Jenkins—and a general good time. Guy Bolton and P. G. Wodehouse were always funny fellows. It does them no harm to be associated with Cole Porter, Howard Lindsay, Russel Crouse and a thundering good song-and-dance show.

**OPPOSITE:** William Gaxton, Ethel Merman, and Victor Moore. **BELOW:** Ethel Merman as Reno Sweeney with members of the cast.

## REVIVAL

October 20, 1987

# Anything Goes

By FRANK RICH

Forget about the Colosseum, the Louvre museum, a melody from a symphony by Strauss—Patti LuPone is the top. As Reno Sweeney, the sassy nightclub singer in the Lincoln Center revival of *Anything Goes*, Ms. LuPone has her first sensational New York role since *Evita* in 1979, and, given that Cole Porter is the evening's buoyant guiding spirit, you don't have to fear that she'll succumb to death scenes in the second act.

With her burst of Lucille Ball red hair, a trumpet's blare in her voice and lips so insinuatingly protruded they could make the Pledge of Allegiance sound lewd, Ms. LuPone's Reno is a mature, uninhibited jazz dame: loose, trashy, funny, sexy. Ethel Merman she's not—the difference in belting power is mainly apparent in "Blow, Gabriel, Blow"—but who is? Ms. LuPone has her own brash American style and, most of all, a blazing spontaneity: With this Reno, everything goes. At the end of Act I, which should by all rights conclude with the full-throttle dance number accompanying the title song, she has the audacity to upstage the entire company and bring down the act with a broad wink into the Vivian Beaumont's auditorium. By then, most of the crowd is ready to take Ms. LuPone home, and not necessarily to mother.

Although the star and her share of unbeatable Porter standards (did I fail to mention "I Get a Kick Out of You"?) are the essential sparks for this *Anything Goes*, the production, directed by Jerry Zaks and choreographed by Michael Smuin, has its other lightheaded though inconsistent virtues. Indeed, yesterday's performance by the stock market may allow the show to serve the same escapist mission in 1987 that it did in 1934, when it tickled those Depression audiences who could still laugh at jokes about suicide leaps on Wall Street.

April 7, 2011

# A GLIMPSE OF STOCKING? SHOCKING!

By BEN BRANTLEY

Who needs a brass section when you've got Sutton Foster? As the nightclub evangelist Reno Sweeney in the zesty new revival of *Anything Goes*, which opened on Thursday night at the Stephen Sondheim Theatre, Ms. Foster has the voice of a trumpet and a big, gleaming presence that floods the house. When she leads the show-stopping "Blow, Gabriel, Blow," you figure that if no horn-tooting archangel appears, it's only because he's afraid of the competition.

Ms. Foster is playing a part originated by the all-time musical-comedy queen of brass, Ethel Merman, who was said to be the heart and soul (as well as lungs) of *Anything Goes* when it opened on Broadway in 1934. Certainly that is the role served to the brimming point by Ms. Foster in Kathleen Marshall's production of this willfully silly tale of love, deception and celebrity-chasing on the high seas, which features a deluxe candy box of songs by Cole Porter.

Both goofy and sexy, shruggingly insouciant and rigorously polished, Ms. Foster's performance embodies the essence of escapist entertainment in the 1930s, when hard times called for bold smiles, tough wisecracks and defiant fantasies of over-the-top opulence. That's the tone that Ms. Marshall is going for in this Roundabout Theatre Company production. And to achieve it she's enlisted a team that includes Derek McLane (for the bright Deco sets), Martin Pakledinaz (for the matching sassy costumes) and the peerless Rob Fisher (for the musical supervision and vocal arrangements).

No revisionist shadows for this version of the show that gave us the immortal standards "You're the Top," "I Get a Kick Out of You" and "Anything Goes," among others. Ms. Marshall and her singing dancers and comic actors—a motley crew that includes Joel Grey, Jessica Walter, Adam Godley and John McMartin—are here not to make sense of the world but to help us forget it for a couple of hours.

. . . . . . . . . . . . . . . . . . . . . . . . . . . . . .

**OPPOSITE:** Patti LuPone in the 1987 revival of *Anything Goes*. **ABOVE:** Sutton Foster (center) and members of the cast in the 2011 revival of *Anything Goes*.

October 11, 1935

# *Porgy and Bess*

By BROOKS ATKINSON

After eight years of savory memories, *Porgy* has acquired a score, a band, a choir of singers and a new title, *Porgy and Bess*, which the Theatre Guild put on at the Alvin last evening. Du Bose and Dorothy Heyward wrote the original lithograph of Catfish Row, which Rouben Mamoulian translated into a memorable work of theatre dynamics. But *Porgy and Bess* represents George Gershwin's longing to compose an American folk opera on a suitable theme. Although Mr. Heyward is the author of the libretto and shares with Ira Gershwin the credit for the lyrics, and although Mr. Mamoulian has again mounted the director's box, the evening is unmistakably George Gershwin's personal holiday. In fact, the volume of music he has written during the last two years on the ebony fable of a Charleston rookery has called out a whole brigade of Times Square music critics, who are quite properly the masters of this occasion. Mr. Downes, soothsayer of the diatonic scale, is now beetling his brow in the adjoining cubicle. There is an authoritative ring to his typewriter clatter tonight.

In these circumstances, the province of a drama critic is to report on the transmutation of *Porgy* out of drama into music theatre. Let it be said at once that Mr. Gershwin has contributed something glorious to the spirit of the Heywards' community legend. If memory serves, it always lacked the glow of personal feeling. Being a fairly objective narrative of a neighborhood of Negroes who lived a private racial life in the midst of a white civilization, *Porgy* was a natural subject for theatre showmanship. The groupings, the mad fantasy of leaping shadows, the panic-stricken singing over a corpse, the evil bulk of the buzzard's flight, the screaming hurricane—these large audible and visible items of showmanship took precedence over the episode of Porgy's romance with Crown's high-steppin' gal.

Whether or not Mr. Gershwin's score measures up to its intentions as American folk opera lies in Mr. Downes's bailiwick. But to the ears of a theatre critic Mr. Gershwin's music gives a personal voice to Porgy's loneliness when, in a crowd of pitying neighbors, he learns that Bess has vanished into the capacious and remote North. The pathetic apprehension of the "Where's My Bess" trio and the manly conviction of "I'm on My Way" add something vital to the story that was missing before.

These comments are written by a reviewer so inured to the theatre that he regards operatic form as cumbersome. Why commonplace remarks that carry no emotion have to be made in a chanting monotone is a problem in art he cannot fathom. Even the hermit thrush drops into conversational tones when he is not singing from the topmost spray in a tree. Turning *Porgy* into opera has resulted in a deluge of casual remarks that have to be thoughtfully intoned and that amazingly impede the action. Why do composers vex it so? "Sister, you goin' to the picnic?" "No, I guess not." Now, why in heaven's name must two characters in an opera clear their throats before they can exchange that sort of information? What a theatre critic probably wants is a musical show with songs that evoke the emotion of situations and make no further pretensions. Part of the emotion of a drama comes from the pace of the performance.

And what of the amusing little device of sounds and rhythms, of sweeping, sawing, hammering and dusting, that opens the last scene early one morning? In the program it is solemnly described as "Occupational Humeresque." But any music hall would be glad to have it without its tuppence colored label. Mr. Mamoulian is an excellent director for dramas of ample proportions. He is not subtle, which is a virtue in showmanship. His crowds are arranged in masses that look as solid as a victory at the polls; they move with simple unanimity, and the rhythm is comfortably obvious.

Mr. Gershwin knows that. He has written the scores for innumerable musical shows. After one of them he was presented with the robes of Arthur Sullivan, who also was consumed with a desire to write grand. To the ears of a theatre critic there are intimations in *Porgy and Bess* that Mr. Gershwin is still easiest in mind when he is writing songs with choruses. He, and his present reviewer, are on familiar ground when he is writing a droll tune like "A Woman Is a Sometime Thing," or a lazy darky solo like "I Got Plenty o' Nuttin'," or made-to-order spirituals like "Oh, de Lawd Shake de Heaven," or Sportin' Life's hot-time number entitled "There's a Boat That's Leavin' Soon for New York." If Mr. Gershwin does not enjoy his task most in moments like this, his audience does. In sheer quality of character they are worth an hour of formal music transitions.

For the current folk opera Sergei Soudeikine has prepared Catfish Row settings that follow the general design of the originals, but have more grace, humor and color. In the world of sound that Mr. Gershwin has created the tattered children of a Charleston byway are still racy and congenial. Promoting *Porgy* to opera involves considerable incidental drudgery for theatre-goers who agree with Mark Twain that "classical music is better than it sounds." But Mr. Gershwin has found a personal voice that was inarticulate in the original play. The fear and the pain go deeper in *Porgy and Bess* than they did in penny plain *Porgy*.

ABOVE: From left, John W. Bubbles as Sportin' Life,
Todd Duncan as Porgy, and Anne Wiggins Brown as
Bess in *Porgy and Bess*.

**LEFT:** A scene from the original Broadway production of *Porgy and Bess*, 1935.

# JUMBO

By BROOKS ATKINSON

Right this way, ladies and gentlemen, for the latest bulletin of *Jumbo*, which finally opened the doors of the Hippodrome Saturday evening. Colossal in scope, childish in its affection for the gaudy tumult of the circus, it is downright enjoyable. For months Billy Rose and his tanbark rabble have been grimly at work behind the venerable walls of the Hippodrome on one of the most extravagant, crack-brained works of foolishness the town has devised in years; and here it is, not so much *Jumbo* as mumbo-jumbo—handsome, original and happily endearing.

It is circus in odor and appearance. Although Hecht and MacArthur have devised a sentimental story to bind the actors, acrobats and animals together, and Rodgers and Hart have hammered out a calliope of good tunes, the main business of *Jumbo* is evoking the wonder of the circus amid the glamour of imaginative showmanship. The Hippodrome has been transformed into a warm and red arena. The stage is a circus ring in the pit, roofed by a canopy, where the trapeze artistes risk their necks for a pay envelope. After Paul Whiteman has made a festive entrance on a white horse and led his band in a brassy fanfare, *Jumbo* settles down to a solid evening of feats of skill, clowning, daring and John Murray Anderson pageantry. If, in your middle years, you have been churlish enough to wish that the circus were as good-humored as your idea of the circus, *Jumbo* deserves your fond attention.

What Jimmy Durante and Arthur Sinclair are up to is acting an innocuous backstage story in a style of free-hand drawing. Considine's circus, which is our circus, is threatened by Mulligan's circus, which is corrupt, predatory and snide. Our circus is nearly sold out by the United States Marshal for non-payment of income

tax. All this amounts to very little at the Hippodrome, for wit and romance look pretty lonely amid the enormous spaces of a circus tent. But it is sufficiently useful to draw a personal point on the proceedings, to perch Mr. Sinclair on the amiable back of an entrancing elephant and to renew an old liking for the raucous ebullience of Jimmy Durante. As Claudius B. (for Brains) Bowers, Jimmy is in grand form, a friendly, strutting, stretch-mouthed comic who manages to make a cheering personal impression against the handicap of so much untenanted space. Mr. Sinclair's rich voice and Irish vehemence also leave a pleasant impression; and Gloria Grafton and Donald Novis are as romantic a pair of love-birds as ever sang of passion from a circus ring.

Don't let that misguide you into thinking of *Jumbo* as a musical play with a big tent background. The circus acts are that celebrated elephant's meat, drink and peanuts—bareback riders, performing ponies, fire-eaters, wire-walkers, whip-snappers, jugglers, supermen of the iron-jaw, four lions, a bridle procession of animals of all nations. In the title role "Big Rosie" plays with so much amiable beauty and patience that she deserves to be the toast of the town all Winter. And for genuine circus clowning this column has never seen the equal of A. Robins, whose mummery is "terrific," as Jimmy would say.

If constructive criticism is tolerable today, this column prays that Mr. Rose find another spot for Mr. Robins in the second act. Otherwise *Jumbo* is perfect as Mr. Rose has staged it—a gargantuan antic, a fool's paradise of bizarre and plain enjoyment. Ladies and gentlemen, don't forget the free menagerie downstairs—the most astonishing, the most pungent, the most— Well, don't forget the wild and domestic animals in the basement. Come one, come all.

Scenes from *Jumbo*. **ABOVE:** Members of the cast, including puppets and Big Rosie the Elephant. **OPPOSITE:** Jimmy Durante and Big Rosie.

80

April 15, 1937

# Babes in Arms

By BROOKS ATKINSON

School being out, the Broadway professors of the song and dance have assembled a show from among the footloose brats and urchins, "Babes in Arms," which was put on at the Shubert last evening. If it is fresh faces you want, any number of shining ones can be discovered among the bantling performers in this good-humored musical show, and also any number of nimble dancing feet and one or two unsullied voices. For Mr. Wiman and his associates have recruited a singularly pleasant cast of youths in their dewy teens and creaking twenties, and Rodgers and Hart have invented the sort of book that they deserve. Not an inspired book, perhaps; not so terse as a Broadway playgoer might like it—but a book that is full of good feeling and a score that is altogether superb. Pardon the performers for the atrocious crime of being young. With the proper direction from Robert Sinclair they have put on a warm-hearted and lively show.

It is the authors' notion to present them as Summer orphans somewhere on Long Island, where a work camp for children keeps willowy imps out of mischief. And it is the children's notion to escape work camp by pooling their ingenuity. They are not altogether successful, nor are the authors, for the book of *Babes in Arms* is a long succession of promises that are parsimoniously rewarded. But it does involve an original ballet or two, several textual promontories for the singing of some excellent songs, and it is always in the best of taste. There is very little of Broadway in it.

There are some good kids in it, however. Notably, there is Wynn Murray, a fat girl of sixteen, with a sunny expression becoming to her years and a voice as full and sweet as her personality. "Way Out West on West End Avenue" is the title of the jaunty ballad the authors have entrusted to her larynx, and she sings it with the most

infectious gusto. According to the program, Duke McHale is twenty, and must soon begin to think of retiring. In the meantime, he dances with admirable skill and earnestness an ingenuous dream ballet that has been imaginatively designed. Mitzi Green, the retired infant prodigy from Hollywood, has a sophisticated assurance, which is a little hard to endure in such genuine company, but it results in one of the most exultant song items in the production—"The Lady Is a Tramp," in the swinging style of Ethel Merman.

Ray Heatherton may be all of twenty-five or twenty-six, which is superannuated-ism, or something of the sort, but he is not too old to do a good job of male leadership in Mr. Wiman's kindergarten. Among the Harlem pickaninnies there are two dancing fools, Harold and Fayard Nicholas, who clatter across the stage with the rhythmic frenzy that only the Negroes can conjure out of a Broadway night. Pay some attention also to Douglas Perry, who is round in shape and short-panted by age and who makes impertinent rejoinders without sounding precocious. Although Rollo Pickert puts up his dukes with alarming eagerness, he is another attractive lad in a show that might be coy without the presence of a gamecock just under the draft age.

For the story of *Babes in Arms* is a catalog of the well-washed and starched performers and a bulletin on one of the most contagious scores Rodgers and Hart have written. No gags worth mentioning; no blackouts; no scandal. But they have provided a cheerful evening in the presence of as nice a group of youngsters as ever dove into an ice cream freezer at a birthday party. Without condescending from the sublime heights of maturity, Mr. Rodgers and Mr. Hart have written a genial and buoyant show for them.

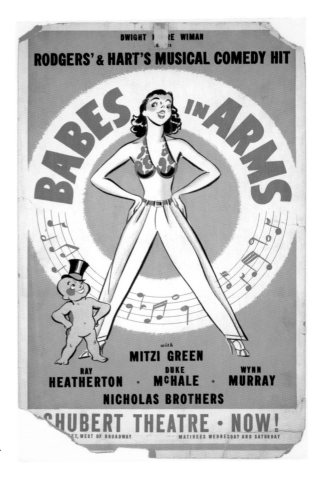

Scenes from *Babes in Arms*. **OPPOSITE, CLOCKWISE FROM TOP:** Members of the cast in a dance number; Wynn Murray and Alfred Drake; and from left, Mitzi Green, Alex Courtney, Alfred Drake, Aljan de Loville, Ray Heatherton, and Wynn Murray. **ABOVE:** Souvenir program, 1937.

# I'D RATHER BE RIGHT

By BROOKS ATKINSON

Mr. Roosevelt should feel very happy about his part in *I'd Rather Be Right*, which opened at the Alvin last evening. On the whole, George S. Kaufman and Moss Hart feel very tender about him. Apart from their affectionate treatment of him in the plot and lines of their musical comedy, they have engaged George M. Cohan to impersonate the President, which is a dispensation devoutly to be desired by anyone who wants to please an audience. For Mr. Cohan is an amiable gentleman whose services to the theatre and whose personality have long held him dear in the affections of Gotham playgoers. Put him in as head man in a political garden party, and the President of the United States is bound to emerge as a buoyant, tactful man-about-town with a soft spot in his heart for young lovers and a feeling of general confusion about the government. As a matter of fact, Mr. Cohan has never been in better form. The audience was his, and lovingly his, all last evening.

If the authors had held council with Jim Farley, they could hardly have felt in better humor about our country. Although advance reports seemed to indicate that *I'd Rather Be Right* might discharge a lampoon at the follies of current politics, it turns out to be a pleasant-spoken musical comedy that leisurely ambles away the evening. There is some brisk stuff here and there—a capital object lesson in the effects of taxation, which is worthy of the Living Newspaper technique; a quip or two about the Federal Theatre, "Wherever we see three people together we are supposed to give a show"; a poke at Walter Lippmann and a few frolicsome skirmishes with the Supreme Court. But there have been Marx Brothers shows in the past that were more hilariously antic than this pastoral in Central Park, and *Of Thee I Sing* was enormously more versatile and dynamic. *I'd Rather Be Right* is playful; and, all questions of political opinion to one side, that is hardly enough for a first-rate musical show.

Richard Rodgers, the composer, and Lorenz Hart, maker of rhymes, have come closer to the spirit of the topical merry-go-round. All their political ditties are keen ones—"A Homogeneous Cabinet," "A Little Bit of Constitutional Fun," "We're Going to Balance the Budget," "Labor Is the Thing" and "Off the Record," this one for Mr. Cohan's voice. They have also written the romantic "Have You Met Miss Jones?" which Joy Hodges and Austin Marshall sing with a good deal of footlights rapture; a piece of tuneful mockery, "Spring in Vienna," which Joseph Macaulay sings with flamboyant humor, and a song or two for Mary Jane Walsh, who has the style and volume of an able chorus drum-major.

There are some varied dances for tapping and twirling, including one tedious bit of documentation entitled "American

Couple." Irene Sharaff has done the costumes with her usual vivacity, and Donald Oenslager has designed a masque scene for Central Park. The cast includes Taylor Holmes and Marion Green as members of the Cabinet, a fussy Ma Perkins by Bijou Fernandez and a droll Jim Farley by Paul Parks. Florenz Ames does something lively in defense of the harassed business man. In fact, every one has conspired to make *I'd Rather Be Right* a clever and generally likable musical comedy. But it is not the keen and brilliant political satire most of us have been fondly expecting.

. . . . . . . . . . . . . . . . . . . . . . . . . . . . . .

Scenes from *I'd Rather Be Right*. **OPPOSITE:** George M. Cohan as the president of the United States. **ABOVE:** From left, Joseph Macaulay, Austin Marshall, George M. Cohan, and Joy Hodges.

# CRADLE WILL ROCK
## *WILL CONTINUE RUN*
### OPERA ORIGINALLY PLANNED BY WPA TO GO ON
### "SO LONG AS PUBLIC SUPPORTS IT"

*The Cradle Will Rock*, an opera by Marc Blitzstein, which was originally intended for a WPA production and was taken over on Friday by a private management when the WPA ruled against the opening of any new productions until after July 1, will continue at the Venice Theatre "so long as the public supports it," John Houseman, managing producer, said yesterday.

The actors in the company had obtained two weeks' leave of absence from the WPA to engage in the privately financed enterprise, but this may be extended indefinitely should the attraction prove successful, he said.

At an emergency performance on Wednesday night and again at the first performance under private management on Friday night, the opera was presented with Mr. Blitzstein playing the score on a piano in lieu of an orchestra and with the actors, minus make-up or costumes, singing their parts from seats in the audience. This technique will be used throughout the run of the attraction, said Mr. Houseman.

"There has always been the question," he said, "of how to produce a labor show so the audience can be brought to feel that it is a part of the performance. This technique seems to solve the problem and is exactly the right one for this particular piece. It will also make it possible to play this show in any sort of theatre or auditorium any place in the country."

The price scale at the Venice Theatre will be from $1.10 to 35 cents. Mr. Houseman said that any WPA worker will be admitted for 25 cents.

**ABOVE:** Olive Staunton. **OPPOSITE:** Howard Da Silva and Olive Staunton as Larry Foreman and Moll.

December 6, 1937

# THE CRADLE WILL ROCK

By BROOKS ATKINSON

After drifting from pillar to post since last July Marc Blitzstein's *The Cradle Will Rock* had an official opening at the Mercury last evening. Written with extraordinary versatility and played with enormous gusto, it is the best thing militant labor has put into a theatre yet. Although Mr. Blitzstein's story of big industry corruption and labor union gallantry is an old one in the working-class theatre, he has transmuted it into a remarkably stirring marching song by the bitterness of his satire, the savagery of his music and the ingenuity of his craftsmanship. At last the comrades of the insurgent theatre can feel sure that they have a fully awakened artist on their side. What *Waiting for Lefty* was to the dramatic stage, *The Cradle Will Rock* is to the stage of the labor battle song.

This is the opera about steel unionization which the Federal Theatre discreetly dropped after an extensive rehearsal period last Summer. For a time it was put on al fresco without costumes or scenery at the Adelphi Theatre, where it made friends rather than money. Last week-end it had two performances at the Mercury Theatre as the first item in the projected Worklight Theatre, which is designed to give auditions to unusual pieces that are homeless. Since it was insufficiently rehearsed last week, the critics were asked to stay away—a form of charity they are always willing to extend on Sunday evenings. But last night it was sufficiently rehearsed to raise a theatregoer's basic metabolism and blow him out of the theatre on the thunder of the finale. *The Cradle Will Rock* rocked a great many things, including the audience.

One can understand the Federal Theatre's embarrassment. For the second time we have proof that a theatre supported by government funds cannot be a free agent when art has an insurgent political motive. *The Cradle Will Rock* is a summons to battle and a cry of warning, directed impartially at the steel industry. Since Big Steel has signed on the dotted line, Mr. Blitzstein's broadside is presumably directed at Little Steel, which has not yet reached for its fountain pen. Briefly, *The Cradle Will Rock* is the story of a steel magnate who unscrupulously consolidates a united front of newspapers and citizens' liberty committees against a union campaign to organize his plant.

Although *The Cradle Will Rock* has arrived at its official opening, it is still without costumes or scenery. Mr. Blitzstein sits at the piano on the rim of the stage. Behind him sit three rows of actors and singers in street clothes. They are individually introduced at the opening of the performance. As the opera progresses they go downstage to act their scenes, returning to their chairs when they are finished. To the casual playgoer this may seem like a negation of the theatre. As a matter of fact, it lays a very grave emphasis upon the deadly earnestness of this operatic pitch battle. Possibly *The Cradle Will Rock* would lose some of its direct fury in a normally accoutred performance.

If Mr. Blitzstein looks like a mild little man as he sits before his piano his work generates current like a dynamo. Most of it is caustically satiric in rhyme scheme and score. He can write anything from tribal chant to Tin Pan Alley balladry; the piano keys scatter scorn, impishness and pathos according to the capricious mood of his story. And when Mr. Blitzstein settles down to serious business at the conclusion his music box roars with rage and his actors frighten the aged roof of the miniature Mercury Theatre.

Since most of the actors are not singers the music of *The Cradle Will Rock* gets only a noisy hearing. The voices are generally strained and some of them are harshly disagreeable. Theatregoers unhappily seated down front are entitled to ear muffs and shower curtains. But if *The Cradle Will Rock* is intended to arouse the rabble by malicious caricature and battle-line thunder it may be temperately reported as a stirring success. It is also the most versatile artistic triumph of the politically insurgent theatre.

May 1, 1983

# A NEW LOOK AT THE CRADLE THAT ROCKED BROADWAY

By ROBERT LEITER

In a rehearsal hall on West 46th Street, John Houseman and alumni of his Acting Company are preparing a revival of Marc Blitzstein's *The Cradle Will Rock*, which starts performances Thursday and runs through May 29 at the American Place. The rehearsal is relaxed, and there is evident camaraderie among the players. Mr. Houseman, sitting to one side of the room, never takes his eyes from the players, his head moving in time to the piano accompaniment. He is evidently a happy man.

The convivial mood is dramatically different from the frenetic atmosphere that surrounded the original production of *Cradle*, which Mr. Houseman produced (and Orson Welles directed) in 1937 under the auspices of the Government-funded Federal Theatre Project. During those first rehearsals the play came to generate so much controversy that, as opening night approached, it took on, in Mr. Houseman's version of the story, the nature of a theatrical time bomb.

Blitzstein's subject matter accounted for most of the problem. *The Cradle Will Rock* is a paean, in a deliberately one-dimensional, agitprop manner of the '30s, to unionism. (Some have even described the work as a musical *Waiting for Lefty*.) The play is set in Steel Town, U.S.A., where Mr. Mister rules everyone. His only opposition comes from Larry Foreman, the working-class hero, who by evening's end announces the triumph of the workers over their

corrupt boss.

All the trouble began when, after four months of rehearsals, it was rumored that Washington considered *Cradle* "dangerous." Then on June 12, 1937—only four days before the first public preview—Mr. Welles and Mr. Houseman received a memo announcing that, "because of impending cuts and reorganization," the opening of any new play was prohibited.

Within three days their theater, the Maxine Elliott at 39th and Broadway, was invaded by a dozen uniformed W.P.A. guards bearing strict orders prohibiting the removal of such Government property as scenery, props and costumes. Houseman, Welles and Blitzstein then retreated to the theater's basement—the one area off limits to the WPA people—and spent the next 36 hours trying to devise a scheme for privately producing *The Cradle Will Rock*.

The obstacles seemed insurmountable. The Musicians Union had announced that if the play were moved to another theater, then the orchestra members had to be paid full Broadway salaries. And Equity made it clear that its actors, having rehearsed the work under the auspices of the Federal Theatre, could not perform for new management without approval of the first producers.

Mr. Welles and Mr. Houseman knew they could meet neither of these demands. But on the morning of June 16 they assured everyone that the performance would go on,

even if Blitzstein had to play the piano and sing every part. (He had actually done this countless times while trying to interest producers in the work.)

A theater broker was then brought to the pink powder room; but after five hours of phone calls his list of available theaters had sunk to zero. He was brushed aside by Mr. Welles and Mr. Houseman; yet he managed to stay on, unobtrusively making his own phone calls and offering suggestions which no one heeded.

At 5 o'clock Jean Rosenthal, the production manager, was given $10 and told to rent a piano. Having accomplished this she was then told to hire a truck, load the piano onto it and keep calling in every 15 minutes for instructions.

Next, Mr. Welles and Mr. Houseman spoke to the actors. Mr. Houseman explained the legal difficulties confronting them. But he added, "There is nothing to prevent you from entering whatever theater we find, then getting up from your seats, as U.S. citizens, and speaking or singing your piece when your cue comes." The responses were mixed, with many actors fearing that such insubordination would lose them their jobs with the Federal Theatre Project.

By 7:30 things looked bleak. Jean Rosenthal called in to say that her truck driver was threatening to quit. It was then, in Mr. Houseman's words, that "the miracle occurred." The theater broker announced that he was leaving. He also said he couldn't understand why no one wanted to use the Venice Theatre. It was open, empty and available, and he'd been offering it to them for three hours.

Everyone pounced upon him. Money changed hands and the necessary announcements were made inside and outside the theater. Curtain time was being changed to 9 P.M., as there were 21 city blocks between the two theaters. The mass of ticket holders who had gathered outside the Maxine Elliott Theatre cheered as they made their way north, many of them on foot. Mr. Welles and Mr. Houseman drove the distance in someone's white Nash roadster with the poet Archibald MacLeish at the wheel.

By 10 minutes to 9 there wasn't an empty seat in the Venice Theatre. With Blitzstein waiting at the piano, Mr. Welles and Mr. Houseman stepped out in front

of the curtain. Mr. Houseman spoke first, insisting—disingenuously—that the company's defiance was artistic, not political. Mr. Welles then set the scene of the play, described the characters and announced: "We have the honor to present—with the composer at the piano—*The Cradle Will Rock*!"

The curtain rose. The spotlight caught Blitzstein at the piano in his shirtsleeves, his suspenders showing. "A street corner—Steel Town, U.S.A.," he said. Then he began to sing the Moll's opening lines.

It took a few moments for people to realize that someone else besides Blitzstein was singing. The spotlight moved off stage and came to rest on the lower left box where Olive Stanton, the original Moll, stood singing. As Mr. Houseman admits, it remains impossible "at this distance in time, to convey the throat-catching, sickeningly exciting quality of that moment." Years later Hiram Sherman, who played Junior Mister

that night, wrote to Mr. Houseman to say that "if Olive Stanton had not risen on cue in the box, I doubt if the rest of us would have had the courage to stand up and carry on. But once that thin, incredibly clear voice came out, they all fell in line." Blitzstein filled in for those actors who had decided not to perform. And the rest became history.

"We're trying to re-create as much of that famous opening night as we can," Mr. Houseman explains during a break in the rehearsal. "I've decided to begin each performance with a 10-minute narrative recounting how the play was originally banned. We're also having a pianist on stage, a young man named Michael Barrett, who was recommended to me by Leonard Bernstein. Michael will impersonate Marc in his shirtsleeves and red suspenders."

The current production will also be done on a bare stage with props kept to a minimum. There will be no attempt made to

manufacture period costumes. Instead, Mr. Houseman has encouraged his actors to shop around for appropriate clothing.

Mr. Houseman is aware that some theatergoers may consider the play a dated piece of propaganda but he dismisses the argument. "The only aspect of the work that's dated is Marc's excessive love of unions," he says. "There are other themes—the fact that artists sometimes sponge off the rich and that doctors and newspaper editors don't always have the most impeccable morals—which still make sense to us today. Actually, the play's only message is that a town run by a boss is not a good town. It's really that simple."

**ABOVE:** Patti Lupone as Moll with members of the cast in the 1983 revival of *The Cradle Will Rock*.

September 23, 1938

# HELLZAPOPPIN

By BROOKS ATKINSON

Folks, it is going to be a little difficult to describe this one. *Hellzapoppin* is what they call it and it was discharged at the Forty-sixth Street Theatre last evening. Deciding that it might be a good idea to put on a show, Ole Olsen and Chic Johnson, a pair of vaudeville knockabouts, stood on the corner of the street and stopped every third man. Those were their actors. Taking an old broom, they went up to the attic and swept out all the gags in sight. Those were their jokes. Dropping into an ammunition store downtown, they picked up several boxes of blank cartridges. Those were to indicate that the jokes had been told and that it was time to start laughing. Then they moved everything in sight into the Forty-sixth Street Theatre, got an audience down front

and set them to laughing. Anything goes in *Hellzapoppin*—noise, vulgarity, practical joking—and about every third number is foolish enough for guffawing.

Very prominent in the proceedings are Olsen and Johnson, a pair of college cut-ups now well on toward middle life without much flowering of their culture. As far as they are concerned, it is house-cleaning day in vaudeville. After a hilarious motion-picture prologue, in which some grotesque sounds and words come out of the pictures of F. D. R., the Little Flower, Hitler and Mussolini, Olsen and Johnson make their entrance in a clownish automobile and trailer and the uproar begins. It pops out of all parts of the house. Up and down the aisles of the orchestra a persistent woman keeps shouting, "Oscar, Oscar!" in a tenement voice. A ticket speculator starts hawking good seats for *I Married an Angel*. Eggs and bananas are tossed out to the audience, and when the lights go out the audience is besieged with spiders and snakes in the darkness. There is no relief even in the intermission. For that is the time when a clown starts paddling up the aisle and haunting unwary customers.

Probably the entertainment ought to show a higher trace of talent. The taste of *Hellzapoppin* runs to second-rate vaudeville turns, with chorus dancing of no particular consequence and some artful warbling by a pair of damsels sweetly billed as "The Starlings." Ornithologically speaking, starlings are likely to be shot or poisoned. But you can see some mighty fine monocycling by Walter Nilsson and some roguish tap dancing by Hal Sherman, and you can hear some lymphatic fiddling by Shirley Wayne, who looks as though she were just on the point of frying a mess of doughnuts. Hardeen is there to astonish the innocent with some prodigious feats of magic.

But this is mainly a helter-skelter assembly of low-comedy gags to an ear-splitting sound accompaniment—some of it ugly, all of it fast. It is a revue concocted of what Al Graham described in yesterday's Conning Tower as "stewed fish-eyes and ragfoam." *I'll Say She Is* was funnier these many years ago because the Marx Brothers were in it. But if you can imagine a demented vaudeville brawl without the Marx Brothers, *Hellzapoppin* is it, and a good part of it is loud, low and funny.

Scenes from *Hellzapoppin*. **OPPOSITE:** Chic Johnson
(center) and Ole Olsen (right). **ABOVE:** Walter Nilsson,
billed as "a loose nut on wheels."

# The Boys from Syracuse

By BROOKS ATKINSON

Taking a swift glance at Shakespeare's *The Comedy of Errors*, George Abbott, who is the jack-of-all-trades in the theatre, has written and staged an exuberant musical comedy, *The Boys from Syracuse*, which was put on at the Alvin last evening. Nothing so gutsy as this has come along for a week. Nothing so original has come along for a much longer period than that. For Mr. Abbott has a knack of giving everything he touches freshness, spontaneity and spinning pace. Rodgers and Hart have written him a versatile score. Jimmy Savo, who is usually lost when he strays away from his own routines, gives an immensely comic performance. And for the other parts, Mr. Abbott has again found attractive and bustling young people whose styles are never hackneyed. Add to this some volatile dancing under George Balanchine's direction, some of the most light-footed settings Jo Mielziner has recently designed and some gorgeous costumes by Irene Sharaff, and the local theatre wakes up to a beautiful feast of rollicking mummery this morning.

As things have turned out, it was a good notion to pilfer Shakespeare's idea and leave his text alone. Against a pseudo-classical setting, which is valuable for costumes and settings, Mr. Abbott has told a knavish tale of twin brothers and twin servants who have been separated for years and are now in the same town unbeknownst to each other. Since one pair of Antipholuses and Dromios is married and the other single, the mistaken identity results in ribald complications that suffuse this column in rosy blushes of shame. Someone will have to call out the fire department to dampen down the classical ardors of this hilarious tale.

Before rushing to the alarm box, however, consider the droll people Mr. Abbott has put to temptation. First of all, there is Savo, the pantomime genius, whose humorous gleams and fairy-tale capers have never been so delighted and disarming. As his master, Eddie Albert, whose boyishness and sparkle of comedy are altogether winning; as Luce, Wynn Murray, the fat Sapolio girl, who beams a song as much as she sings it; as the distressed wife, Muriel Angelus, who is beautiful in figure and voice; as her sister, the lovely Marcy Wescott, who has an enchanting way with a sentimental tune; as the incontinent Antipholus, Ronald Graham, who can master a song without cheapening it, and as the second Dromio, Teddy Hart, brother of the lyricist and an old hand with knockabout comedy—these are the principal people of the plot and they are all genial company.

Giving Shakespeare a commendable assist in the modern vernacular, Mr. Abbott has found plenty for them to do. Richard Rodgers, seated at his composing spinet, and Lorenz Hart, thumbing the rhyming dictionary, have distributed some of their gayest songs. Let us pass over their bawdries with decorous reserve, pausing only to remark that they are vastly enjoyable, and let us praise them extravagantly, for such a romantic song as "This Can't Be Love" and such gracious mischief as the "Sing for Your Supper" trio. Not that Mr. Rodgers and Mr. Hart are averse to the down beat and the thumping of good music hall balladry. To their way of thinking, Ephesus is the home of carnival.

Nor is the dancing a clever afterthought. George Balanchine has designed and staged it. In Betty Bruce and Heidi Vosseler he has a pair of dancers who are extraordinarily skillful and who can translate the revelry of a musical rumpus into dainty beauty. Particularly at the close of the first act Mr. Balanchine has found a way of turning the dancing into the theme of the comedy and orchestrating it in the composition of the scene. Not to put too solemn a face on it, the dancing is wholly captivating.

As the lady to the left remarked, kiss *The Boys from Syracuse* hello.

. . . . . . . . . . . . . . . . . . . . . . . . . . . . .

**OPPOSITE:** A scene from *The Boys from Syracuse*. **RIGHT, TOP:** Eddie Albert and Jimmy Savo as Antipholus and Dromio. **RIGHT, BOTTOM:** Marcy Wescott, Wynn Murray, and Muriel Angeles.

December 26, 1940

# PAL JOEY

By BROOKS ATKINSON

If it is possible to make an entertaining musical comedy out of an odious story, *Pal Joey* is it. The situation is put tentatively here because the ugly topic that is up for discussion stands between this theatregoer and real enjoyment of a well-staged show. Taking as his hero the frowsy nightclub punk familiar to readers of a series of sketches in *The New Yorker*, John O'Hara has written a joyless book about a sulky assignation. Under George Abbott's direction some of the best workmen on Broadway have fitted it out with smart embellishments.

Rodgers and Hart have written the score with wit and skill. Robert Alton has directed the dances inventively. Scenery out of Jo Mielziner's sketchbook and costumes off the racks of John Koenig—all very high class. Some talented performers also act a book that is considerably more dramatic than most. *Pal Joey*, which was put on at the Ethel Barrymore last evening, offers everything but a good time.

Whether Joey is a punk or a heel is something worth more careful thinking than time permits. Perhaps he is only a rat infested with termites. A night club dancer and singer, promoted to master of ceremonies in a Chicago dive, he lies himself into an affair with a rich married woman and opens a gilt-edged club of his own with her money. Mr. O'Hara has drawn a pitiless portrait of his small-time braggart and also of the company he keeps; and Gene Kelly, who distinguished himself as the melancholy hoofer of *The Time of Your Life*, plays the part with remarkable accuracy. His cheap and flamboyant unction, his nervous cunning, his trickiness are qualities that Mr. Kelly catches without forgetting the fright and gaudiness of a petty fakir. Mr. Kelly is also a brilliant tap dancer—"makes with the feet," as it goes in his vernacular—and his performance on both scores is triumphant. If Joey must be acted, Mr. Kelly can do it.

Count among your restricted blessings Vivienne Segal who can act with personal dignity and can sing with breeding. In a singularly sweet voice she sings some scabrous lyrics by Lorenz Hart to one of Richard Rodgers's most haunting tunes—"Bewitched, Bothered and Bewildered." June Havoc applies a broad, rangy style to some funny burlesques of nightclub routines and manners. Jean Casto satirizes the strip-tease with humorous condescension. As a particularly rank racketeer Jack Durant, who is a sizable brute, contributes a few amazing and dizzy acrobatics. This department's paternal heart goes out especially to Leila Ernst who is the only uncontaminated baggage in the cast.

Occasionally *Pal Joey* absents itself a little from depravity and pokes fun at the dreariness of nightclub frolics, and at the close of the first act it presents an admirable dream ballet and pantomime. Joey's hopeful look into a purple future is lyrically danced by Mr. Kelly. There is a kind of wry and wistful beauty to the spinning figures of Mr. Alton's dance design. But the story of *Pal Joey* keeps harking back to the drab and mirthless world of punk's progress. Although *Pal Joey* is expertly done, can you draw sweet water from a foul well?

Scenes from *Pal Joey*. **ABOVE:** Gene Kelly, Stanley Donen, and Leila Ernst. **OPPOSITE:** June Havoc.

January 24, 1941

# Lady in the Dark

By BROOKS ATKINSON

All things considered, the American stage may as well take a bow this morning. For Moss Hart's musical play, *Lady in the Dark*, which was put on at the Alvin last evening, uses the resources of the theatre magnificently and tells a compassionate story triumphantly. Note the distinction between "musical play" and "musical comedy." What that means to Mr. Hart's mind is a drama in which the music and the splendors of the production rise spontaneously out of the heart of the drama, evoking rather than embellishing the main theme.

Although the idea is not new, since *Cabin in the Sky* and *Pal Joey* have been moving in that direction this year, Mr. Hart and his talented associates have carried it as close to perfection as anyone except an academician can require. Eschewing for the moment his blistering style of comedy, Mr. Hart has written a dramatic story about the anguish of a human being. Kurt Weill has matched it with the finest score written for the theatre in years. Ira Gershwin's lyrics are brilliant. Harry Horner's whirling scenery gives the narrative a transcendent loveliness. As for Gertrude Lawrence, she is a goddess: that's all.

What brings this about is the emotional confusion of the woman editor of a smart women's magazine. Up to now she has been contented, living happily with a married man whose wife would not divorce him, and

absorbed in work at which she is conspicuously successful. But suddenly everything has gone awry. Frightened by the jangle of her nerves, she goes to a psychoanalyst. *Lady in the Dark* is the drama of the strange images he draws out of her memories. In the end the analyst resolves her confusion into an intelligible pattern—proving, incidentally, that you never know whom you love, which is a terrifying prospect, but that is neither here nor there.

If that sounds like a macabre theme, you can rely upon Mr. Hart's lightness of touch and his knack for tossing in a wisecrack to keep the narrative scenes buoyant. And the long, fantastic interludes when the editor is exploring her memories carry *Lady in the Dark* into a sphere of gorgeously bedizened make-believe that will create theatrical memories for every one who sees them. Mr. Weill's score is a homogenous piece of work, breaking out into song numbers over a mood of dark evocation—nostalgic at times, bursting also into humor and swing. And Mr. Gershwin, in turn, has written his lyrics like a thoroughbred. Uproariously witty when the time is right, he also writes in impeccable taste for the meditative sequences.

To carry the burden of such a huge production, Mr. Horner has set his scenery on four revolving stages that weave naturalism and fantasy into a flowing fabric; and Hassard Short, as usual, has lighted it regally. The

production is a rhapsody in blue and gold, giving reality an unreal size, shape and color, and Irene Sharaff's costumes are boldly imaginative. As the mistress of the choreography, Albertina Rasch has designed vivid lines of dance movement, and the staging is full of grace and resourcefulness.

No one but Miss Lawrence could play a virtuoso part of such length and variety. She is on stage almost at curtain-rise, and she is never off it long—leaping from melancholy to revelry with a swiftness that would be bewildering if she could not manage caprices so well. She sings, she dances. After playing a scene as a mature woman, she steps across the stage to play a scene as a schoolgirl without loss of enchantment. Sometimes Miss Lawrence has been accused of overacting, which is a venial sin at most. But no one will accuse her of being anything but superb in *Lady in the Dark*. She plays with anxious sincerity in the narrative scenes and with fullness and richness in the fantasy. For good measure, she sings "The Saga of Jenny" like an inspired showgirl.

The cast, under Mr. Hart's direction, is excellent throughout. As a comic fashion photographer, Danny Kaye, who was cutting up in *The Straw Hat Revue* last year, is infectiously exuberant. Macdonald Carey, who played in the Globe Shakespeare at the World's Fair, acts the part of an aggressive magazine man with a kind of casual forthrightness. As a glamorous movie hero, Victor Mature is unobjectionably handsome and affable. Margaret Dale has an amusing part as a fashion editor and plays it with dry humor, and Natalie Schaffer has some fun with a super-modish gadabout. In the unwelcome part of the sympathetic lover, Bert Lytell gives a good performance, and Donald Randolph, as the analyst, also behaves like a gentleman.

All these actors and variegated items of a show have been pulled into place by a theatre that has been put on its mettle by an occasion. *Lady in the Dark* is a feast of plenty. Since it also has a theme to explore and express, let's call it a work of theatre art.

Scenes from *Lady in the Dark*. **OPPOSITE, CLOCKWISE FROM TOP:** Danny Kaye (center) and members of the cast; Gertrude Lawrence; and Victor Mature.

And then there was Rodgers and Hammerstein. That sentence does not contain an error in subject-verb agreement. Rodgers and Hammerstein consisted of two distinct individuals with earlier (and impressive) independent careers—the composer Richard Rodgers and the lyricist and book writer Oscar Hammerstein II. But it was as a single entity that they transformed the American musical and ruled its world, indomitably, for more than a decade.

For their first collaboration, *Oklahoma!*, which opened in 1943, the *Times* reviewer Lewis Nichols piled on all sorts of flattering adjectives ("delightful," "wonderful," "infectious"). And he sensed a turning point for Rodgers (previously best known as the saucy collaborator of Lorenz Hart), whose score, he noted (using a word that would come to enfold *Oklahoma!* as snugly as skin), had seldom before been as "integrated."

But it was after *Oklahoma!* had settled into the first sold-out weeks of what would be a run of 2,212 performances that Broadway began to register the depth of the impression left by this story of life amid the cornfields and cow pastures. By 1944, reviewing *On the Town*, Nichols described it, with arch nostalgia, as the "most engaging musical show to come this way since the golden day of *Oklahoma!*" And *Oklahoma!* remains, even now, the touchstone by which the significance of a musical is measured.

But why? Well, for one thing it was serious about subjects like love and death, and it is important to remember that America was by this time at war again. There would always be a place for frivolous, escapist song-and-dance shows during and after that war. But *Oklahoma!* wasn't just escapist. Here, with song and dance (choreographed by Agnes de Mille) flowing naturally out of conventional dialogue, this show seemed to lend a dimension of grandeur to prosaic lives, and to suggest that the pain and love and fear that ordinary Americans had inside them deserved to be translated into music that soars to the skies. It was easier and homier than opera, but it had that ennobling touch of the heroic. When a mere two years later the creators of *Oklahoma!* came up with another musical about Americans in love and in danger—this one set in New England and called *Carousel*—Nichols led his review by saying, "Richard Rodgers and Oscar Hammerstein II, who can do no wrong, have continued doing no wrong."

At least a couple of other shows had set the tone and the stage for the ascendancy of *Oklahoma!* (Its most direct ancestor, *Show Boat*, by Kern and Hammerstein, was too long past by Broadway's bustling standards to be taken into consideration just then.) Moss Hart and Kurt Weill's *Lady in the Dark*, a "musical drama" that set psychoanalysis to music, had opened in 1941, inspiring Atkinson to make claims for its artistic greatness that Nichols did not put forth for *Oklahoma!* (at least not in his opening night review).

But there was another show, of another stripe altogether, that may have helped to dissolve the musical's boundaries between the silly stage and earnest daily life and to encourage theatergoers to regard a good-time gal of a genre with the kind of sentimental respect reserved for Mother. It was *This Is the Army*, Irving Berlin's 1942 revue of military-themed songs and sketches cast from the ranks of American soldiers preparing for war. Atkinson wrote that the show was "a by-product of something infinitely greater" than the usual show-business fare. Irving Berlin, he said, had made another memorable contribution to "the genius of America," adding, "His chief virtues are the simplicity and sincerity of his style. He does not aspire to sophistication."

That down-to-earth sincerity, or the illusion of it, was certainly part of the appeal of *Oklahoma!* and *Carousel*. The same sensibility was evident even in the smart-aleck *On the Town*, the Betty Comden–Adolph Green romp about three sailors on shore leave in Manhattan, which featured music by Leonard Bernstein and choreography by Jerome Robbins.

E. Y. Harburg, Fred Saidy, and Burton Lane's *Finian's Rainbow* (1947) had a populist heart, too, but it also injected a surprising, politically barbed whimsy into its story of an Irish leprechaun in the American South. Atkinson called it "a raree-show of enchantment, humor and beauty, to say nothing of enough social significance to hold the franchise." He was just as impressed by the more solemn *Street Scene*, adapted from Elmer Rice's Pulitzer Prize–winning drama of tenement life, with songs by Kurt Weill and Langston Hughes. "Mr. Weill is writing serious music enkindled by the excitement of New York," said Atkinson, who called the production "a musical play of magnificence and glory."

Not that overt sophistication was banished altogether, not as long as Cole Porter was still around. His backstage musical *Kiss Me, Kate* (1948), an innuendo-dripping romp about narcissistic stars performing *The Taming of the Shrew*, was an instant smash. And a lucre-loving refugee from the 1920s, the wide-eyed gold digger Lorelei Lee, was reincarnated in the audacious form of Carol Channing in *Gentlemen Prefer Blondes*. Atkinson called Channing's performance "the most fabulous comic creation of this dreary period in history." Those words might have rankled Ethel Merman, who had opened three years earlier as the rowdy, sharp-shooting heroine of Berlin's *Annie Get Your Gun*. Still, Nichols's review had asserted that Merman remained "heaven's gift to the musical show" and could still "scream out the air of a song so that the building trembles."

The promising new songwriting team Alan Jay Lerner and Frederick Loewe scored a critical and popular hit with the fairy-tale airiness of *Brigadoon*. But as the 1940s drew to a close, it was clear once again that the decade belonged to Rodgers and Hammerstein, whose *South Pacific*—a musical of culture clashes as experienced by Americans overseas during World War II—would win the Pulitzer Prize. Atkinson made the point that this "tenderly beautiful idyll of genuine people inexplicably tossed together in a strange corner of the world" was not just "an assembled show." It was, he said, in words that seemed to assess the distance the musical had come since he began reviewing, a "thoroughly composed musical drama."

**OPPOSITE:** Marc Platt and Katharine Sergava in the original Broadway production of *Oklahoma!*, 1943.

# THIS IS THE ARMY

By BROOKS ATKINSON

Call it taste. In *This Is the Army* Irving Berlin completely understands what he is doing. Given the Army on the one hand and the theatre on the other, he has joined them perfectly in a swift, clean-cut and candid soldier show. In spite of the title, this is not all of the Army, of course. For the Army has been recruited from the States for a grimmer purpose. We could not take the show even frivolously if the Army and Navy were not spreading across the face of the earth on a terrible errand that has nothing to do with the gayety of the theatre. Although the Army has left its heart at the Stage Door Canteen, it is putting its back into war against tyranny.

Mr. Berlin understands that. But he has not forgotten that a citizens' Army is composed of all sorts of men who are young and skylarking—tall and short, black and white, plain and good-looking, full of humor and energy. A few of them have talent for show business; all of them have a longing for revelry. There is a suggestion of the iron of Army discipline in the first part of the show. Two guards with rifles stand rigidly at either end of the stage; and at the end of every number the guard is changed with military ceremony. Between guard mounts the fun is broad, good-humored and lusty, like the tomfoolery of a bunch of young Americans pulled loose from home. *This Is the Army* is ebullient and normal. Mr. Berlin has had the genius to understand that young men can be serious without being solemn. Under the uniforms, beneath the military decorum, there is an abundance of life in his show.

In a way his task has been simplified. He does not have to be heroic. If he were writing for Broadway actors costumed in military uniforms he might feel impelled to praise democracy, bless America or wave the flag. Broadway does not take these fundamental things for granted. But the men for whom he is writing need no introduction. Since they are wearing the uniform we know where they stand, and Mr. Berlin can go on from there. The songs he has written for them and the nonsense they have contributed out of their own abundance acquire prestige from the fact that they are soldiers. Whether we are conscious of it or not, *This Is the Army* is a by-product of something infinitely greater, and that fact colors our responses to it.

Mr. Berlin is just the man for the job. As every one knows, he wrote *Yip, Yip, Yaphank* in the last war with the insight of an enlisted man. But his chief virtues are the simplicity and sincerity of his style. He does not aspire to sophistication. Take "I Left My Heart at the Stage Door Canteen," which has become especially popular. It is a natural song: it has melody and sentiment. It is pleasant to hear and easy to remember. Once you have heard it, it sounds as though it had always been written. Or, take "This Is the Army, Mr. Jones," which makes sense in a soldiers' show and can be sung without taking a special course in music. It is a natural expression of a common state of mind. Mr. Berlin can write for soldiers because he does not have to woo them or condescend to them and because he is not personally ambitious. *This Is the Army* is completely on the level.

Being an honest expression of animal high spirits, it is not witty, brilliant or clever. Two soldiers compete in telling tall tales. A soldier juggles potatoes and a paring knife. There is some comic dialogue between Private Julie Oshins, Sergeant Ezra Stone and Corporal Philip Truex. First Class Private Joe Cook Jr. tosses in a fleet echo of his old man's bountiful good cheer. Corporal James A. Cross and some other Negro soldiers set a Lenox Avenue blaze to "What the Well-Dressed Man in Harlem Will Wear." Next to closing, Mr. Berlin and a platoon of aging Upton boys revive "Oh, How I Hate to Get Up in the Morning," from the old *Yaphank* show.

No wonder *This Is the Army* leaves the audience in a glow of enjoyment and loyalty. For Mr. Berlin's taste is perfect. He knows what the Army means to all of us today; and he also knows soldiers and audiences. With all those things absorbed into his system, he has contributed another memorable show to the genius of America.

. . . . . . . . . . . . . . . . . . . . . . . . . . . . . . . . . . .

**LEFT:** A scene from *This Is the Army.*

April 1, 1943

# *Oklahoma!*

By LEWIS NICHOLS

For years they have been saying the Theatre Guild is dead, words that obviously will have to be eaten with breakfast this morning. Forsaking the sometimes somber tenor of her ways, the little lady of Fifty-second Street last evening danced off into new paths and brought to the St. James a truly delightful musical play called *Oklahoma!* Wonderful is the nearest adjective, for this excursion of the Guild combines a fresh and infectious gayety, a charm of manner, beautiful acting, singing and dancing, and a score by Richard Rodgers which doesn't do any harm either, since it is one of his best.

*Oklahoma!* is based on Lynn Riggs's saga of the Indian Territory at the turn of the century, *Green Grow the Lilacs*, and, like its predecessor, it is simple and warm. It relies not for a moment on Broadway gags to stimulate an appearance of comedy, but goes winningly on its way with Rouben Mamoulian's best direction to point up its sly humor, and with some of Agnes de Mille's most inspired dances to do so further. There is more comedy in one of Miss de Mille's gay little passages than in many of the other Broadway tom-tom beats together. The Guild has known what it is about in pursuing talent for its new departure.

Mr. Rodgers's scores never lack grace, but seldom have they been so well integrated as this for *Oklahoma!* He has turned out waltzes, love songs, comic songs and a title number which the State in question would do well to seize as an anthem forthwith. "Oh, What a Beautiful Morning" and "People Will Say" are headed for countless juke-boxes across the land, and a dirge called "Pore Jud"—in which the hero of the fable tries to persuade his rival to hang himself—is amazingly comic. "The Farmer and the Cowman" and "The Surry with the Fringe on the Top" also deserve mention only because they quite clearly approach perfection; no number of the score is out of place or badly handled.

The orchestrations are by Russell Bennett, who knows his humor and has on this occasion let himself go with all the laughter he can command.

To speak and sing the words—Oscar Hammerstein II contributed the book and lyrics—the play has an excellent collection of players, none of whom yet is world-famous. Alfred Drake and Joan Roberts as the two leading singers are fresh and engaging; they have clear voices and the thought that the audience might also like to hear Mr. Hammerstein's poetry. Joseph Buloff is marvelous as the peddler who ambles through the evening selling wares from French cards to Asiatic perfume—and avoiding matrimony.

Howard da Silva, Lee Dixon, Celeste Holm and Ralph Riggs are some of the others, and Katharine Sergava and Mark Platt are two of the important dancers. Possibly in addition to being a musical play, *Oklahoma!* could be called a folk operetta; whatever it is, it is very good.

. . . . . . . . . . . . . . . . . . . . . . . . . . . . .

Scenes from *Oklahoma!* **OPPOSITE, TOP:** From left, Joan McCracken, Kate Friedlich, Margit DeKova, Bobby Barrentine, and Vivian Smith in the "Out of My Dreams" ballet. **OPPOSITE, BOTTOM:** Joseph Buloff, Celeste Holm, and Ralph Riggs. **ABOVE:** In front, from left, Betty Garde, Joan Roberts, Alfred Drake, Lee Dixon, and Celeste Holm.

LEFT: Lee Dixon (center) and members of the cast in a scene from the original Broadway production of *Oklahoma!*, 1943.

December 29, 1944

# ON THE TOWN

By LEWIS NICHOLS

There can be no mistake about it: *On the Town* is the freshest and most engaging musical show to come this way since the golden day of *Oklahoma!* Everything about it is right. It is fast and it is gay, it takes neither itself nor the world too seriously, it has wit. Its dances are well paced, its players are a pleasure to see, and its music and backgrounds are both fitting and excellent. *On the Town* even has a literate book, which for once instead of stopping the action dead speeds it merrily on its way. The Adelphi Theatre on West Fifty-fourth Street is the new Utopia.

*On the Town* is a perfect example of what a well-knit fusion of the respectable arts can provide for the theatre. Taking a book by Betty Comden and Adolph Green as a base, Leonard Bernstein has composed all manner of songs—some in Tin Pan Alley's popular style, some a bit removed. Jerome Robbins, whose idea was the basis for the show—it came from his ballet *Fancy Free*—has supplied perfect dances and found Sono Osato and others to do them. Oliver Smith's simple settings are in keeping with the spirit of the book and tunes. And finally, since the other participants were not experienced theatre people, George Abott was invited to put the whole thing together. Mr. Abbott has done one of his perfect jobs.

*On the Town* is the story of three sailors on a twenty-four hour pass from the Brooklyn Navy Yard. In the subway they see a picture of Miss Turnstiles, and in the effort to find her in person they give Miss Comden and Mr. Green a chance to roam through New York. As half of The Revuers, those two know their city. The book they have fashioned makes cheerful fun of Miss Turnstiles, the museums, night clubs and the upper floors of Carnegie Hall, where culture learns to cult. They are serious about nothing, and oftentimes they offer only suggestions of ideas, allowing the audience to fill in the thought. It has been a long time since a musical comedy audience has been allowed to enjoy a musical comedy book.

Only last spring, Mr. Bernstein was earning the Music Critics' annual prize for the best new composition of the year; this morning he will start up the ladder of ASCAP. He has written ballet music and songs, background music and raucously tinny versions of the blues. It is possible that none of the individual numbers may spend a year on the Hit Parade, but "Lonely Town" is strict Broadway, "Lucky to Be Me" is strict torch. For a scene in Times Square he has provided the roar of that crossroads of the world. The music has humor and is unpedantic; Mr. Bernstein quite understands the spirit of *On the Town.*

So does the cast, of course. Miss Osato brought down the highest rafters when she appeared a year ago in *One Touch of Venus,* and there is no reason to replace any of those rafters now. Her dancing is easy and her face expressive. Any day now her picture will be in the trains as Miss Subway. Nancy Walker also is wonderful as a tough, firm, taxi driver who collects one of the sailors. She can shrill out a ballad like "Come Up to My Place" with all the harshness of a Coney Island barker and all the verve of—well, Nancy Walker. Miss Comden, in the role of another girl who likes the Navy, also is good at it; Adolph Green, Cris Alexander and John Battles are the sailors.

But the charm of *On the Town* is not so much in the individual performances as in the whole. The chorus and ballet numbers, many of them done with an edge of satire, are easy and graceful. Mr. Abbott permits no lags in his evening, and down in the pit and up on the stage everything always is in order. It is an adult musical show and a remarkably good one.

· · · · · · · · · · · · · · · · · · · · · · · · ·

**OPPOSITE, CLOCKWISE FROM TOP:** A scene from *On the Town;* Sono Osato (standing on her head) as Ivy; and Betty Comden and Adolph Green as Claire and Ozzie.

WAR & POST-WAR

# Carousel

By LEWIS NICHOLS

Richard Rodgers and Oscar Hammerstein II, who can do no wrong, have continued doing no wrong in adapting *Liliom* into a musical play. Their *Carousel* is on the whole delightful. It spins and whirls across the stage of the Majestic, now fast and rousing, now nostalgic and moving. To it, the composer of the team has brought one of the most beautiful Rodgers scores, and the lyricist some of his best rhymes. The Theatre Guild, offering the play as its farewell to the season and on its twenty-sixth birthday, has given it an excellent production, with Rouben Mamoulian to direct, and Agnes de Mille for the dances. The Majestic is across the street from the St. James, where *Oklahoma!* is stationed; the pair of Rodgers-Hammerstein shows will be able to wink at one another for a long time to come.

In deciding to make a musical play of Ferenc Molnár's *Liliom*, the pair automatically adopted a couple of heavy millstones. One is *Oklahoma!* and they got around that by not trying to imitate themselves. The other is the familiarity most audiences have with *Liliom*. This they conquered by following the story quite closely as to incident, changing only the time and locale. *Carousel* is set on the New England coast toward the end of the nineteenth century. Its principal figure still is a barker in a carnival, he still commits suicide after an abortive holdup, he goes to heaven and comes back again to do his one good deed. There is a new ending, but one which does not violate the spirit of the original.

At the beginning of the play, where scene and mood must be established, *Carousel* moves a little slowly, but as soon as Mr. Rodgers has warmed his keyboard and Mr. Hammerstein his pen, chance complaints evaporate. The composer is offering all types of song. "June Is Bustin' Out All Over" is a cheerful, rousing number; "If I Loved You" is excellent of the type implied by its name.

"What's the Use of Wond'rin'" is very good, so is "You'll Never Walk Alone." There is ballet music, soft music and sentimental, and connecting themes. Mr. Hammerstein has worked hard on his lyrics; some of them are funny, some factual, some aiming at nothing higher than to be pleasant. In the lyric to "This Was a Real Nice Clam Bake" he can make his audience hungry for an immediate shore dinner.

As lyricist, Mr. Hammerstein must have a great admiration for the cast, which sings the words audibly and well. John Raitt is Liliom under the name of Billy Bigelow. He has an excellent and powerful voice and is not afraid to use it. He perhaps is not as good an actor as singer; he lacks the easy swagger and arrogance which goes with the character. Jan Clayton is a charming Julie, and can also sing; Jean Darling is Julie's friend and Eric Mattson the latter's husband. Christine Johnson is fine in the role derived from that of the photographer with whom Julie and Liliom lived, and Jean Casto has the part of the carousel's owner.

Miss de Mille has built up two main dances. One is a hornpipe, which is light and gay; the other is a ballet which Billy sees as he looks down from heaven upon his daughter. This last is perhaps not up to Miss de Mille's final score, although Bambi Linn, late of the rival across the street, is in it. Mr. Mamoulian has directed the whole thing so as to stress the music, which is eminently proper, and to set forth every pleasant angle possible. *Carousel* lacks comedy in its usual sense, only one role—that of Billy's nemesis and played by Murvyn Vye—approaching the normal forms of musical play humor. Jo Mielziner has designed good settings, simple for a New England seacoast, whimsical for heaven, and Miles White has costumed everyone nicely. But *Carousel* remains a Rodgers-Hammerstein offering, and as such a good turn on and to the spring theatre.

**OPPOSITE:** Jean Darling as Carrie Pipperidge, John Raitt as Billy Bigelow, and Jan Clayton as Julie Jordan in *Carousel*. **ABOVE:** Poster, 1945.

May 17, 1946

# ANNIE GET YOUR GUN

By LEWIS NICHOLS

The inadvertently postponed *Annie Get Your Gun* finally arrived at the Imperial last evening, and turned out to be a good professional Broadway musical. It has a pleasant score by Irving Berlin—his first since *This Is the Army*—and it has Ethel Merman to roll her eyes and to shout down the rafters. The colors are pretty, the dancing is amiable and unaffected, and Broadway by this time is well used to a book which doesn't get anywhere in particular. *Annie,* in short, is an agreeable evening on the town, and it takes little gift for prophecy to add that it, and she, will chant their saga of the sharpshooting lady for many months to come.

By now, Miss Merman is regarded as heaven's gift to the musical show, and there is nothing about the new one to detract from that reputation. They have given her the part of Annie Oakley, who shot with Buffalo Bill's show, and Miss Merman is deadly with a rifle over her shoulder. She can scream out the air of a song so that the building trembles; and she can be initiated into an Indian tribe in such a way the event is singularly funny. Herbert and Dorothy Fields, as librettists, quite often have left her working in something of a void, but she has worked there before and can handle the situation

adequately. Her inflections give a leering note to even sedate lyrics, and the toss of her head would be a credit to Bill's show, as it is to that of Rodgers and Hammerstein.

Mr. Berlin's return to home ground is news of high and important order. For that homecoming, he has written a good, steady score, with numbers which fit the events and the story. There is nothing like "White Christmas" or "Easter Parade" among them, but several which have a place a bracket or so below. "They Say It's Wonderful" is the love song, and that will be heard around; and "Moonshine Lullaby," "I'm an Indian Too," "Show Business" and "Sun in the Morning" all are good. Abandoning the piano for the accompanying pencil of the lyricist, Mr. Berlin has fitted gay, brisk words to his tunes, and he is blessed by singers who can enunciate them.

Although the shooting of *Annie Get Your Gun* is done most affably by Miss Merman and Mr. Berlin, there are others involved to a more or less important extent. Jo Mielziner's settings are in the style of lavish musical shows, colorful and complete. The costumes by Lucinda Ballard are summery, bright, Indian, wild West and when the time is ripe, sardonic. Helen Tamiris has designed dances

which probably will not be studied at formal ballet schools but fit agreeably into the proceedings. The contributors all are professionals.

In any Merman show the other members of the acting company habitually take on the harassed air of the losing horses in a steeplechase. Ray Middleton is the Frank Butler of *Annie,* Frank being the lady's rival and sweetheart, and Mr. Middleton offering a voice to Mr. Berlin and no great acting ability otherwise. William O'Neal is a dignified Buffalo Bill; Marty May is energetic as his manager; Harry Bellaver is fine as Chief Sitting Bull. The young people are played by Betty Anne Nyman and Kenny Bowers. The chorus is pleasant to look upon, the orchestrations are good, and if there are abrupt pauses with some frequency—well, Miss Merman must change costumes and Mr. Berlin is not writing continuous opera.

· · · · · · · · · · · · · · · · · · · · · · · · ·

**OPPOSITE, CLOCKWISE FROM TOP:** A dance scene from *Annie Get Your Gun;* Ethel Merman as Annie; and sheet music for "There's No Business like Show Business."

March 25, 1994

# A CAROUSEL *FOR THE '90S FULL OF GRIT AND PASSION*

By DAVID RICHARDS

*Carousel* will be 50 next year, but as of this morning it is the freshest, most innovative musical on Broadway. It is also the most beautiful.

Time and again you will marvel at the way the British director Nicholas Hytner and his designers transform the curved stage of the Vivian Beaumont Theater at Lincoln Center, where the production opened last night. Sculptors of space, they summon out of the star-flecked darkness breathtaking images of a 19th-century seacoast town in Maine. In the scheme of things, this brawling little world is nothing, a mere speck in the cosmos, ignored by the indifferent moon overhead. But it is so full of life and love struggling to make itself felt that it is everything. Clearly, a rueful philosopher abides deep within the immensely gifted Mr. Hytner.

Just as often, you will gasp at the bold moves and risky choices made by Richard Rodgers and Oscar Hammerstein II. The success of *Oklahoma!* two years earlier had proved their partnership worthy. *Carousel* would sanctify it. As much a musicalized play as a musical, it explores in some of the team's most enduring songs the troubled souls of Billy Bigelow, carnival barker and ne'er-do-well, and Julie Jordan, the millworker who falls for him and then suffers his abuse with a kind of helpless fortitude.

"What's the Use of Wondr'in'," Julie's attempt to explain the unexplainable bond between them, may be the sweetest surrender to fate ever penned. But then, this is a luminescent musical shot through with pain and bewilderment, an uplifting musical in which the lives of most of the major characters are either miserable or misspent. The paradoxes and contradictions are precisely

what keep *Carousel* alive and vital. The simpler-minded entertainments tend to die young.

There is one big obstacle to your enjoyment, however, and you should probably know it right now. With a few exceptions, this *Carousel*, which originated in late 1992 in London at the Royal National Theatre, is indifferently sung. Those who fondly remember John Raitt or Gordon MacRae in the role of Billy, or the likes of Barbara Cook and Shirley Jones as Julie, will find the evening short on vocal luster. The most powerful voice in the company belongs to the mezzo-soprano Shirley Verrett, who appears as the warm-hearted Nettie Fowler. But the diva seems uncomfortable belting out "June Is Bustin' Out All Over" and only slightly more sure of herself with "You'll Never Walk Alone."

Mr. Hytner's blanket solution to this problem is to have the performers approach the songs as monologues, sound the lyrics for their hidden impulses and then simply act the stuffing out of them. Over the years, Rodgers and Hammerstein have come to stand for a corn-fed American goodness and the more saccharine forms of optimism. It's an erroneous impression, largely spawned by *The Sound of Music* and Hammerstein's moralistic injunctions to "climb ev'ry mountain" or "whistle a happy tune." Mr. Hytner will have none of it. He wants to restore the grittiness to *Carousel* and, in that respect, gorgeous singing matters less to him here, I suspect, than the proletarian authenticity of the characters.

That Michael Hayden, who plays Billy, comes across as a boy in a man's part is no doubt intentional. Billy is callow and

unthinking, a touseled idol for 19th-century teenage girls. He really doesn't start to grow up until he dies and goes to purgatory. The strapping first-act "Soliloquy" has the character bursting with the wonder and pride of impending fatherhood. As Mr. Hayden sings the number, however, what registers is fear and confusion, eating away at the soaring melody. Sally Murphy is a more assured singer, but her Julie has a wan and slightly unkempt air. She is attracted to danger and instinctively flouts authority. She would probably get along with Tonya Harding.

By darkening the characters in this fashion, Mr. Hytner allows his actors to work with a denser subtext than usual. Romance can turn rough and sweaty. Quick tempers keep undermining the Puritan proprieties: When, speaking of Billy, Julie admits to her friend Carrie Pipperidge, "Last Monday he hit me," the flat, emotionless confession may come out of the blue, but it comes as no surprise. You won't cotton to Mr. Hytner's method if you like Rodgers and Hammerstein for their sunniness. On every front, a heightened dialectic between light and shadow, decency and prurience is central to the vision and gives the production its distinction.

The very first sight to greet you, during the pantomimed prologue that opens the show, is a huge clock. Under it, Julie and seven other women, exhausted automatons, slave away at a massive loom. The clock strikes 6. The women let out a whoop of liberation, run to exchange their drab smocks for more festive garb and make their raucous way out the factory gates.

All the while, the stage is revolving. Then, as if in a giant kaleidoscope, the garish elements of a carnival begin to float into view—Uncle Sam on stilts, a dancing bear, the gaping jaws of a fun-house door and finally the wooden steeds of the carousel itself—propelled in great circles by a headstrong waltz and the tipsy excitement in the air.

Simpler in design, but visually no less arresting, is the spectacle of the townsfolk packed into rowboats of brightest red, heading out to their island clambake on an inky sea. Bob Crowley's sets and costumes and Paul Pyant's lighting go beyond picturesque. They are art. Even when they have the sober truth and plain purpose of New England about them, they can be sinfully lovely.

The secondary leads, Carrie Pipperidge and Enoch Snow, inhabit more traditional musical-comedy terrain, although Mr. Hytner has seen fit to make their eight children into a walking United Colors of Benetton ad. Audra Ann McDonald, the real find of this production, has a welcomingly open manner

as Carrie, a vigorous voice and a ready sense of comedy, while Eddie Korbich stays on the likable side of pomposity as her beau. By the second act, they've become a rich, stuffy bourgeois couple, another not-exactly-happy ending, if you think about it. Fisher Stevens, sounding like steel wool on sandpaper as that drunk and bad influence, Jigger Craigin, and Jeff Weiss, as a Starkeeper out of Star Trek, both successfully buck convention, which calls for more folksy interpretations of the roles.

After the dazzling prologue, you can forgive the production for not reaching the heights again until well into the second act. But hit them it does in the dream ballet, which shows Billy and Julie's young daughter, Louise, being seduced by a strutting fairground boy. Choreographed by Sir Kenneth MacMillan in and around the wreckage of a carousel, the dance is a torrid affair. At the preview I saw, the sullen bravura of Jon

Marshall Sharp and the daredevil petulance of Dana Stackpole, an understudy, were a highly flammable combination.

The explosion of sexual energy in the pas de deux is Billy and Julie's story one generation later. By this time, Billy, of course, is a ghost. Julie just looks like one. Love can do that to people. Mr. Hytner, you shouldn't forget, is the man who staged "Miss Saigon," another tumultuous story of doomed love.

Better singing voices no doubt could have made this a Carousel for the ages. Instead, it is a Carousel for our times, which is still a considerable achievement. In any case, you will leave the Vivian Beaumont humming the sets. Normally, that's a joke. Here, it isn't. Consider it the highest of compliments.

. . . . . . . . . . . . . . . . . . . . . . . . . . . .

**BELOW:** Audra Ann McDonald, Michael Hayden, and Sally Murphy in the 1994 revival of *Carousel*.

May 17, 1946

# ANNIE GET YOUR GUN

By LEWIS NICHOLS

The inadvertently postponed *Annie Get Your Gun* finally arrived at the Imperial last evening, and turned out to be a good professional Broadway musical. It has a pleasant score by Irving Berlin—his first since *This Is the Army*—and it has Ethel Merman to roll her eyes and to shout down the rafters. The colors are pretty, the dancing is amiable and unaffected, and Broadway by this time is well used to a book which doesn't get anywhere in particular. *Annie,* in short, is an agreeable evening on the town, and it takes little gift for prophecy to add that it, and she, will chant their saga of the sharpshooting lady for many months to come.

By now, Miss Merman is regarded as heaven's gift to the musical show, and there is nothing about the new one to detract from that reputation. They have given her the part of Annie Oakley, who shot with Buffalo Bill's show, and Miss Merman is deadly with a rifle over her shoulder. She can scream out the air of a song so that the building trembles; and she can be initiated into an Indian tribe in such a way the event is singularly funny. Herbert and Dorothy Fields, as librettists, quite often have left her working in something of a void, but she has worked there before and can handle the situation

adequately. Her inflections give a leering note to even sedate lyrics, and the toss of her head would be a credit to Bill's show, as it is to that of Rodgers and Hammerstein.

Mr. Berlin's return to home ground is news of high and important order. For that homecoming, he has written a good, steady score, with numbers which fit the events and the story. There is nothing like "White Christmas" or "Easter Parade" among them, but several which have a place a bracket or so below. "They Say It's Wonderful" is the love song, and that will be heard around; and "Moonshine Lullaby," "I'm an Indian Too," "Show Business" and "Sun in the Morning" all are good. Abandoning the piano for the accompanying pencil of the lyricist, Mr. Berlin has fitted gay, brisk words to his tunes, and he is blessed by singers who can enunciate them.

Although the shooting of *Annie Get Your Gun* is done most affably by Miss Merman and Mr. Berlin, there are others involved to a more or less important extent. Jo Mielziner's settings are in the style of lavish musical shows, colorful and complete. The costumes by Lucinda Ballard are summery, bright, Indian, wild West and when the time is ripe, sardonic. Helen Tamiris has designed dances

which probably will not be studied at formal ballet schools but fit agreeably into the proceedings. The contributors all are professionals.

In any Merman show the other members of the acting company habitually take on the harassed air of the losing horses in a steeplechase. Ray Middleton is the Frank Butler of *Annie,* Frank being the lady's rival and sweetheart, and Mr. Middleton offering a voice to Mr. Berlin and no great acting ability otherwise. William O'Neal is a dignified Buffalo Bill; Marty May is energetic as his manager; Harry Bellaver is fine as Chief Sitting Bull. The young people are played by Betty Anne Nyman and Kenny Bowers. The chorus is pleasant to look upon, the orchestrations are good, and if there are abrupt pauses with some frequency—well, Miss Merman must change costumes and Mr. Berlin is not writing continuous opera.

· · · · · · · · · · · · · · · · · · · · · · · · ·

**OPPOSITE, CLOCKWISE FROM TOP:** A dance scene from *Annie Get Your Gun;* Ethel Merman as Annie; and sheet music for "There's No Business like Show Business."

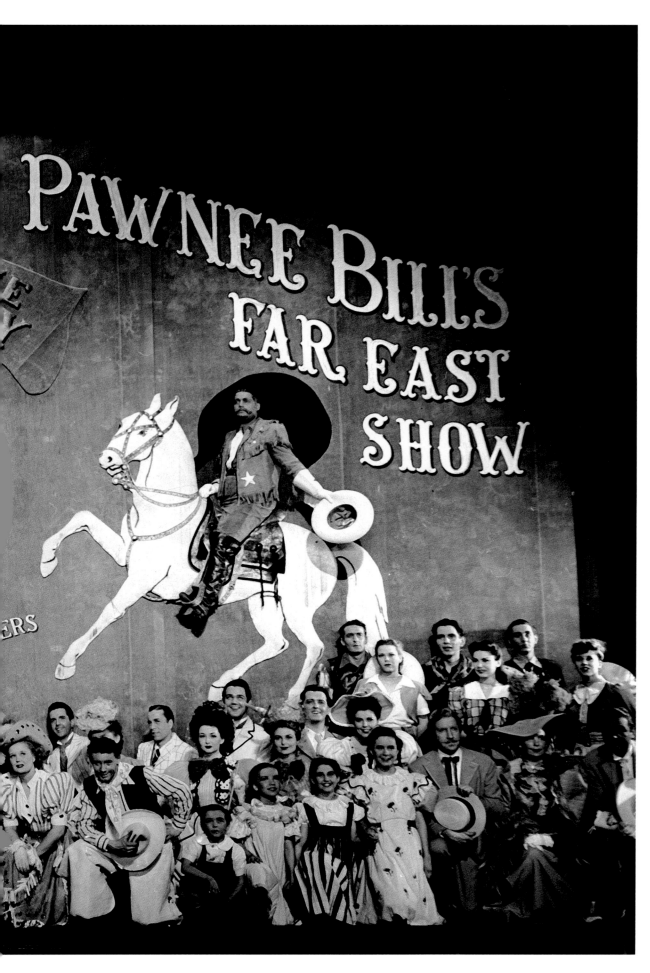

LEFT: A scene from the original Broadway production of *Annie Get Your Gun*, 1946.

January 10, 1947

# STREET SCENE

### By BROOKS ATKINSON

Add to the text of Elmer Rice's *Street Scene* a fresh and eloquent score by Kurt Weill and you have a musical play of magnificence and glory. Sung by a superb cast, it opened at the Adelphi last evening. Eighteen years ago Mr. Rice's ballad of a dingy side street in New York rose high above the horizon of the theatre, and it has always remained there as a cherished masterpiece. For nothing else has recaptured so much of the anguish, romance and beauty of cosmopolis.

Now Mr. Weill, the foremost music maker in the American theatre, has found notes to express the myriad impulses of Mr. Rice's poem and transmuted it into a sidewalk opera; and Langston Hughes has set it to affectionate lyrics. Mr. Weill's record includes some notable scores for *Johnny Johnson, Knickerbocker Holiday* and *Lady in the Dark*. But obviously this is the theme he has been waiting for to make full use of his maturity as a composer.

For he has listened to the main street cries of Mr. Rice's garish fable—the hopes, anxieties and grief of people trying to beat a humane existence out of the squalor of a callous city. The main theme he has conveyed in the rueful wonder of the song Mrs. Maurrant sings in the summer moonlight—"Somehow I Never Could Believe"; in her daughter's romantic lament—"What Good Would the Moon Be?"; in the janitor's brooding song and in the horror-stricken choral entitled "The Woman Who Lived Up There." In these songs, and in the ominous orchestrations that accent the basic moods of the drama, Mr. Weill is writing serious music enkindled by the excitement of New York.

But he is a Broadway virtuoso with a love for the trivia as well as the grandeur of his theme. For relish of life in the streets there is nothing more enchanting than his tone poem to ice cream and his gay dance for the street urchins. As a poet Mr. Hughes also relishes the people whose lives spill out of packed buildings on to the pavements. His lyrics communicate in simple and honest rhymes the homely familiarities of New York people and the warmth and beauty of humanity. Acting as popular song writers, as well as artists, Mr. Weill and Mr. Hughes have tossed off one down-beat hot number, called "Moon-faced, Starry-eyed," to which Sheila Bond and Danny Daniels dance a superb American apache number that outranks any of the current show tunes on Broadway.

Not long ago the local managers were complaining that they could no longer find actors who could sing. The producers of *Street Scene* have had no such trouble. They have found superb singers who have helped to make this one of the memorable nights in theatre going. Polyna Stoska, who plays Mrs. Maurrant, has a brilliant soprano voice that contains both the sadness and sweetness of the part. As her daughter, Anne Jeffreys sings and acts with equal beauty. Norman Cordon conveys in his baritone singing the violence and sullenness of Mr. Maurrant.

There is an abundance of fine singing all through the play—Creighton Thompson as the janitor, Brian Sullivan as the restless law student, Irving Kaufman as the amusing Jewish intellectual. Hope Emerson is vastly entertaining as the garrulous old crone; and Peggy Turnley and Ellen Carleen ably sing the tabloid lullaby.

Jo Mielziner, who designed the celebrated setting for the original production, has designed another of lighter texture—the garishness more sympathetically stated. And perhaps this is something of what the opera contributes to the old drama. With its music and dances, its chorals and lyrics, it finds the song of humanity under the argot of the New York streets.

. . . . . . . . . . . . . . . . . . . . . . . . . . . . .

**LEFT:** Norman Cordon (with gun) as Mr. Maurrant with members of the cast in *Street Scene*.

January 11, 1947

# FINIAN'S RAINBOW

By BROOKS ATKINSON

Jettisoning most of the buncombe of the traditional musical show, B. Y. Harburg and Fred Saidy have written an original and humorous fantasy, *Finian's Rainbow*, which was put on at the Forty-sixth Street last evening. Do not be terrified by the news that it whirls around a leprechaun and a magic pot of gold. For Mr. Harburg and Mr. Saidy wrote *Bloomer Girl* two seasons ago, and that was no sissy show.

With some clarion music by Burton Lane and some joyous dancing by a company of inspired sprites, the authors have conjured up a raree-show of enchantment, humor and beauty, to say nothing of enough social significance to hold the franchise. It puts the American musical stage several steps forward for the imagination with which it is written and for the stunning virtuosity of the performance.

Ella Logan, with her pair of potent pipes, is bellowing some rapturous Irish songs as the daughter of a crack-brained Irish spell-maker—"How Are Things in Glocca Morra?" being her most beguiling number. As the central mischief-maker, the producers have had the good sense to import a rare Irish entertainer, Albert Sharpe. Mr. Sharpe is a high-stepping and sagacious comic who radiates merriment and who plunges into the *Finian's Rainbow* fable with the most infectious good humor.

Add to Miss Logan and Mr. Sharpe a leprechaun whose sense of humor does not destroy the purity of the fairy story, and you have an incomparable band of unhackneyed performers. The leprechaun is played by David Wayne, who has a grin just a trifle too worldly for complete innocence. His best song, sung once with Miss Logan, is entitled "Something Sort of Grandish." It and he should be inscribed in the Hall of Fame.

If the American musical stage continues to improve, it will no longer be necessary

for anyone to speak dialogue on the stage. Everything essential can be said in song and dancing. Against a wide and rhapsodic setting by Jo Mielziner, the ballet dancers of *Finian's Rainbow* begin the evening with some lyrical springtime rites of real glory. If notes of music could leap across the stage, they would be no lighter or lovelier than this joyous ballet of a young and free people. Mr. Kidd has designed it with skill and enthusiasm. The leading dancer is Anita Alvarez, a performer in a style of dancing gossamer. Mr. Kidd and his band of dancers have interpreted the theme of *Finian's Rainbow* like thoroughbreds and artists.

Not all of *Finian's Rainbow* is on the highest level. It concludes the first act with a conventional finale calculated to split your eardrums. In the second act it gives you an eyeful of tawdry musical show enticements

descended from Ziegfeld. And its stubborn shotgun marriage of fairy-story and social significance is not altogether happy. The capriciousness of the invention does not last throughout the evening.

But those are minor reservations to the enjoyment of a highly original evening in the theatre in the presence of a stageful of good companions. Although the production is large and varied, Bretaigne Windust has ably put it together and set it a happy pace. Thanks for a refreshing theatre party.

. . . . . . . . . . . . . . . . . . . . . . . . . . . . . . .

Scenes from *Finian's Rainbow*. **OPPOSITE:** Anita Alvarez as Susan and David Wayne as Og. **ABOVE:** David Wayne and Ella Logan as Sharon.

March 14, 1947

# *Brigadoon*

By BROOKS ATKINSON

To the growing list of major achievements on the musical stage add one more—*Brigadoon*, put on at the Ziegfeld last evening. For once the modest label "musical play" has a precise meaning. For it is impossible to say where the music and dancing leave off and the story begins in this beautifully orchestrated Scotch idyll. Under Bob Lewis' direction all the arts of the theatre have been woven into a singing pattern of enchantment.

According to the book by Alan Jay Lerner, two American boys on a holiday stumble into a quaint Scottish village called Brigadoon on the morning of a fair and on the day of a wedding. Although Brigadoon seems pleasant and hospitable it also seems like a strange anachronism; and finally the local dominie tells them why. Brigadoon is a spectral village that comes to life one day every century; and while the rest of the world wears itself out, the villagers of

Brigadoon live on from century to century in neighborly enjoyment and in a remote corner of time.

In less imaginative hands this fable might yield nothing more than entertainment for guffawing. But the fathers of *Brigadoon* are spreading the sorcery of their village into a plastic work of art that carries dialogue into dancing and dancing into music with none of the practical compromises of the Broadway stage. There are two or three good Broadway songs in Frederick Loewe's score. "Almost Like Being in Love," sung rapturously by David Brooks and Marion Bell, is an able swing number; and "There But for You Go I," sung by Mr. Brooks, is good Broadway romance.

But most of the score, which lays the emphasis on string instruments, has a traditional background of bagpipe skirling and a melodic air. "Waitin' for My Dearie" is a

lyrical romance and "I'll Go Home With Bonnie Jean" is a village festival number. Mr. Loewe has also written some lively airs for country dancing, like those for the wedding dance and the sword dance.

This is where Agnes de Mille comes in. For a kind of idyllic rhythm flows through the whole pattern of the production, and Miss de Mille has dipped again into the Pandora's box where she keeps her dance designs. Some of the dances are merely illustrations for the music. One or two of them are conventional, if lovely, maiden round dances. But some of them, like the desperate chase in the forest, are fiercely dramatic. The funeral dance to the dour tune of bagpipes brings the footstep of doom into the forest. And the sword dance, done magnificently by James Mitchell, is tremendously exciting with its stylization of primitive ideas.

Oliver Smith's settings in low colors are commonplace and convey little of the magic common to the rest of the production. With a fresh locale to work in, David Ffolkes has designed some spirited Scotch costumes, which is probably no more than an exercise in autobiography for him. The cast has been chosen with the same taste that prevails throughout the performance. Pamela Britton for the impudence, Virginia Bosler for the innocent bride, Lee Sullivan for the tenor songs, Lidija Franklin for the solo dances, William Hansen for the village elder, George Keane for the ironic Yankee—these are the actors with the most conspicuous parts.

But it undermines the motive of *Brigadoon* to pick and choose among the performers. For this excursion into an imagined Scottish village is an orchestration of the theatre's myriad arts, like a singing storybook for an idealized country fair long ago.

. . . . . . . . . . . . . . . . . . . . . . . . . . . .

Scenes from *Brigadoon*. **ABOVE:** From left, Edward Cullen, Marion Bell, Virginia Bosler, Will Hansen, Lee Sullivan, and Paul Anderson. **OPPOSITE:** James Mitchell as Harry.

December 31, 1948

# KISS ME, KATE

By BROOKS ATKINSON

Taking an obliging hint from Shakespeare, the makers of *Kiss Me, Kate* have put together a thoroughly enjoyable musical comedy, acted at the New Century last evening. Shakespeare has supplied a few bedraggled scenes from *The Taming of the Shrew*. Using these as a springboard into festivity, Bella and Samuel Spewack have contrived an authentic book which is funny without the interpolation of gags.

Cole Porter has written his best score in years, together with witty lyrics. Under Hanya Holm's direction, the dancing is joyous. And Lemuel Ayers has provided carnival costumes and some interesting scenery.

Occasionally by some baffling miracle, everything seems to drop gracefully into its appointed place, in the composition of a song show, and that is the case here. No one has had to break his neck to dazzle the audience with his brilliance, and no one has had to run at frantic speed to get across the rough spots. As far as the Spewacks are concerned, *Kiss Me, Kate* is the story of a vainglorious actor and his temperamental ex-wife who are starring in a revival of *The Taming of the Shrew* in Baltimore. Although the Shakespeare circus has had some bad performances, none has been worse than the burlesque Alfred Drake and Patricia Morison have inflicted on it here.

The Italian setting has another practical advantage. It gives Mr. Porter an opportunity to poke beyond Tin Pan Alley into a romantic mood. Without losing his sense of humor, he has written a remarkable melodious score with an occasional suggestion of Puccini, who was a good composer, too. Mr. Porter has always enjoyed the luxury of rowdy tunes, and he has scribbled a few for the current festival—"Another Op'nin', Another Show," "We Open in Venice," "Too Darn Hot" and "Brush Up Your Shakespeare," which is fresh out of the honky-tonks. All his lyrics are literate, and as usual some of them would shock the editorial staff of *The Police Gazette*.

But the interesting thing about the new score is the enthusiasm Mr. Porter has for romantic melodies indigenous to the soft climate of the Mediterranean. Although "Wunderbar" is probably a little north of the Mediterranean Sea, the warm breezes flow through it; and "So in Love Am I" has a very florid temperature, indeed.

The plot device concentrates the acting and singing in four people, and fortunately they are all uncommonly talented. As a greasepaint hussy, Miss Morison is an agile and humorous actress who is not afraid of slapstick and who can sing enchantingly. She has captured perfectly the improvised tone of the comedy, and she plays it with spirit and drollery. Lisa Kirk plays a subordinate part in a style that might be described as well-bred impudence. Given a sardonic song like "Always True to You (in My Fashion)," she can translate it into pert and gleaming buffoonery.

We have all been long acquainted with Mr. Drake as headman in musical shows. In the part of the egotistical actor who plays Petruchio on stage, Mr. Drake's pleasant style of acting and his unaffected singing are the heart of the show. By hard work and through personal sincerity. Mr. Drake has become about the most valuable man in his field. In the secondary male role, Harold Lang, who is principally a dancer, also gives a versatile and attractive performance.

Under the supervision of John C. Wilson there are other treasures in this humorous phantasmagoria of song—the torrid pavement dancing of Fred Davis and Eddie Sledge, the bland gunman fooling of Harry Clark and Jack Diamond, the antic dancing masquerade that serves as first scene to *The Taming of the Shrew* sequence.

All these items have been gathered up neatly into the flowing pattern of a pleasant musical comedy. To filch a good notion from *The New Yorker*, all you can say for *Kiss Me, Kate* is that it is terribly enjoyable.

OPPOSITE: Alfred Drake and Patricia Morison in *Kiss Me, Kate*. **ABOVE:** Poster for *Kiss Me Kate*, 1946.

April 8, 1949

# SOUTH PACIFIC

By BROOKS ATKINSON

No one will be surprised this morning to read that Richard Rodgers, Oscar Hammerstein II and Joshua Logan have written a magnificent musical drama. Even before they set pencil to paper and chose *South Pacific* for the title, alert theatregoers very sensibly started to buy tickets for it. With Mary Martin and Ezio Pinza in the leading parts, the opening performance at the Majestic last evening amply confirmed preliminary expectations and brought the town a wonderfully talented show.

Although Mr. Rodgers and Mr. Hammerstein are extraordinarily gifted men, they have not forgotten how to apply the seat of the pants to the seat of the chair. One thing that makes *South Pacific* so rhapsodically enjoyable is the hard work and organization that have gone into it under Mr. Logan's spontaneous direction. They have culled the story from James Michener's *Tales of the South Pacific*, which in some incredible fashion managed to retain sensitive perceptions toward the Pacific Islands and human beings in the midst of the callous misery, boredom and slaughter of war.

The perception has been preserved in this sombre romance about a French planter and an American nurse from Arkansas. Writing for Broadway, Mr. Rodgers and Mr. Hammerstein have not forgotten to entertain the customers with some exuberant antics by humorously sullen American Seabees who resent everything they have to endure. But essentially this is a tenderly beautiful idyll of genuine people inexplicably tossed together in a strange corner of the world; and the music, the lyrics, the singing and the acting contribute to this mood.

If the country still has the taste to appreciate a masterly love song, "Some Enchanted Evening" ought to become reasonably immortal. For Mr. Rodgers' music is a romantic incantation; and, as usual, Mr. Hammerstein's verses are both fervent and simple. Mr. Pinza's bass voice is the most beautiful that has been heard on a Broadway stage for an eon or two. He sings this song with infinite delicacy of feeling and loveliness of tone. As a matter of fact, Mr. Pinza is also a fine actor; and his first appearance on the one and only legitimate stage is an occasion worth celebrating.

Since we have all been more or less in love with Miss Martin for several years, it is no surprise to find her full of quicksilver, pertness and delight as the Navy nurse. She sings some good knockabout melodies with skill and good nature, making something particularly enjoyable out of the stomping jubilee of "I'm Gonna Wash That Man Right Outa My Hair" and blowing out the walls of the theatre with the rapture of "I'm in Love With a Wonderful Guy." In the opinion of one inquiring theatregoer, there seems to be a little of Annie Oakley, the gun-girl, left in Miss Martin's attack on a song, and perhaps this should be exorcised by slow degrees. For the Navy nurse is a few cuts above Annie socially. Miss Martin is the girl who can make her captivating without deluging her in charm.

Since *South Pacific* is not an assembled show, but a thoroughly composed musical drama, you will find high standards of characterization and acting throughout. Take Juanita Hall, for example. She plays a brassy,

greedy, ugly Tonkinese woman with harsh, vigorous, authentic accuracy; and she sings one of Mr. Rodgers' finest songs, "Bali Ha'I," with rousing artistry.

After wasting his talents on stereotyped parts for several years, Myron McCormick has a good one as a braggart, scheming Seabee, and plays it with great comic gusto. *South Pacific* naturally does well by the ruffians who saved democracy amid groans of despair in the Eastern ocean, and "There Is Nothing Like a Dame" ought to go down as their theme song.

As evidence of the care that has gone into this drama take note of the part of Capt. George Brackett, U. S. N. The part is written with real invention on the model of a human being, and Martin Wolfson plays him admirably.

Jo Mielziner has provided entrancing settings that presumably have a Polynesian accent. Russell Bennett has written orchestrations, especially for the overtures, that are rich and colorful in instrumental sound. For the authors and producers have a high regard for professional skill, and everything they have put their hands to is perfectly wrought. Fortunately, Mr. Rodgers and Mr. Hammerstein are also the most gifted men in the business. And *South Pacific* is as lively, warm, fresh and beautiful as we had all hoped that it would be.

· · · · · · · · · · · · · · · · · · · · · ·

Scenes from *South Pacific*. **OPPOSITE, CLOCKWISE FROM TOP:** Ezio Pinza, Barbara Luna, Michael De Leon, and Mary Martin; Mary Martin; and Juanita Hall, Betta St. John, and William Tabbert.

# REVIVAL

April 4, 2008

# OPTIMIST AWASH IN THE TROPICS

By BEN BRANTLEY

Love blossoms fast and early in Bartlett Sher's rapturous revival of Rodgers and Hammer-stein's *South Pacific*, which opened Thursday at the Vivian Beaumont Theater at Lincoln Center. And while you may think, "But this is so sudden," you don't doubt for a second that it's the real thing.

I'm talking partly about the chemistry between the production's revelatory stars, Kelli O'Hara and Paulo Szot, in the opening scene of this tale from 1949 of men and women unmoored by war. But I'm also talking about the chemistry between a show and its audience.

For this *South Pacific* re-creates the unabashed, unquestioning romance that American theatergoers had with the American book musical in the mid-20th century, before the genre got all self-conscious about itself. There's not an ounce of we-know-better-now irony in Mr. Sher's staging. Yet the show feels too vital to be

a museum piece, too sensually fluid to be square.

I could feel the people around me leaning in toward the stage, as if it were a source of warmth on a raw, damp day. And that warmth isn't the synthetic fire of can-do cheer and wholesomeness associated (not always correctly) with Rodgers and Hammerstein. It's the fire of daily life, with all its crosscurrents and ambiguities, underscored and clarified by music.

During the past couple of decades directors have often felt the need to approach the Rodgers and Hammerstein classics with either a can of black paint or misted-up rose-colored glasses. (This has been especially true in London, with the National Theatre's celebrated darkness-plumbing productions of *Carousel* and *Oklahoma!*, and the current sugar-glazed cash-cow of a revival of *The Sound of Music* in the West End.) Mr. Sher, who heralded the

return of full-blown lyricism to musicals with his exquisite production of Adam Guettel and Craig Lucas's *Light in the Piazza* several years ago, puts his trust unconditionally in the original material.

It's as if a vintage photograph had been restored not with fuzzy, hand-colored pretti-ness but with you-are-there clarity. Though Michael Yeargan's perspective-stretching beachscape of a set isn't photo-realist, you somehow accept it as more real than real, just as the score performed by the sumptuously full orchestra (with musical direction by Ted Sperling) feels from the beginning like thought made effortlessly audible.

Scenes from the 2008 revival of *South Pacific*.
**OPPOSITE, TOP:** Paulo Szot, Laurissa Romain, Luka Kain, and Kelli O'Hara. **OPPOSITE, BOTTOM:** Loretta Ables Sayre (center) and members of the cast. **ABOVE:** Kelli O'Hara (center) and members of the cast.

December 9, 1949

# Gentlemen Prefer Blondes

By BROOKS ATKINSON

Happy days are here again. The musical version of *Gentlemen Prefer Blondes*, which lighted the Ziegfeld last evening, is a vastly enjoyable song-and-dance antic put on with humorous perfection. Millions of people doted on Anita Loos' comic fable when it appeared as a play in 1926 with a memorable cast and the laughs pitched fairly low in the diaphragm.

Fortunately they are going to have an opportunity to enjoy it again in a thoroughly fresh treatment. For Miss Loos and Joseph Fields have now fitted it to the formula of an old-fashioned rowdydow with Tin Pan Alley tunes by Jule Styne and some brassy and amusing lyrics by Leo Robin.

Staged expertly in a festive manner by John C. Wilson, it brings back a good many familiar delights to a street that has been adding art to the musical stage for quite a long time. But thanks to the clowning of Carol Channing, it also brings us something new and refreshing. Let's call her portrait of the aureate Lee the most fabulous comic creation of this dreary period in history.

You will recall Lorelei Lee as the flapper gold-digger who made her way through masculine society with a good deal of success in the Twenties. In Miss Channing's somewhat sturdier image, Lorelei's rapacious innocence is uproariously amusing. Made-up to resemble a John Held creature, she goes through the play like a dazed automaton—husky enough to kick in the teeth of any gentleman on the stage, but mincing coyly in high-heel shoes and looking out on a confused world through big, wide, starry eyes. There has never been anything like this before in human society.

Miss Channing can also act a part with skill and relish. They have given her a funny autobiographical ballad, "A Little Girl From Little Rock," which she translates into a roaringly entertaining number. She has something original and grotesque to contribute to every number. She can also speak the cock-eyed dialogue with droll inflections. Her Lorelei is a mixture of cynicism and stupidity that will keep New York in good spirits all winter.

Having good taste in general, the producers of *Gentlemen Prefer Blondes* have hired Yvonne Adair to appear with Miss Channing as Dorothy, the more cautious brunette; and Jack McCauley to play the part of Lorelei's protector. Since they are both expert performers with a sense of humor, this turns out to be very happy casting. A pleasure-mad, teetering old lady by Alice Pearce; a handsome, genteel young man from Philadelphia by Eric Brotherson; a philandering Britisher by Rex Evans, and an indecently healthy zipper manufacturer by George S. Irving—round out the principal performers of a singularly affable cast.

Although the tone of *Gentlemen Prefer Blondes* is old-fashioned, the spirit is modern and the pace is swift. Oliver Smith has provided a suite of good travelogue settings, combining the best features of New York and Paris. And Miles White has designed stunning costumes with a humorous accent.

Agnes de Mille has done the ballets with a light touch—managing somehow to combine precision dancing with gay improvisations in her pleasant folk style. Anita Alvarez sweeps in and out of the show with a whole series of impish dances, performing one of the best with Kazimir Kokic. As a matter of fact, there is a lot of entertaining and expert dancing through the many scenes of this plausible burlesque of one of the most ancient rackets of the world.

Every part of it is alive and abundantly entertaining. And above it all towers the blonde thatch of Miss Channing, who is batting her big eyes, murdering the English language and carrying the whole golden world along with her by sheer audacity. *Gentlemen Prefer Blondes* was always funny. It is even funnier, now that the lustrous Miss Channing has taken such a strangle hold on the part.

. . . . . . . . . . . . . . . . . . . . . . . . . . . .

**OPPOSITE:** Carol Channing and Yvonne Adair in *Gentlemen Prefer Blondes.*

# IV. THE FIFTIES

The 1950s would be the last consistently fertile decade for what we now think of as the classic American musical, the model that Rodgers and Hammerstein perfected. By now, it was taken for granted that song should spring seamlessly from plot and that dance could be used not just for decorative flourish but to propel and amplify a story. American composers and book writers plied this formula with a confidence that would never be theirs again, and rang up a remarkable range of variations.

These were the years, after all, that triumphed with tales of both singing gangsters à la Damon Runyon (in *Guys and Dolls*) and a semi-singing, snobbish professor of phonetics à la George Bernard Shaw (in *My Fair Lady*). A nineteenth-century royal Siamese court (*The King and I*) and a Major League Baseball field (*Damn Yankees*); Main Street, U.S.A., in sunny, old-timey Iowa (*The Music Man*) and the mean streets of contemporary, racially divided New York (*West Side Story*)—these were all settings for shows that combined commercial and critical appeal. And *Times* reviewers threw their hats into the air so often, it's a wonder they had any headgear left by 1959.

Rodgers and Hammerstein showed they still had the stuff to come up with hits, bookending the decade with two of them: *The King and I* (1951) and *The Sound of Music* (1959). But while they were accorded the respect due founding fathers, there were murmurs when *The Sound of Music* opened that the old boys were getting a little stale and even retrogressing. That show's scenario, wrote Brooks Atkinson, "has the hackneyed look of the musical theater that Richard Rodgers and Oscar Hammerstein II replaced with *Oklahoma!* in 1943."

Old masters like Cole Porter (*Silk Stockings*) and Irving Berlin ("*Call Me Madam*") remained on the scene. So did old-master directors like George Abbot and George S. Kaufman. But a new slew of talents were coming into their own, including the songwriter Frank Loesser, whose *Guys and Dolls* (1950) is still considered a nigh-perfect high point of the integrated musical. (His *The Most Happy Fella*, in 1956, didn't generate anything like the same box office success, but its operatic ambitions and sensitive probing of character through music inspired Atkinson to pronounce: "Broadway is used to heart. It is not accustomed to evocations of the soul.") And with *Damn Yankees* and *The Pajama Game*, the team of Richard Adler and Jerry Ross delivered smashes, perennials that remain in the revival repertory as well as a clutch of songs that became standards.

Also on the rise was a new hybrid of choreographer and director, who at their best stamped each show with an auteur's signature and consistency of vision. The most spectacular example of the species was Jerome Robbins, whose successes in the 1950s improbably and exhaustingly included *The Pajama Game* and *Peter Pan* (1954), *Bells Are Ringing* (1955), *West Side Story* (1957), and *Gypsy* (1959). Atkinson gracefully evoked the essence of Robbins' work in *West Side Story*,

writing, "Most of the characters, in fact, are dancers with some images of personality lifted out of the whirlwind—characters sketched on the wing." (Working with Robbins on *The Pajama Game* was the up-and-coming Bob Fosse, who would later take the role of director-choreographer to ever more stylized extremes.)

Two shows, above all, stood out for their daring and seemed to promise that no subject might be beyond the musical's reach. No one (including George Bernard) would have thought that a typically talky play by George Bernard Shaw would translate with any fluency to the musical stage. Yet in reviewing Lerner and Loewe's *My Fair Lady* (1956), adapted from Shaw's *Pygmalion* and starring Rex Harrison and Julie Andrews, Atkinson felt compelled to call the show "wonderful" in both his opening and closing paragraphs, while observing that "probably for the first time in history a typical musical comedy audience finds itself absorbed in the art of pronunciation." The unexpectedness of another musical's subject the following year gave Atkinson pause. Of *West Side Story*, which featured a ravishing score by Leonard Bernstein and poetic lyrics by a newcomer named Stephen Sondheim, he said, "Although the material is horrifying, the workmanship is admirable."

*West Side Story* would be adapted to film (in 1961) and win an Oscar for the year's best motion picture; so would *The Sound of Music* (in 1965). In fact, nearly all of the shows mentioned above would be made into movies. Broadway was still one of the essential go-to places for Hollywood producers in search of inspiration. In the next century, that equation would be reversed, with films regularly serving as the basis for stage musicals. For now, though, one detects a certain suspicion of things cinematic in *Times* reviews of Broadway. *Kismet* (1953) is dismissed for resembling "nothing so much as a supercolossal Hollywood wonderwork," while Robbins is taken to task for infusing scenes in *Peter Pan* with "a Hollywood-like lust for production for production's sake."

In this decade the musical started to make use of its own self-consciousness about itself and its origins. The first thoroughgoing pastiche musical to become a hit, Sandy Wilson's *The Boy Friend*, shows up in 1954 (with a very young Julie Andrews in the lead), as an homage to and send-up of the straight-faced silliness of shows of the 1920s. And in 1959, *Gypsy* uses the vocabulary of vaudeville and burlesque and subtitles itself "a musical fable." It also, in its portrayal of the monstrous stage mother Momma Rose (played by Ethel Merman, in a legendary career-capping performance), delivered what Clive Barnes later called "one of the few truly complex characters in the American musical." And so as the 1950s drew to its end, it provided what would come to be regarded by many as the greatest of all American musicals.

**OPPOSITE:** Workers installing the neon lettering for the Shubert Theatre's 2003 revival of *Gypsy*.

November 25, 1950

# Guys and Dolls

### By BROOKS ATKINSON

Out of the pages of Damon Runyon, some able artisans have put together a musical play that Broadway can be proud of. *Guys and Dolls* they call it out of one corner of the mouth. It opened at the Forty-sixth Street last evening. With a well-written book by Jo Swerling and Abe Burrows, and a dynamic score by Frank Loesser, it is a more coherent show than some that have higher artistic pretensions.

But you can count as its highest achievement the fact that it has preserved the friendly spirit of the Runyon literature without patronizing and without any show-shop hokum. It is the story of some gamblers and their unfortunate women who try to fit into the shifty pattern of Broadway life some of the stabilizing factors of marriage and love-making.

Let one playgoer remark in passing that there is something a little disconcerting about the casual attitude this story takes toward a religious mission which is trying to save a few souls in the neighborhood. But even this intrusion on the way of life of some street-corner salvationists is redeemed by the hearty camaraderie of all the characters of the book. Although they are gamblers, showgirls, cops and adult delinquents, they have their ethics, too, and live in a gaudy, blowzy world that is

somehow warm and hospitable. After all, the Broadway culture is simple and sentimental but has a better heart than some cultures that are more literate.

Everyone concerned with *Guys and Dolls* has cast the show with relish and originality; and George S. Kaufman has never been in better form in the director's box. As the executive officer of the oldest floating crap game in town, Sam Levene gives an excitable and hilarious performance. Vivian Blaine makes something comic out of the lively vulgarity of a nightclub leading lady, singing her honky-tonk songs in a shrill but earnest voice. Isabel Bigley does as well by a missionary sergeant who astonishes herself by falling in love with an itinerant gambler. She plays a few enticing tricks on one of Mr. Loesser's most rollicking songs—"If I Were a Bell." As the tall, dark and handsome gambler, Robert Alda keeps the romance enjoyable, tough and surly.

The Runyon milieu is rich in startling types, and *Guys and Dolls* has the most flamboyant population of any show in town. Stubby Kaye, as a rotund sidewalk emissary; Johnny Silver, as a diminutive horse philosopher; B. S. Pully, as a big gun-and-blackjack man from Chicago—are sound, racy members of hallway society; and at last

Tom Pedi has got a part that runs more than five minutes as Harry The Horse, executive secretary for a thug. No one could make a more lovable salvationist than Pat Rooney Sr., who sings "More I Cannot Wish" with cordial good-will.

Everything is all of a piece in this breezy fiction which has been organized as simply and logically as a Runyon story. Michael Kidds' comic ballets of night club production numbers and crap games belong to the production as intimately as Jo Mielziner's affable settings and Alvin Colt's noisy costumes. Mr. Loesser's lyrics and songs have the same affectionate appreciation of the material as the book, which is funny without being self-conscious or mechanical.

From the technical point of view we might as well admit that *Guys and Dolls* is a work of art. It is spontaneous and has form, style and spirit. In view of the source material, that is not astonishing. For Damon Runyon captured the spirit of an idle corner of the town with sympathetic understanding and reproduced it slightly caricatured in the sketches and stories he wrote. *Guys and Dolls* is gusty and uproarious, and it is not too grand to take a friendly, personal interest in the desperate affairs of Broadway's back-room society.

Scenes from *Guys and Dolls*. **CLOCKWISE FROM TOP:** Johnny Silver (foreground, left), Stubby Kaye (center), and Netta Packer (far right); Stubby Kaye and Vivian Blaine; and Robert Alda and Isabel Bigley.

April 15, 1992

# *Guys and Dolls;* Damon Runyon's New York Lives Anew

By FRANK RICH

If you have ever searched Times Square to find that vanished Broadway of lovable gangsters, wisecracking dolls and neon-splashed dawns, you must not miss the *Guys and Dolls* that roared into the old neighborhood last night. As directed with a great eye and a big heart by Jerry Zaks and performed by a thrilling young company that even boasts, in Faith Prince, the rare sighting of a brand-new musical-comedy star, this is an enchanting rebirth of the show that defines Broadway dazzle.

It's hard to know which genius, and I do mean genius, to celebrate first while cheering the entertainment at the Martin Beck. Do we speak of Damon Runyon, who created the characters of *Guys and Dolls* in his stories and with them a whole new American language? Or of Frank Loesser, who in 1950 translated Runyon into songs with melodies by turns brash and melting and lyrics that are legend? This being the theater department, please forgive my tilt toward Loesser, whose musical setting of phrases like "I got the horse right here" and "a person could develop a cold" and "the oldest established permanent floating crap game in New York" are as much a part of our landscape as the Chrysler Building and Radio City Music Hall.

The thing to remember about Runyon is that he was born in Kansas and didn't reach Manhattan until he was twenty-six. His love for his adopted town is the helplessly romantic ardor of a pilgrim who finally found his Mecca. That romance is built into the text of *Guys and Dolls*, in which the hoods and chorus girls engage in no violence, never

mention sex and speak in an exaggeratedly polite argot that is as courtly as dese-and-dose vernacular can be.

Runyon's idyllic spirit informs every gesture in this production. Mr. Zaks, the choreographer Christopher Chadman and an extraordinary design team led by Tony Walton give the audience a fantasy Broadway that, if it ever existed, is now as defunct as such *Guys and Dolls* landmarks as Klein's, Rogers Peet and the Roxy. Yet it is the place

we dream about whenever we think of Runyon and Loesser or anyone else who painted New York as a nocturnal paradise where ideas and emotions are spelled out sky-high on blinking signs and, to quote another lyric, "the streetlamp light fills the gutter with gold."

Scenes from the 1992 revival of *Guys and Dolls*. **OPPOSITE:** Faith Prince as Miss Adelaide. **ABOVE:** Faith Prince and Nathan Lane.

March 30, 1951

# THE KING AND I

### By BROOKS ATKINSON

Nearly two years having elapsed since they invaded the South Pacific, Richard Rodgers and Oscar Hammerstein II have moved over to the Gulf of Siam. *The King and I,* which opened at the St. James last evening, is their musical rendering of Margaret Landon's *Anna and the King of Siam.* As a matter of record, it must be reported that *The King and I* is no match for *South Pacific,* which is an inspired musical drama.

But there is plenty of room for memorable music-making in the more familiar categories. Strictly on its own terms, *The King and I* is an original and beautiful excursion into the rich splendors of the Far East, done with impeccable taste by two artists and brought to life with a warm, romantic score, idiomatic lyrics and some exquisite dancing.

As the English governess who comes out from England in the Eighteen-Sixties to teach the King's children, Gertrude Lawrence looks particularly ravishing in some gorgeous costumes and acts

an imposing part with spirit and an edge of mischief. Yul Brynner plays the King with a kind of fierce austerity, drawn between pride of office and eagerness to learn about the truth of the modern world from a "scientific foreigner." Apart from the pleasures of the musical theatre, there is a theme in *The King and I*, and, as usual, Mr. Rodgers and Mr. Hammerstein have developed it with tenderness as well as relish, and with respect for the human beings involved.

Part of the delight of their fable derives from the wealth of beauty in the Siamese setting; and here Jo Mielziner, the Broadway magnifico, has drawn on the riches of the East; and Irene Sharaff has designed some of her most wonderful costumes. As a spectacle, *The King and I* is a distinguished work. In the direction, John van Druten has made something fine and touching in the elaborate scene that introduces the King's charming children to their English school marm. Jerome Robbins, serving as choreographer, has put together a stunning ballet that seasons the liquid formalism of Eastern dancing with some American humor. Yuriko, the ballerina, is superb as the Siamese notion of Eliza, in *Uncle Tom's Cabin.*

Mr. Rodgers is in one of his most affable moods. For Miss Lawrence he has written several pleasant and ingratiating numbers which she sings brightly—"Hello, Young

Lovers!" "The Royal Bangkok Academy" and "Shall I Tell You What I Think of You?" Dorothy Sarnoff does something wonderful with "Something Wonderful," which is one of Mr. Rodgers' most exultant numbers. Probably the most glorious number is "I Have Dreamed," which Doretta Morrow and Larry Douglas sing as a fervent duet. Mr. Brynner is no great shakes as a singer, but he makes his way safely through a couple of meditative songs written with an agreeable suggestion of Eastern music.

Say a word of thanks to Russell Bennett for his colorful orchestrations that make a fresh use of individual instruments and that always sound not only interesting but civilized. His orchestration should be especially appreciated in the long and enchanting scene that brings on the children one by one.

Don't expect another *South Pacific* nor an *Oklahoma!* This time Mr. Rodgers and Mr. Hammerstein are not breaking any fresh trails. But they are accomplished artists of song and words in the theatre; and *The King and I* is a beautiful and lovable musical play.

Scenes from *The King and I.* **ABOVE:** Charles Francis (far left), Gertrude Lawrence (second from right), Sandy Kennedy (far right), and members of the cast. **OPPOSITE:** Yul Brynner and Gertrude Lawrence as the King and Anna.

**RIGHT:** From right of center, Dorothy Sarnoff (standing), Gertrude Lawrence (seated), Johnny Stewart (bowing), and Yul Brynner in a scene from the original Broadway production of *The King and I*, 1951.

Scenes from *Wonderful Town*. **ABOVE:** Rosalind
Russell and members of the cast. **LEFT:** Rosalind
Russell and George Gaynes. **OPPOSITE:** From left,
Rosalind Russell, Dot Clark, Edith Adams, George
Gaynes, and Chris Alexander.

February 26, 1953

# *Wonderful Town*

By BROOKS ATKINSON

According to the Constitution, Rosalind Russell cannot run for President until 1956. But it would be wise to start preparing for her campaign at once. For she can dance and sing better than any President we have had. She is also better looking and has a more infectious sense of humor.

She can remain in residence until 1956 at the Winter Garden. *Wonderful Town*, which opened there last evening, is the most uproarious and original musical carnival we have had since *Guys and Dolls* appeared in this neighborhood. Joseph Fields and Jerome Chodorov have founded the book on their comedy, *My Sister Eileen*, which was founded in turn on Ruth McKenney's wryly comic stories. That noble lineage in laughter accounts for the humorous literacy of the story.

But everyone is more inspired than usual in the administration of *Wonderful Town*. Leonard Bernstein has written it a wonderful score. Dispensing with hurdy-gurdy techniques, he has written a bright and witty score in a variety of modern styles without forgetting to endow it with at least one tender melody and a good romantic number. Orchestrated by Don Walker, conducted by Lehman Engel, the score carries forward the crack-brained comedy of the book with gaiety and excitement.

If you remember that Mr. Bernstein also wrote the music for *On the Town* a decade ago, you will be glad to know that Betty Comden and Adolph Green are associated with him again. They have written some extraordinarily inventive lyrics in a style as unhackneyed as the music. And Donald Saddler has directed the most exuberant dances of the season. Sometimes gifted people never quite get attuned to each other in the composition of a musical circus. But in *Wonderful Town* everyone seems to have settled down joyfully to the creation of a beautifully organized fandango—the book,

the score and the ballets helping each other enthusiastically. George Abbott, ring-master of numberless musical shows, has put everything together in a robust, high-spirited performance.

No doubt you know already that this is the saga of two sisters from Ohio who settle down in an aguish Greenwich Village basement as the first step toward achieving careers in New York. The musical version is a little more elaborate than the prose version, and it gives Raoul Pene du Bois an opportunity to design some congenial Village scenery, to say nothing of a whole wardrobe of fantastic costumes.

Despite the elaborations of the book, the experiences the sisters have in the Village are as bizarre as they were originally. They include a festive conga line with the Brazilian sailors that brings down the first act curtain on a notable rumpus. As Sister Eileen, Edith Adams is absolutely perfect. She is both demure and coquettish; she is simple and frank, good company and well mannered. And she sings with a sweetness that represents the character delightfully. The hill-billy lament for "Ohio" that Miss Russell and she sing early in the show is not

merely funny; it tells with great skill the folk background of this sophisticated folk tale.

Everyone else is in the right key, also: George Gaynes as a magazine editor with a fine baritone voice; Dort Clark as an aggressively cynical newspaper man; Chris Alexander as a refined drugstore manager; Henry Lascoe as a combination fake painter and phony landlord; Ted Beniades as nightclub charlatan. As restaurant cooks, waiters, cadets and assorted individuals, Nathaniel Frey, Delbert Anderson, David Lober and Ray Dorian are all right, too. As a husky, illiterate football player, Jordan Bentley is a very hearty buffoon. They make the Village a good deal more warm-hearted and insane than it is in nature.

At the head of all this bedlam Miss Russell gives a memorably versatile comic performance. She is tall, willowy and gawky; she is droll, sardonic and incredulous. Her comedy can be broad and also subtle. For she radiates the genuine comic spirit. In *Wonderful Town* she makes the whole city wonderful; and she will make the whole country wonderful when she is elected President in 1956.

# THE THREEPENNY OPERA

By LEWIS FUNKE

For those who have been wondering whether Marc Blitzstein's adaptation of *The Threepenny Opera* would stand up in a dramatic performance in the theatre as well as it did in concert form at the Brandeis University Festival in 1952, the answer was provided last night in Greenwich Village's Theatre de Lys. The answer is that it does. Indeed, it stands up beautifully and to Mr. Blitzstein this morning this department extends heartfelt thanks.

The score of *The Threepenny Opera,* which the late Kurt Weill wrote to the German-language book and lyrics of Bert Brecht, is, of course, one of the authentic contemporary masterpieces. It is full of beauty, of humor, of compassion, and what Mr. Blitzstein has done is to retain that score while putting the text into English. It is a remarkable contribution.

To be sure, others have rendered the Brecht words into English, too. But this reviewer has never heard these efforts, and comparisons are impossible. The important point of the moment is what Blitzstein has done. And what he has done is to provide words that fit the music, words that retain the bite, the savage satire, the overwhelming bitterness underlying this work from its original forebear, John Gay's *The Beggar's Opera.*

The company which has been assembled for the present production is young, full of vigor and goodwill. Vocally, it is entirely satisfactory. Dramatically its performance is somewhat rough along the edges and there is evidence of inexperience. From time to time it is difficult to avoid being conscious of a lack of bite and style. But this only indicates how much lurks in this opera.

Among those who have a complete comprehension and mastery of the work is, naturally, Lotte Lenya, widow of Mr. Weill. Miss Lenya, appearing as Jenny, the part she created in the original Berlin production in 1928, delivers her role with the

necessary strength and authority. Charlotte Rae as Mrs. Peachum is excellent and so are Jo Sullivan as Polly, Beatrice Arthur as Lucy and Scott Merrill as Macheath.

An eight-piece orchestra provides the accompaniment, and within the confines of the tiny Theatre de Lys it is just right.

*The Threepenny Opera,* which Bert Brecht set in Victorian England, a period Mr. Blitzstein has retained, appears to be indestructible. Its commentary on human beings and life retains a persistent vitality. To hear it rendered in language clear and comprehensible is an added pleasure.

Scenes from *The Threepenny Opera.* **OPPOSITE:** Scott Merrill and Beatrice Arthur as Macheath and Lucy. **ABOVE:** Lotte Lenya as Jenny with Scott Merrill.

May 14, 1954

# THE PAJAMA GAME

By BROOKS ATKINSON

The last new musical of the season is the best. It is *The Pajama Game*, which opened at the St. James last evening with all the uproar of a George Abbott show. He and Richard Bissell put the book together out of Mr. Bissell's recent novel, *7¼ Cents*. Applying the good old football spirit to a strike in a pajama factory, the book is as good as most though no better.

For, like the customers who are now going to pour into the St. James, Mr. Abbott is really interested in the color, humor and revelry of a first-rate musical rumpus. *The Pajama Game* fits those specifications exactly.

Richard Adler and Jerry Ross have written an exuberant score in any number of good American idioms without self-consciousness. Beginning with an amusing satire of the work tempo in a factory, they produce love songs with more fever than is usual this year; and they manage to get through a long evening enthusiastically in other respects also. "Once a Year Day" is a jubilee number with a very rousing finish; "There Was Once a Man" takes the goo out of love expertly. Mr. Adler and Mr. Ross write like musicians with a sense of humor; and Don Walker, who has provided imaginative orchestrations, shares their high spirits.

Fortunately, the people who manufacture pajamas are wonderful company in the theatre. The head-man is John Raitt, with the deep voice and the romantic manner; and the head-woman is Janis Paige, whose voice is almost as exhilarating as her shape. Entangled in some love-and-union hokum,

they make mating seem attractively normal, and they sing as though they meant it.

Eddie Foy Jr., a true clown who can strut standing still, is immensely funny as a factory time-keeper and a mighty friendly man in a dance. Reta Shaw and he contribute one amiable soft-shoe dance that made the audience explode last evening.

*The Pajama Game* has been staged by Mr. Abbott and Jerome Robbins, both of whom like motion on the stage. That may account for the lightness and friskiness of the performance. And that may also help to explain why Bob Fosse's ballets and improvised dance turns seem to come so spontaneously out of the story. This is the place to express considerable gratitude to Carol Haney. In the cast she is the secretary to the boss of the plant.

But in fact she is a comic dancer of extraordinary versatility. Shaggy-haired and gamin-like, she suits the mode of the season except that she substitutes carica-ture for glamour. Her burlesque strip-tease for a funny number called "Her Is" is

effortless and convulsing. With Buzz Miller and Peter Gennaro, she introduces the second act with a swift, high-pressure vaudeville that is terrific. Both as dancer and actress Miss Haney is superb.

The Pajama Game includes all the usual properties of a loud and ample musical carnival. The costumes and scenery are by Lemuel Ayers, who can make even a factory workroom look theatrical. There is a union picnic for purposes of festive spectacle in the first act, and a restaurant called "Hernando's Hideaway" where the second act goes pleasantly insane.

Mr. Bissell, former tow-boat skipper, and currently boss of a shirt and pajama factory, is a more original writer than you would suspect in the book of this show. Beaten into shape for Broadway, his tale of factory labor problems looks a good deal like dear old Siwash. But say this for the book: it provides an original setting. And, as usual, Mr. Abbott has provided the noise, speed, guffaws and excitement of an energetic, amusing show.

Scenes from *The Pajama Game*.
**OPPOSITE:** John Raitt and Janis Paige (center) flanked by Carol Haney (left), and Eddie Foy, Jr. (right). **ABOVE:** Eddie Foy Jr., Shirley MacLaine (third from left), and members of the cast. **RIGHT:** John Raitt and Janis Paige.

# REVIVAL

February 24, 2006

# THE PAJAMA GAME

## DRESSES ARE FINE, BUT PAJAMAS ARE DIVINE

By BEN BRANTLEY

"Tell me!" Seen in cold print, these may not look like two of the sexiest words in the English language. But as spoken, shouted and sung by Harry Connick Jr. and Kelli O'Hara in Kathleen Marshall's delicious reinvention of *The Pajama Game,* the 1954 musical that gave new meaning to labor-management relations, that simple little phrase transforms the private pleasures of pillow talk into a heady public celebration. And a little novelty number called "There Once Was a Man" becomes a rockabilly pelvis pumper that turns the thermostat way up on a show that has already been generating plenty of steam heat.

What's this? Sexual chemistry in a Broadway musical? Isn't that illegal now? If it were, then Mr. Connick and Ms. O'Hara (not to mention their red-handed director and choreographer, Ms. Marshall) would be looking at long jail terms. But as long as these stars are on the stage of the American Airlines Theatre, where this frisky tale of a union dispute at a pajama factory opened last night, grown-up audiences have the chance to witness something rarely seen anymore: a bona fide adult love affair, with all its attendant frictions, translated into the populist poetry of hummable songs and sprightly dance.

Scenes from the 2006 revival of *The Pajama Game.*
**OPPOSITE, TOP:** From left, Peter Benson, Joyce Chittick, Harry Connick Jr., and Kelli O'Hara.
**OPPOSITE, BOTTOM:** Kelli O'Hara and members of the cast. **ABOVE:** Harry Connick Jr. and Kelli O'Hara as Sid and Babe.

October 1, 1954

# The Boy Friend

By Brooks Atkinson

Out of some clichés from the foolish Twenties, Sandy Wilson has written a delightful burlesque, *The Boy Friend*, which opened at the Royale last evening. He wrote it originally for British audiences who have been enjoying it ever since.

There seems to be no reason why their American counterparts should not enjoy it here. For Mr. Wilson's light cartoon of the standard musical play of the Twenties is extremely well done in manuscript as well as on stage. He has written book, songs and lyrics with satirical inventiveness; and someone has directed it with great ironic skill.

For it is hard to say which is funnier: the material or the performance. With a covetous eye on the follies of the Twenties, Mr. Wilson has knocked together an old-fashioned book as maudlin as they were in those days. It tells the story of a rich little girl who falls in love with a charming messenger boy, who, fortunately, in the last act turns out to be the son of Lord and Lady Brockhurst.

Writing the music and lyrics in the same skimming, sardonic vein, Mr. Wilson has composed a tinny score in a jazzy style with amusingly innocuous lyrics.

*I could be happy with you*
*If you could be happy with me,*
his lovers sing with bogus rapture. Some other awful though plausible lines come across the footlights: "Skies will not always be blue," for example. Mr. Wilson has a knack for coating the obvious with humor.

The staging is superb. Dressed in the flapper, knee-length gowns of the Twenties, with cloche hats, and made up in the garish stage style of the period, the girls are grotesquely funny to look at before the show properly begins. But there is a lot more to the caricature than costumes. For the director has revived all the coy stage routines of the day, and they are hilarious.

The toothy charm, the girlish shrugs, the screeching laughter, the fraudulently innocent glee—they are all present or

accounted for, the more horrible, the more uproarious. Was the musical stage as silly as this in the Twenties? Well, it was. We are all guilty, if only because we liked it that way.

According to the program, Vida Hope, who directed the London production, has directed the American facsimile. Since this department does not know all the details of the intramural rumpus during the rehearsal period, it will take the program at face value and give Miss Hope credit for a brisk, witty performance.

Many of the performers have come from England, and they are wonderful. The saucy girls who begin the festivities with squealing, grimacing and dancing are very funny. Ann Wakefield, who does a fast Charleston and flirts with all the boys, is vastly amusing. Dilys Lay, another pony soubrette, is a miniature Beatrice Lillie.

Ruth Altman, a Gothamite in good standing, plays and sings a breezy coquette of middle years. John Hewer, as a tap-dancing romantic lead, acts with the arch good nature of the period.

But it is probably Julie Andrews, as the heroine, who gives *The Boy Friend* its special quality. She burlesques the insipidity of the part. She keeps the romance very sad. Her hesitating gestures and her wistful, shy mannerisms are very comic. But, by golly, there is more than irony in her performance. There is something genuine in it, too. Some-times her romantic sadness is almost moving. One theatregoer found himself sorry for her and just on the verge of believing *The Boy Friend*; and he was happier than she was when she found Prince Charming in the last buttery scene.

But that is obviously an illegal attitude to take toward Mr. Wilson's pastiche. *The Boy Friend* is a caricature of the hokum musical comedy of the Twenties, and a mighty good one, too.

Scenes from *The Boy Friend*. **OPPOSITE:** Julie Andrews and John Hewer. **ABOVE:** Members of the cast perform a dance number.

October 21, 1954

# PETER PAN

By BROOKS ATKINSON

If Mary Martin is satisfied, so are the folks out front. The musical version of *Peter Pan*, which opened at the Winter Garden last evening, is a vastly amusing show.

Barrie wrote the libretto. But a lot of the exuberance of Texas has stolen into the legend now. For Miss Martin, looking trim and happy, is the liveliest Peter Pan in the record book. She has more appetite for flying and swinging than any of her more demure predecessors, and she performs as actor, dancer and singer with skill and enjoyment. Peter Pan may have been a proper Victorian originally. He is a healthy, fun-loving American now.

As the bloodthirsty Captain Hook, Cyril Ritchard gives a superb performance in the grand manner, with just a touch of burlesque. Among the other stars of the production, put Jerome Robbins' name high on the list. Mr. Robbins began as a choreographer. Without taking leave of that profession, he has directed this phantasmagoria with inventiveness and delight. The adventures of Peter Pan are marvelously enlivened in Never Never Land by any number of comic ballets for children, Indians and pirates—rushing and winning in style, though never alien to the innocent spirit of Barrie. Mr. Robbins has done a wonderful job.

There is room for some arguments about this full-gauged show. By the time the third act comes round, it begins to look over produced. Peter Larkin's scenery is magical, as are Motley's costumes and all the other impedimenta of a big carnival. But a Hollywood-like lust for production for production's sake makes things look ponderous toward the end.

Nor has the music much taste. The songs and the lyrics have been contributed by many hands, and some of them are suitable. The opening nursery fugue, called "Tender Shepherd," is a lovely piece that promises a charming evening. There is a highly comic tango for the pirates, and a sweet-tempered waltz for Liza (who is Mary Martin's daughter) in the second act. But most of the music sounds as though it had come out of Tin Pan Alley tune factories. It lacks distinction and has no audible fondness for Barrie.

Although the taste in showmanship and in music is common, the taste in performers is impeccable. Kathy Nolan's round-faced beaming Wendy is perfect—girlish without sentimentality. As the mother of the Darling children, Margalo Gillmore gives a beautiful performance. Sondra Lee, as Tiger Lily, the Indian maid, is uproarious. She dances and acts a sort of gutter Indian with a city accent that is mocking and comical.

The orphan boys are well cast, particularly in the case of one begoggled little shaver with a tooth missing who teeters gravely through the dances. Among the pirates is Joe E. Marks, a short man who looks constantly worried and more like a homebody than any pirate should. Norman Shelly's maternal-minded dog, Don Lurio's disdainful kangaroo, Richard Wyatt's scholarly lion and Joan Tewkesbury's gossipy ostrich are very cheerful company.

Altogether it is a bountiful, good-natured show with a lot of disarming child's play, and Miss Martin flying through the scenery. *Peter Pan* with a Texas accent is fun.

**OPPOSITE:** Mary Martin and, below, from left, Kathy Nolan, Joseph Stafford, and Robert Harrington in *Peter Pan*.

May 6, 1955

# DAMN YANKEES

By LEWIS FUNKE

As shiny as a new baseball and almost as smooth, a new musical glorifying the national pastime slid into the Forty-sixth Street Theatre last night. As far as this umpire is concerned you can count it among the healthy clouts of the campaign.

It is called *Damn Yankees* and it tells about how Casey Stengel's stalwarts are brought down to defeat by the Washington Senators in the final game of the season with the American League bunting the prize. But even the most ardent supporters of Mr. Stengel's minions should have a good time. And, as for that Dodger crowd, well you can just imagine.

Heading the board of strategy for this outfit is that shrewd manipulator of talent, George Abbott. He acts as general manager of the proceedings on the stage in addition to having collaborated on the book with Douglass Wallop, from whose novel, *The Year the Yankees Lost the Pennant*, this merry romp was taken.

To be sure, like any other manager in the course of a long season, Mr. Abbott has not been able to iron out all the kinks in his combination. In spite of his emphasis on speed afoot and timing there is a tendency every now and then for things to settle down a bit flatly on the ground. But the story of how Joe Boyd leases his soul to the Devil in order to become Joe Hardy, champion home-run hitter and inspiration of the Washington Senators, succeeds in being a sufficiently satisfactory vehicle on which to hang some highly amusing antics and utilize some splendid performers.

There is for instance that enchantress, Gwen Verdon, who socked a home run two years ago in *Can-Can*. Miss Verdon is the devil's handmaiden called upon to aid in sealing the fate of Joe Hardy's soul. It is difficult to understand how Joe was able to hold out for so long. For Miss Verdon is just about as alluring a she-witch as was ever bred in the nether regions. Vivacious, as sleek as a car on the showroom floor, and as nice to look at, she gives brilliance and sparkle to the evening with her exuberant dancing, her wicked, glistening eyes and her sheer delight in the foolery.

For the Devil there is the impeccable Ray Walston, a suave and sinister fellow who knows how to be disdainful of the good in man, whose pleasure, as you might expect, is to make humans squirm. Authoritative and persuasive, he does not overdo a role that easily could become irritating in less expert hands. Stephen Douglass, as Joe Hardy, is a completely believable athlete, clean-cut and earnest about his work. And, although it is impossible to spread the full credits to a large and vigorous cast, mention must be made of the effective contributions by Jean Stapleton as an autograph hound, Nathaniel Frey and Jimmy Komack as a couple of ball hawks, and Rae Allen as a nervy feminine sports writer.

In the music department Richard Adler and Jerry Ross have provided a thoroughly robust score to fit the occasion. The music has the spirit and brass that you'd expect to find out at the ball park and the lyrics are appropriate and smart. "Heart" is a humorous ode to the need for courage on the athletic field and it is done splendidly by Russ Brown, the sturdy manager of the Senators, along with the Messrs. Komack, Frey and Albert Linville. "The Game" is a humorous hymn to athletic abstinence. And "Shoeless Joe From Hannibal, Mo." sets the stage for a splendid hoedown for Robert Fosse, who attended to the choreography.

Mr. Fosse, with Miss Verdon's aid, is one of the evening's heroes. His dance numbers are full of fun and vitality. In "Whatever Lola Wants," there is a first-class gem in which music, lyrics and dance combine to make a memorable episode of the femme fatale operating on the hapless male. "Who's Got the Pain" involves Miss Verdon and Eddie Phillips in a mambo and "Two Lost Souls" puts on a torrid and rowdy bacchanal just to prove everyone's versatility.

William and Jean Eckart, assigned to the scenery and costume department, have decked out the whole affair handsomely. There is a considerable amount of talent in this entertainment and it makes up for some of the wide-open spaces that pop up every now and then. Looks like Mr. Abbott has another pennant winner.

Scenes from *Damn Yankees*. **OPPOSITE, TOP:** Stephen Douglass (center) and members of the cast. **OPPOSITE, BOTTOM:** Stephen Douglass and Gwen Verdon as Joe Hardy and Lola.

March 16, 1956

# My Fair Lady

By BROOKS ATKINSON

Bulletins from the road have not been misleading. *My Fair Lady*, which opened at the Mark Hellinger last evening, is a wonderful show.

Alan Jay Lerner has adapted it from Shaw's *Pygmalion*, one of the most literate comedies in the language. Many other workmen have built the gleaming structure of a modern musical play on the Shaw fable. They are Frederick Loewe, the composer who collaborated with Mr. Lerner on *Brigadoon* and *Paint Your Wagon*; Oliver Smith, who has designed a glorious production; Cecil Beaton, who has decorated it with ravishingly beautiful costumes; Moss Hart, who has staged it with taste and skill.

Although their contributions have been bountiful, they will not object if this column makes one basic observation. Shaw's crackling mind is still the genius of *My Fair Lady*. Mr. Lerner has retained the same ironic point of view in his crisp adaptation and his sardonic lyrics. As Professor Higgins and Eliza Doolittle, Rex Harrison and Julie Andrews play the leading parts with the light, dry touch of top-flight Shavian acting.

*My Fair Lady* is staged dramatically on a civilized plane. Probably for the first time in history a typical musical comedy audience finds itself absorbed in the art of pronunciation and passionately involved in the proper speaking of "pain," "rain" and "Spain."

And yet it would not be fair to imply that *My Fair Lady* is only a new look at an old comedy. For the carnival version adds a new dimension; it gives a lift to the gaiety and the romance. In his robust score, Mr. Loewe has made the Covent Garden scenes more raffish and hilarious. Not being ashamed of old forms, he has written a glee-club drinking-song, and a mock hymn for Alfred Doolittle's wedding.

Not being afraid of melody, he has written some entrancing love music, and a waltz; and he has added something to

Professor Higgins' characterization in a pettish song entitled "A Hymn to Him." All this is, no doubt, implicit in *Pygmalion*. But Mr. Loewe has given it heartier exuberance. Although the Old Boy had a sense of humor, he never had so much abandon. *Pygmalion* was not such a happy revel.

In the choreography and in the staging of the musical numbers, Hanya Holm has made a similar contribution. The "Ascot Gavotte" at the races is a laconic satire of British reserve in the midst of excitement, and very entertaining, too. "The Embassy Waltz" is both decorous and stunning.

Despite all the rag-tag and bobtail of a joyous musical show, Mr. Hart and his associates have never lost their respect for a penetrating comedy situation. Some things of human significance are at stake in *My Fair Lady*, and some human values are involved. Thanks to the discerning casting, the values have been sensitively preserved. As Professor Higgins' sagacious mother, Cathleen Nesbitt carries off her scenes with grace and elegance.

As Alfred P. Doolittle, the plausible rogue, Stanley Holloway gives a breezy performance that is thoroughly enjoyable. And Robert Coote is immensely comic as the bumbling Colonel Pickering.

But it is the acting of Miss Andrews and Mr. Harrison in the central roles that makes *My Fair Lady* affecting as well as amusing. Miss Andrews does a magnificent job. The transformation from street-corner drab to lady is both touching and beautiful. Out of the muck of Covent Garden something glorious blossoms, and Miss Andrews acts her part triumphantly.

Although Mr. Harrison is no singer, you will probably imagine that he is singing when he throws himself into the anguished lyrics of "A Hymn to Him" in the last act. By that time he has made Professor Higgins' temperament so full of frenzy that something like music does come out of him.

**ABOVE:** Rex Harrison and Julie Andrews in *My Fair Lady*. **OPPOSITE:** Julie Andrews as Eliza Doolittle.

**LEFT:** Julie Andrews (center), Cathleen Nesbitt (to
Andrews's right), and members of the cast in the
original Broadway production of *My Fair Lady*, 1956.

By BROOKS ATKINSON

May 4, 1956

# THE MOST HAPPY FELLA

By BROOKS ATKINSON

Having selected a fine theme, Frank Loesser has composed a fine music drama.

The theme comes from Sidney Howard's memorable *They Knew What They Wanted*, produced in 1924. In Mr. Loesser's music version, it is called *The Most Happy Fella*, which was put on at the Imperial last evening.

The term "music drama" is used here advisedly. After having written the scores for two wonderful musical comedies, *Where's*

*Charley?* and *Guys and Dolls*, Mr. Loesser has now come about as close to opera as the rules of Broadway permit. He has told everything of vital importance in terms of dramatic music. He has written about the longest score that Broadway has had since *Porgy and Bess*. In its most serious moments *The Most Happy Fella* is a profoundly moving dramatic experience.

Nothing could be much simpler than the original story—the legend of a

mail-order bride in California about thirty years ago. The characters are simple. They consist of a middle-aged, unattractive, highly emotional Italian who owns a vineyard in Napa Valley, and of a tired, rather commonplace waitress who is looking for a way out. She accepts his proposal of marriage without knowing him. Shocked by the difference between what she sees and what she had expected, she has a wild, brief affair with a young man of her own age. By the

time she finds herself genuinely in love with her husband, she knows that she is carrying the child of another man.

Since the characters are simple and genuine, since the episodes are commonplace, homely and fundamental, the story is extraordinarily touching. As a composer, Mr. Loesser has range and depth enough to give it an overwhelming musical statement. The fiery and passionate arias he has written for the husband and the wife manage to concentrate the emotions in simple, direct, powerful, musical sound, and give *The Most Happy Fella* great dramatic stature. Without severing his connections with Broadway, Mr. Loesser has given Broadway some musical magnificence.

The leading parts could hardly be better acted and sung. As Tony, the volatile, good-hearted husband, Robert Weede sings with skill and conviction in a superbly trained voice. As Rosabella, the shy, timid mail-order bride, Jo Sullivan also sings beautifully, and is likely to break the hearts of the audience as thoroughly as Tony's. Having sung Julie in *Carousel*, which is an equivalent

music drama, Miss Sullivan has just the right experience for her present role.

Although *The Most Happy Fella* is obviously a rare achievement for the theatre, this department has a few reservations about the work as a whole. Mr. Loesser and Joseph Anthony, the director, have tried to make the best of two worlds— the world of music drama, the world of Broadway entertainment. Here and there it seems to be overproduced and overacted; some of the sequences are too facile, too slick and overblown, in the Broadway style that always tries to top everything in town. It is as if Mr. Loesser did not altogether trust the rueful and lovely fable they borrowed from Sidney Howard.

Even when the story is not concerned with Tony and Rosabella, *The Most Happy Fella* is best when it is simplest. The spaghetti music sung exuberantly by Rico Froehlich, Arthur Rubin and John Henson; the drugstore-cowboy song sung by Shorty Long, Alan Gilbert, Mr. Henson and Roy Lazarus; the original ballad sung by Art

Lund, and all the songs sung with good humor by Susan Johnson, are in the happiest vein of *The Most Happy Fella*. Although Dania Krupska's choreography is interesting, it is one part of the play that to this department seems overdone, as if it were more concerned with conquering the audience than developing the theme. Although Jo Mielziner's scenery is imposing, it is crowded and heavy.

But in everything that is vital to the theme, the work is first-rate. For the pathetic story of the mail-order bride and the man who loves her is a piece of dramatic literature. Mr. Loesser has caught the anguish and the love in some exalting music. Broadway is used to heart. It is not accustomed to evocations of the soul.

· · · · · · · · · · · · · · · · · · · · · · · · · · · · ·

Scenes from *The Most Happy Fella*. **OPPOSITE:** Susan Johnson, Robert Weede, Jo Sullivan, and Rico Froelich. **ABOVE:** From left, Rico Froelich, Arthur Rubin, and John Henson.

November 30, 1956

# BELLS ARE RINGING

By BROOKS ATKINSON

Judy Holliday is even more talented than you may have suspected. In *Bells Are Ringing*, which was put on at the Sam S. Shubert last evening, she sings, dances, clowns and also carries on her shoulders one of the most antiquated plots of the season.

Nothing has happened to the shrill little moll whom the town loved when Miss Holliday played in *Born Yesterday*. The squeaky voice, the embarrassed giggle, the brassy naïveté, the dimples, the teeter-tot-ter walk fortunately remain unimpaired.

As the romantic girl in a telephone-answering service, Miss Holliday now adds a trunk-full of song-and-dance routines. Possibly they derive in part from the days when she was one of The Revuers, with Betty Comden and Adolph Green, authors of *Bells Are Ringing*. Without losing any of that doll-like personality, she is now singing music by Jule Styne and

dancing numbers composed by Jerome Robbins and Bob Fosse. She has gusto enough to triumph in every kind of music hall antic.

She needs the gusto. And Sydney Chaplin needs the warmth, taste, skill and grace that make him an admirable leading man. For this is the season when the writers seem to be breaking down all over town, leaving the burden of comic entertainment to the performers. Miss Comden and Mr. Green have chosen an original subject—a telephone-answering service that leads into the personal lives of several people. That is how the dream girl played by Miss Holliday meets her sweet-heart, and brings a number of other bizarre people together.

But there have not been so many sur-prised hellos, inept song cues and dance signals since *Oklahoma!* drove hackneyed musical comedy out of business. This brand of labored plot complication and manipulation is where we all came in many years ago. It leaves *Bells Are Ringing* on the level of a routine vaudeville show.

As vaudeville, it has virtues. Although Mr. Styne's taste in melody is conventional, he can often come up with a good production number, and the lyrics by Miss Comden and Mr. Green are always jaunty. "It's a Simple Little System" turns out to be a rousing piece of knavery, with Eddie Lawrence belting out the music enthusiastically. Apart from her

skill with such pleasant numbers as "Bells Are Ringing" and "Is It a Crime?" Miss Holliday brings the evening to a flaring conclusion when she tosses all kinds of vaudeville revelry into a number entitled "I'm Goin' Back." Mr. Chaplin also has a winning musical style in "On My Own," "You've Got to Do It" and all his numbers with Miss Holliday.

Trust Mr. Robbins and Mr. Fosse to provide the regulation good ballet numbers—notably a sort of fandango in a subway, a crisply-performed Spanish number and some less original parodies of nightclub roistering. Since Raoul Pene du Bois has a rich sense of color, the costumes are attractively simple and fresh. His sets are not as distinctive as most of his work.

Miss Holliday is a fantastic entertainer with a personality that is both amusing and endearing. As leading man, Mr. Chaplin is not only versatile but also honest. It is easy to believe everything he does and says. Last eve-ning's audience seemed to have enormous enthusiasm for the show and for Miss Holliday in particular. But this department confesses to a feeling of disenchantment. The old writing routines are back; they are no gayer than they used to be.

Scenes from *Bells Are Ringing.* **OPPOSITE:** Judy Holliday as Ella Peterson. **ABOVE:** Judy Holliday and members of the cast in a dance number.

December 3, 1956

# Candide

By BROOKS ATKINSON

Since Voltaire was a brilliant writer, it is only right that his *Candide* should turn out to be a brilliant musical satire.

Pooling their talents, Lillian Hellman, the literary lady, and Leonard Bernstein, the music man, have composed an admirable version of Voltaire's philosophical tale, which opened at the Martin Beck on Saturday evening. Add to the honor roll Tyrone Guthrie, who has staged the production, Oliver Smith, who has designed it beautifully, and Irra Petina, Robert Rounseville, Barbara Cook and Max Adrian, who sing the chief parts gloriously. For the performance is a triumph of stage arts molded into a symmetrical whole.

Let's admit that the eighteenth-century philosophical tale is not ideal material for a theatre show, for it is plotless and repetitious. And let's further concede that the Candide that Miss Hellman, Mr. Bernstein and Mr. Rounseville have created is not the blithering idiot whom Voltaire invented. He is more like a disillusioned hero.

But the authors of the musical work are quite right in supposing that Voltaire's contemptuous satire on optimism is modern in spirit, as, indeed, it must always be. Its cynical acceptance of war, greed, treachery, venery, snobbishness and mendacity as staples of civilization provokes no feeling of disbelief in the middle of the twentieth century.

Although Miss Hellman has not covered quite so much territory as Voltaire, she has transported Candide away from the mawkish idealism of Westphalia to Lisbon, Paris, Buenos Aires and back to Venice, with a return to a ruined Westphalia in the last scene.

Bit by bit, Dr. Pangloss' devotion to the best in the best of all possible worlds becomes hollow and ridiculous. Battered by their cruel travelers, Dr. Pangloss' ragged band of followers settles down in the last scene to cultivating the garden of the only kind of life that is possible.

Toward the end of a long evening, the philosophical tale that always makes the same point in a different context does lose the freshness of the opening scenes. But Candide's sorry journey has stimulated Mr. Bernstein into composing a wonderful score all the way through. None of his previous theatre music has had the joyous variety, humor and richness of this score. It begins wittily. It parodies operatic music amusingly. But it also has a wealth of melody that compensates for the intellectual austerity of Voltaire's tale. While Candide is learning about life the hard way, Mr. Bernstein is obviously having a good time.

Under Mr. Guthrie's bountiful direction, the acting and the singing are magnificent. As the raffish, ribald beldame, Miss Petina is tremendously entertaining—splendid as a singer, virtuoso as a comic performer in a happily broad style. Miss Cook is also a lustrous singer, particularly in Mr. Bernstein's own version of how a jewel song should be written. And her acting portrait of a lyrical maiden who quickly learns how to connive with the world is sketched with skill, spirit and humor.

Mr. Rounseville is a sensitive romantic singer with a captivating voice. If he gives us a more disarming Candide than Voltaire intended, no objections are raised in this corner, for the Rounseville Candide is excellent. Mr. Adrian, who plays both Dr. Pangloss, the egregious optimist, and Martin, the bitter pessimist, is a lean, ascetic actor with a chilling grin and a saturnine style. He can also sing agreeably. As a sort of Janus, he comments on Candide's journey with ironic drollery. The large cast, which is without exception a notable one, includes William Olvis, a powerful singer and a good actor, as the languid Governor of Buenos Aires.

Mr. Smith's fabulous scene designs and Irene Sharaff's vigorous costumes help to make *Candide* the most stunning production of the season. Everything has been done with taste and vitality. A couple of centuries have been frittered away since Voltaire wrote *Candide*. He can still put the various departments of the modern theatre on their professional toes.

Scenes from *Candide*. **ABOVE:** Max Adrian (center) as Dr. Pangloss with members of the cast. **OPPOSITE:** William Olvis as the Governer of Buenos Aires and Barbara Cook as Cunegonde.

September 27, 1957

# WEST SIDE STORY

### By BROOKS ATKINSON

Although the material is horrifying, the workmanship is admirable.

Gang warfare is the material of *West Side Story*, which opened at the Winter Garden last evening, and very little of the hideousness has been left out. But the author, composer and ballet designer are creative artists. Pooling imagination and virtuosity, they have written a profoundly moving show that is as ugly as the city jungles and also pathetic, tender and forgiving.

Arthur Laurents has written the story of two hostile teen-age gangs fighting for supremacy amid the tenement houses, corner stores and bridges of the West Side. The story is a powerful one, partly, no doubt, because Mr. Laurents has deliberately given it the shape of *Romeo and Juliet*. In the design of *West Side Story* he has powerful allies.

Leonard Bernstein has composed another one of his nervous, flaring scores that capture the shrill beat of life in the streets. And Jerome Robbins, who has directed the production, is also its choreographer.

Since the characters are kids of the streets, their speech is curt and jeering. Mr. Laurents has provided the raw material of a tragedy that occurs because none of the young people involved understands what is happening to them. And his contribution is the essential one. But it is Mr. Bernstein and Mr. Robbins who orchestrate it. Using music and movement they have given Mr. Laurents' story passion and depth and some glimpses of unattainable glory. They have pitched into it with personal conviction as well as the skill of accomplished craftsmen.

In its early scenes of gang skirmishes, *West Side Story* is facile and a little forbidding—the shrill music and the taut dancing movement being harsh and sinister. But once Tony of the Jets gang sees Maria of the Sharks gang, the magic of an immortal story takes hold. As Tony, Larry Kert is perfectly cast, plain in speech and manner; and as Maria, Carol Lawrence, maidenly soft and glowing, is perfectly cast also. Their balcony scene on the fire escape of a dreary tenement is tender and affecting. From that moment on, *West Side Story* is an incandescent piece of work that finds odd bits of beauty amid the rubbish of the streets.

Everything in *West Side Story* is of a piece. Everything contributes to the total impression of wildness, ecstasy and anguish. The astringent score has moments of tranquillity and rapture, and occasionally a touch of sardonic humor. And the ballets convey the things that Mr. Laurents is inhibited from saying because the characters are so inarticulate. The hostility and suspicion between the gangs, the glory of the nuptials, the terror of the rumble, the devastating climax—Mr. Robbins has found the patterns of movement that express these parts of the story.

Most of the characters, in fact, are dancers with some images of personality lifted out of the whirlwind—characters sketched on the wing. Like everything also in *West Side Story*, they are admirable. Chita Rivera in a part equivalent to the Nurse in the Shakespeare play; Ken Le Roy as leader of the Sharks; Mickey Calin as leader of the Jets; Lee Becker as a hobbledehoy girl in one gang—give terse and vigorous performances.

Everything in *West Side Story* blends—the scenery by Oliver Smith, the costumes by Irene Sharaff, the lighting by Jean Rosenthal. For this is one of those occasions when theatre people, engrossed in an original project, are all in top form. The subject is not beautiful. But what *West Side Story* draws out of it is beautiful. For it has a searching point of view.

Scenes from *West Side Story*. **LEFT:** The Jets.
**OPPOSITE:** Larry Kert and Carol Lawrence.

**ABOVE:** Chita Rivera (center) and members of the cast in the original Broadway production of *West Side Story*, 1957.

December 20, 1957

# THE MUSIC MAN

By BROOKS ATKINSON

Dollars to doughnuts, Meredith Willson dotes on brass bands.

In *The Music Man*, which opened last evening at the Majestic, he has translated the thump and razzle-dazzle of brass-band lore into a warm and genial cartoon of American life. Since the style is gaudy and since David Burns plays a small town mayor with low-comedy flourishes, *The Music Man* is a cartoon and not a valentine.

But Mr. Willson's sophistication is skin-deep. His heart is in the wonderful simplicities of provincial life in Iowa in 1912, and his musical show glows with enjoyment. Mr. Willson's music is innocent; the beat is rousing and the tunes are full of gusto. The dances, improvised by Onna White, are rural and festive. Raoul Pene du Bois' country costumes are humorously hospitable. With Robert Preston in top form in the leading part, the cast is as exuberant as opening day at a county fair.

If Mark Twain could have collaborated with Vachel Lindsay, they might have devised a rhythmic lark like *The Music Man*, which is as American as apple pie and a Fourth of July oration.

It is the story of a traveling-salesman charlatan who cannot read music or play any instrument, but who sells the boys of River City a brass band and gorgeous uniforms. His motives are dishonest. But during the weeks when he is mulcting the customers, he transforms a dull town into a singing and dancing community. In the last scene the law is hot on his heels. But, don't worry. Mr. Willson approves of his charlatan as thoroughly as he loves the town librarian, the barber shop quartet, the kids, the ladies, the railroad, and the vitality of life in the Middle West.

In other hands, this could easily look like an assembly job, clever, smart and spurious. Serving as his own librettist, composer and lyric-writer, Mr. Willson has given it the uniformity of a well-designed crazy-quilt in which every patch blends with its neighbor. By some sort of miracle, his associates have caught his point of view exactly. Morton Da Costa's droll, strutting direction; Don Walker's blaring orchestrations; Howard Bay's jovial scenery, including a racing locomotive that drowns the orchestra players in steam when the curtain goes up—these aspects of the production have Mr. Willson's own kind of gaiety.

As the infectious bunko man, Mr. Preston could hardly be improved upon. His expansive energy and his concentration on the crisis of the moment are tonic. Since the music is unpretentious, he has no trouble in making it sound hearty. When the music is romantic, Barbara Cook is on hand to sing it beautifully. She is also a beguiling actress in fresh and pleasant fashions.

But the cast is attractive in every instance. Pert Kelton as a harsh-voiced Irish widow; Iggie Wolfington as a breathless conspirator; little Eddie Hodges as a lisping youth and little Marilyn Siegel as a girl who can play cross-hand on the piano, Al Shea, Wayne Ward, Vern Reed and Bill Spangleberg as close-harmonizers—are immensely entertaining.

For Mr. Willson has given them lively, artless things to do, and they keep him good company. Like Richard Bissell, another Iowa playwright, Mr. Willson has a fresh slant on Americana. Although he does not take it seriously, he loves it with the pawkiness of a liberated native. *The Music Man* is a marvelous show, rooted in wholesome and comic tradition.

. . . . . . . . . . . . . . . . . . . . . . . . . . . . . . . . . .

**OPPOSITE:** Robert Preston as Harold Hill.

# Once Upon a Mattress

By BROOKS ATKINSON

Spring having definitely arrived, some attractive people have declared a pleasant holiday at the Phoenix.

Don't be deceived by the tasteless title of the show that opened last evening. *Once Upon a Mattress*, as they have dubbed it, refers to nothing more ribald than the fairy-story of the princess who could not sleep because there was a pea under her mattress—twenty mattresses in the current version.

Like the title, the story that Jay Thompson, Marshall Barer and Dean Fuller have written under it is no masterpiece. A humorous version of the old legend, it has some of the annoying precociousness of a college show, and it is a little self-conscious in its coyness.

But two of the ladies enmeshed in the plot have remarkably fresh talent. Mary Rodgers, the composer, has written a highly enjoyable score. For the record, it must be reported that she is a daughter of Richard Rodgers. But nothing she has written sounds like his portfolio. She has a style of her own, an inventive mind and a fund of cheerful melodies; and *Once Upon a Mattress* is full of good music.

Some of it is sung by a breezy comedienne who comes brawling into the story about half way through the first act and gives it a wonderful lift for the rest of the evening. She is Carol Burnett. She is making her debut in musical comedy, but she has already made an enduring contribution to international polity. She sang "I Made a Fool of Myself Over John Foster Dulles."

Miss Burnett is a lean, earthy young lady with a metallic voice, an ironic gleam and an unfailing sense of the comic gesture. As a singer, she discharges Miss Rodgers' music as though she were firing a field mortar. As a performer, she is bright and entertaining.

*Once Upon a Mattress* is a yarn about an overbearing queen who is trying to frustrate all the princesses who want to marry her son. Although it is good-natured, it is neither witty nor dynamic. But it provides the

background for a handsome production by William and Jean Eckart—simple though splendid scenery and entrancing fairy-story costumes. In place of luxurious materials, the Eckarts have substituted impeccable taste and imaginative design.

And George Abbott is on hand to show how easily a first-rate director can give shape and pace to a performance and make every actor look like a genius. The mood is gaily naïve; the tempo is light and the total impression beguiling.

All the actors look like good companions who know how to behave on a festive occasion. As the king, who is a mute, Jack Gilford is an amusing pantomimist. A queen with the evil smile of a dragon by Jane White; a hang-dog prince by Joe Bova; a delightful singing minstrel by Harry Snow and a delightful dancing jester by Matt Mattox; a

distressed princess by Anne Jones—these are the principal parts, all well performed by winning young people.

Although *Once Upon a Mattress* is a small show, it has not economized on craftsmanship. Joe Layton's dances are joyous. The band, under Hal Hastings' direction, is expert, and the orchestrations by several hands have spirit and color.

Don't be distressed by the title, and don't expect much from the libretto. But be comforted by the fact that the musical theatre has acquired a genuine new composer and a funny new clown. April may be a cruel month, but May is kind.

........................................................

Scenes from *Once Upon a Mattress*. **ABOVE:** Carol Burnett as Princess Winnifred. **OPPOSITE:** Jack Gilford and Jane White as King Sextimus the Silent and Queen Aggravain.

May 22, 1959

# GYPSY

By BROOKS ATKINSON

Since Ethel Merman is the head woman in
*Gypsy*, which opened at the Broadway last
evening, nothing can go wrong. She would
not permit *Gypsy* to be anything less than
the most satisfying musical of the season.

She is playing the indomitable mother
of Gypsy Rose Lee, a stripper with a difference; and Miss Merman, her pipes resonant
and her spirit syncopated, struts and bawls
her way through it triumphantly.

Ever since *Annie Get Your Gun*, it has
been obvious that she is an actress in addition
to being a singer. In the book Arthur Laurents
has written for her (based on the memoirs of
Gypsy Rose Lee) she is the female juggernaut
who drives her two daughters into show business and keeps their noses to the grindstone
until one of them is a star.

*Gypsy* is a musical tour of the hotel
rooms and backstages of the seamy side of
show business thirty years ago when vaudeville was surrendering to the strip-tease. Jo
Mielziner has designed a savory production.
Jule Styne has supplied a genuine show-business score, and Stephen Sondheim has set
amusing lyrics to it.

Under the genial direction of Jerome
Robbins, who is willing to take time to
enjoy what he is doing, the performance is
entertaining in all the acceptable styles
from skulduggery to the anatomy of a ter-
magant. There are some very funny scenes
in the beginning when Jacqueline Mayro,
as a baby star, makes all the clichés of juvenile performing wonderfully garish and
plausible.

As Mother Rose's shoestring act sinks
lower in the profession, *Gypsy* descends into
the inferno of a burlesque joint where the
grind sisters—notably Maria Karnilova and
Faith Dane—contribute some ludicrous exer-
cises in vulgarity. No one could improve
much on the scene Mr. Robbins and Mr.
Mielziner have devised to portray one of
Minsky's most elegant show pieces. It fairly
explodes with rhinestone splendor.

The cast is delightful. Lane Bradbury
plays with gusto the part of June, the baby
star who wrecks the act by running off to be
married. Jack Klugman, kindly and worried,
plays Herbie, the combination boy friend and
booking agent. As Gypsy, Sandra Church
gives a lovely performance. A slight young
lady with small features and a delicate style
of acting, she conveys with equal skill the
shyness of the adolescent and the tough
assurance of the lady who becomes a star.

But *Gypsy* is Miss Merman's show. Mr.
Styne has given her some good greased-horn
music, which she delivers with earthy magnificence in her familiar manner. There are
some sticky scenes toward the end when
*Gypsy* abandons the sleazy grandeur of show
business and threatens to become belles-
lettres. It deserts the body and starts cultivating the soul. Things look ominous in the
last ten minutes.

But trust Ethel. She concludes the proceedings with a song and dance of defiance.
Mr. Styne's music is dramatic. Miss Merman's
performance expresses her whole character—
cocky and aggressive, but also sociable and
good-hearted. Not for the first time in her fabulous career, her personal magnetism electri-
fies the whole theatre. For she is a performer
of incomparable power.

*Gypsy* is a good show in the old tradition of musicals. For years Miss Merman has
been the queen.

Scenes from *Gypsy*. **OPPOSITE:** Jack Klugman and
Ethel Merman as Herbie and Mother Rose. **ABOVE:**
Ethel Merman and Sandra Church as Gypsy.

September 24, 1974

# *GYPSY* BOUNCES BACK WITH ZEST AND LILT

By CLIVE BARNES

Lightning never strikes twice! Right? Wrong! At the Winter Garden Theatre last night, Angela Lansbury shattered the town (theatrically speaking, of course) in *Gypsy*. And yet on May 21, 1959, at the Broadway Theatre, just up the road, Ethel Merman did the same trick in the same show. But it was a different lightning.

Broadway has opened its season with *Gypsy*, and although this is a sort of revival, it is the kind of revival we cannot have too much of. Everything about *Gypsy* is right. The Jule Styne score has a lilt and a surprise to it. The music bounces out of the pit, assertive, confident and cocky, and has a love affair with Stephen Sondheim's elegantly paced, daringly phrased lyrics. And then there is the book by Arthur Laurents. But really the book is first.

Have you noticed how many good musicals have a backstage setting? Partly it is because show-business people like writing about show-business people, and they also have a love and reverence for the shows of the past. Yet above this, as a genre the backstage musical has a great deal going for it. Its dramatic rhythmic beats of alternating failure and success are apposite for the musical form, and the singing and dancing emerge naturally from the story.

*Gypsy* is one of the best of musicals and it improves with keeping. After all, 1959 was a very good year. Now *Gypsy* starts the new season with a musical to think about, ponder and love.

. . . . . . . . . . . . . . . . . . . . . . . . . . . . . .

**RIGHT:** Angela Lansbury in the 1974 revival of *Gypsy*.
**OPPOSITE:** Christa Moore (left) and Tyne Daly in the 1989 revival of *Gypsy*.

# REVIVAL: TYNE DALY

November 17, 1989

# *Gypsy* Is Back on Broadway With a Vengeance

By FRANK RICH

If someone asked me to name the best Broadway musical, I'd gladly equivocate on any side of a debate embracing *Guys and Dolls*, *My Fair Lady*, *Carousel*, *Porgy and Bess* and—well, you know the rest. But I've always had only one choice in the category of favorite musical. It is *Gypsy*, and as I sat at its scorching new revival starring Tyne Daly, once again swept up in its goosebump-raising torrents of laughter and tears, I realized why, if anything, this 30-year-old show actually keeps improving with age.

*Gypsy* may be the only great Broadway musical that follows its audience through life's rough familial passages. A wrenching fable about a tyrannical stage mother and the daughters she both champions and cripples—yet also a showcase for one classic Jule Styne–Stephen Sondheim song and rousing Jerome Robbins vaudeville routine after another—*Gypsy* is nothing if not Broadway's own brassy, unlikely answer to *King Lear*. It speaks to you one way when you are a child, then chases after you to say something else when you've grown up.

Like *Lear*, it cannot be done without a powerhouse performance in its marathon parental role. Ms. Daly, a television actress who might seem inappropriate to the task, follows Angela Lansbury in proving that not even Ethel Merman can own a character forever. Ms. Daly is not Merman, and she is not Ms. Lansbury. Her vocal expressiveness and attack have their limits (most noticeably in "Mr. Goldstone"), and warmth is pointedly not her forte. But this fiercely committed actress tears into—at times claws into—Mama Rose, that "pioneer woman without a frontier," with a vengeance that exposes the darkness at the heart of *Gypsy* as it hasn't been since Merman.

# REVIVAL: BERNADETTE PETERS

May 2, 2003

# *NEW MOMMA TAKES CHARGE*

By BEN BRANTLEY

You can tear down the black crepe, boys. Take the hearse back to the garage, and start popping Champagne corks. Momma's pulled it off, after all—big time.

Playing a role that few people thought would ever fit her and shadowed by vultures predicting disaster, Bernadette Peters delivered the surprise coup of many a Broadway season in the revival of *Gypsy* that opened last night at the Shubert Theatre.

Ms. Peters, a beloved eternal daughter of the American musical, has taken on that genre's most daunting maternal role: Momma Rose, the ultimate stage mother in the ultimate backstage show and a part cast in bronze by Ethel Merman more than four decades ago. Working against type and expectation under the direction of Sam Mendes, Ms. Peters has created the most complex and compelling portrait of her long career, and she has done this in ways that deviate radically from the Merman blueprint.

There have been many illustrious successors to Merman as Rose: Angela Lansbury and Tyne Daly on Broadway, Rosalind Russell on screen and Bette Midler on television.

Only Ms. Peters, however, can be said to have broken the Merman mold completely. And she does so without cracking or distorting the nigh perfect shape of what may be the greatest of all American musicals.

. . . . . . . . . . . . . . . . . . . . . . . . . . . . .

**ABOVE:** Bernadette Peters in the 2003 revival of *Gypsy*. **OPPOSITE:** Patti LuPone in the 2008 revival of *Gypsy*.

## REVIVAL: PATTI LUPONE

March 28, 2008

# CURTAIN UP! IT'S PATTI'S TURN AT *GYPSY*

By BEN BRANTLEY

Watch out, New York. Patti LuPone has found her focus. And when Ms. LuPone is truly focused, she's a laser, she incinerates. Especially when she's playing someone as dangerously obsessed as Momma Rose in the wallop-packing revival of the musical *Gypsy*, which opened on Thursday night at the St. James Theatre.

In July, when an earlier version of *Gypsy* starring Ms. LuPone had a limited run as part of the Encores! summer series, this powerhouse actress gave a diffuse, narcissistic performance that seemed to be watching itself in a mirror. She was undeniably Patti with an exclamation point, the musical cult goddess, offering her worshipers plenty of polished brass, ululating notes and winking sexiness. But Rose, the ultimate stage mother of Gypsy Rose Lee's memoirs, was as yet only a wavering gleam in her eye.

What a difference eight or nine months makes. And yes, that quiet crunching sound you hear is me eating my hat. As directed by Arthur Laurents, this latest incarnation of *Gypsy*, the 1959 fable of the last days of vaudeville, shines with a magnified transparency that lets you see right down to the naked core of characters so hungry for attention that it warps them.

November 17, 1959

# The Sound of Music

By BROOKS ATKINSON

From the Trapp Family Singers, the makers of *The Sound of Music* have acquired two valuable assets—legendary personal courage and a love of singing.

By no particular chance, those are the most winning characteristics of the bountiful musical drama that Mary Martin brought to the Lunt-Fontanne Theatre last evening. Although Miss Martin, now playing an Austrian maiden, has longer hair than she had in *South Pacific*, she still has the same common touch that wins friends and influences people, the same sharp features, goodwill and glowing personality and the same plain voice that makes music sound intimate and familiar.

Using *The Trapp Family Singers* as their source book, Howard Lindsay and Russel Crouse have provided her with the libretto of an operetta. Unfortunately, it is conventional in its literary point of view. The story of the novice from the abbey who becomes governess of seven motherless children and teaches them how to sing is an attractive one; especially when, as the wife of their father, she

helps to lead them out of Austria away from the Nazis into Switzerland.

But the scenario of *The Sound of Music* has the hackneyed look of the musical theatre that Richard Rodgers and Oscar Hammerstein II replaced with *Oklahoma!* in 1943.

The best of *The Sound of Music* is Rodgers and Hammerstein in good form. Mr. Rodgers has not written with such freshness of style since *The King and I*. Mr. Hammerstein has contributed lyrics that also have the sentiment and dexterity of his best work.

Since *The Sound of Music* opens in an Austrian abbey it begins with some religious music. Fortunately, Patricia Neway is on hand as the Mother Abbess to give the church an exalting purity of tone and feeling.

But the basic theme has had the happy effect of releasing Mr. Rodgers' endless fund of cheerful melodies—a charming, wistful song called "My Favorite Things"; a touching song for the children called "Do Re Mi" (in the friendly mood of "Getting to Know You"); an Alpine ballad entitled "The Lonely Goatherd"; an antic piece for the children, dubbed "So

Long, Farewell," and the theme song, which is the most captivating of all. In the second act as well as the first, the play is rich in music.

As performance and production, *The Sound of Music* is off the top shelf. You are likely to lose your heart to the seven singing children who range from the doll-like adolescent of Lauri Peters to the chubby innocence of Evanna Lieu. In his stage direction, Vincent J. Donehue is not above being cute with the children (and coy with Miss Martin), for the direction has the stereotyped quality of the libretto. But no one could mask the natural beauty and high spirits of the Trapp boys and girls.

The cast is excellent throughout. Theodore Bikel as the serious, high-minded Baron Von Trapp, Kurt Kasznar as a witty, animated friend of the family, who accepts the Nazis, Marion Marlowe as a stunning lady of wealth who sees no point in resisting the invaders—they are all well cast and they bring taste and skill to the production.

In his settings Oliver Smith has provided opulent décor—none of it finer than the lovely opening scene. Lucinda Ballard's costumes are up to her own standard. Russell Bennett's dainty orchestrations and Frederick Dvonch's fine conducting uphold the traditions of musical production on a high level.

It is disappointing to see the American musical stage succumbing to the clichés of operetta. The revolution of the Forties and Fifties has lost its fire. But *The Sound of Music* retains some of the treasures of those golden days—melodies, rapturous singing and Miss Martin. The sound of music is always moving. Occasionally it is also glorious.

Scenes from *The Sound of Music*. **ABOVE:** Mary Martin as Maria with nuns from the abbey. **OPPOSITE:** Clockwise from top left, William Snowden, Joseph Stewart, Mary Susan Locke, Marilyn Rogers, Lauri Peters, Kathy Dunn, Evanna Lien, and Mary Martin.

In 1968, Clive Barnes heralded the arrival of "the first Broadway musical in some time to have the authentic voice of today rather than the day before yesterday." The show was *Hair*, an import from the Public Theater downtown, and it really was all about sex, drugs and rock 'n' roll—well, rock 'n' roll retooled and retuned for midtown ears. And it represented Broadway's most successful bid of the decade to translate what young Americans were listening to on the radio into what audiences might hear on stage.

Broadway was suddenly feeling middle-aged, and it was doing its best to get into—what was it the young people called it?—the groove. Before *Hair*, it had flirted (although only in fun) with Elvis-style pelvis shaking in *Bye Bye Birdie* (1960), a satirical look at Presley mania in which a tuneful, sunny score (by Charles Strouse) prevails over the more raucous sounds of an Elvis stand-in. And in the same year that *Hair* opened, Broadway brought into its fold the finger-snapping Top 40 songwriters Burt Bacharach and Hal David with *Promises, Promises,* a show (with a book by the hit-maker Neil Simon) about sex and martinis and easy listening, set on Madison Avenue.

But the biggest blockbusters of that decade, both of which opened in 1964, were sentimental Rodgers and Hammerstein–style shows: *Hello, Dolly!*, adapted from Thornton Wilder's cozy comedy *The Matchmaker*, and *Fiddler on the Roof*, which set Sholem Aleichem's homespun stories of life on the shtetl to song. They also both happened to star performers who had outsized, almost grotesque stage presences: Carol Channing (as Dolly) and Zero Mostel (as Tevye the milkman in *Fiddler*).

The musicals of the 1960s were big on stars with big personalities, exotic and exaggerated creatures who were the spiritual children of Ethel Merman and might be described, to use a word that was just coming into vogue, as "camp": Tammy Grimes in *The Unsinkable Molly Brown* (1960), Robert Morse in *How to Succeed in Business Without Really Trying* (a Pulitzer Prize winner from 1961), Barbra Streisand as Fanny Brice in *Funny Girl* (1964), Barbara Harris in *On a Clear Day You Can See Forever* (1965) and Gwen Verdon in *Sweet Charity* (1966).

And despite the box-office magnetism of the hippies of *Hair*, by the early 1970s Broadway was retreating into what it presented as a happier, sillier, more innocent time. The 1971 revival of *No, No, Nanette* (1925), starring the 1930s movie musical sweetheart Ruby Keeler, prompted Barnes to observe, "Nostalgia may prove to be the overriding emotion of the seventies, with remembrance of things past far more comfortable than the realization of things present." But he—and Broadway audiences—enjoyed themselves at *Nanette*, as they did at the 1973 revival of *Irene* (1919) with Debbie Reynolds.

Barnes wasn't as impressed by a brand-new 1971 show called *Follies*, which looked back to the age of Nanette—and Florenz Ziegfeld. "It carries nostalgia to where sentiment finally engulfs it in its sickly maw," he wrote. Yet this production, which explored the midlife crises of four characters through the hopeful songs of their youth, embodied a new direction in musicals. Three of its creators—its composer, Stephen Sondheim, and its

directors, Harold Prince and the choreographer Michael Bennett—had already established themselves as the most influential pathfinders for that direction, and would remain so for years to come.

The name for the type of show with which these men were associated was "the concept musical," a vague and catchall term for works that replaced naturalism with productions that wore their governing metaphors on their sleeves. These notably included the Prince-directed, neo-Brechtian *Cabaret*, which featured songs by the rising stars John Kander and Fred Ebb and used a decadent nightclub as a microcosm of decadent Weimar Germany. (Bob Fosse, who directed the film version of *Cabaret*, employed much the same format, and the same songwriting team, for *Chicago* in 1975.) And Prince and Sondheim collaborated on a series of shows in the 1970s that fractured the musical form to examine divided souls in divided cultures, from the neuroses-torn, chic Manhattan of *Company* (1970) to the hypocrisy-ridden Victorian London of *Sweeney Todd* (1979).

Bennett, in the meantime, went his own way and came up with an unexpected, sui generis show that captured perfectly the self-conscious spirit of the 1970s (aka the Me Decade) and provided Broadway with what would become (for a while) its longest-running hit. Assembled from long, taped interview sessions with Broadway dancers, *A Chorus Line* transformed an audition for a musical into a stylish but heartfelt orgy of self-revelation, expressed in emotional monologues, song and—but of course—dance. "We have for years been hearing about innovative musicals," wrote Barnes; "now Mr. Bennett has really innovated one."

Yet Barnes also felt compelled to note, "*Oklahoma!* it isn't." And as dazzling and lovable as *A Chorus Line* was, it was pretty much inimitable, with a formula that belonged to its moment and did not sustain repetition. The other shows that drew crowds in the 1970s were a motley lot: the commedia dell'arte–styled *Pippin* (1972), a showcase for the prestidigitation of Bob Fosse; *The Wiz* (1975), which retold *The Wizard of Oz* with African American characters and a Motown beat; and the immensely popular *Annie* (1977), an unapologetically old-fashioned musical inspired by the comic strip *Little Orphan Annie*. And, oh, yes, there were two attention-grabbing shows in 1971 starring Jesus: *Godspell* (which became an Off-Broadway favorite) and *Jesus Christ Superstar*.

The latter was the work of a British composer who was just beginning to flex his muscles, Andrew Lloyd Webber. At the end of the 1970s, Lloyd Webber had audiences, if not critics, nigh swooning over his luscious, Puccini-flavored pop (which Walter Kerr said sounded "as though Max Steiner had arranged it for Carmen Miranda") for *Evita*, a biomusical (directed by Prince) about Eva Perón, the first lady of Argentina. Mrs. Perón (played by a fierce new star named Patti LuPone) would settle in for a long stay in Manhattan. Who knew that this Latina heroine would be the harbinger of a British conquest of Broadway in the decade to come?

**OPPOSITE:** Barbara Streisand in the original Broadway production of *Funny Girl*, 1964.

April 15, 1960

# BYE BYE BIRDIE

By BROOKS ATKINSON

Things are complicated in *Bye Bye Birdie*, which opened at the Martin Beck last evening. Things are also uneven.

Ostensibly, Michael Stewart has written a comic libretto about the impact on the country of a swaying singer, like Elvis Presley. Ostensibly, Charles Strouse, composer, Lee Adams, lyricist, and Gower Champion, choreographer and director, have the same thing in mind.

There are some ludicrous scenes that show teenagers screaming and adult ladies swooning when the great voice bellows "Honestly Sincere" and "One Last Kiss" with stupefying ferocity.

Dick Gautier plays the primitive singer with pompadour, sideburns, gaudy costumes, a rugged voice and a contemptuous vulgarity that are funny—a good, unsubtle cartoon of hideous reality. As the one damsel in America whom he is going to kiss on TV (*The Ed Sullivan Show*, no doubt replacing the Sean O'Casey interview) Susan Watson is charming.

As her resentful father, Paul Lynde contributes to the merriment of the nation by simulating indignation and provincial fatuity. *Bye Bye Birdie* is most enjoyable when Mr. Lynde and members of the family caterwaul "Hymn for a Sunday Evening," and make fools of themselves on a national hookup. Say a grateful word or two also in praise of Michael J. Pollard's teen-age swain, struggling gauchely against the infectious romanticism of a hillbilly singer.

But what has this to do with the frustrated idyll of an unresponsive business manager and his torrid secretary, played by Dick Van Dyke and Chita Rivera? Mr. Van Dyke is a likable comedian, who has India-rubber joints; and Miss Rivera is a flammable singer and a gyroscopic dancer.

Mr. Champion has provided original things for them to do—particularly a dream ballet in which the male dope is assassinated by wish-fulfillments of macabre nature. For Miss Rivera he has contrived a Mack Sennett jumping-jack vaudeville that is expertly danced by a number of buffoons.

But these sequences of *Bye Bye Birdie* have little relevance to the main business of the evening. Kay Medford is the most satisfactory element in them. She plays the poisonously doting mother of the business manager—coarse, deliberate, dead-pan and vocally abrasive. Miss Medford is a very funny dame.

Last evening the audience was beside itself with pleasure. This department was able to contain itself. *Bye Bye Birdie* is handsomely produced with gay scenery by Robert Randolph and animated costumes by Miles White. In the sequences devoted to the mercurial temperament and idol-worshiping of the female teenagers Mr. Champion has contrived a number of funny mass scenes, balanced against droll interludes that isolate individuals.

But as a production, *Bye Bye Birdie* is neither fish, fowl nor good musical comedy. It needs work.

Scenes from *Bye Bye Birdie*. **OPPOSITE:** Dick Gautier as Conrad Birdie with members of the cast. **ABOVE:** The telephone number. **RIGHT:** Dick Van Dyke, Kasimir Kokich, Chita Rivera (standing), and Kay Medford.

May 4, 1960

# *Fantasticks*

By BROOKS ATKINSON

Having won a lot of admirers with a short version of *The Fantasticks*, Tom Jones has expanded it for the production that opened at the Sullivan Street Playhouse last evening.

Although it is ungrateful to say so, two acts are one too many to sustain the delightful tone of the first. After the intermission, the mood is never quite so luminous and gay.

The remark is ungrateful because the form of a masque seems original in the modern theatre. Harvey Schmidt's simple melodies with uncomplicated orchestrations are captivating and the acting is charming. Throughout the first act *The Fantasticks* is sweet and fresh in a civilized manner.

According to the program, it is based on Rostand's *Les Romanesques*. In the form of a dainty masque, designed in modern taste by Ed Wittstein, it is a variation on a Pierrot and Columbine theme. A boy and a girl, who are neighbors, are in love as long as a wall separates them and they believe that their fathers disapprove. Actually, their fathers want them to marry. To create an irresistible romantic mood, the fathers arrange a flamboyant abduction scene in the moonlight.

Although the story is slight, the style is entrancing in Word Baker's staging. It seems like a harlequinade in the setting of a masque. The characters are figures in a legend, acted with an artlessness that is winning. As the

Narrator, the Girl and the Boy, Jerry Orbach, Rita Gardner and Kenneth Nelson, respectively, sing beautifully and act with spontaneity, not forgetting that they are participating in a work of make-believe.

After the intermission the author substitutes sunshine for moonlight. Disillusion destroys the rapture of the introductory scene. Pierrot and Columbine have combed the stardust out of their hair. But it seems to this theatregoer that the second act loses the skimming touch of the first. As an aging ham actor, Thomas Bruce is not so funny as he is in his first appearance, and the conceits of the staging become repetitious.

Perhaps *The Fantasticks* is by nature the sort of thing that loses magic the longer it endures. Any sign of effort diminishes it. But for the space of one act it is delightful. The music, played on piano and harp, has grace and humor. All the actors are thoroughbreds.

**ABOVE:** From left, George Curley, Hugh Thomas, Kenneth Nelson, Jerry Orbach (top), Rita Gardner, William Larsen, and Thomas Bruce in *The Fantasticks*.

January 9, 2002

# FOR LITTLE MUSICAL THAT COULD, A 42-YEAR RUN

By PETER MARKS

Before there was a Unisphere in Flushing Meadow Park or a bridge dedicated to an explorer named Verrazano, before the Beatles cut their first single or the Soviets spirited missiles into Cuba, a small band of actors filed nightly into a tiny theater in Greenwich Village to perform a romantic little musical about a boy, a girl and the travails of young love.

The week it opened, in May 1960, its producer was advised to close the show: the reviews were only so-so, and ticket sales were disappointing. But he decided to try to hang on for a spell, to the relief of the cast of unknowns. One of them, an actor named Jerry Orbach with a creamy baritone, imagined that if it had time to develop a following, the show might flourish. "I thought," Mr. Orbach recalled, "it could run for like five years."

He was off by only thirty-seven.

*The Fantasticks* would go on to defy every convention of the here-today-gone-tomorrow ethos of the theater, staying longer in New York than many New Yorkers. It would not only outrun virtually every entertainment venture of its time but also outlast nine presidents, six mayors, four decades and enough city blackouts, bailouts and blizzards to fill a stack of almanacs. On the *Fantasticks* timeline, *Cats*, which ran for 18 years, was a flash in the pan. Only *The Mousetrap* in London, soon to celebrate its 50th anniversary, has endured longer.

And now, on Sunday evening, after 17,162 performances—an American record that, like Joe DiMaggio's consecutive-game hitting streak, may never be equaled—*The Fantasticks* will do the one thing that few thought it capable of. It will close. For one last time, the two-piece band of piano and harp will strike up the score, the actor playing the dashing El Gallo will sing the signature opening song, "Try to Remember"; the eight-member cast will enact the simple, two-act fable on the white-tiled floor of the Sullivan Street Playhouse; and then the ancient-looking stage lights will be switched off on an essential piece of theater history.

"Haven't we earned the right to retire gracefully?" asked Tony Noto, the show's associate producer and son of its chief producer, Lore Noto. If he sounded slightly exasperated, it may have been because in the months since word of the closing began to spread, die-hard fans have been telling the Notos that justice would be served only if *The Fantasticks* were allowed to run perpetually, a kind of theatrical Niagara Falls.

But the Notos are *Fantastick*-ed out. And so perhaps are most theatergoers. It is no secret that this war horse has been limping along for years, surviving chiefly on out-of-towners lured by, among other things, the sheer length of its celebrated run. Even then, it has been difficult to fill the 150-seat theater. There was the memorable low point of a matinee a few years back, the younger Mr. Noto recalled, when the actors did the entire show for a paying audience of one.

So when a new landlord recently bought the building that houses the theater and talked of large-scale renovation of the property—the show has a lease that allows it to stay for as long as it continues to run—the Notos decided to settle with the owner and move on. (They say they are bound by the deal not to discuss its terms.)

Still, the intriguing question about *The Fantasticks* has less to do with why it is leaving than with why it, among the thousands of shows that have risen and fallen over the years, should be the Methuselah of musicals, having been presented in more than 15,000 productions around the country and the world.

During its 42-year run it has been made into a television special and a feature film, employed actors who went on to win Tonys, Emmys and Oscars, and had its melodies recorded by the likes of Harry Belafonte and Barbra Streisand. Once, years ago, when Ed Ames sang "Try to Remember" on the *Tonight* show, the response was so overwhelming that Johnny Carson asked him back to sing it again.

And of course this Off Broadway show has provided an income to countless theatrical journeymen, William Tost among them. He is a record holder himself, having played Bellomy, the Girl's father, since Nov. 6, 1982. "I can't think of any other show that I could be in this long," he said, standing in a spartan communal dressing room at the Sullivan Street Playhouse. "I don't think I could have been in *Death of a Salesman* for 19 years and remained sane."

Like those centenarians who attribute their survival to a regimen of wine and goose fat, *The Fantasticks* is a specimen whose longevity is a mystery to the experts. Even its creators, the composer Harvey Schmidt and the lyricist and book writer Tom Jones, cannot really put their fingers on it. Some unique mixture of ingredients is the best anyone can come up with: a timeless story, a simple setting, an eternally magical score, a producer with a stubborn streak, who nearly closed the show in 1986, then relented.

"It's meant to be a celebration and a sendup of young love," Mr. Jones said during a joint interview with Mr. Schmidt. "It's supposed to touch you and also make you think how stupid it all is."

Mr. Schmidt and Mr. Jones, who went on to write musicals like *I Do! I Do!* and *110 in the Shade*, toiled on *The Fantasticks* for years in the late 1950s. Its eccentricities began with its working title, *Joy Comes to Deadhorse*. Inspired by a largely forgotten work, *Les Romanesques* by Edmond Rostand, the author of *Cyrano de Bergerac*, the young songwriters drew on a variety of theatrical styles and themes, from commedia dell'arte to *A Midsummer Night's Dream*, to devise the parablelike story of Matt and Luisa, an everyboy and -girl, who learn about delight only by discovering pain.

"It's such a beautiful love story," said Rita Gardner, the original Luisa, the dreamy ingénue who sings of wanting to "go to town in a golden gown/And have my fortune told."

"The show had all those gorgeous songs,

and it was done in a simple way without sets," she said. "And there was empathy for everyone involved. Word Baker, the director, would let us do the show and he would say, 'I'll take that, that and that.' He was the editor, and he allowed us to be free."

Baker died in 1995 but is still listed as the director. The original Matt, Kenneth Nelson, also died a few years ago; Mr. Orbach, now a star of *Law and Order*, played the suave narrator El Gallo, the part that made his name. Mr. Jones, under the pseudonym Thomas Bruce, originated the part of Henry, the Old Actor.

He and Mr. Schmidt eventually settled on *The Fantasticks*, which was also the name of the English version of the Rostand play, as their title. "I really loved the K; it really gave it such zing," declared Mr. Schmidt, who trained as a graphic artist and designed the type for the show's logo. (In the 1960s *The Fantasticks* protested when a cleaning product with a name spelled similarly came on the market. The songwriters said that in a compromise the manufacturer agreed to drop the C in its name.)

*The Fantasticks* was never a success of the magnitude of, say, *The Producers*. "It's never officially been a hit," Mr. Schmidt said. The piece bruises easily; in lazy productions, the artsy conceits—the stylized language, the character of the Mute—fall prey to preciousness.

It has also been altered over the years to conform to contemporary sensibilities. El Gallo's first-act showstopper "It Depends on What You Pay," in which he lists the ways he might beguile and steal off with Luisa, is better known as the rape song. Rape is used in the number to mean seduction, but it became a more loaded term as time wore on.

The show in all its manifestations has made a comfortable living for its authors, but it's not the jackpot. "It's not been a joy ride," said the elder Mr. Noto, who bristles at the suggestion that *The Fantasticks* has made a mint. In 1980, for example, the show made a profit of $24,000, he said. The profit for 1990, distributed among all of his investors, was $199,000.

Still, the original 44 investors have done well. The show's official Web site, www .thefantasticks.com, says they have received a 19,465 percent return on their collective investment of $16,500. Even so, parting with a piece after 42 years is not all business. "I

have a joke now that it's harder closing a show than opening one," Lore Noto said.

The timing of the final bow of course is especially poignant, given the terrible deaths of other enduring city monuments in recent months. The message of *The Fantasticks* proved to be eerily resonant in the days after Sept. 11. El Gallo's opening words could have been written that very week:

> *Try to remember the kind of September*
> *When life was slow and oh so mellow.*

Paul Blankenship, who was playing El

Gallo at the time, said he could hardly force the words out. The actors report that there was not a dry eye in the theater during those performances. On Sunday night, there probably won't be one, either.

. . . . . . . . . . . . . . . . . . . . . . . . .

Scenes from *The Fantastics*. **ABOVE:** Natasha Harper, and Jeremy Ellison Gladstone, 2001. **OPPOSITE:** From left, Martin Vidnovic, Santino Fontana, Sara Jean Ford, and Leo Burmester in a 2006 revival, which opened Off Broadway at the Snapple Theater Center.

December 5, 1960

# Camelot

By HOWARD TAUBMAN

Although its people are handsome and its vistas beautiful, *Camelot* is a partly enchanted city.

At the outset, the new musical, which opened at the Majestic Theatre Saturday night, glows with magic. The impossible seems to have happened. The inspired creators of *My Fair Lady*—Alan Jay Lerner and Frederick Loewe, with Moss Hart in charge of the staging—appear to have passed another miracle.

We are transported to a hilltop near Camelot. The castle soars in the distance, and in the foreground is a gracefully stylized tree, gleaming in fairyland silver. The populace, assembled to greet Guenevere, who is to be Queen, looks as if it has stepped, elegant and smiling, out of the exquisite illuminated pages of a priceless manuscript.

Tradition requires ceremonial meetings to take place on the hilltop, but in a happy never-never land it is easy to declare a new precedent. Whereupon a procession forms, and in deliciously stiff and humorous dance movement, it sets out for the bottom of the hill. The arts of the theatre unite to make an enchanting modern comment on the legendary past.

Arthur jumps from his hiding place in the tree at the call of Merlyn. The young king is a child of nature—sturdy, manly, warmhearted and a bit dull-witted—and, as bodied forth by Richard Burton, he is a winning figure. After some discourse by Merlyn, necessary exposition but the authors are wise to get rid of the old windbag early in the evening, Arthur returns to his hiding place in the tree.

Guenevere runs in. She has escaped from her carriage and is fleeing the fearsome formalities. In the slim, airy person of Julie Andrews, a lovely actress and true singer, she is regal and girlish, cool and eager. Arthur may be dull, but he is no fool. He

drops from the tree. She does not know who he is but is attracted and urges him to make advances. In the title song, "Camelot," they sing of the wonders of enchantment, and we, too, are enchanted.

Almost two hours of playing time elapse before we arrive at a similarly enchanted scene between these two. In a charming song, "What Do Simple Folk Do?", they muse on how ordinary people spend their time, and they test each diversion. They whistle, sing, dance and, in the end, sit morosely and wonder what royal folks do. Miss Andrews and Mr. Burton perform with winning lightness. Again there is magic in *Camelot*.

Visually, *Camelot* is never less than a thing of beauty. Oliver Smith's architecture and cloths are royally lavish and impeccably tasteful. The costumes by Adrian and Tony Duquette have the magnificence of knighthood in flower. Hanya Holm's choreography, except for a disappointing affair in the forest of Morgan Le Fey, has style. Feder's lighting bathes the scenes in fresh dimensions of illusion.

A celebration of May Day becomes an appealing design of color in motion. There is courtly elegance in the jousting field with its lofty grandstand, even if the musical account of the tournament is handled somewhat like the Ascot scene in *My Fair Lady*. There is grandeur in the scenic composition of the Great Hall, with its impressive throne and its floating balconies.

Unfortunately, *Camelot* is weighed down by the burden of its book. The style of the story-telling is inconsistent. It shifts uneasily between light-hearted fancy and uninflected reality.

A good deal of the humor is obvious. Much reliance is placed on a stock comic English numbskull; he is called Pellinore, but could be Colonel Pickering, and is played,

indeed, by Robert Coote, of *My Fair Lady* fame.

Lancelot, sung and played splendidly though he is by Robert Goulet, is a pompous bore. Were it not for the personal communication of Miss Andrews and Mr. Burton, Guenevere and Arthur would not be very engaging. Their use of appellations like Jenny and Lance offers the spurious intimacy of Broadway, rather than the magic Camelot should have. And the conception of Morgan Le Fey, played by the seductive M'el Dowd, as a temptress with a sweet tooth is unimaginative.

Mr. Lerner's lyrics are fashioned cleverly. Mr. Loewe has written some pleasant tunes, including "How to Handle a Woman" and "Before I Gaze at You Again." But "Fie on Goodness!" is a sonorous male chorus, the musical essence of which is as old-fashioned as "The Vagabond King."

"The Seven Deadly Virtues," an inventive number for Mordred, played with a flair by Roddy McDowall, is set to a tinkly rhythm, when it should have diabolical brilliance. And "Guenevere," which the authors undoubtedly use to replace a lot of narrative, is oratorio without a trace of genius.

Graceful and sumptuous though it is, *Camelot* leans dangerously in the direction of old-hat operetta. It has intervals of enchantment, as it must with talented men like Lerner, Loewe and Hart in charge. It would be unjust to tax them with not attaining the heights of *My Fair Lady*, but it cannot be denied that they badly miss their late collaborator—Bernard Shaw.

. . . . . . . . . . . . . . . . . . . . . . . . . . . . .

**OPPOSITE:** Robert Goulet, Julie Andrews, and Richard Burton in *Camelot*.

# HOW TO SUCCEED IN BUSINESS WITHOUT REALLY TRYING

By HOWARD TAUBMAN

*How to Succeed* is as impudent as a competitor who grabs off a fat contract and as cheerful as the tax collector who gets his cut no matter who makes the deal. Its irreverence is as bracing as a growth stock that matures into a nice capital gain.

Not a bypath in the honored folkways of big business avoids a going over. The mailroom, plans and system, personnel, advertising, the president, chairman of the board, the executive conference, secretaries, stenographers, cleaning women, the coffee break and even the executive washroom are sources of anything but innocent merriment. Not even love is sacred, but being shrewd showmen, the authors don't knock it.

*How to Succeed* arrives bearing precious gifts of an adult viewpoint and consistency of style. Abe Burrows, sly and robust magician of the musical theatre, has directed brilliantly as well as helped Jack Weinstock and Willie Gilbert in drawing the story from Shepherd Mead's book. Frank Loesser has written lyrics with an edge and tunes with a grin. Bob Fosse's staging, like the dances, sets and costumes, is gaily in the spirit of the production.

There are dividends of diverting comment everywhere, even in extra musical touches. When boy and girl meet in a long, tender kiss, the orchestra in the pit, as if rebuking Mr. Loesser's song for not feeling the moment keenly enough, breaks into a lush theme from a piano concerto of the romantic school. As the executives solemnly march into the conference room for a fateful meeting, an organ plays a soulful voluntary as if to fix a fitting mood for the highest meditations.

Imagine a collaboration between Horatio Alger and Machiavelli and you have

It's an open question whether big business in America should be warier of trust busters than of the new musical that frolicked into the Forty-sixth Street Theatre Saturday night.

The antitrust watchdogs can crack a mean whip, but *How to Succeed in Business Without Really Trying* applies a gigantic hotfoot. It stings mischievously and laughs uproariously.

Big business is not likely to be the same again. If it isn't guarding self-defensively against invoking the old team try and the sanctified corporate image, it will be so busy chuckling at its reflection in this impish mirror of a musical that it won't have time to do big business. But you can bet that this show will. It belongs to the blue chips among modern musicals.

Finch, the intrepid hero of this sortie into the canyons of commerce. As played with unfaltering bravura and wit by Robert Morse, he is a rumpled, dimpled angel with a streak of Lucifer. Butter couldn't melt in his mouth because he is so occupied spreading it on anyone who can help him up a rung of that ladder you've heard about.

Finch starts his climb to glory by bumping into J. B. Biggley, president of World Wide Wicket Company, Inc., and being knocked down by him. J. B. is played with admirable shortness of patience and temper by Rudy Vallee, looking austere behind a pince-nez. Only a few things melt J. B.—flattery, a luscious dish named Hedy and the enduring joy of being an alumnus—therefore, a Groundhog—of dear, old Ivy.

When J. B. and his Hedy (Virginia Martin looking like come-hither alabaster poured into garments that cling and caress) join in a heartrending ballad, "Love from a Heart of Gold," and Hedy belts out the top tones like a Valkyrie sopping with emotion, you know that passion has had it. When J. B. and Finch strut through "Grand Old Ivy," you know that the rousing heartfelt tributes to Alma Mater have had it, too. And when Mr. Vallee cups his hands to his mouth like a megaphone, for a moment the years roll back on our youth when we listened to him sing the "Maine Stein Song" with as much sentiment as he poured into it.

On his painless way up Finch meets Rosemary, charmingly played by Bonnie Scott, who loves him instantly and forever. With gentle forbearance he crosses swords with J. B.'s nephew, Frump. Charles Nelson Reilly plays the villain with a wonderful sneaky relish. As he lays his dark plans and chortles fiendishly, "I shall return," you realize that the machinations in the towers of industry have more melodrama than the Westerns they sponsor.

When you enter the Park Avenue office building of World Wide Wicket and find the staff in frozen attitudes, like manikins in a store window, you know that *How to Succeed* is bent on fun with a helping of malice. It never lets up; indeed, it becomes livelier and funnier as it moves up the ladder with Finch.

A coffee break without coffee undermines free enterprise. An ingenious dance celebrating the point that a stenographer is not a toy keeps a tongue in cheek. The

authors pay their good-humored and biting respects to Paris originals that aren't, to a Madison Avenue presentation full of sound, fury, and maybe a lot of truth, to the in-fighting that flows over into the executive washroom and to the sort of entertainment big business concocts for television.

As in modern musicals of quality, the songs in *How to Succeed* sharpen the ridicule. "Cinderella, Darling" is a hymn sung by grateful—and hopeful—secretaries to the occasional bosses who make them honest

women. "I Believe in You" is a torch song to self-esteem. And "Brotherhood of Man" is a jubilant, twinkling ode that will leave you as happy as if you owned a piece of the show. Let Wall Street and Madison Avenue tremble as the rest of us rejoice.

Scenes from *How To Succeed in Business Without Really Trying.* **OPPOSITE:** Robert Morse as Finch. **ABOVE:** Virginia Martin as Hedy.

## REVIVAL

March 24, 1995

# CLIMBING THE LADDER, SONG BY SONG

By VINCENT CANBY

Call it gospel or just good news: *How to Succeed in Business Without Really Trying* is as fast, funny and glitzy as it ever was. Nearly 34 years after its premiere at the 46th Street Theatre, the Frank Loesser–Abe Burrows chef-d'oeuvre is back at the same house (since renamed the Richard Rodgers), where the pristine revival opened last night.

Times have since coarsened, public morals have become looser and political attitudes have been corrected. Yet the musical's skeptical wit and cheerfully amoral heart remain forever young. You might almost suspect that this 1961 fable of blind business ambition had been ahead of its time. Not really.

*How to Succeed* isn't about the corporate raiders, the arbitragers and the creative bookkeepers who so captivated the 1980s. Its world is enclosed entirely within the glass-and-steel tower that is the World Wide Wicket Company headquarters in Manhattan. The show's gifts and concerns are timeless. Under the classy, intelligent guidance of Des McAnuff, the director, and Wayne Cilento, whose choreography recalls Bob Fosse's original dances without imitating them, the show is a triumph of contemporary Broadway know-how.

Most important, it has the marvelous Loesser score and an unusually crafty book, at the center of which is the most endearingly flawed character ever to scheme his way from window-washer to the top of the corporate ladder. He's J. Pierrepont Finch, the role that made a star of Robert Morse and now provides the deceptively gentle-mannered Matthew Broderick with the breakout opportunity of his theatrical career. Beneath that earnest boy-next-door exterior, J. Pierrepont Finch is an epically gifted opportunist, a fellow with both eyes on the main chance when he arrives at World Wide Wicket.

Mr. Broderick sings. He dances. He comes on to strangers as if he were Tom Sawyer, although he's more like Huck Finn in a three-button suit. He deceives with such innocent, deadpan relish that he threatens the stability of the house. Mr. Broderick never suggests the gap-toothed, moon-faced mania that made Mr. Morse so funny. Instead he gives a supremely legitimate performance that also happens to be priceless.

Scenes from the 1995 Broadway revival of *How To Succeed in Business Without Really Trying.* **OPPOSITE, TOP:** Victoria Clark, Matthew Broderick, and Megan Mullally. **OPPOSITE, BOTTOM:** Members of the cast performing "A Secretary Is Not a Toy."

THE SIXTIES & SEVENTIES

# A FUNNY THING HAPPENED ON THE WAY TO THE FORUM

By HOWARD TAUBMAN

Know what they found on the way to the forum? Burlesque, vaudeville and a cornucopia of mad, comic hokum.

The phrase for the title of the new musical comedy that arrived at the Alvin last night might be, caveat emptor. *A Funny Thing Happened on the Way to the Forum* indeed! No one gets to the forum; no one even starts for it. And nothing really happens that isn't older than the forum, more ancient than the agora in Athens. But somehow you keep laughing as if the old sight and sound gags were as good as new.

Heed the Roman warning. Let the buyer beware if he knew burlesque and vaudeville and the old comic hokum and found nothing funny in it. For him the knockabout routines at the Alvin will be noisy and dreary.

A plastic-faced, rolling-eyed, Falstaff-like character like Zero Mostel playing zany follow-the-leader with three centurions ordered to keep an eye on him? A rubber-faced, murmurous David Burns playing an enamored old goat and cooing like an antiquated turtle dove? A bewigged and fluttering Jack Gilford got up in a shimmering white gown and pretending to be a dead, yet agitated, virgin? A lank, deep-voiced Shakespearean like John Carradine pretending to be a timid though agile dealer in courtesans?

If stuff like that—wonder what word they had in the Colosseum for corn?—doesn't joggle your funny bone, keep away from the Alvin. For the rest of us who were young and risible in the days when comedians were hearty and comedy was rough and tumble and for the new generations who knew not the untamed gusto of this ancient and honorable style of fooling, it will be thumbs up for this uninhibited romp.

Burt Shevelove and Larry Gelbart, authors of the book, are willing to pay full credit, if not royalties, to Plautus, their distinguished antecedent. They admit they helped themselves to his plays. Who hasn't among

comic writers in the last two millenniums? And whom did Plautus crib from?

Their book resorts to outrageous puns and to lines that ought to make you cringe. Like having a slave of slaves remark, "I live to grovel." Like having a domineering matron tell a slave holding a sculpture of her, "Carry my bust with pride." Like having a stately courtesan named Gymnasia bark at a eunuch, "Don't you lower your voice at me!"

George Abbott, who has been around a long time but surely staged nothing for the forum mob, has forgotten nothing and remembered everything. He has engineered a gay funeral sequence to a relentlessly snappy march by Stephen Sondheim. He has used mixed identities, swinging doors, kicks in the posterior, double takes and all the rest of the familiar paraphernalia with the merciless disingenuousness of a man who knows you will be defenseless.

Mr. Sondheim's songs are accessories to the pre-meditated offense. With the Messrs. Mostel, Gilford, Burns and Carradine as a coy foursome, "Everybody Ought to Have a Maid" recalls the days when delirious farceurs like the Marx Brothers could devastate a number. When Mr. Mostel, the slave with a nimble mind and a desire to be free, persuades Mr. Gilford, the nervous straw boss of the slaves, to don virgin's white, the two convert the show's romantic and pretty "Lovely" into irresistible nonsense.

Ruth Kobart as a large-voiced, domineering wife, Brian Davies as the juvenile lead, Preshy Marker as a dumb but beautiful virgin, Ronald Holgate as a captain who admits to being a legend in his own time and Raymond Walburn as a confused old citizen of Rome are among the cheerful participants.

There are six courtesans, who are not obliged to do much but have a great deal to show. There is choreography by Jack Cole— it says here—but not much. The set? Who needs more than a single simple one for a whole show? Plautus probably managed with less. Since Tony Walton didn't get to design much scenery, he has had his little joke with the odd assortment of leotards, tunics, togas, gowns and wreaths that pass for Roman duds.

Say all the unkind and truthful things you wish about *A Funny Thing*. It's noisy, coarse, blue and obvious like the putty nose on a burlesque comedian. Resist these slickly paced old comic routines, if you can. Try and keep a straight face as Zero Mostel explains to the sacrificial Jack Gilford that an impending pyre is only "a fire pyre."

Scenes from *A Funny Thing Happened on the Way to the Forum*. **OPPOSITE:** From left, John Carradine, Jack Gilford, David Burns, and Zero Mostel. **ABOVE:** Gloria Kristy as Gymnasia and Zero Mostel as Pseudolus.

# Hello, Dolly!

By HOWARD TAUBMAN

As a play Thornton Wilder's *The Matchmaker* vibrated with unheard melodies and unseen dances. Michael Stewart, Jerry Herman and Gower Champion apparently heard and saw them, and they have conspired ingeniously to bring them to shining life in a musical shot through with enchantment.

*Hello, Dolly!*, which blew happily into the St. James Theatre last night, has qualities of freshness and imagination that are rare in the run of our machine-made musicals. It transmutes the broadly stylized mood of a mettlesome farce into the gusto and colors of the musical stage. What was larger and droller than life has been puffed up and gaily tinted without being blown apart. *Hello, Dolly!* is the best musical of the season thus far.

It could have been more than that. Were it not for lapses of taste, it could have been one of the notable ones. But Mr. Champion, whose staging and choreography abound in wit and invention, has tolerated certain cheapnesses, like the vulgar accent of a milliner's clerk, like the irritating wail of a teenager crying for her beau, like the muddled chase in the midst of a series of tableaux vivants. Mr. Stewart's book has settled for some dull and cheap lines the musical would not miss.

It is a pity because *Hello, Dolly!* does not need such crutches. One can understand, of course, why offenses against taste creep into an essentially imaginative musical. The stakes are so high that there is a tendency to whip things up, as if the public could not be trusted. But only musicals without ideas or talent must resort to desperate measures, which don't help anyhow.

But enough of peevishness. Let us rejoice in the blessings *Hello, Dolly!* bestows.

The conception as a whole, despite an occasional excess of exuberance that turns into turbulence, is faithful to the spirit of Mr. Wilder's broad, chuckling jest. Mr. Stewart's book holds fast to Mr. Wilder's atmosphere and style even if it trots off into Broadwayese now and then. Mr. Herman's songs are brisk and pointed and always tuneful.

Mr. Champion's direction at its happiest darts and floats on stylized, yet airborne patterns of choreography. Oliver Smith's sets with their back-drops that unroll like screens have the elegance of pen-and-ink drawings and the insouciance of a rejuvenated old New York. Freddy Wittop's costumes join Mr. Smith's designs in an extravagance of period styles and colors.

The basic story, deliberately calculating in its simplicity, is unchanged. Here in a shrewdly mischievous performance by Carol Channing is the endlessly resourceful widow, Mrs. Dolly Gallagher Levi, matchmaker and lady-of-all-trades, who sets her enormous bonnet crested by a huge pink bird for the half-millionaire, Vandergelder, and lands him on her pleasure-loving terms.

Miss Channing's Dolly is all benevolent guile. She can talk faster than a con man without losing her big-eyed innocent gleam. She can lead Vandergelder to the widow Molloy and manage to rub noses with him enticingly.

She can teach "Dancing" to Mr. Herman's gliding three-four muse. Resplendent in scarlet gown embroidered with jewels and a feathered headdress, and looking like a gorgeous, animated kewpie doll, she sings the rousing title song with earthy zest and leads a male chorus of waiters and chefs in a joyous promenade around the walk that circles the top of the pit.

Here is David Burns as the curmudgeon Vandergelder, bellowing nasally like W. C. Fields redivivus. His intransigence in the face of warmth and kindness is a comfort in a Pollyanna world. When he roars that he is "rich, friendless and mean, which in Yonkers is as far as you can go," you are bound to share his pride. And when, standing on a dismantled parade float that is being pulled out of sight, he roars, "Where are you taking me?", he has the righteous wrath of a Horatius defending a sinking bridge.

Charles Nelson Reilly and Jerry Dodge as two of Vandergelder's oppressed clerks loose on the town sing and dance agreeably, and their buffoonery would be funnier if it were toned down. Eileen Brennan is as pretty and desirable a widow Molloy as one could wish—with a voice, too. Igors Gavon is another performer with a big, resonant voice.

What gives *Hello, Dolly!* its special glow is its amalgamation of the lively theater arts in the musical numbers. Mr. Champion has provided fragments of dance for the overture-less opening that are all the more attractive because they are spare and unexpectedly spaced.

When he fills the stage for the ebullient "Put on Your Sunday Clothes" at the Yonkers Depot and has his lavishly garbed cast promenading along the oval runway out front, the theater throbs with vitality. As if to put a cherry on the sundae, the stage magicians have provided a railroad car pulled by an engine that spits smoke and ashes.

For a 14th Street parade Mr. Champion has deployed his forces in a cheerful old New York version of medieval guilds. To a bouncing gallop by Mr. Herman, Mr. Champion has set a corps of waiters with trays, spits and jeroboams at the ready, dancing a wild, vertiginous rout. To Mr. Herman's lightly satirical "Elegance," Mr. Champion has fashioned a delightfully mannered routine for his quartet of singers—Miss Brennan, Sondra Lee, Mr. Reilly and Mr. Dodge.

Making the necessary reservations for the unnecessary vulgar and frenzied touches, one is glad to welcome *Hello, Dolly!* for its warmth, color and high spirits.

**OPPOSITE:** Carol Channing as Dolly.

## REVIVAL

October 20, 1995

# IT'S JUST ONE ROLE, BUT IT'S CHANNING'S

By VINCENT CANBY

Not since Joseph Jefferson, who played Rip Van Winkle for most of the second half of the 19th century, has any American performer been so long identified with a single role as Carol Channing with Dolly Levi, nee Gallagher, in *Hello, Dolly!*

Ms. Channing first played the formidable matchmaker in the show's premiere Broadway engagement starting in January 1964. With occasional time off for other theater work, several movies, some television specials and nightclub appearances, she has been playing Dolly ever since. In this country, abroad, and maybe on a nearby planet or two.

For this reason, it's not exactly a surprise that she has turned up on the stage of the Lunt-Fontanne Theatre, the scene of her 1978 revival, to have yet another go at the part in a new production set to tour the world from Japan to Australia and maybe Lapland.

The only surprise was my surprise when I saw a preview performance. There I sat with some embarrassment as if chemically stimulated: helpless with pleasure and turned into a goon, wearing a dopey, ear-to-ear grin from the moment of her entrance through her pricelessly delivered remarks at the curtain call. At that point, I was even ready to swear that she had written every one of those seemingly impromptu lines herself.

World, beware: it's possible this woman is a substance that should be legally controlled.

Though I hadn't seen Ms. Channing since the first *Dolly* production, I have over the years (always in the line of duty) been forced to watch at least two of her replacements (Betty Grable and Ginger Rogers) and Barbra Streisand, who starred in the screen adaptation, one of the iciest musicals ever made by Hollywood.

Ms. Channing and the show, which officially opened last night, are the real thing.

Scenes from the 1995 revival of *Hello, Dolly!* **OPPOSITE:** Carol Channing as Dolly. **BELOW:** Members of the cast.

March 27, 1964

# FUNNY
# GIRL

By HOWARD TAUBMAN

Who wouldn't want to resurrect Fanny Brice? She was a wonderful entertainer.

Since Fanny herself cannot be brought back, the next best thing is to get Barbra Streisand to sing and strut and go through comic routines à la Brice. Miss Streisand is well on her way to becoming a splendid entertainer in her own right, and in *Funny Girl* she goes as far as any performer can toward recalling the laughter and joy that were Fanny Brice.

If the new musical that arrived last night at the Winter Garden were dedicated entirely to the gusto and buffoonery of Fanny Brice, all would be well nigh perfect this morning. But *Funny Girl* also is intent on telling the story of how Fanny loved and lost Nick Arnstein, and part of the time it oozes with a thick helping of sticky sentimentality.

But that's show-business sagas for you. They rarely can untrack themselves from the hokum and schmaltz that authors and, for all one knows, show people consider

standard operating procedure. As for the public, it often is a pushover for the glamour of the stage and the romances of show folk. Say for *Funny Girl* that it has not reached to be neck deep in show business. It has every right to be there.

*Funny Girl* is most fun when it is reveling in Fanny's preoccupation with show business. Miss Streisand as a young Brice bursting with energy and eagerness to improve her routines is an impudent dancing doll who refuses to run down. Miss Streisand imagining herself in a radiant future in "I'm the Greatest Star," an appealingly quirky song, is not only Fanny Brice but all young performers believing in their destinies.

Then there are the production numbers that recall the theater before World War I. Miss Streisand and a wildly agitated chorus, set loose in a pattern designed by Carol Haney, do the explosive "Cornet Man" in a way that would startle the music halls of old but does not betray their spirit.

For an evocation of the stately *Ziegfeld Follies*, which Miss Brice brightened with her exuberance, there are two big nostalgic numbers. One glorifies the bride, with beautiful girls, draped and undraped, fixed in the scenery and rippling on a lofty flight of stairs topped by candelabra, and with Miss Streisand turning the overblown "His Love Makes Me Beautiful" into a spoof. The other, using the same stairway, shoots soldiers and soldierettes into a furious drill to a military "Rat-Tat-Tat-Tat," with Miss Streisand doing her bit as a comic veteran.

Fanny's friends making merry with a block party on Henry Street after her debut in the *Follies* are festive company. And Miss Streisand as Fanny hamming it up in her first rendezvous with Sydney Chaplin in a private room in a swank restaurant is almost as funny as the funny girl herself might have been. She uses a fan with mock coyness; she arranges herself on a chair like a rachitic femme fatale; she walks across the room with a wiggle Mae West would envy.

These maneuvers nevertheless to a Brice or a Streisand are the small tricks of the clown's trade. What makes Miss Streisand's manipulation of them in this scene particularly impressive is that she conveys a note of honest emotion underneath the clowning. Indeed, at this point the romance of Fanny and Nicky is as charming as young love.

Isobel Lennart's book skirts sentimentality reasonably well until Fanny and Nick turn serious, get married and run into troubles. By the end *Funny Girl* is drenched in tears.

Fortunately, Miss Streisand can make a virtue out of suffering, if she is allowed to sing about it. Jule Styne, who has written one of his best scores, has provided her with bluesy tunes like "Who Are You Now?" and she turns them into lyrical laments.

Miss Streisand can also draw rapture from the yearning "People." For a change of pace she makes her raffish share of "You Are Woman," for which Bob Merrill has done smiling lyrics, worthy of the performer she impersonates.

Mr. Chaplin is a tall, elegant figure as Nick, gallant in courting and doing his best when he must be noble. Kay Medford, who seems to be a stage mother every time you see her in a musical, is dry and diverting as Fanny's shrewd parent. Danny Meehan is agreeable as a hoofer who befriends the young Fanny.

Garson Kanin gets credit for being the director and Jerome Robbins for being the production supervisor, and only they and the company know what their contributions were. Say for both of them that *Funny Girl* behaves as if it takes its hokum seriously and that its show-business sequences framed in Robert Randolph's cheerful sets move at a pace hard to resist.

It's the authentic aura of show business arising out of Fanny Brice's luminous career that lights up *Funny Girl*. Much of the spoken humor is homespun—that is, East Side homespun. The true laughter in this musical comes from the sense of truth it communicates of Fanny Brice's stage world. And Fanny's personality and style are remarkably evoked by Miss Streisand. Fanny and Barbra make the evening. Who says the past cannot be recaptured?

**OPPOSITE:** Barbara Streisand as Fanny Brice.

# Fiddler on the Roof

By HOWARD TAUBMAN

It has been prophesied that the Broadway musical theater would take up the mantle of meaningfulness worn so carelessly by the American drama in recent years. *Fiddler on the Roof* does its bit to make good on this prophecy.

The new musical, which opened last night at the Imperial Theatre, is filled with laughter and tenderness. It catches the essence of a moment in history with sentiment and radiance. Compounded of the familiar materials of the musical theater—popular song, vivid dance movement, comedy and

emotion—it combines and transcends them to arrive at an integrated achievement of uncommon quality.

The essential distinction of *Fiddler on the Roof* must be kept in mind even as one cavils at a point here or a detail there. For criticism of a work of this caliber, it must be remembered, is relative. If I wish that several of the musical numbers soared indigenously, if I find fault with a gesture that is Broadway rather than the world of Sholem Aleichem, if I deplore a conventional scene, it is because *Fiddler on the Roof* is so fine that it

deserves counsels toward perfection.

But first to the things that are marvelously right. The book that Joseph Stein has drawn from the richly humorous and humane tales of Sholem Aleichem, the warmhearted spokesman of the poor Jews in the Russian villages at the turn of the century, is faithful to its origins.

It touches honestly on the customs of the Jewish community in such a Russian village. Indeed, it goes beyond local color and lays bare in quick, moving strokes the sorrow of a people subject to sudden tempests of vandalism and, in the end, to eviction and exile from a place that had been home.

Although there is no time in a musical for a fully developed gallery of human portraits, *Fiddler on the Roof* manages to display several that have authentic character. The most arresting, of course, is that of Tevye, the humble dairyman whose blessings included a hardworking, if sharp-tongued, wife, five daughters and a native philosophical bent.

If Sholem Aleichem had known Zero Mostel, he would have chosen him, one is sure, for Tevye. Some years ago Mr. Mostel bestowed his imagination and incandescence on Tevye in an Off-Broadway and television version of Sholem Aleichem's stories. Now he has a whole evening for Tevye, and Tevye for him. They were ordained to be one.

Mr. Mostel looks as Tevye should. His full beard is a pious aureole for his shining countenance. The stringy ends of his prayer shawl hang from under his vest; the knees of his breeches are patched, and his boots are scuffed. On festive occasions he wears a skull cap and kaftan that give him an appearance of bourgeois solidity. But he is too humble to put on airs.

A man of goodwill, Mr. Mostel often pauses to carry on a dialogue with himself, arguing both sides of a case with equal logic. He holds long conversations with God. Although his observations never are disrespectful, they call a spade a spade. "Send us the cure," he warns the Lord, "we got the sickness already."

When Maria Karnilova as his steadfast but blunt wife breaks in on one of these communions with a dry greeting, "Finally home, my breadwinner!", he is polite enough for a parting word to God, "I'll talk to You later."

Mr. Mostel does not keep his acting and singing or his walking and dancing in separate compartments. His Tevye is a unified, lyrical conception. With the exception of a grimace or a gesture several times that score easy laughs, Tevye stays in character.

The scope of this performance is summed up best in moments made eloquent through music and movement. When Mr. Mostel sings "If I Were a Rich Man," interpolating passages of cantillation in the manner of prayer, his Tevye is both devout and pungently realistic. When Tevye chants a prayer as the good Golde tries to convey an item of vital news, Mr. Mostel is not only comic but evocative of an old way of life. When Tevye hears the horrifying word that his third daughter has run away with a gentile, Mr. Mostel dances his anguish in a flash of savage emotion.

The score by Jerry Bock and the lyrics by Sheldon Harnick at their best move the story along, enrich the mood and intensify the emotions. "Sabbath Prayer" is as hushed as a community at its devotions. "Sunrise, Sunset" is in the spirit of a traditional wedding under a canopy. When Tevye and Golde after 25 years of marriage ask themselves, "Do You Love Me?", the song has a

Scenes from *Fiddler on the Roof.* **OPPOSITE:** Zero Mostel as Tevye. **BELOW:** Beatrice Arthur (center) as the matchmaker with members of the cast.

touching angularity. But several of the other romantic tunes are merely routine.

Jerome Robbins has staged *Fiddler on the Roof* with sensitivity and fire. As his own choreographer, he weaves dance into action with subtlety and flaring theatricalism. The opening dance to a nostalgic song, "Tradition," has a ritual sweep. The dances at the wedding burst with vitality. A dream sequence is full of humor. And the choreographed farewells of the Jews leaving their Russian village have a poignancy that adds depth to *Fiddler on the Roof*.

Boris Aronson's sets provide a background that rings true; they give the work an unexpected dimension of beauty in scenes like "Sabbath Prayer," the wedding and the epilogue.

Joanna Merlin, Julia Migenes, Tanya Everett as three of the daughters, Beatrice Arthur as a busybody of a matchmaker, Austin Pendleton as a poor tailor, Bert Convy as a young radical, Michael Granger as a well-to-do butcher and Joe Ponazecki as the gentile suitor are among those who sing and act with flavor.

Richness of flavor marks *Fiddler on the Roof*. Although it does not entirely eschew the stigmata of routine Broadway, it has an honest feeling for another place, time and people. And in Mr. Mostel's Tevye it has one of the most glowing creations in the history of the musical theater.

. . . . . . . . . . . . . . . . . . . . . . . . . . . . . . . . . . .

**RIGHT:** Maria Karnilova and Zero Mostel (in bed) with members of the cast in the original Broadway production of *Fiddler on the Roof*, 1964

November 23, 1965

# MAN OF LA MANCHA

By HOWARD TAUBMAN

And now Cervantes and his ineffable Don Quixote have been transported to the popular musical theater. With the exception of a few vulgarities and some triteness, they have made the transition in *Man of La Mancha* with remarkable spirit and affection.

Virtually every medium of communication has attempted to seize Don Quixote in its own language and imagery. The fond and foolish knight, his quest and his adventures have been turned into film, opera, symphonic tone poem, what you will. The results, sometimes distinguished and often not, depended on the genius of the new form and the capacities of the transformers.

The dire perils to Don Quixote if cheap, rude hands were laid on him are readily apparent. But no such fate befalls the Don himself in *Man of La Mancha*, which opened last night at the ANTA Washington Square Theatre. As Dale Wasserman has written him, Albert Marre directed him and Richard Kiley plays him, he is admirably credible—a mad, gallant, affecting figure who has honestly materialized from the pages of Cervantes.

One can quibble about other aspects of *Man of La Mancha*. Irving Jacobson is a sympathetic, gentle Sancho, but it is difficult to shake the uneasy feeling that he is a Spaniard with a Jewish accent.

Mitch Leigh and Joe Darion have made every conscientious effort to integrate their songs into the texture of action and character. Indeed, the program eschews the usual list of numbers. But their muse, though it aspires, does not always soar in the imaginative vein of Cervantes and Quixote.

Yet *Man of La Mancha* rates far more plusses than minuses. At its best it is audacious in conception and tasteful in execution. Many of the familiar adventures of Don Quixote are caught in evocative scenes. Howard Bay's use of the thrust stage, where the Lincoln Center Repertory Theater endured its first struggles, is sparing in its furniture and props and, thanks to the employment of light, rich in illusion. Mr. Marre and his choreographer, Jack Cole, have conjured up some impressive pictures in action and repose.

Best of all is Mr. Kiley, who has never given a finer performance. We meet him at the beginning as Cervantes being led down a huge stairway, which has been lowered from on high, into a large prison cell.

After the guards are gone, he is attacked by his fellow inmates, who rob him, find his immortal manuscript and prepare to cast it into the flames. To save it, Cervantes goes on trial before this jury of the condemned, and he tells them the story of Don Quixote.

Seated on a box before a crude mirror, Cervantes turns himself into Don Quixote, as he pastes on mustache, pointed beard and thick eyebrows, dons a battered cuirass and arms himself with a lance. As the musical play progresses, Mr. Kiley shuttles back and forth between Cervantes and Don Quixote, and the transformation always is amazingly apt.

As Cervantes he is a man of spirit with a quizzical humor and a keen flexible intelligence. Shading into Quixote, he becomes the amiable visionary, childlike in his pretensions and oddly, touchingly gallant. His eyes take on a wild, proud, otherworldly look. His posture is preternaturally erect. His folly becomes a kind of humbling wisdom.

Watch him as he and Mr. Jacobson sit on their wooden mounts, pulled by actors wearing delicious masks of horses' heads. This is the innocent, radiant knight errant ready for any derring-do. Mr. Kiley also can sing, and he delivers the confident "I am Don Quixote of La Mancha" with a marchlike stride.

Watch Mr. Kiley as he arrives at the inn, which he imagines to be the castle where he is to be dubbed a knight. With a blossom in his plumed helmet and a green sprig in his lance, he appears with the delicate pride and conviction of a lighthearted soul about to meet its destiny. Listen to him serenade Joan Diener as the strumpet of a servant, who is to become his dream Dulcinea. The song itself is ordinary, but the Quixote has endearing credibility.

Mr. Kiley defends his Dulcinea against the muleteers in stout combat that is a little too stagy for comfort, but how true, disarming and amusing he is when he sends the bewildered girl to bind up the enemy's wounds. The binding up of the wounds, by the way, is turned in a blistering, orgiastic dance for the muleteers and the shapely, mobile Miss Diener, who is dragged and hauled as violently as any performer in town.

Mr. Kiley's finest scene is at the end. Now an old man, feeble and dying, he has forgotten his days of knighthood. But his Dulcinea comes to his bedside. She whispers the words of the song he once sang, "To Dream the Impossible Dream." The memory of Quixote floods the old man's consciousness. He rouses himself, stands up: he is for a last precious moment Don Quixote again.

One could dispense with the added bit where Mr. Kiley, with arms around Mr. Jacobson and Miss Diener, belts out a chorus in operetta style. One wishes Mr. Kiley did not mutter a banal, modern "Yegh" in an earlier scene as he glances at a pot on the fire. One could do without other reminders of show biz here and there that traduce the essential atmosphere.

Ray Middleton as a fellow inmate and as innkeeper plays and sings with sturdy forthrightness. Robert Rounseville, who used to sing tenor leads in opera, reminds us how exhilarating it is to hear a real voice in the popular musical theater, and he has a tender, moving "De Profundis" to sing for the departed Don Quixote.

Whatever concessions *Man of La Mancha* has made to easy popularity, it has not filled the stage with an extraneous chorus line or turned Don Quixote into an oafish clown. One does not expect complete fidelity to Cervantes outside his pages—who reads him these days?—but there are charm, gallantry and a delicacy of spirit in this reincarnation of Quixote.

· · · · · · · · · · · · · · · · · · · · · · · ·

**OPPOSITE:** Ray Middleton and Richard Kiley in *Man of La Mancha*.

January 31, 1966

# SWEET CHARITY

By STANLEY KAUFFMANN

It is Bob Fosse's evening at the Palace. That newly refurbished theater, clad in several becoming shades of red, re-opened on Saturday night with a musical called *Sweet Charity*. The show's chief attractions are the staging and the dances by Mr. Fosse, which have style and theatrical vitality. The same cannot be said for the book or the score.

The book was adapted from Federico Fellini's film *Nights of Cabiria* (1957), to which it has retained some resemblances. The heroine has been changed from a sentimental Roman tart to a sentimental New York dance-hall hostess, but the story begins and ends with her abandonment by a man; she spends one evening with a famous actor; there is a "religious" pilgrimage to a jazz revival meeting.

Beyond that, the material has been supplied by Neil Simon and, in the main, without the wit—or even the wise-cracks—that have previously marked his comedies. Possibly Mr. Simon is hampered by working on someone else's ideas. In any event, the result is a series of pattern scenes, generally with pattern characters filling in the shape of the scene with pattern dialogue.

The occasional good line is poorly treated. A man who is trapped in a stalled elevator begins to panic, and says: "I'd be all right if I could just get out for a few minutes." As we laugh, we hear the joke being explained into the ground—and we stop laughing.

But the chief trouble with the show is that it is so patently designed from Moment One to be a heart-tugger. Gwen Verdon, in the name role, appears in silhouette and dances forward as title "credits" are lowered from the flies. The signs read: "The Story of a Girl Who Wanted to be Loved." It is a typographical error: this is the story of a show that wants to be loved.

From this first game-gamine appearance, as we follow Charity through her first betrayal, her glimpse of glamour through an encounter with a film star, her meeting with Mr. Right who eventually does her wrong, up to the very last scene where she literally pleads on her knees for affection, there is scarcely any let-up in this show's appeal to us to smother it with love. Wistful, coy, tremulously plucky, Charity tugs and tugs and tugs at our hearts, and the exercise builds up some pretty stiff resistance.

Miss Verdon, as Charity, has a marathon role in which she is rarely off stage. She is a first-class performer: a good singer, an excellent dancer, a thorough, stage-taking professional. But—and this is partly Mr. Fosse's fault—she plays so unremittingly in the brave-pathetic vein that, abetted by a narrative, nondramatic script, she frequently repeats effects.

The principal male of the evening, John McMartin, tries hard to give conviction to a neurotic swain, in the face of a final switch that is as artificially sad as any Hollywood ending was ever artificially happy. McMartin does particularly well with his comic moments in the stalled elevator.

Helen Gallagher is tough, all right, as another dance hostess, and so is Thelma Oliver. Together—and in a trio with Miss Verdon—they operate smartly.

Mr. Fosse's staging of numbers is often superb. "Big Spender," in which the hostesses line up at a railing that has arisen just behind the footlights, is a splendid mobile frieze of floozies. "Rich Man's Frug" and "Rhythm of Life," the "religious" beatnik number with a sharp vocal arrangement, are electric uses of jazz. Mr. Fosse also employs nice silent-movie touches—subtitles flashed overhead, stopped motion, a little dance satire of film comedy (executed by Miss Verdon).

Cy Coleman here joins the company of the many current show composers who supply appropriate rhythms but no tunes that can be remembered. There is not even a tune that one would *want* to remember. Dorothy Fields's lyrics are no more than serviceable. Irene Sharaff's costumes, as we have come to expect from her, are much more than serviceable—vivid yet not overstated cartoons.

Robert Randolph's lighting and settings are good. I particularly admired the airy outlines (apparently wrought iron) of trees and façades that are lowered from time to time against back-lighting. (Much of this show is done in silhouettes with lighting from back and sides; and Mr. Fosse has conceived much of the dancing and staging with emphasis on elongated profile arrangements.)

But *Sweet Charity* grows tedious between its brightest numbers, despite Mr. Fosse's work and Miss Verdon's professionalism, because it so heavily emphasizes the adjective in the title. The good-hearted dumb broad is one of the oldest of stage clichés. She reappeared only last week in one of Stanley Mann's one-act plays at the Cherry Lane. Here she is paraded as if, merely by recognizing her again, we ought to adore her.

Writing of that same basic cliché in the Fellini original, the English critic John Russell Taylor said: "Right at the film's conception there is something wrong; perhaps it is that while setting up a model of perfect Christian charity and humility Fellini cannot himself believe in it as a human possibility."

Here the sense of that disbelief is greatly increased. Not to ask too much of a musical, we can still note a quickly implanted sense that Charity is merely a theatrical device. No one connected with this show persuades us that she is anything more than a mechanism with which they hope to "get" the audience. Despite all the heat and skill applied, the mechanism remains mechanical.

· · · · · · · · · · · · · · · · · · · · · · · · ·

**OPPOSITE:** Gwen Verdon as Charity.

May 25, 1966

# Mame

By STANLEY KAUFFMANN

*Mame* is back, with music—probably to stay as long as last time when it was *Auntie Mame,* without music. As show biz goes, this is good news. It opened last night at the Winter Garden (I saw the last preview), replete with lively song and dance, an exceptionally able cast, and a splendidly splashy production. Even the scenery is entertaining.

There may be a few benighted Eskimos who still need to be told that the story comes, originally, from Patrick Dennis's novel; was dramatized by Jerome Lawrence and Robert E. Lee and was then filmed. It concerns (dear Eskimo readers) a zesty Manhattan lady of the nineteen-twenties, wealthy and ingratiatingly wild, who inherits a young nephew from her deceased brother and shortly afterward inherits the Depression.

Through thick and several thins, the large-minded lady and the adoring boy make their difficult ways, until she marries a rich

Southerner. After some years of honeymooning abroad, she returns to find Patrick grown and in the grip of a blond suburban bore.

Mame knocks the stuffing out of the prospective stuffy marriage and steers Patrick into a more likely one. At the end, she works her world-opening wiles on Patrick's young son, preparing to Mame him happily for life.

This star vehicle deserves its star, and vice is very much versa. No one can be surprised to learn that Angela Lansbury is an accomplished actress, but not all of us may know that she has an adequate singing voice, can dance trimly, and can combine all these matters into musical *performance.*

In short, Miss Lansbury is a singing-dancing actress, not a singer or dancer who also acts. (Somewhat surprisingly, there is even more character color in her singing than in her spoken dialogue.) In this marathon role she has wit, poise, warmth, and a very taking coolth. The visceral test, I suppose, is whether one is jealous of little Patrick growing up with an aunt like that. I was green.

Then there is little Patrick himself. Child actors in important roles are the chanciest of theater chances. (Two musicals in a row have taken this chance.) Frankie

Michaels, as Patrick, is fine: no saccharin, complete conviction, a good enough singer, and he even dances a little (a tango!). The hazard with young performers is that either they look coached or, if they are gifted, are show-offs. Young Mr. Michaels is neither. He is simply a competent member of the cast, and I'm sure that Miss Lansbury would be the first to assert how difficult her job would be with a lesser nephew.

But grown-ups can be crackerjack professionals, too. Beatrice Arthur plays a sodden stage star, the bosom pal of Mame and a viper in her bosom. Miss Arthur gives a caustic musical-comedy performance that is fluent in skill and superb in timing. There is a particularly long pause that Miss Arthur takes—a very risky moment—that she judges to fine-hair exactness and crowns with a perfect payoff.

Jane Connell is Agnes Gooch, the comic secretary, and this part, as written, is still too broad for me, particularly in the change from chastity to chase. But Miss Connell, another singing actress, plays it better than it deserves, with the caricature rather than character that it asks.

The mature Patrick is firm-jawed Jerry Lanning. Special praise for Diane Coupe in the small role of the girl he eventually marries. With a very few lines Miss Coupe establishes swiftly and sweetly that Patrick is making the right move at last.

Messrs. Lawrence and Lee have applied a neat distilling touch to their original play-script, allowing for what is supplied by songs and dances. In fact, the accidental death of Mame's husband is handled better here than it was in play or film—it is slipped less bumpily into the comic proceedings.

Jerry Herman's score has music that is strongly rhythmic and sufficiently tuneful, and lyrics that are generally deft. I could have done with one less cheer-up number in the first act ("We Need a Little Christmas"). And although the duet between Mame and Patrick after her stage flop is essential, "My Best Girl" has a bit more goo than is good for it.

Still "The Man in the Moon" is the best of the many recent parodies of old-fashioned operettas, "Bosom Buddies" (Mame and her actress friend) is a sharp duelling duet, and the show's title song is a foursquare twenties-type number that whams us into grinning submission. My own favorite, however, is Mame's solo, "If He Walked into My Life," in which she wonders whether she is responsible for the grown Patrick's mistakes—a good song well done by an *actress*.

Gene Saks has directed with inventiveness and an unstrained sense of pace. Onna White's choreography is not startlingly original (after all, she had to do a lot of nineteen-twenties numbers) but it is always spirited. The scenery by William and Jean Eckart is not only pretty but mobile (most of it changes interestingly before your eyes), and the costumes by Robert Mackintosh are gorgeously exaggerated.

Like some other recent musicals, *Mame* is a bit too long, particularly in the first act—which puts an extra burden on the second act. Like most others, it comes to our ears through an amplifying system of which we are never unaware. Like most others, it is, fundamentally, one more trip through material that most of us know very well already; and this is not necessarily a cheery comment on the State of the Theater or the State of Us.

But, whatever those truths may be, the present truth is that *Mame* does its job well with plenty of effective theatrical sentiment, laughs and vitality.

And with Miss Lansbury.

Scenes from *Mame*. **OPPOSITE:** Angela Lansbury and Beatrice Arthur. **BELOW:** Angela Lansbury as Mame with members of the cast.

# CABARET

By WALTER KERR

*Cabaret* is a stunning musical with one wild wrong note. I think you'd be wise to go to it first and argue about that startling slip later.

The first thing you see as you enter the Broadhurst is yourself. Designer Boris Aronson, whose scenery is so imaginative that even a gray green fruit store comes up like a warm summer dawn, has sent converging strings of frosted lamps swinging toward a vanishing point at upstage center. Occupying the vanishing point is a great geometric mirror, and in the mirror the gathering audience is reflected. We have come for the floor show, we are all at tables tonight, and anything we learn of life during the evening is going to be learned through the tipsy, tinkling, angular vision of sleek rouged-up clowns, who inhabit a world that rains silver.

- - - - - - - - - - - - - - - - - - - - - - -

Scenes from *Cabaret*. **ABOVE:** Jack Gilford and Lotte Lenya. **OPPOSITE:** The Kit Kat Club band.

This marionette's-eye view of a time and place in our lives that was brassy, wanton, carefree and doomed to crumble is brilliantly conceived. The place is Berlin, the time the late '20s when Americans still went there and Hitler could be shrugged off as a passing noise that needn't disturb dedicated dancers. Adapted by Joe Masteroff from the Christopher Isherwood–John van Druten materials that first took dramatic form as *I Am a Camera*, the story line is willing to embrace everything from Jew baiting to abortion. But it has elected to wrap its arms around all that was troubling and all that was intolerable with a demonic grin, an insidious slink and the painted-on charm that keeps revelers up until midnight making false faces at the hangman.

Master of Ceremonies Joel Grey bursts from the darkness like a tracer bullet, singing us a welcome that has something of

the old *Blue Angel* in it, something of Kurt Weill, and something of all the patent-leather nightclub tunes that ever seduced us into feeling friendly toward sleek entertainers who twirled canes as they worked. Mr. Grey is cheerful, charming, soulless and conspiratorially wicked. In a pink vest, with sunburst eyes gleaming out of a cold-cream face, he is the silencer of bad dreams, the gleeful puppet of pretended joy, sin on a string.

No matter what is happening during the evening, he is available to make light of it, make sport of it, make macabre gaiety of it.

Perhaps an amoral chanteuse with the mind of a lightning bug ("I guess I am a really strange and extraordinary person") is installing herself without warning in the rented apartment of an American writer, ready to share bed and bread but not for long. Perhaps the landlady is shyly and ruefully succumbing to a proposal of marriage from a Jewish grocer (she is rueful because she is old now, singing "When you're as old as I—is anyone as old as I?") and perhaps the Jewish grocer is beginning to feel the bite of things to come. Precisely as a brick is hurled through her suitor's shop window, Mr. Grey comes bouncing from the portals to grab a gorilla in rose tulle. The two spin into a hesitation waltz with the prim and stately delicacy of partners well-met. Let the world lose its mind, let the waltz go on.

Under choreographer Ronald Field's beautifully malicious management, Mr. Grey is superb, as are the dancers, the four girls who bang at instruments and call themselves the Kit Kat Klub Kittens (even the piano seems to wear feathers), and the unending supply of tenors to give an Irish lilt ("Tomorrow Belongs to Me") to a contrapuntal pause in the tacky, rattling, bizarre and bankrupt goings-on. With the exception of an unlucky last song for landlady Lotte Lenya, the John Kander–Fred Ebb tunes snatch up the melodic desperation of an era and make new, sprightly, high-voltage energy of it,

providing the men of the company with a table-to-table telephone song that comes to seem rhythm in a state of shock, and offering Miss Lenya several enchantingly throaty plaints, notably a winning acceptance of the way things are, called "So What?"

Miss Lenya has never been better, or if she has been, I don't believe it. Suitor Jack Gilford, with just enough hair left to cross his forehead with spitcurls and gamely spinning his partner in spite of clear signs of vertigo, makes his first-act wrap-up, a rapid-fire comic turn called "Meeskite," one of the treasures of the occasion. Bert Convy, as the American with a small whirlwind on his hands, not only acts well but opens his throat for "Why Should I Wake Up?" with the belief and the urgency of a singer who'd never given acting a second thought.

We are left now with the evening's single, and all too obvious, mistake. One of the cabaret tables is empty, the table reserved for heroine Sally Bowles. Sally Bowles, as the narrative has it, is a fey, fetching, far-out lassie with a head full of driftwood and a heart she'd rather break than shackle. She is a temperament, and she needs a temperament to play her.

Producer-director Harold Prince, in a totally uncharacteristic lapse of judgment, has miscast a pretty but essentially flavorless ingenue, Jill Haworth, in the role. Miss Haworth has certain skills and may be able to use them in other ways. Wrapped like a snowball in white fur and sporting that pancake tam that girls of the '20s used to wear whenever they were going to be photographed having snowball fights, she succeeds—at some angles—in looking astonishingly like Clara Bow. But her usefulness to this particular project ends there. She is trim but neutral, a profile rather than a person, and given the difficult things *Cabaret* is trying to do, she is a damaging presence, worth no more to the show than her weight in mascara.

. . . . . . . . . . . . . . . . . . . . . . . . . . . .

**RIGHT:** Joel Grey (center) and members of the cast in the original Broadway production of *Cabaret*, 1966.

March 20, 1998

# Desperate Dance at Oblivion's Brink

By BEN BRANTLEY

Sally Bowles has just stepped into the spot-light, which is, you would imagine, her very favorite place to be. Yet this avidly ambitious chanteuse recoils when the glare hits her, flinching and raising a hand to shade her face. Wearing the barest of little black dresses and her eyes shimmering with fever, she looks raw, brutalized and helplessly exposed. And now she's going to sing us a song, an anthem to hedonism, about how life is a cabaret, old chum. She might as well be inviting you to hell.

Not exactly an upbeat way to tackle a showstopper, is it? Yet when Natasha Richardson performs the title number of *Cabaret*, in the entertaining but preachy revival of the 1966 Kander-Ebb show that opened last night, you'll probably find yourself grinning in a way you seldom do at musicals these days. For what Ms. Richardson does is reclaim and reinvent a show-biz anthem that is as familiar as Hamlet's soliloquy.

She hasn't made the number her own in the way nightclub performers bring distinc-tive quirky readings to standards. Instead, she has given it back to Sally Bowles. Ms. Richardson, you see, isn't selling the song; she's selling the character. And as she forges ahead with the number, in a defiant, metallic voice, you can hear the promise of the lyrics tarnishing in Sally's mouth. She's willing herself to believe in them, and all too clearly losing the battle.

For pleasurable listening, you would of course do better with Liza Minnelli, who starred in the movie version. But it is to Ms. Richardson's infinite credit that you don't leave the theater humming the tune to *Cabaret*, but brooding on the glimpses it has provided of one woman's desperation.

Desperation, and not of the quiet variety, is the watchword of this revival, which has been staged for the Roundabout Theatre Company by the hot young English director Sam Mendes and the American choreographer Rob Marshall. Presented in the Henry Miller Theatre, which the designer Robert Brill has refashioned in the image of the lurid club of the play's title with stage-side tables replacing the orchestra seats, the production pushes hard to remind us that the decadence of Weimar Berlin was far from divine.

This *Cabaret* is seedier, raunchier and more sinister than either the original ground-breaking Broadway version, directed by Harold Prince, or the 1970 movie by Bob Fosse. But it is also, in the long run, less effec-tive. Like its heroine, Sally Bowles, it wants nothing more than to shock, and as with Sally, the desire winds up seeming more naive than sophisticated.

That doesn't mean that you should pass on this *Cabaret*. You would be foolish, first of all, to miss the extraordinary Ms. Richardson, the English stage and film actress last seen on Broadway in *Anna Christie*, who is here giving what promises to be the performance of the season. Her Sally Bowles is a dazzling example of how star power can be harnessed to create a devastating portrait of someone who is definitely not a star. You find yourself thinking less of Ms. Minnelli's winning screw-ball gamine in the same part than of Laurence Olivier in *The Entertainer*.

What's more, in the role of the androgy-nous M.C., who acts as a Brechtian guide to the play's seamy universe, Alan Cumming commits grand theatrical larceny by comman-deering a character that promised to be eter-nally the property of Joel Grey. Mr. Cumming, a Scottish actor making his New York debut, studiously avoids impersonating Mr. Grey's satanic marionette of the Broadway and film versions. Instead, he presents an M.C. with a human face, bruisable beneath the white grease paint and pandering smile.

Scenes from the 1998 revival of Cabaret. **OPPOSITE:** Alan Cumming and members of the cast. **ABOVE:** Natasha Richardson and Alan Cumming.

April 30, 1968

# HAIR

By CLIVE BARNES

What is so likable about *Hair,* that tribal-rock musical that last night completed its trek from downtown, via a discothèque, and landed, positively panting with love and smelling of sweat and flowers, at the Biltmore Theatre? I think it is simply that it is so likable. So new, so fresh and so unassuming, even in its pretensions.

When *Hair* started its long-term joust against Broadway's world of Sigmund Romberg it was at Joseph Papp's Public Theater. Then its music came across with a kind of acid-rock, powerhouse lyricism, but the book, concerning the life and times of hippie protest, was as rickety as a knock-kneed centipede.

Now the authors of the dowdy book—and brilliant lyrics—have done a very brave thing. They have in effect done away with it altogether. *Hair* is now a musical with a theme, not with a story. Nor is this all that has been done in this totally new, all lit-up, gas-fired, speed-marketed Broadway version. For one thing it has been made a great deal franker. In fact it has been made into the

frankest show in town—and this has been a season not noticeable for its verbal or visual reticence.

Since I have had a number of letters from people who have seen previews asking me to warn readers, and, in the urbanely quaint words of one correspondent, "Spell out what is happening on stage," this I had better do. Well, almost, for spell it out I cannot, for this remains a family newspaper. However, a great many four-letter words, such as "love," are used very freely. At one point—in what is later affectionately referred to as "the nude scene"—a number of men and women (I should have counted) are seen totally nude and full, as it were, face.

Frequent references—frequent approving references—are made to the expanding benefits of drugs. Homosexuality is not frowned upon—one boy announces that he is in love with Mick Jagger, in terms unusually frank. The American flag is not desecrated—that would be a Federal offense, wouldn't it?—but it is used in a manner that not everyone would call respectful. Christian ritual also comes in for a bad time, the authors approve enthusiastically of miscegenation, and one enterprising lyric catalogues somewhat arcane sexual practices more familiar to the pages of the *Kama Sutra* than *The New York Times.* So there—you have been warned. Oh yes, they also hand out flowers.

The show has also had to be adapted to its new proscenium form—and a number of new songs have been written, apparently to fill in the gaps where the old book used to be. By and large these new numbers are not quite the equal of the old, but the old ones—a few of them sounding like classics by now—are still there, and this is a happy show musically. Galt MacDermot's music is merely pop-rock, with strong soothing overtones of Broadway melody, but it precisely serves its purpose, and its noisy and cheerful conservatism is just right for an audience that might wince at "Sergeant Pepper's Lonely Hearts Club Band," while the Stones would certainly gather no pop moss.

Yet with the sweet and subtle lyrics of Gerome Ragni and James Rado, the show is the first Broadway musical in some time to have the authentic voice of today rather than the day before yesterday. It even looks different. Robin Wagner's beautiful junk-art setting (a blank stage replete with

broken-down truck, papier-mâché Santa Claus, juke box, neon signs) is as masterly as Nancy Potts's cleverly tattered and colorful, turned-on costumes. And then there is Tom O'Horgan's always irreverent, occasionally irrelevant staging—which is sheer fun.

Mr. O'Horgan has worked wonders. He makes the show vibrate from the first slow-burn opening—with half-naked hippies statuesquely slow-parading down the center aisle—to the all-hands-together, anti-patriotic finale. Mr. O'Horgan is that rare thing: a frenetic director who comes off almost as frequently as he comes on. Some of his more outlandish ideas were once in a while too much, but basically, after so many musicals that have been too little, too much makes a change for the good.

But the essential likability of the show is to be found in its attitudes and in its cast. You probably don't have to be a supporter of Eugene McCarthy to love it, but I wouldn't give it much chance among the adherents of Governor Reagan. The theme, such as it is, concerns a dropout who freaks in, but the attitudes are those of protest and alienation. As the hero says at one point: "I want to eat mushrooms. I want to sleep in the sun."

These attitudes will annoy many people, but as long as Thoreau is part of America's heritage, others will respond to this musical that marches to a different drummer.

You don't have to approve of the Yip-Yip-Hooray roaring boys to enjoy *Hair,* any more than you have to approve of the Royal Canadian Mounted Police to enjoy *Rose Marie,* and these hard-working and talented actors are in reality about as hippie as Mayor Lindsay—no less. But the actors are beguiling. It would be impossible to mention them all, so let me content myself with Mr. Rado and Mr. Ragni, actors and perpetrators both, Lynn Kellogg and Shelley Plimpton—one of the comparatively few holdovers from the original production—who does marvels with a lovely Lennon and McCartney–like ballad, "Frank Mills."

Incidentally, the cast washes. It also has a delightful sense of self-mockery.

**OPPOSITE:** A scene from *Hair.*

Excerpt from August 8, 2008

# *LET THE SUNSHINE IN, AND THE SHADOWS*

By BEN BRANTLEY

It is deep summer in the late 1960s in Central Park, and nobody is keeping off the grass. A heady concentration of anarchic youth has come out to play, flooding the shaggy green patch of turf that has been made of the stage at the open-air Delacorte Theater. And the whiff of hedonism that this crowd emanates induces a serious contact high in anyone who comes near it.

The pure hormonal vitality that courses through the Public Theater's exuberant production of *Hair*, which officially opened Thursday night, is enough to make it the pick-me-up event of New York's dog days this year. But middle-aged audience members who revisit this landmark work from 1967 in search of the feckless flower children they once were are likely to uncover more than they bargained for.

What's so excitingly eye-opening about Diane Paulus's interpretation of *Hair* isn't that it's fun. Put a bunch of kids with decent pipes, lithe bodies and adolescent energy on a stage and let 'em loose on Galt MacDermot's abidingly infectious score, and a certain amount of giddy pleasure is guaranteed.

Mr. MacDermot, after all, once described *Hair* as "the *Hellzapoppin* of its generation," referring to a zany hit revue of the late 1930s. Sure enough, Gerome Ragni and James Rado's book and lyrics, with their quick-sketch comic routines and satiric musical pastiches, suggest good old American vaudeville filtered through a mescaline haze. And Ms. Paulus, who was one of the creators of the long-running Off-Broadway romp *The Donkey Show*, does full justice to this show's madcap friskiness.

But she also locates a core of apprehension in *Hair* that reveals it to be much more than a time-capsule frolic, a *Babes in Arms* for head trippers. The lively teenage rebels of *Hair* may be running headlong after a long good time. But in this production, more than any I've seen, it's clear that they're also running away, and not just from what they see as the dead-end lives of their parents and a man-eating war in Vietnam.

The hippies of this *Hair* are also struggling against a nascent sense that no party can last forever, and that they have no place to go once it's over. The wonderful cast here, led by Jonathan Groff and Will Swenson, present their characters as being subject to the laws of youth as described by the poet Babette Deutsch: "The young whose lips and limbs are time's quick-colored fuel."

Seen 40 years after it first stormed the middle-class citadel of musical comedy, *Hair* registers as an eloquent requiem not only for the idealism of one generation but also for the evanescence of youth itself. It's still the "tribal love-rock" celebration it was always advertised as being. But in suggesting the dawning Age of Aquarius is already destined for nightfall, this production establishes the show as more than a vivacious period piece. *Hair*, it seems, has deeper roots than anyone remembered.

Scenes from the 2008 Public Theater revival of *Hair*. **OPPOSITE, TOP:** Will Swenson (center, left) and members of the cast. **OPPOSITE, BOTTOM:** Will Swenson and Jonathan Groff. **ABOVE:** Tommar Wilson, Will Swenson, and Bryce Ryness.

# Promises, Promises

By CLIVE BARNES

Yes, of course, yes! The Neil Simon and Burt Bacharach musical *Promises, Promises* came to the Sam S. Shubert Theatre last night and fulfilled them all without a single breach. In fact it proved to be one of those shows that do not so much open as start to take root, the kind of show where you feel more in the mood to send it a congratulatory telegram than write a review.

Neil Simon has produced one of the wittiest books a musical has possessed in years, the Burt Bacharach music excitingly reflects today rather than the day before yesterday, and the performances, especially from Jerry Orbach as the put-upon and morally diffident hero, contrive, and it's no easy feat, to combine zip with charm.

Also it is a "new musical" that does, for once, seem entitled to call itself "new." To an extent the new element is to be found in the book, for although ancestors can be found for the story in *How to Succeed in Business* and *How Now, Dow Jones*, the intimacy of the piece is fresh. Even more, there is the beat of the music; this is the first musical where you go out feeling rhythms rather than humming tunes.

The story is based upon the screenplay by Billy Wilder and I. A. L. Diamond for the film *The Apartment*, starring Jack Lemmon and Shirley MacLaine, that has the perhaps enviable reputation of being either one of the most immoral films ever made or else a slashing satire against the American way of business life.

The hero is not a nice man. In fact he is a kind of mouse-fink, who decides to sleep his way to the top in business without really lying. The sleeping is done—in a manner of speaking—not by him but by the senior executives in the life insurance firm in which he works. He gives them the key to his apartment and they give him the key to the executive washroom. They find a haven for their girls, and he finds a haven for his aspirations.

Curiously enough, deep down where it matters he has a kind of battered integrity that suffers from nothing so much as moral color-blindness. Then he falls in love. He falls in love with a girl who is on visiting terms with his apartment but not with him. Guess what happens? You are right the first time.

Mr. Simon's play (and revealingly I find myself thinking of it as much as a play with music as a musical) crackles with wit. The jokes cling supplely to human speech so that they never seem contrived. The whole piece has a sad and wry humanity to it, to which the waspishly accurate wise cracks are only a background.

It is also interesting to see how Mr. Simon wins our sympathy, even our empathy, for his morally derelict hero. In a dramatic trick half as old as time, or at least half as old as Pirandello, he has this dubious young man address the audience direct. The same dubious young man—he must have been great at selling life insurance—takes us so far into his lack of confidence that we feel sorry for him. We even forgive his half-baked way of talking to invisible audiences. Mr. Simon, you see, is a very resourceful man, and persuasive. He wouldn't even have to sell you the Brooklyn Bridge; you would be prepared to rent it.

The music is modern pop and delightful. Mr. Bacharach—always helped by Hal David's happily colloquial lyrics—is no musical revolutionary. Yet the score does have a new beat. It is tense rather than lyrical, and it is fond of bolero rhythms and hidden celestial choirs.

It is Mr. Bacharach who gives the musical its slinky, fur-coated feel of modernity, but it is certainly a feel that has been taken up and even exploited by the staging. Robin Wagner's settings are so architecturally and decoratively perfect for time, place and period that they seem to absorb the characters like the blotting paper style

backgrounds of top class advertisements, while Donald Brooks's costumes look so apt that they will probably need to be changed every three months to keep up.

Even more considerable is the success of Robert Moore, who has directed his first musical with all the expertise of a four-armed juggler. He has dovetailed Michael Bennett's most imaginatively staged musical numbers into the whole, and given the musical notable pace and style.

The cast was virtually perfect. Mr. Orbach has the kind of wrists that look as though they are about to lose their hands, and the kind of neck that seems to be on nodding acquaintanceship with his head. He makes gangle into a verb, because that is just what he does. He gangles. He also sings most effectively, dances most occasionally, and acts with an engaging and perfectly controlled sense of desperation.

Jill O'Hara, sweet, tender and most innocently beddable, looks enchanting and sings like a slightly misty lark, and Edward Winter is handsome and satisfyingly caddish as the man who betrays her, and is finally given his deserts by our worm-turning hero.

Of the rest I enjoyed Paul Reed, Norman Shelly, Vince O'Brien and Dick O'Neill as a quartet of tired business men hoping to get themselves tireder, and two beautifully judged character performances from A. Larry Haines as a doctor in a more than usually general practice, and Marian Mercer as a tiny-voiced hustler with a heart as big as a saloon. I liked finally the girl, Donna McKechnie, who led the dance number at the end of the first act with the power and drive of a steam hammer in heat.

**OPPOSITE:** Jill O'Hara as Fran and Jerry Orbach as Chuck Baxter.

April 27, 1970

# COMPANY

By CLIVE BARNES

With the always possible exception of Vladivostok, Manhattan must surely be the most masochistic village in the world. We expect visitors to our grubby canyons to come to us, exhausted by our pollution, soused by our martinis, maimed by our muggers, and to say: "This *is* hell on earth. How do *you* stand it?"

We agree, feel a little bit prouder, like some survivors from a national catastrophe, and straighten our shoulders for the next day's battle in the streets, in the offices and in the bedrooms of the place that calls us home.

*Company*, a show that opened last night at the Alvin Theatre, and about which I have some personal reservations, deserves to be a hit in a lean season. It is a very New York show and will be particularly popular with tourists—especially those from Vladivostok and Westchester—who will get the kind of insight into New York's jungle that you perceive in the survival-kit information provided by *New York* magazine. Indeed, if you like *New York* magazine you will probably love *Company*.

The musical, directed and produced by Harold Prince, with music and lyrics by Stephen Sondheim and book by George Furth, is about the joys and pains of married love in New York City. Particularly the pains.

Five apparently childless and seemingly unemployed couples are visited by their friend Robert, a Peter-Pannish young man of 35 and a bachelor of fascinating eligibility. Robert seems the only worthwhile thing in these uncertain marriages. He flirts with the principals, introduces a couple of them to pot, watches a karate demonstration between another couple, watches one couple get divorced (they stay together, of course, as man and mistress) and another couple (who had, of course, been living together) get married. He proposes to one girl, is propositioned by another.

In case you had any doubts about his sexual inclinations—and I am not sure that I did—he has three girls on the side. One of them is vulgar enough actually to work for a living. She is an airline stewardess, but luckily takes her hat off in bed.

Creatively Mr. Sondheim's lyrics are way above the rest of the show; they have a lyric suppleness, sparse, elegant wit, and range from the virtuosity of a patter song to a kind of sweetly laconic cynicism in a modern love song. The music is academically very interesting. Mr. Sondheim must be one of the most sophisticated composers ever to write Broadway musicals, yet the result is slick, clever and eclectic rather than exciting. It is the kind of music that makes me say: "Oh, yeah?" rather than "Gee whiz!" but I readily concede that many people will consider its sheer musical literacy as offsetting all other considerations.

Mr. Furth's book is a strange mixture of lines almost witty enough to be memorable and other phrases that more decorously might have been left on the road. The dialogue is starched with a brittle facetiousness that with luck might be confused with a barbed and savage humor. Still, it never talks down to us; indeed, it rises to talk up.

The conception has two difficulties. In the first place these people are just the kind of people you expend hours each day trying to escape from. They are, virtually without exception—perhaps the airline stewardess wasn't too bad—trivial, shallow, worthless and horrid.

Go to a cocktail party before the show, and when you get to the theater you can have masochistic fun in meeting all the lovely, beautiful people you had spent the previous two hours avoiding. You might enjoy it. At least this lot goes away with the curtain, and doesn't know your telephone number.

The second fault is a structural one. Here is a series of linked scenes, all basically similar to one another, and it is left to the director to find a variety of pace and character, and to impose a satisfactory unity on the show. This Mr. Prince has not done. It may not be his fault. The odds were against him.

The setting by Boris Aronson is admirable—a mixture between an East Side multiplex, Alcatraz and an exhibition display of some 20 years ago demonstrating the versatility of elevators. It is all in a tasteful shade of Perspex, and looks better than it sounds.

Michael Bennett is one of those artists who carry the past into the future, and stylizes his view of it into a signature. Of course you can see the influence of Gower Champion, and all the other champions, yet his choreography has genuine vitality, and it is one of the major joys of the show.

The cast, apart from the leading man, Dean Jones, is excellent. In a role that needed a mixture of Dean Martin and Tom Jones, Dean Jones might be thought to have something going for him. He is very amiable, but in this role, at least, he needs more charisma. He needs to be the cynosure of all eyes, the aspiration of all hearts. He comes over as the kind of guy you would be delighted to encounter in a cabaret.

The others are all fine . . . Elaine Stritch, with her den-mother arrogance, is superb. She gives bland lines a bite, and sharp lines the kind of blinding accuracy line-writers dream of. I liked the whole cast, the men perhaps more than the women, Charles Kimbrough, Steve Elmore and Charles Braswell, putting in particularly good work, but I also admired Pamela Myers (given Sondheim's most perfect and imaginative song, "Another Hundred People") and Susan Browning as the wistfully wistful airline stewardess who is doubtless eternally on her way to Barcelona.

I was antagonized by the slickness, the obviousness of *Company*. But I stress that I really believe a lot of people are going to love it. Don't let me put you off. Between ourselves, I had reservations about *West Side Story*.

. . . . . . . . . . . . . . . . . . . . . . . . .

**OPPOSITE:** Larry Kert (who replaced Dean Jones soon after opening night), Elaine Stritch (seated behind Kert), and members of the cast in a scene from *Company*.

April 5, 1971

# *Follies*

By CLIVE BARNES

The musical *Follies*, which opened last night at the Winter Garden, is the kind of musical that should have its original cast album out on 78s. It carries nostalgia to where sentiment finally engulfs it in its sickly maw. And yet—in part—it is stylish, innovative, it has some of the best lyrics I have ever encountered, and above all it is a serious attempt to deal with the musical form.

A theater is being torn down. Between the wars—tap, tap, tap, slurp, slurp, slurp—it was the home of Weismann's Follies where, it seems, that every pretty girl was so much like a melody that the melodies themselves did not matter too much.

Weismann, himself retired and seeing the theater about to take its place among the more attractive parking lots of New York City, throws a first and last reunion party—and all the Weismann girls out of the graveyard and the geriatric ward get together for one final bash. They sing a few of their old numbers and open up a few of their old sores.

Among them are Buddy and Sally, and Ben and Phyllis. Years ago, in 1941, Buddy loved Sally, Sally loved Ben, Phyllis loved Ben, and Ben loved Ben. Buddy married Sally, Ben married Phyllis, but their marriages are not working out. (They rarely do in Stephen Sondheim musicals.)

Now meeting again after 30 years, the girls have left show business, and Buddy is a moderately unsuccessful salesman, while, so far as I can tell, Ben is a world-famous Foundation head who has just written a coffee-table book about someone called Wilson. He has made a fortune and he and his wife bask in Braques, Utrillos and Georgian silver. Their lives though are empty. The other pair's are also empty but in a smaller size.

For a moment it looks as though intellectual Ben will take off with silly little Sally, but they then get involved in some Follies extravaganza and all four end up going off into the bleak Broadway dawn to live unhappily ever after, with their lawful spouses.

James Goldman's book is well enough written; indeed one of its problems is that the writing is far better than the shallow, narrow story, raising expectations that are never fulfilled. When, to give this all-too-eternal quadrilateral dramatic dimension, Mr. Goldman first has their lives intercut with the ghosts of their earlier selves, and finally puts all eight of them into an ironic Follies routine that is meant to comment on their personal and marital plights—by the faded beard of Pirandello he has gone too far.

Mr. Sondheim's music comes in two flavors—nostalgic and cinematic. The nostalgic kind is for the pseudo-oldie numbers, and I must say that most of them sound like numbers that you have almost only just forgotten, but with good reason. This non-hit parade of pastiche trades on camp, but fundamentally gives little in return. It has all the twists and turns of yesteryear, but none of the heart—and eventually the fun it makes of the past seems to lack something in affection. The cinematic music is a mixture of this and that, chiefly that. I doubt whether anyone will be parodying it in 30 or 40 years' time.

The lyrics are as fresh as a daisy. I know of no better lyricist in show-business than Mr. Sondheim—his words are a joy to listen to, even when his music is sending shivers of indifference up your spine. The man is a Hart in search of a Rodgers, or even a Boito in search of a Verdi.

The production has been directed by Harold Prince and Michael Bennett, the latter also arranging the *Late Late Show* style dances. It is all very stylish, with Boris Aronson's beautifully decrepit scenery moving in and out like a TV studio, and Florence Klotz having provided the best costumes to be seen on Broadway.

The first-night audience—which someone should hire intact for openings—adored many of the old-timers. Fifi D'Orsay, Mary McCarty and Ethel Shutta all stopped the show with their gutsy Broadway routines, but although I admired all three, I also felt a little uncomfortable at the nature of my admiration.

It is a carefully chosen cast—which, oddly enough, performed better when I first saw the show Wednesday afternoon—that works very hard. Gene Nelson, who injured himself and last night was unable to perform his flashily effective thirties-style acrobatic dance solo, makes an attractively battered loser out of Buddy; Dorothy Collins, with a simmering torch-song to end, is woebegonely flighty as Sally; John McMartin makes a rakishly and seedily convincing Ben, and Yvonne De Carlo was blowsily adorable as a surviving movie star who had seen better days and worse nights.

My personal favorite was Alexis Smith, however. She looks wonderful—O.K., let's say it, she still looks wonderful—and she has a mixture of ice and vitality that is tantalizingly amusing. She also sings and dances with style and acts with commanding serenity.

There are many good things here—I think I enjoyed it better than the Sondheim/Prince last torn marriage manual *Company*, and obviously everyone concerned here is determined to treat the musical seriously as an art form, and such aspiration must be encouraged.

**OPPOSITE:** A member of the chorus in *Follies*.

# *Flipping Over Follies*

By MARTIN GOTTFRIED

Neither Clive Barnes nor Walter Kerr liked *Follies* and they are this newspaper's drama critics. I am not about to say that they were "wrong," and right and wrong, rave and pan are the least of theater criticism anyway. I do believe, though, that every artwork is either good or it isn't, and I am convinced that *Follies* is monumental theater. Not because I say so but because it is there for anybody to see. Moreover, its importance as a *kind* of theater transcends its interest as an example of a musical. I mean to notice this in *The New York Times* because if this truly great work is not recognized in these pages, then a part of reality will have gone unrecorded there.

*Follies* is not just another hit show. Had it not succeeded so tremendously at what it was trying to do, the attempt alone—the very idea—would have made it a landmark musical. At a time when our musical theater is in a frightful state, devoid of even its traditional professionalism, this production has moved it to a new plateau, has reminded us that the musical is a theater *form*. For those who take the musical theater as seriously as it deserves, this show will henceforth be the standard. Aspirations to opera are now obviously absurd. The musical stage is unique and capable of the mighty.

*Follies* is a *concept musical*, a show whose music, lyrics, dance, stage movement and dialogue are woven through each other in the creation of a tapestry-like theme (rather than in support of a plot). This has been a conscious development in a line of musicals that began with *West Side Story* (whose concept was New York street gangs) and included *Gypsy* (vaudeville), *A Funny Thing Happened on the Way to the Forum* (the relationship between Roman comedies and American burlesque), *Fiddler on the Roof* (Jewish traditions),

*Anyone Can Whistle* (sanity and individuality), *Cabaret* (pre-war German degeneracy), *Zorba* (modern and classic Greece) and *Company* (New York frigidity). Some of these were more conceptual than others, some worked better than others and *Whistle*, one of the most brilliant, was brutally unappreciated, but the idea continued to be developed, even with the abandonment of the theater by its originator, Jerome Robbins.

The concept behind *Follies* is theater nostalgia, representing the rose-colored glasses through which we face the fact of age. In exploring this idea—the fancied past and the painful reality—Harold Prince and Stephen Sondheim have carried the musical theater into size, into grandeur. *Follies* is awesome, it looms out of the Winter Garden's shadows like a giant ghost ship.

This is an appropriate image because the show is conceived in ghostliness. At its very start, ghosts of Follies showgirls stalk the stage, mythic giants in winged, feathered, black and white opulence. Similarly, ghosts of Twenties shows slip through the evening as the characters try desperately to regain their youth through re-creations of their performances and inane theater sentiments of their past.

The book is weak. Admitted. James Goldman's device of a reunion of old Follies girls in a theater being torn down is a clumsy instigation for the action, and his comparative study of two soured marriages is awkward and trite. But Mr. Prince, who is heading toward the inevitable elimination of musical books, has stripped this story down, making the production itself the main event. So, Goldman's four unhappy people are haunted by memories—brought to life by four young actors as their ghosts. They are frightened by the reality of age and the impossibility of regaining old choices, and are forced, finally, to realize that their recollections are as sentimental, as untrue and as dead as the theater that once celebrated such innocence. Fashions of the past are but pages from a calendar (so any criticism of *Follies* as camp is really missing the point—there is nothing gay in this realism). Prince has snatched away the gauze curtain from our nostalgia to reveal the present as a crumbling monument to the past, a decaying body painted over with flaky primary colors.

The very actors in the show are of the past themselves, cast perhaps cruelly. Alexis Smith, Gene Nelson, Dorothy Collins, Yvonne De Carlo, Mary McCarty are people we knew when they were young. Now we see them 20, 30 years older, in contrast to their youth (and ours). In this sense, these actors are used, but of course they must perform too. Miss Smith is astounding, a true, charismatic star and breathtakingly beautiful. Dorothy Collins, *Hit Parade* jokes notwithstanding, has a voice of impressive versatility and range. John McMartin is the one lead with no roots in our youth but, having always had something oddly of the past in his presence and being one of the few singing actors in the theater, he is impeccably cast.

The sets are by Boris Aronson, by anyone's standard the artist of theater designers, and his basic setting is an old theater whose natural decay is being helped along by the wrecker's ball (a little something for the symbolists). Among his sliding platforms and suggested cobwebs, Prince has magnificently used the Twenties musical as a metaphor for one's past (and what else are these "concepts" for musicals but metaphors? Isn't it chilling to realize the mythic in our own and recent history?). One by one, the Follies veterans, reunited at an onstage party, go through their old turns, giving Sondheim his longed-for chance—he is a compulsive satirist—to write Rodgers songs, Arlen songs, Kern songs, De Sylva, Brown & Henderson songs.

Sondheim's qualities as a theater composer can hardly be overstated. He is constantly extending his vision, a composer applying a trained imagination to a stage he intimately understands. He works with, perhaps, the finest orchestrator in our theater's history, Jonathan Tunick, who uses ingenious and sympathetic instrumental combinations to bring out Sondheim's inner voices, his fresh turns of harmony, his inventive meters and surprising resolutions. Sondheim's music is modern even when it is nostalgic and Tunick understands this. Moreover, by writing his own, virtually perfect, lyrics, Sondheim matches the words to the (musical and intellectual) personality of his music as no partner lyricist could possibly do (Porter, Berlin and Loesser are equivalent examples of the unity in a composer-lyricist).

Michael Bennett's dazzling dance memories and perpetually musical staging are as seamlessly woven into that personality, just as they are into Prince's immensely creative general direction. This team has integrated itself so thoroughly as to create a whole, indivisible into its parts, a panorama of a papier-mâché past.

Because of the show's need for song numbers, Sondheim has had to turn from the free-form theater music of *Whistle* and *Company* to pastiches of 32-bar standards (somewhat similar to his score for *Forum* and the song, "You Could Drive a Person Crazy," in *Company*). Given the wonderful accuracy of these pastiches, with their uncanny mixture of the originals' composing idiosyncrasies and Sondheim's Stravinsky-Ravel-Copland orientation, this diversion from his own, ambitious style is only charming.

The charm show criss-crosses with the ghost show like people in a square dance, the two colliding as if one of those dancers had

missed a beat. The disappointed, imperfect reality upsets the nostalgic, perfect dream in the inevitable full-scale Follies that is the production's climax.

Now the carousel runs amok. Mr. Aronson drops down the tinsel and mirrors, Florence Klotz costumes the memories in crimson and satin, the chorus line comes up in top hats and tap shoes. The rememberers in the present dance with their memories. Bewildered, they watch their younger selves sing innocently of romance, the lyrics simultaneously mimicking the past and mocking the present. The whole machine cracks—like the theater in which it is set, like the kind of theater that is being buried, like the recalled bodies, like the optimism, cheerfulness and trust celebrated by the old show business. The *Follies* ghost materializes in ruins as the ground wrenches beneath it. The follies within the Follies within *Follies* turn grotesque and horrific. The characters stumble, confronting each other and their

pasts, going through the Follies acts themselves, some of their ghosts careening in drag (Prince can be excused his own ghost memory of *Cabaret* in this).

Finally, the nightmare-dream passes, the sun comes up and shines through the theater-set's demolished rear wall. The couples leave to live with their wounds, accepting the loss of youth with some of age's wisdom (I'll grant demerits there for pure baloney).

So, *Follies* has its imperfections. It seems overlong because of the lack of an intermission; this is an imposition on the audience and a pause would not have hurt the show's continuity anyhow. The story, though minimized by production, is undeniably simpleminded. Even so, *Follies* is truly awesome and, if it is not consistently good, it is always great.

. . . . . . . . . . . . . . . . . . . . . . . . . . . . . . .

**ABOVE:** John McMartin and members of the chorus in a scene from *Follies*.

**LEFT:** A scene from the original Broadway production of *Follies*, 1971.

## REVIVAL

September 12, 2011

# DARKNESS AROUND THE SPOTLIGHT

By BEN BRANTLEY

Somewhere along the road from Washington to Broadway, the Kennedy Center production of "Follies" picked up a pulse. A vigorous heart now beats at the center of this revitalized revival of James Goldman and Stephen Sondheim's 1971 musical, which opened on Monday night at the Marquis Theater. And though the subject is the ghosts of show business past, don't expect gentle nostalgia. This "Follies" looks back as much in anger as in fondness. That's what makes it so vibrant.

Set in a decaying theater that once housed the Ziegfeld-style Weismann musical revues, "Follies" asks us to measure the warping weight of three decades upon the onetime Weismann performers who reunite "for a final chance to glamorize the old days," as one character says. But there's another, happier computation to consider. That's the changes wrought not by 30 years but by three or four months.

As directed by Eric Schaeffer, "Follies" seemed sleepy and slow when I caught it in Washington in May. Though it perked up in its second act, much of the production felt unfocused and unresolved. Two of its stars, Jan Maxwell and Danny Burstein, were excellent, but you had to question some of the other casting choices. Bernadette Peters, that eternally blooming rose of the American theater, as a faded, dowdy housewife? The hearty Ron Raines as a high-strung businessman on the verge of a nervous breakdown?

I am happy to report that since then, Ms. Peters has connected with her inner frump,

Mr. Raines has found the brittle skeleton within his solid flesh, and Ms. Maxwell and Mr. Burstein have only improved. Two new additions to the cast, Jayne Houdyshell and Mary Beth Peil, are terrific. This production has taken on the glint of crystalline sharpness. If it still has a few soft spots, it is by and large a taut creation, one that finds a white-hot here and now in the shadows of lost time.

When the original "Follies" opened in 1971, it was very much of its time and a breathtaking departure. Broadway was then specializing in nostalgic musicals (like "No, No, Nanette") and dramas of middle-aged disenchantment (paging Edward Albee) — a dichotomy appropriate to the sour years of Vietnam and Watergate. "Follies" took on both sides of the equation. And Goldman's book and especially Mr. Sondheim's songs captured an almost pathological tension between the two.

Directed by Harold Prince and Michael Bennett — and staged with a sumptuousness that would be unthinkable today — the 1971 "Follies" was Broadway's ultimate ghost story, steeped in a hungry and shimmering darkness. In Mr. Schaeffer's version neither the ghosts nor the darkness loom as large. Though gorgeously costumed by Gregg Barnes, the spectral showgirls don't really seem to know why they're there. And Mr. Carlyle's period choreography, though often charming, lacks the grandeur and precision of Bennett's.

Where this "Follies" excels is in its psychological portraiture and character-defining use of Mr. Sondheim's intricately layered songs. (James Moore is the sensitive musical director.) Though few of the performers are natural pastiche artists, they evoke enough of yesteryear's modes and moods to suggest that they've been around. And they skillfully illuminate the tug of war — between youth and age, optimism and cynicism — that swirls within Mr. Sondheim's score.

That tension surfaces most benignly in the showstopping "Who's That Woman," in which the former Weismann Girls, led by a first-rate Terri White, recreate an old production number. Watch their faces as they go though nearly forgotten paces, embracing, and recoiling from, the blithe young things they once were.

Not all the characters are similarly at ease with what they have become, and they fail to heed the show's central admonition, "Never look back" (touchingly sung here by

Rosalind Elias with Viennese-operetta flourishes). As Ms. Paige performs "I'm Still Here" — with a galvanizing fierceness that makes this much-performed song sound fresh and stinging — it's not just an anthem of survival but also of rage against ravaging time.

A performance-honing anger defines each of the four central characters too. Ms. Peters, who in Washington looked entirely too sexy to be Sally, now has the eloquently crestfallen aspect of a woman who's almost given up on life but sees the glimmer of a last chance. The new wig and dress help to play down her natural radiance, but it's the fractured quality in her singing voice (most affectingly deployed in the torchy "Losing My Mind") and line readings that puts across the character as someone for whom resentment is sliding into madness.

Mr. Burstein does his best work to date as the chatty, glad-handing Buddy, whose disappointment chills his every smile. His fantasy number, "Buddy's Blues," becomes a blistering diatribe against unshakable ambivalence. And Mr. Raines, though saddled with some of Goldman's more tedious "smart" dialogue, exudes the fever-pitched heartiness you see in politicians just before their careers crash.

As for Ms. Maxwell, she gets better every time I see her. Her Phyllis (the part for which Alexis Smith won a Tony) is the show's most dazzling embodiment of someone trying both to reclaim and to move beyond her receding past. Her "Could I Leave You?," Phyllis's lacerating assertion of independence to her husband, overflows with both tenderness and hostility.

You see, the girl who fell in love with Ben still lurks anxiously beneath the glossy veneer that Phyllis has since acquired. The younger selves of Phyllis, Ben, Sally and Buddy are dexterously incarnated here by Kirsten Scott, Nick Verina, Lora Lee Gayer and Christian Delcroix. But they're almost superfluous. The four stars of this "Follies" give X-ray performances, in which lives past and souls divided can be seen clearly beneath the skin. Like Mr. Sondheim's music, they make harmony out of the jangling contradictions that come with being alive.

Scenes from the 2011 Broadway revival of *Follies*. **OPPOSITE, TOP:** Bernadette Peters and members of the ensemble. **OPPOSITE, BOTTOM:** From left, Jan Maxwell, Bernadette Peters, and Ron Raines.

# JESUS CHRIST SUPERSTAR

### By CLIVE BARNES

Nothing could convince me that any show that has sold two-and-one-half million copies of its album before the opening night is anything like all bad. But I must also confess to experiencing some disappointment when *Jesus Christ Superstar* opened at the Mark Hellinger Theatre last night.

It all rather resembled one's first sight of the Empire State Building. Not at all uninteresting, but somewhat unsurprising and of minimal artistic value.

Not for the first time has Jesus Christ been made big business. This musical—already very successful on records—tells the story of the Passion of Christ in contemporary terms and accompanied by pop music, ranging from rock-salt to icing-sugar. The story will doubtless be familiar to most. The lyrics are by Tim Rice and the music by Andrew Lloyd Webber. They are young Englishmen of obvious talent, and it is apparent that this midcult version of the Passion story is seriously and sincerely intended.

Mr. Rice's intention was clearly to place Christ's betrayal and death into a vernacular more immediate perhaps to our times. His record sales would presumably indicate his success in this aim, but he does not have a very happy ear for the English language. There is a certain air of dogged doggerel about his phrases that too often sounds as limp as a deflated priest.

It is surely unfortunate, even bathetic, to have Christ at his moment of death remark solemnly: "God forgive them! They don't know what they are doing." The sentiments are unassailable, but the language is unforgivably pedestrian. Again—in another lyric—we have Christ complaining bitterly:

"My time is about through—little left to do—After all I've tried for three years . . . seems like 30 . . . seems like 30."

Well, of course, it sounds better set to music, but not, I feel, better enough.

The music itself is extraordinarily eclectic. It runs so many gamuts it almost becomes a musical cartel. Mr. Lloyd Webber is an accomplished musician—he is one of those rare birds, a Broadway composer who produces his own orchestrations—and he has emerged with some engaging numbers.

The title song, "Superstar," has a bounce and exaltation to it, an almost revivalist fervor that deserves its popularity. I also much admire the other hit of the show, "I Don't Know How to Love Him." This also shows Mr. Rice at his best as a lyricist, although it is perhaps surprising to find this torch ballad sung by Mary Magdalene to Jesus Christ—even a Jesus Christ Superstar. There is a certain vulgarity here typical of an age that takes a peculiar delight in painting mustaches on the *Mona Lisa* and demonstrating that every great man was a regular guy at heart.

Most of the music is pleasant, although unmemorable. It has a pleasing texture, although the orchestral finale, which sounds something like a church-organ voluntary inspired by Vaughan Williams and Massenet, may be a little hard to take for musical ears. The pastiches of the Beatles are far more acceptable, but this is not an important rock score in the manner of *Tommy* by The Who. It is, unhappily, neither innovative nor original.

The music does have the bustling merit of vitality, which is what has made its records sell, and what Tom O'Horgan has seized upon in his monumentally ingenious staging. Ever since his beginning at La Mama, Mr. O'Horgan has tried to startle us. Once he startled us with small things, now he startles us with big things. This time, the things got too big.

There were too many purely decorative effects, artistic excrescences dreamed up by the director and his designers, Robin Wagner and Randy Barcelo, that seemed intended to make us gasp and our blood run cold. The stage is full of platforms, carriages descend from the heavens, and even the

stars over Gethsemene are captured in a blue plastic box. The total effect is brilliant but cheap—like the Christmas decorations of a chic Fifth Avenue store.

It is unfortunate that the sound equipment—which sounded rather blurred, incidentally—involved the use of hand-mikes, which, while dressed up as pieces of rope, and occasionally handed around from actor to actor like holy chalices, remained unmistakably mikes—not least when Jesus jumps up dramatically to seize one, in the approved TV spectacular manner.

For me, the real disappointment came not in the music—which is better than run-of-the-mill Broadway and the best score for an English musical in years—but in the conception. There is a coyness in its contemporaneity, a sneaky pleasure in the boldness of its anachronisms, a special, undefined air of smugness in its daring. Christ is updated, but hardly, I felt, renewed.

The performances played second fiddle to the memories of the record album and the virtuosity of Mr. O'Horgan's own performance. Christ was made into a shrill-voiced neurotic, who looked like all the right pictures. He was played with some dignity by Jeff Fenholt. But it was not a rewarding view of Christ, although at one with the limp-wristed, rosily maquillaged Herod, the obviously conniving Caiaphas, or the spitefully Roman Pilate. This last was a good performance by Barry Denen, and I admired the tortured Judas of Ben Vereen, and the well-sung Mary Magdalene of Yvonne Ellman—one of the few survivors from the album.

For all this, *Superstar* seemed to me less than super—but the novelty of its aspirations should win it many adherents.

. . . . . . . . . . . . . . . . . . . . . . . . . . . . . . .

**OPPOSITE:** Jeff Fenholt and members of the cast in *Jesus Christ Superstar.*

February 15, 1972

# Grease

By CLIVE BARNES

They are starting to be nostalgic about 1959 now—and almost all I can remember about it is that it was a great year for Burgundy. However, it was probably quite good for Coca-Cola as well, and last night at the Eden Theatre we had the opening of *Grease*, a rock 'n' roll musical that tries to transport us back to those dear dead days when Elvis still had his pelvis, butter didn't melt in Sandra Dee's mouth, hair styles looked like James Dean's and Marlon Brando rode a motorcycle.

It was, as historians say, a time of transition. America was between wars and popular music had become influenced by the rhythm 'n' blues style of singers such as Chuck Berry, so rock 'n' roll was starting to rock. But the Beatles and their successors had not yet arisen to give rock the sophistication it was later to acquire.

*Grease*, which originated in Chicago, is a parody of one of those old Elvis Presley campus movies—and if that is what you think you are ready for, please don't let me stop you.

It is said to be set at a reunion of a high school class of 1959, but very little is made of the reunion aspect. However, as most of the so-designated teenagers look trustworthily over 30, perhaps they were meant to be playing their past.

The show has been written, book, music and lyrics, by Jim Jacobs and Warren Casey. It is perhaps most successful in its suggestion of attitude and period, and there are times when *Grease* catches the flavor of its time. The gang fights—remember *West Side Story*? The authors do—and the shy emergence of the new morality that made the summer of '59 different for teenagers from the summer of '42.

The story is about the guy who should have been Elvis Presley getting his girl after a certain degree of misunderstanding. Not even Elvis Presley himself could ever have thought it an interesting story—and it still isn't.

The music is the loud and raucous noise of its time. It is meant to be funnier than it is, but the authors are forever being frustrated by the nature of what they are satirizing and its comparative nearness to contemporary pop music. Interestingly, the score is usually at its best when we are being given comic versions of tearjerking ballads—such as the heroine's plaintive lament: "It's Raining on Prom Night."

There is a cosy aggressiveness to the show, a deliberately loud-mouthed and facetious tastelessness that some will find attractive, especially, I imagine, those who were teenagers in Middle America at the end of the 1950s. But the show is a thin joke. As with almost all pastiches, once the initial joke has been established, it is bound to wear thin.

The production is a good one. Douglas W. Schmidt's settings, making clever use of photo-montage, are both effective and adaptable; Carrie F. Robbins's costumes and Jim Sullivan's hair styles ruthlessly re-create the sartorial and tonsorial monstrosities of the time; Tom Moore's direction and, best of all, Patricia Birch's engagingly fresh dances, both make a great contribution.

The cast worked hard and well, with an almost manic enthusiasm. The men, in particular, caught the right, cool attitude of the period—that nodding of the head and smoky disdain of the eyes. As the hero and heroine, Barry Bostwick and Carole Demas could not have been better; as the tough second couple, Adrienne Barbeau and Timothy Meyers were good as well as tough, and Alan Paul as a pop singer showed flair and style.

If there is a place in New York for a modern 1950s rock parody musical from Chicago, then *Grease* might well slide into it. If there is a place. The first-night audience seemed genuinely to enjoy it, so perhaps there is.

Scenes from *Grease*. **BELOW:** Carole Demas and Barry Bostwick. **OPPOSITE:** Adrienne Barbeau (center) and Barry Bostwick (top right).

## TRANSFER TO BROADWAY

June 4, 1972

# GREASE? GROOVY

By HARRIS GREEN

The kind of musical that Broadway has needed for some time will finally get there this week—after playing for quite a while Off Broadway. On Wednesday, *Grease* transfers from the Eden Theatre on Second Avenue to the Broadhurst on West 44th Street. Singularly unappetizing as its title is, the show should prove most nourishing for Broadway. Somehow, it has managed to combine the two commodities everyone agrees our theater most requires: younger audiences and what I can best describe—not too ponderously, I trust—as "older virtues." That is, *Grease* deserves the adjectives we once awarded shows like *Pal Joey*, *Kiss Me, Kate*, *Guys and Dolls* and *The Pajama Game* but haven't had much call for recently.

This season, rock has come to be considered so potent an esthetic form that it has been treated as if it were suitable for any subject, even for texts as demanding as Euripides or the New Testament. This is also the season when a social conscience became so fashionable on Broadway that matters such as slum clearance, drug addiction and criminal insanity were felt to be toe-tapping topics for song and dance. For several seasons we haven't had many musicals that deserve to be hailed as "brash . . . charming . . . unsentimental . . . light-hearted . . . spunky . . . high-spirited . . . unpretentious." Good word, that "unpretentious"! Thanks to *Grease*, all are applicable once more. The musical comedy is both musical and comic once more. The younger audiences supporting it may not realize how good the show they are seeing is, and the—to be as tactful as possible—older audiences who are

avoiding it certainly do not know what they are missing.

An older theatergoer's reluctance to see *Grease* is understandable. Its producers advertised it, for a while, as "the new '50s rock 'n' roll musical," so one might have received the impression that its creators, Jim Jacobs and Warren Casey, are fondly recalling the raunchy puerilities of the Jerry Lee Lewis-Sandra Dee era one would just as soon forget. Actually, Jacobs and Casey view the period with that rare blend of affection and consternation that Sandy Wilson brought to *The Boy Friend*.

They are so unsentimental about the brutishness of Elvis and the inanities of Annette that it wouldn't surprise me to learn they'd dashed the whole show off one weekend—possibly after watching an old beach-party flick on TV—when the pluperfect mindlessness of what they'd once taken seriously struck them with such force that each sprang to his typewriter or guitar, writhing with inspiration. Nowhere in *Grease* is there that mad delight in the insipid past that has permitted nostalgia to rage like a plague on Broadway.

And if my older theatergoer protests that an evening spent with "a bunch of foul-mouthed young louts and sluts" strikes him as unpromising, I must remind him that a show about a garment strike did not sound

any too rewarding in 1954, either, yet who but the most arteriosclerotic member of the N.A.M. was pained by *The Pajama Game*? And would anyone care to guess what that little musical would be like today, if it were to be created in the tuneless, plotless, radical-chic manner Melvin Van Peebles used for his aptly titled *Ain't Supposed to Die a Natural Death*? Or the more songful but just as incongruous revue form Tom O'Horgan employed for his late, unlamented *Inner City*?

Some may feel the musical has come a long way, indeed, when its composers take on topics like urban angst, paranoia and others, equally gay, which would have given Mahler and Berg pause. I fear those who create such musicals, along with their long-suffering public, are smitten with what I call "charity-ball syndrome," which allows the show-biz types to make a buck and their fans to spend one and all to ease their social consciences by believing "it's for a good cause."

The musical, I think we need to be reminded, is not a sociological thesis with a sense of rhythm or an opera gone slumming—or the highest form of theater, for that matter. But the special diversion it offers is always welcome, if it's high-spirited and unpretentious. *Grease*, for the most part, is. It deserves to be moved to Broadway, as a reminder, if nothing else.

October 24, 1972

# PIPPIN

By CLIVE BARNES

An amiable and racy musical, *Pippin*, which arrived at the Imperial Theatre last night, has three great things to commend it. It is one of the best musical stagings to be seen on Broadway in years, it is most beautifully designed and it might well do for the actor Ben Vereen what *Cabaret* did for Joel Grey.

*Pippin* is about Pippin, or, if we are going to be historically accurate, Pepin. But the musical is not going to be historically accurate, and it is none the worse for that. Pippin, or Pepin, was the son of Charlemagne, and this musical is set in the year 780 and concerns the Holy Roman Empire, but not too holily or imperially.

The book has been written by Roger O. Hirson and the music and lyrics are by Stephen Schwartz, composer of the international hit *Godspell*. The concept, and it is a conceptual musical of the type people are fond of dubbing "innovative," has Pippin's career spelled out for him by a troupe of Callot-like commedia dell'arte clowns. There is someone, a solitary figure in modern dress, who is called the Leading Player, and is a cross between master of ceremonies, manager of the troupe and God. He tells us of the life and times of Pippin.

Pippin is an extraordinary young man, the son of a great Emperor, talented and handsome. Yet he feels the "need to be completely fulfilled." He tries war, sex, revolution and domesticity. All to no avail. As a grand finale he is offered the ultimate transfiguration of fire, death by immolation in a magician's hoop. Not unpredictably he refuses this and settles back for domesticity, wife and family.

It is, I felt, a trite and uninteresting story with aspirations to a seriousness it never for one moment fulfills. It is a commonplace set to rock music, and I must say I found most of the music somewhat characterless.

What will certainly be memorable is the staging by Bob Fosse. This is fantastic. It takes a painfully ordinary little show and launches it into space.

From the first moment until almost the last (for nothing can totally redeem the book's lame duck ending) Mr. Fosse never loses his silk and velvet grasp on the show. He works desperately—and successfully—hard to give the tired old idea of a group of clowns some artificial resuscitation—he even makes sense of the superhuman commentator and he gives the show the pace of a roller derby and the finesse of a conjuror. Yet nothing seems strained or exaggerated.

Mr. Fosse has achieved complete continuity between his staging and his choreography, and his dances themselves have art and imagination. They swing with life. Mind you, Mr. Fosse has two master collaborators in Tony Walton and Patricia Zipprodt.

Mr. Walton's scenery manages an almost impossible combination of Holy Roman Empire and Fifth Avenue chic. He has also provided scenery that will slide, fold, make itself scarce when necessary, and when equally necessary even adaptable. This is exactly suited to Mr. Fosse's pell-mell dazzle. Miss Zipprodt has accomplished her task with equal adroitness and elegance—her clowns look Italian and Fellini and her girls look French and naked. It is probably just right for the Holy Roman Empire.

The cast also lives up to Mr. Fosse rather than down to its material. Eric Berry is fun as the bibulous, cynical Charlemagne, Leland Palmer splendid as his Jewish mother of a wife and Jill Clayburgh all sweet connivance as the widow out to get her man. Irene Ryan has one tremendous show-stopper as a geriatric swinger and John Rubinstein possesses all the natural grace and radiance needed for this Candide-like hero.

It was, I felt, Mr. Vereen who really held the show together. His mocking presence and voice, his deft dancing and easy authority, make his performance one of the most impressive aspects of the evening.

The book is feeble and the music bland, yet the show runs like a racehorse. It was probably Mr. Fosse's night, and playgoers contemplating an evening of theatrical prestigiditation, a handful of most pleasing performances and a few notably pretty girls (I'd wondered whatever happened to Jennifer Nairn-Smith after she left the New York City Ballet) will not be disappointed.

**LEFT:** Kathryn Doby, Ben Vereen, and Candy Brown in a scene from *Pippin*.

# A LITTLE NIGHT MUSIC

By CLIVE BARNES

At last a new operetta! At last resonances and elegances in a Broadway musical. *A Little Night Music*, which opened at the Shubert Theatre last night, is heady, civilized, sophisticated and enchanting. It is Dom Perignon. It is supper at Laserre. It is a mixture of Cole Porter, Gustav Mahler, Antony Tudor and just a little of Ingmar Bergman. And it is more fun than any tango in a Parisian suburb.

It is set in Sweden at the turn of the century. It is also the turn of the year. Those mysterious white nights in Sweden, when people smile and go mad to the sound of the folk dancing and the breaking of hearts and schnapps glasses.

Hugh Wheeler, who has written the book, got his suggestion from that old and lovely Bergman movie—one of the director's few comedies—*Smiles of a Summer Night*. It is not too like the film, which in a musical works to its advantage.

A lawyer has married some 30 years beneath him, and after 11 months of marriage his child-bride, beautiful, delicate and wondering, is still a virgin. On impulse he visits an old—but not too old—actress friend of his, and is discovered, most compromisingly, by her hussar lover. The hussar's wife offers to put everything right, by establishing the fidelity of her husband's mistress. The actress's mother,

who takes care of her daughter, is persuaded to invite the lawyer, his son, who is madly in love with his mother-in-law, and, of course, the wife, together with a strayly amorous servant, to a country weekend at her villa. The hussar, and his loyal wife, intrude.

And that is only the first act.

Mr. Wheeler's book is uncommonly urbane and witty. The jokes are funny, and the very real sophistication has considerable surface depth. Yet perhaps the real triumph belongs to Stephen Sondheim, who wrote the music and lyrics. The music is a celebration of ¾ time, an orgy of plaintively memorable waltzes, all talking of past loves and lost worlds.

Despite the idea of a waltz-musical, which somehow suggests one of Strauss's, or the title, so redolent of Mozart, it seems that Mr. Sondheim is aiming at the lilt of Mahler. There is a peasant touch here, a sense of country values. For all its sophistication it is a story in which the stables are more important than the chandeliers.

Then, of course, there are Mr. Sondheim's breathtaking lyrics. They have the kind of sassy, effortless poetry that Cole Porter mastered. The mother announces grandly: "I acquired some position—plus a tiny Titian," and this is coming from a lyricist who only seconds before has dazzlingly made "raisins" rhyme with "liaisons." Grace is abounding—who but Mr. Sondheim would dare: "The hip-bath, the hip-bath, how can you trip and slip into a hip-bath." You have to be very hip, and Mr. Sondheim is.

It is also a particular triumph for the producer and director, Harold Prince. For years he has been attempting to bring—or so it has seemed to me—something of the sensibility of the serious lyric theater, specifically perhaps the ballet, into American musicals. Here he has pulled it off in a way he didn't in *Follies* or *Company*.

The mood is here perfectly placed. The choreography—subtly, almost unnoticeably, contrived by Patricia Birch—helps, but the profile of the show, its style and pattern, is practically palpable. People have long been talking about Mr. Prince's conceptual musicals; now I feel I have actually seen one of the actual concepts.

Boris Aronson's scenery is, oddly enough, good only in patches. The swiftly shifting patterns of the show (which reveals its cinematic derivation here) have given Mr. Aronson the difficulty of constantly changing scenes, which he solves with screens of silver birches.

These, while decorative enough, become a little tiresome. However, his villa is a delight, and he has devised a front-cloth that is pure Swedish Drottningholm baroque. The costumes by Florence Klotz are sumptuous and knowingly aware, while the lighting by Tharon Musser puts all the soft and cold smiles into this particular summer night.

Finally, but not least, the performances. Casting, in the past, has not always been as princely as this producer's other activities.

Here he gets it right, first time around. Hermione Gingold is immeasurably grande dame as the almost Proustian hostess (I haven't loved her so much since she sang about the Borgia orgies 30 years ago) and all are cut to style.

The misty-voiced and glistening-eyed Glynis Johns was all tremulous understanding as the actress, and Len Cariou was delightfully and jauntily battered as the husband whose wife doesn't even know him, let alone understand him.

Laurence Guittard was a splendidly stuffed hussar, Patricia Elliott decently spirited as his wife, Victoria Mallory all sugar as the virgin wife, and D. Jamin-Bartlett sensationally all spice as the less than virgin maid.

*A Little Night Music* is soft on the ears, easy on the eyes, and pleasant on the mind. It is less than brash, but more than brassy, and it should give a lot of pleasure. It is the remembrance of a few things past, and all to the sound of a waltz and the understanding smile of a memory. Good God!—an adult musical!

. . . . . . . . . . . . . . . . . . . . . . . . . . . .

Scenes from *A Little Night Music*. **OPPOSITE:** From left, Glynis Johns, Laurence Guittard, Hermione Gingold, Patricia Elliott, and William Daniels. **ABOVE:** Glynis Johns and Len Cariou.

January 6, 1975

# THE WIZ

By CLIVE BARNES

Criticism is not objective. This does not mean that a critic cannot see qualities in a work that does not evoke much personal response in himself. A case in point is *The Wiz*, a black musical that opened last night at the Majestic Theatre. It has obvious vitality and a very evident and gorgeous sense of style. I found myself unmoved for too much of the evening, but I was respectfully unmoved, not insultingly unmoved. There is a high and mighty difference.

L. Frank Baum's *The Wonderful Wizard of Oz* has been a standard children's story almost since its first publication in 1900. A year later Baum himself made a theatrical adaptation of the piece, and there have been other stage versions. But it was in Victor Fleming's 1939 movie, starring Judy Garland as the little Kansas girl whisked away on a cyclone along the yellow brick road to the Land of Oz, that the story received what was really its definitive treatment.

The idea of the present staging appears to have been that of the producer, Ken Harper, and one can easily see his line of thought. With a musical mixture of rock, gospel and soul music, written by Charlie Smalls, who provided both score and lyrics, *The Wiz* is intended as a new kind of fantasy, colorful, mysterious, opulent and fanciful. It was also obviously meant to be a fantasy for today—very modern, a dream dreamed by a space-age child.

The concept is very good in theory, but the practice is not made perfect. Mr. Smalls's music—vastly overamplified by the way—sounded all too insistent and oddly familiar. It had plenty of verve but it lacked individuality.

It is the over-all style of *The Wiz* that gives it its overriding impact. It has all been very carefully conceived and shaped. Not only is Mr. Smalls's music all of a piece but the visual aspect of the production—with handsomely stylized settings by Tom H. John and vibrantly colored and wackily imaginative

costumes by Geoffrey Holder—offers a fresh and startling profile. This is first-rate and highly innovative.

Unfortunately, with the blaring, relentless rhythms of Mr. Smalls's music and the visually arresting but rather tiring scenic spectacle, the total result is a little cold. This is not helped by a somewhat charmless book by William F. Brown.

It is eventually the story, or more correctly the treatment of the story, that I found tiresome. A fairy tale, to work, has to have magic. We have to give ourselves up to it, to suspend our cynical disbeliefs and, to some extent, identify with the characters. To me, this proved impossible in *The Wiz*. The little girl in the film played by Miss Garland was an utterly real person. The Dorothy in *The Wiz* never for a moment has those dimensions. And the Scarecrow, the Tinman and the Lion (who, in memory, must always be Bert Lahr), while fantastic, are rarely amusing.

None of this was the fault of the performers. Stephanie Mills, however, who plays Dorothy, while having a really wonderful voice, unusually mature for a 15-year-old, did not have a very persuasive personality. The singing throughout was first-class, particularly from Mabel King and Dee Dee Bridgewater, who both have big and beautiful voices.

The rest of the cast is admirable, including Tiger Haynes, Ted Ross and the gracefully loose-limbed Hinton Battle as the comic trio helping Dorothy on her way to the Emerald City, and Andre de Shields as the sardonic Wiz. Nor can fault be found with the staging. Mr. Holder (who took the assignment while the show was on the road) has directed *The Wiz* with a characteristic feel for movement, and the vibrant choreography by George Faison (here making his Broadway debut) is almost invisibly meshed in with the general staging.

When so much is individually good it is difficulty to justify a personal sense of disappointment. Perhaps it is, at least for me, that fantasy is enthralling only when it is rooted in experience. Also the stylistic unity of the show, which may prove very exciting to many Broadway theatergoers, is, of course, familiar to me from years of going to the ballet and the opera, so its originality is diluted. There are many things to enjoy in *The Wiz*, but, with apologies, this critic noticed them without actually enjoying them.

. . . . . . . . . . . . . . . . . . . . . . . . . . . . . . . .

Scenes from *The Wiz*. **ABOVE:** Stephanie Mills (in white), Clarice Taylor (far right), and members of the cast. **OPPOSITE:** Andre de Shields as the Wiz with members of the cast.

# A Chorus Line

By CLIVE BARNES

The conservative word for *A Chorus Line* might be tremendous, or perhaps terrific. Michael Bennett's new-style musical opened at the Newman Theater of the New Shakespeare Festival Public Theater on Lafayette Street last night, and the reception was so shattering that it is surprising if by the time you read this, the New York Shakespeare Festival has got a Newman Theater still standing in its Public Theater complex on Lafayette Street. It was that kind of reception, and it is that kind of a show.

We have for years been hearing about innovative musicals; now Mr. Bennett has really innovated one. *A Chorus Line* takes a close, hard squint at Broadway babies on parade—here and now. The scene is a Broadway gypsy encampment—and the chorus, and how to get into it, is the line of battle.

It is easy to see from where *A Chorus Line* evolved. It is in direct succession to Harold Prince's *Company*, and, to a lesser extent, *Cabaret* and *Follies*. The debt is unmistakable, but it has been paid in full. What makes *A Chorus Line* so devastatingly effective is its honesty of subject matter—so that even its faults can work for it.

Show-business musicals always start with a certain advantage. Even their clichés can pass for justifiable observation of the form, and Mr. Bennett was obviously aware of this when he had his idea. But the idea is bright—indeed, it glows like a beacon heavenward. Like most great ideas it is simple. It is nothing but the anatomy of a chorus line. And the gypsies themselves—those dear, tough, soft-bitten Broadway show dancers, who are the salt and the earth of the small white way—are all neatly dissected as if they were a row of chickens. Their job-hunger, their sex lives, their failures (because even the best of them never thought of themselves forever in the chorus but 99 percent of them will be there until they drop or drop out),

their feeling toward dancing, why they started and what they might do when they stop—all is under a coruscatingly cruel microscope.

Of course, the show—which has been brilliantly written by James Kirkwood and Nicholas Dante—has a long streak of sentimentality where its heart might have been, but this is show business, baby, and even the sentimentality is true to form. We accept it—and rightly so—as part of the scene. For Mr. Bennett has found a marvelous set-up for his exploration into the life and times of the contemporary show dancer. It is an audition.

The director of a new show has whittled down his choice of 24 people to 17. The 17 are lined up before him. He needs eight, or what he calls "four and four." Four boys and four girls—and "how about us women?" as one of the girls says. One by one—as he calls them out—he has them step from the line and talk. Talk about themselves—what they are doing there in that rehearsal hall on that morning. It is psychological striptease, and slowly the kids undress in a series of sad if funny vignettes. There is the girl who wanted to be a ballerina, the boy who discovered he was homosexual, the girl who flunked Stanislavsky motivation at the High School of Performing Arts and the somewhat elderly Puerto Rican boy who never had his father call him son until he found him working in a drag show. (Try to get the Stanislavsky motivation for that one—it is beyond me.)

Even the director has a story to tell. His girl, fearful of the saccharine smell of his success, walked out on him, and now, after failure and heartbreak in Los Angeles, she is back, in the audition, trying to win a way back onto the chorus line. Yet somehow all the hokum works—because it is undisguised and unapologetic.

The music by Marvin Hamlisch is occasionally hummable and often quite cleverly drops into a useful buzz of dramatic recitative.

Mr. Hamlisch is not such a good composer as he was in the movie *The Sting* when he was being helped out by Scott Joplin, but he can pass, and the lyrics by Edward Kleban do more than that, they pass with a certain distinction, while the look of the show (an explosion of mirrors that may owe something to the *Cabaret* set but is still food for reflection) and the cast is 105 percent marvelous.

One simply must mention a few—Donna McKechnie as the prodigal chorine, for example, is wonderfully right, as are Clive Clerk as the reluctant drag artist, Priscilla Lopez as the histrionic dropout, Carole Bishop as the fast-talking brunette who wasn't even born the day before yesterday, and Robert Lupone as the uptight director, who, like all the others, could be a portrait, or a composite portrait, of so many failed successes. For honesty is the policy of Mr. Bennett's show, and from opening to the stupendous closing chorus, it is, stamped indelibly, as Mr. Bennett's show.

His choreography and direction burn up superlatives as if they were inflammable. In no way could it have been better done.

It is in a small theater and here, at last, is the intimate big musical. Everything is made to work. The groupings are always faultless, the dances have the right Broadway surge, and two numbers, the mirror-dance for Miss McKechnie and the Busby Berkeley–inspired finale, deserve to become classics of musical staging. And talking of classics, while there will be some to find fault, perhaps with a certain reason, with the hard-edged glossiness of *A Chorus Line*, it is a show that must dance, jog and whirl its way into the history of the musical theater. *Oklahoma!* it isn't, but no one with strength to get to the box office should willingly miss it. You will talk about it for weeks.

. . . . . . . . . . . . . . . . . . . . . . . . . . . . . . . .

Scenes from *A Chorus Line*. **OPPOSITE, TOP:** Members of the cast. **OPPOSITE, BOTTOM:** From left, Sammy Williams, Pamela Blair, Donna MacKechnie, Robert LuPone, Carole Bishop, and Priscilla Lopez.

June 15, 1975

# How A Chorus Line Was Born

By ROBERT BERKVIST

"There is *truth* on that stage—nothing monumental or astounding, but truth nonetheless. The audience starts believing in those chorus dancers right away. In fact, people seem to be finding *A Chorus Line* more believable than most plays they've seen recently. It's this experience that makes the show different, makes it innovative."

Michael Bennett, who conceived, choreographed and directed the new musical that is the surprise hit of the season downtown at the Public Theater, was responding to the critics who had almost unanimously hailed his show as a new-style musical. We were talking on the sunny terrace of Bennett's midtown apartment cum office. Bennett, a slight, wiry figure in faded T-shirt and jeans, was relaxing for the first time in months; his bonily ascetic face, with its odd combination of close-trimmed Amish-style chin whiskers and Sicilian mustache, showed the accumulated fatigue of long hours of rehearsal, and the dawning realization of gold-plated success. "I'm trying to keep myself in check," he admitted. "I could spend the rest of my life chasing this show, trying to top myself, and that's a trap I want to stay out of."

A line in the playbill reads, "This show is dedicated to anyone who has ever danced in a chorus or marched in step . . . anywhere." Bennett says he included that tribute as a measure of respect and affection for the dancers who give life and form to his art. At 32, Bennett, a former chorus "boy" himself, is quick to acknowledge his roots and debts. "Broadway dance," he observes simply, "is what I know, what I was, and what I am. In *A*

*Chorus Line*, I tried to show the audience exactly what Broadway dancing is all about, on all its levels."

The show is staged like an audition. Twenty-four dancers are trying out for eight openings in the chorus line of an upcoming musical. The director sizes them up, immediately cuts their number to 17 and then invites the rest to step forward, one by one, and tell him something true about themselves. This they do, telling stories that range from broken homes to homosexuality to dreams of glory sparked by the Moira Shearer dance film *The Red Shoes*. Finally, the director rejects all but four boys and four girls. The others pack up their rehearsal clothes, and their hopes, for another audition.

The intensely personal responses of the candidates to the director's cold interrogation are, of course, a gimmick, a hook upon which to impale the audience's concern. At a real audition, there is neither time nor money for on-stage psychotherapy. But, says Bennett, the dancers' revelations have the effect of a collective biography. "True, some of the show is autobiographical in that it draws on my own experience. For example, my parents took me to dancing school, back home in Buffalo, when I was 3 years old, and even then I knew that it made me special— and that's a nice anecdote for the show, but I hope *A Chorus Line* says more than that. By the way, if you think Zach, the director in the show, is cold and hard, I have to say that the nicest thing a director can be in an audition is businesslike. Don't be friendly, don't raise false hopes; let the rejected candidate walk out with dignity." Bennett himself had lots of practice at this in the course of casting his show, looking for "the best dancers I could find, who could also act." He estimates that more than 300 dancers tried out for fewer than a dozen roles—truly a case of life reflecting art reflecting life.

What was the genesis of *A Chorus Line*? Bennett smiles. "You may not believe this," he says, "but the show grew out of my feelings as I watched the Watergate hearings; it's my reaction to the falsehood and apathy that seemed to grip the country during that period. I was sick of it. I wanted to do something on stage that would show people being honest with one another."

Bennett had also been thinking of creating a show solely with dancers, and the two

impulses came together one weekend in January of 1974 when he invited 24 first-rate dancers to join him at an East Side studio for a midnight workout and rap session. "I had the germ of an idea for a show about people like us," he says. "I brought along a tape recorder and we talked for hours about what we were doing, what we were after, that sort of thing. I asked everybody to tell me the whys and hows of their careers, as truthfully as they could.

"That session was so long and fruitful that we met for another one. We all walked out of those talks feeling that it had been a special time. Dancers, you know, are very open people. I think that's because they spend so much of their lives, from childhood on, practicing in front of a mirror. A dancer has to acknowledge strengths and weaknesses. Not that we're saints—we can be extremely narcissistic—but we're unaccustomed to hiding the truth from ourselves. A mirror doesn't lie."

Bennett came away from those group analysis sessions with about 30 hours of tape-recorded truths—and perhaps a smattering of narcissistic hyperbole. He sat listening to the tapes for several months, wondering what to do with them. "Then I realized," he said, "that what those kids had been doing was auditioning their lives for me." The audition idea took hold. Bennett called in a friend, Nicholas Dante, a dancer turned writer, and the two spent last summer editing and reworking the material into script form. Bennett also went to Joseph Papp and said he had a show he wanted to try out in workshop form at the Public Theater. Papp gave him the go-ahead, which meant that Bennett had a commitment of basic production funds from the Public.

The next step was music. Bennett decided to ask an old friend, Marvin Hamlisch, to do the score. "Marvin had just won all those Oscars for *The Way We Were* and *The Sting*. When I told him I wanted him to come East to do an Off Broadway musical on a workshop basis with no money in sight, well, he really wrestled with the idea for a while." Bennett laughed. "He wrestled with his agent, too." The idea appealed to Hamlisch, a native New Yorker, and he agreed to do the music. Edward Kleban, a newcomer with some Off Broadway experience, was engaged to write the lyrics.

"I started my first workshop at the Public Theater in August. Joe Papp had told me I could have all the time I needed, which was something completely new for me; I've done Broadway musicals with only six weeks for rehearsals. It was a good thing we had the time, because at that point we had ourselves a five-hour play. We knew we had some cutting to do."

Bennett called a halt to the first workshop in September while he went back uptown to direct Neil Simon's comedy, *God's Favorite*, on Broadway. When he picked up *A Chorus Line* again, he asked James Kirkwood, a former actor who is now a novelist and playwright, to help smooth out the show's book. "By that time I knew I needed a playwright's help. Jim settled right in, and we were able to start the second workshop in December. We reworked the material so often, I think we must have discarded six other versions of the show. But things went well. We began previews in April and opened a month later—almost a year and a half after those first all-night talks. *A Chorus Line* is as close as we could come to rendering the truth—the subtext, you could call it—of many hours of discussion among a group of dancers whose lives revolve around Broadway."

Only about half of the dancers who attended the original discussions are in the cast today. Some couldn't afford the luxury of a long-term project and had to find other jobs; others couldn't resist opportunities that arose during the months of preparation. "We were paying only $100 a week," Bennett says. "Now that the show has opened, the kids are making something over $200 a week. The scale is based on the capacity of the theater, and ours seats only 299. We lost $10,000 a week during those low-price previews. Joe raised ticket prices after opening night, but we're still dropping between $1,000 and $2,000 a week; the theater just can't support our big cast and orchestra. When we start performances uptown at the Shubert on July 25, I hope to be able to pay back these people for all the time they've invested in the show. I owe Joe Papp a great debt, too. In the end, the show cost him around $300,000 up to opening night; Broadway conditions would have run the bill close to a million. But we'd never have been given this chance on Broadway."

Bennett swears he is never going back to work under those pressurized Broadway conditions. The toll in terms of wasted creative energy is, he says, much too high. Besides, he likes "being the boss." After working in various capacities on 12 Broadway shows, starting with *A Joyful Noise* in 1966 and including *Company*, *Follies* and *Seesaw*, he is savoring *A Chorus Line* as "the first Michael Bennett musical."

Throughout his career, Bennett's model has been Jerome Robbins (his first job as a dancer was in a touring company of Robbins's *West Side Story*) who, he says, "set a level, a tone I've aimed at. Robbins made dance an integral part of the musical. *West Side Story* had a tremendous impact on me, and on the musical theater. Broadway used to be looked down on by the dance world, but I don't think that's true any more. People like Robbins, like Alvin Ailey, have crossed and recrossed the boundaries between Broadway and ballet."

What's next in the way of boundary-crossing for Bennett himself? "I'd really like to do a movie," he said dreamily. "On the other hand, I might do a ballet for Robert Joffrey, another choreographer whose work I admire and respect. Or ... maybe I'll just rejoin life for a while; I tend to tune out everything when I'm working on a show." And in the more distant future? "Well, when I can't dance any more, I won't choreograph any more. But that's all right, because there'll always be some terrific new kids around to audition for my part."

. . . . . . . . . . . . . . . . . . . . . . . . . . . . . .

**PAGE 245, TOP TO BOTTOM:** Michael Bennett directing *A Chorus Line* with Marvin Hamlisch (right) and company members nearby; Michael Bennett at a rehearsal of *A Chorus Line*; and *A Chorus Line* company members rehearsal.

**RIGHT:** Members of the cast of the Broadway production of *A Chorus Line*, 1975.

June 4, 1975

# *CHICAGO*

By CLIVE BARNES

Form or content, shadow or substance—those classic alternatives of artistic endeavor had their day in court at the 46th Street Theatre last night. Well, not really. For neither content nor substance were truly represented, and the result was a foregone conclusion; Bob Fosse's new musical, *Chicago*, is one of those shows where a great deal has been done with very little. One might be tempted to say that never in the history of the Broadway theater has so much been done by so many for so few final results—but then one remembers *Pippin*.

Indeed, one remembers *Pippin* through quite a lot of *Chicago* and when one is not remembering *Pippin* one is remembering *Cabaret* and when one is not remembering *Cabaret* one is remembering *Roxie Hart*. But I get ahead of myself.

There is a great deal of glossiness to admire in *Chicago*. We are given three superlative, knock-em-in-the-aisles performances by three stars who glitter like gold-dust all evening: Gwen Verdon, Chita Rivera and Jerry Orbach. Even more, there is the incredibly authoritative directorial voice of Mr. Fosse (stentorian, individual and precisely articulated), unfortunately shouting hoarsely over a desert of style. Style is everywhere; *Chicago* drips with it like a dowager with opals.

The three stars and the deft virtuosity (both cool and cold) of Mr. Fosse are far from being the show's only virtues. Indeed, at times the show seems to be stuffed with virtues. Take the music by John Kander and the lyrics (perhaps especially the lyrics) by Fred Ebb. They are often unmemorable—chiefly because they seem already to have been remembered somewhere—but remain bright and clever pastiches of 'twenties music.

There are reminiscences here of Chicago jazz, torch songs, crooners; Mr. Kander clearly knows and loves his period, and, with the help of Mr. Ebb's caustic, mocking lyrics, can reconstruct it with a certainty of style that takes one's breath away. But the whole score induces more admiration than honest pleasure.

Tony Walton's setting, dominated by an orchestra platform with translucent pillars at the side decorated with cut-out images of the period, and Patricia Zipprodt's atmospheric and imaginative costumes are similarly effective, and full of chic, but something more than chic. This is not merely the evocation of a period but a comment on it.

This pervasive suggestion of commentary, of standing aside from a time and a place and hinting at it with a wry, at times even cynical, objectivity, is both the show's salient virtue and also the aspect of it that links it, like an umbilical cord, to *Cabaret*. It can be seen obviously, and at times very rewardingly in Mr. Fosse's directorial or choreographic (for they are much of a muchness) concept.

The slow-motion prowling choreography—that soft-shoe shuffle for chalk-faced ballerinas and mocking song-and-dance men, all given with a sharp-edged and macabre lilt—or those almost monumentally inventive production numbers (give Mr. Fosse a chair, lights and Miss Rivera and he will run you up a show-biz gem) have become the hallmarks of Mr. Fosse's work and style. But where does it all lead? What happens?

In the show's rapidly sinking second half (the first is very markedly its superior) the cast, almost in honest desperation it seems, is given a number in which you can almost hear Mr. Fosse thinking out loud. They whisper softly in unison: "Give them the old hocus-pocus ... razzle-dazzle them and they will never get wise." Say you so? Perhaps. For the sake of *Chicago* I hope so.

At basis the real trouble with *Chicago* is that there is nothing to build it upon. The original play *Chicago*, written in 1926, was a moderately amusing, and for the time quite risqué, novel of newspapers and courts in Chicago in the 'twenties, written by Maurine Watkins, who had herself worked as a Chicago court reporter. It was made into a rather funny Ginger Rogers movie in 1942 by Nunnally Johnson, who called it after its heroine *Roxie Hart*.

A comedy melodrama of a girl who shoots her lover and is then acquitted through the chicaneries of the Chicago criminal system—you can only wonder who ever thought it was suitable for a musical. This is what went wrong. The musical had lost its moorings from the very beginning. It was not the kind of original idea that could support all this lavish embellishment of style, chic and fancy.

So one is left with some beautiful bits and some dazzling pieces, but an eventual feeling of disappointment. All that talent should have been spent polishing up something else; all that love for Chicago should have toddled somewhere lusher and more productive.

The audience adored it—they even applauded when the lights first went down—and there are things, very very positive things, for everyone to adore, not least the performers. Both the girls dance their hearts out, together, singly, or leading the splendid band of gypsies who make up most of the rest of the cast. Miss Verdon's voice, all candy innocence and yet somehow naughtily suggestive of untold viciousness, is perfectly matched by the strangulated tones of Miss Rivera's blasé worldliness. Mr. Orbach, who, as a crooked lawyer, has the worst role in the show, by way of compensation gets the two best production numbers, one supported by fan-dancers and another as a ventriloquist, in both of which he is a knockout.Excellent work is also contributed by Mary McCarty as an often-bitten matron, M. O'Haughey as a transvestite coloratura countertenor and Barney Martin as the unconsidered husband.

*Chicago*, despite its disappointments, is easily one of the best musicals of the season; it is brassy, sassy, raunchy but mechanical. A couple of years ago Mr. Fosse created a one-minute television commercial for *Pippin* that helped the other 119 minutes no end. He should start work on another commercial.

· · · · · · · · · · · · · · · · · · · · · · · · · · · · · · · ·

**OPPOSITE:** Chita Rivera and Gwen Verdon in *Chicago*.

November 15, 1996

# A LIVELY LEGACY, A COME-HITHER AIR

By BEN BRANTLEY

Who would have thought there could be such bliss in being played for a patsy?

In the pulse-racing revival of the musical *Chicago*, which opened last night at the Richard Rodgers Theatre, all the world's a con game, and show business is the biggest scam of all.

It makes a difference, though, when the hustle involves a cast of top-flight artists perfectly mated to their parts and some of the sexiest, most sophisticated dancing seen on Broadway in years.

By the time the priceless Bebe Neuwirth, playing a hoofer turned murderer, greets the audience at the beginning of the second act with the salutation "Hello, suckers!," it's a label we're all too happy to accept. The America portrayed onstage may be a vision of hell, but the way it's being presented flies us right into musical heaven.

This sharp-edged, self-defined tale of "murder, greed, corruption, violence, exploitation, adultery and treachery" received a healthy initial run in the mid-1970s but very ambivalent reviews.

Even with such mesmerizing stars as Gwen Verdon and Chita Rivera, swell vaudeville-pastiche songs by John Kander and Fred Ebb and the acutely stylish direction and choreography of Bob Fosse, *Chicago*

seemed too chilly, in those days, to be truly loved in the way *Oklahoma!* or *A Chorus Line*, its warmhearted contemporary and rival, might be.

Yet this new incarnation, directed by Walter Bobbie and choreographed by Ann Reinking (who also stars), makes an exhilarating case both for *Chicago* as a musical for the ages and for the essential legacy of Fosse, whose ghost has never been livelier than it is here.

There's been talk in the press that theatergoers, in the era of O. J. Simpson and Amy Fisher, are now more likely to accept the work's jaded take on pathological celebrity worship and a fractured justice system. But that's not what makes this *Chicago* so immensely appealing.

What this production makes clear is how much *Chicago* is about the joy of seducing an audience that goes to the theater, above all, to be seduced. Fosse, who had a fiercely conflicted relationship with his profession, may have regarded entertainers as applause-addicted grifters. (Take another look at his autobiographical movie, *All That Jazz*, if you want confirmation.)

Yet he also reveled in the adrenaline rush that comes from singers and dancers doing what they do best, at their best. Every number in this *Chicago* (and most of them are show-stoppers) buzzes with an implicit, irresistibly arrogant declaration: "Watch me. What I'm about to do is going to be terrific, and you're going to love every second of it."

And yet somehow everything feels richer, like an expensive, perfectly constructed sheath from a designer like Mainbocher. It creates the ideal environment for a tribute to the illusions that can be woven out of air by the right combination of music, actors, singers and dancers. And each of the performances has been polished like the Astors' silver.

Much of the credit, of course, goes to Mr. Bobbie, whose delightfully inventive direction sustains just the right tone of heady irony. Ms. Reinking, a former dancer for Fosse (and, for a time, his companion), has brought her own light-handed sparkle in evoking the Fosse spirit, and the corps de ballet couldn't be better, physically capturing the wry, knowing pastiche

of some of Kander and Ebb's best songs.

It's hard to know where to start in singling out cast members. Ms. Reinking's Roxie Hart, the over-the-hill chorine who becomes a star when she murders her straying lover, emerges as the most entertainingly erotic cartoon character since Jessica Rabbit.

Ms. Reinking meets her match, though, in her co-star. As Velma Kelly, a vaudevillian in jail for a bloody crime of passion and Roxie's competitor in publicity seeking, Ms. Neuwirth has translated her deadpan comic persona and technical proficiency as a dancer into an ecstatic benchmark performance.

The deliciously mechanical wriggle in her walk embodies the very soul of the show. And to see her turn her legs into a pair of air-slicing scissors, her face set in a bewitching expression of self-satisfaction, is like falling in love, against your better judgment, with a specialist in breaking hearts.

James Naughton, a superb musical leading man who in another age would have the status of a Robert Preston, brings flawless timing and a velvety crooner's voice to the role of the press-manipulating lawyer.

And as Amos, Roxie's limp dupe of a husband, Joel Grey (best known as the decadent emcee in another Kander-Ebb musical, *Cabaret*) achieves the miracle of turning passivity into pure show-biz electricity, all the more arresting for being kept at a low voltage.

See, the performers seem to be saying, what we're doing is all illusion, and you're falling for it. Or as a line from the song "Razzle Dazzle" has it, "Long as you keep 'em way off balance, how can they spot you got no talents?"

Nonsense. This production isn't smoke and mirrors. It's flesh and blood shaped by discipline and artistry into a parade of vital, pulsing talent. If there's any justice in the world (and *Chicago* insists that there isn't), audiences will be exulting in that parade for many, many performances to come.

· · · · · · · · · · · · · · · · · · · · · · · · · · · · ·

**OPPOSITE:** Bebe Neuwirth and Ann Reinking in the 1996 revival of *Chicago*.

# Annie

By CLIVE BARNES

To dislike the new musical *Annie*, which opened last night at the Alvin Theatre, would be tantamount to disliking motherhood, peanut butter, friendly mongrel dogs and nostalgia. It also would be unnecessary, for *Annie* is an intensely likable musical. You might even call it lovable; it seduces one, and should settle down to being a sizable hit.

It is based on the famous cartoon character Little Orphan Annie, but not all that seriously. This is not a comic-strip show—it is no *Li'l Abner*—indeed, Annie's picaresque adventures would scarcely lend themselves to such a treatment. Rather, the authors have taken her as a symbol—a symbol of the end of the Great Depression and Franklin D. Roosevelt's New Deal in 1933.

The idea apparently was Martin Charnin's—he also wrote the lyrics and directed the show—but the book is by Thomas Meehan, and against my expectations I found it whimsically charming. Because I usually have a healthy, normal, W. C. Fields attitude toward performing children and performing dogs, this means more from me than it would coming from someone who customarily swoons at the theatrical glint of a little girl's petticoat, or the canine grin of a histrionically inclined pooch.

The story starts with Annie caught in an orphanage of Dickensian horrors, presided over by a formidable, liquor-swilling tyrant, Miss Hannigan, a blowsy harridan without an unmalicious thought in her head. Annie, convinced that somewhere in the wide world her parents are alive and wanting her, tries to escape from the orphanage only to be captured and returned to the deadly embrace of Miss Hannigan.

Fate clumps in when Oliver Warbucks, one of the richest men in the world, wants an orphan to spend Christmas with him. His secretary chooses Annie and the rest is history—or at least a long-running comic strip.

The show, which originated, like so many other Broadway musicals, at Michael Price's Goodspeed Opera House in East Haddam, Conn., has a rare kind of gutsy charm. It takes what could be the pure dross of sentimentality and turns it into a musical of sensibility. It presumably owes most to Mr. Charnin's concept of the musical as pop-social document. Mr. Meehan's script abounds with cute but appealing references to the period, and the historical detail of the show—from the search for Dillinger to the villainess smoking Lucky Strike Green—seems formidably accurate. (President Roosevelt had formulated his New Deal before Christmas 1933, but everyone is permitted a little poetic license.)

The music by Charles Strouse is tuneful and supportive. It is neither unduly inventive nor memorable, but the overall impression is distinctly pleasing. It is amiable music that washes over one in a manner both comforting and comfortable.

The worst aspect of the show is Mr. Charnin's lyrics, which are bland to the point of banality; but even this could have been intentional, for obviously nothing is intended to disturb the show's air of amiable nostalgia. It is meant to be a show to experience, not a show to think about.

Where Mr. Charnin, in his capacity as director or, possibly, Mike Nichols in, for him, the unusual capacity of producer, have been superbly effective is in giving the show a style of its own. Here the collaborators are provided with a jet-propelled lift from the settings by David Mitchell. If ever that old joke about leaving the theater humming the scenery was justified, this could be the occasion. The neatly stylized costumes by Theoni V. Aldredge add considerably to the spectacular visual brilliance of the show, which is one of the best-looking Broadway musicals we have had in years.

One of the problems of *Annie* must have been simply the casting of Annie herself. Imagine a Shirley Temple in a red fright-wig, tippy-tapping through the Depression with a brave little smile. Andrea McArdle seems first and foremost refreshingly normal and not at all waiflike.

Her acting is uncalculated and convincing and her singing voice has an attractively rasplike treble to it. Best of all, she is anything but precocious or a brat. And as for the red fright-wig, she doesn't wear it till the last scene, and then, I suppose, it is only a nod to pictorial convention. The dog, Sandy, is disreputable without being obnoxious, and lovable without being maudlin.

As the wicked Miss Hannigan, Dorothy Loudon, eyes bulging with envy, face sagging with hatred, is deliciously and deliriously horrid. She never puts a sneer, a leer or even a scream in the wrong place, and her singing has just the right brassy bounce to it.

Reid Shelton, as Daddy Warbucks, looks a little like an avuncular Otto Preminger and exudes a nice brand of gruff good nature; there is an entrancing 7-year-old moppet, Danielle Brisebois; Robert Fitch and Barbara Erwin are rascally villains; Raymond Thorne proves urbanity personified as F.D.R., and Sandy Faison is particularly appealing as Warbucks's elegant and compassionate secretary.

The Broadway musical was once celebrated all over the world for its sheer efficiency. In recent years this reputation has been somewhat tarnished, despite occasional inspirations, with the machinations of the staging being expected to triumph over any flaws in the material. *Annie* really works on all levels. It is that now rare animal—the properly built, handsomely groomed Broadway musical. And leapin' lizards (sorry, one had to say it somewhere!), you're welcome.

. . . . . . . . . . . . . . . . . . . . . . . . . . . . . . . .

**OPPOSITE:** Andrea McArdle, Reid Shelton, and Sandy in *Annie*.

May 10, 1978

# AIN'T MISBEHAVIN'

### By RICHARD EDER

What whistles, hoots, throws off sparks and moves at about 180 miles an hour even though it is continually stopped?

*Ain't Misbehavin'*.

This musical re-creation of Fats Waller, the jazz singer and pianist, is a whole cluster of marvels. No self-respecting audience could let it go on without interrupting it continually, and if the audience at the Longacre Theatre, where it opened last night, was self-respecting to start off, it ended up in a state of agitated delight.

There are approximately 30 numbers in the show, conceived and directed by Richard Maltby Jr. with a lot of help from some extraordinary talented friends. Most were written by Fats (Thomas) Waller, who died in 1943 on the *Super Chief* after whizzing through the '20s and '30s. Others were songs he recorded, and there are a few purely musical numbers to which Mr. Maltby has set lyrics.

A whole series of the jazz worlds of the time, uptown and downtown, raffish and posh—the posh had an edge of mockery to it—funny and startlingly beautiful, came to life. We are conducted through it by five singers, a gentle-fingered, garter-sleeved pianist named Luther Henderson, and a small band in the background.

The set, by John Lee Beatty, is simple: concentric red arches that concentrate the action on the Longacre's relatively small stage. If the five performers, all of them talented and three of them magnificent, ever flagged in holding the stage, there was always the piano. Tall and ornate as a small cathedral, it had an engaging way of moving around.

When Mr. Henderson got into his most vigorous stride—a two-beat rhythm: bass-note, chord, bass-note, chord—the piano sidled sideways as if being pumped. At the end of the first act, when the cast cake-walked off-stage, the piano bobbed along after them.

The company warms up with the show's title song, engagingly performed. This is ground-level, relatively speaking, pleasant as it is. It leads up to one of the half-dozen totally charged, hair-raising numbers that lift the show from merely delightful to electrifying.

This first peak is "Honeysuckle Rose." Rather, it is Ken Page, portly, loose-jointed and gravel-voiced, holding his stomach so it won't get away and belting out one note that he holds past resuscitation. Having held it, he tastes it, wrinkles his mouth, and looks rueful. And into his arms, like a large parcel mailing itself, sidles Nell Carter. Round-faced and rounder-bodied, she establishes beyond doubt and with metallic lyric conviction that she is unquestionably the honeysuckle rose that all the fuss is about.

Without waiting for the dust to settle they exit, giving the piano a casual twirl; it turns a half-turn, and there, plastered to the back, is the show's third star, Armelia McQueen. She is not merely round but spherical, and she smiles a demure smile that looks as if maggots had broken in overnight and laid eggs in it. Her high, breathy "Squeeze Me" is hilarious parody; she is the baby-doll to put an end to the species.

Nell Carter comes back and with a blaring "OW!" starts "I've Got a Feeling I'm Falling," one of the show's most devastating numbers. Miss Carter can blare like a trumpet, moan like a muted trumpet, and do 100 variations on breathiness. Her "Mean to Me" is sung quietly, but with a silvery, delicate pungency—her round face suddenly becomes a prism of shifting expressions—that could lead an army.

Some of the songs are performed as skits, and some of these are very funny. "How Ya Baby" is a crackling dance performed by Andre De Shields and Charlaine Woodard, who juggles her thin frame as if she were six hoops all in the air at once. Mr.

Page has the show's funniest number, "Your Feet's Too Big," delivered in high indignation and top form.

By comparison with Miss Carter, Miss McQueen and Mr. Page, the other two performers are weaker. Miss Woodard moves marvelously, but she is not a very interesting singer; and it is pure singing that is the heart of this show. Mr. De Shields is quite out of place; he is

bland and mannered and his skill lacks the besotted conviction that makes *Ain't Misbehavin'* behave so beautifully. His "The Viper's Drag," a long number about a man stoned on reefers, is the show's one real failure.

There are two or three other numbers that fall rather flat. Mr. Maltby's lyrics in a couple of pieces—"The Jitterbug Waltz" and "Lounging at the Waldorf" are too wordy, and

they overload the musical line. On the other hand his "Handful of Keys," where the singers vocalize the piano's stride effect, is charming.

These are small faults. They are hard to remember after the show's next-to-last number. The five singers sit perfectly still, hands folded, and break into "Black and Blue." But the plangent harmonies, the polyphonic quality, the majesty of this

setting—the hallucinatory arrangement is by William Elliott—could be a spiritual, a Gesualdo madrigal, or any other musical work that operates on pure spirit. It is the heart of this heart-stopping *Ain't Misbehavin'*.

**ABOVE:** From left: Andre De Shields, Armelia McQueen, Nell Carter, Charlaine Woodard, and Ken Page in a scene from *Ain't Misbehavin'*.

257

March 2, 1978

# SWEENEY TODD

By RICHARD EDER

The musical and dramatic achievements of Stephen Sondheim's black and bloody *Sweeney Todd* are so numerous and so clamorous that they trample and jam each other in that invisible but finite doorway that connects a stage and its audience, doing themselves some harm in the process.

That is a serious reservation, and I will get back to it. But it is necessary to give the dimensions of the event. There is more of artistic energy, creative personality and plain excitement in *Sweeney Todd*, which opened last night at the enormous Uris Theatre and made it seem like a cottage, than in a dozen average musicals.

It is in many ways closer to opera than to most musicals; and in particular, and sometimes too much for its own good, to the Brecht-Weill *Threepenny Opera*. Mr. Sondheim has composed an endlessly inventive, highly expressive score that works indivisibly from his brilliant and abrasive lyrics.

It is a powerful, coruscating instrument, this muscular partnership of words and music. Mr. Sondheim has applied it to making a Grand Guignol opera with social undertones. He has used a legend commemorated in broadsheets, and made into a half-dozen nineteenth-century play versions; and most recently into a modern version written by Christopher Bond and shown in London in the early seventies.

It is the story of a barber, unjustly convicted and transported to Australia by a wicked judge who coveted his wife. Upon his return the barber takes the name Sweeney Todd, and takes his general and particular revenge by slitting the throats of his clients, who are then turned into meat pies by his industrious associate, Mrs. Lovett.

Mr. Sondheim and his director, Harold Prince, have taken this set of rattle-trap fireworks and made it into a glittering, dangerous weapon. With the help of Hugh Wheeler, who adapted the book from Mr. Bond's play, they amplify every grotesque and exaggerated detail and step up its horsepower.

The set, a great contraption like a foundry with iron beams, moving bridges, and clanking wheels and belts, is grim and exuberant at the same time. When a back panel, a festering mass of rusty corrugated iron, lifts, a doleful scene of industrial London is exposed.

In stylized attitudes, and gutter costumes, a whole London underworld appears, serving, in the manner of *The Threepenny Opera*, as populace and as sardonic chorus. In cut-off, laconic phrases they sing verses of the "Sweeney Todd Ballad," a work whose musical strength is deliberately bitten off until it swells out in the bloody finale.

Sweeney, played by Len Cariou, appears from a hole in the ground. He is lit throughout like a corpse. Mr. Cariou, his eyes sad and distracted, his hair parted foppishly in the middle, dresses and carries himself like a seedy failure; but a failure illuminated by a vision.

Mr. Cariou is to some degree the prisoner of his anguish: he slits throats with lordly abstraction but his role as deranged visionary doesn't give him much variety. He is such a strong actor, and such a fine singer, though, that he makes up for it with a kind of glow.

Angela Lansbury has more opportunities as Mrs. Lovett, and she makes towering use of them. Her initial number, in which she sings of selling the worst pies in London, while pounding dough and making as many purposefully flailing gestures as a pinwheel, is a triumph.

Her songs, many of them rapid patter songs with awkward musical intervals, and having to be sung while doing five or ten other things at once, are awesomely difficult and she does them awesomely well. Her voice is a visible voice; you can follow it amid any confusion; it is not piercing but piping. Her face is a comic face; her eyes revolve three times to announce the arrival of an idea; but there is a blue sadness blinking behind them.

Mr. Sondheim's lyrics can be endlessly inventive. There is a hugely amusing recitation of the attributes given by the different professions—priest, lawyer, and so on—to the pies they contribute to. At other times the lyrics have a black, piercing poetry to them.

His score is extraordinary. From the pounding "Sweeney Todd Ballad," to a lovely discovery theme given to Todd's young friend, Anthony, in various appearances, to

the most beautiful "Green Finch and Linnet Bird" sung by Johanna, Todd's daughter, and through many others, Mr. Sondheim gives us all manner of musical strength.

He has strength to burn, in fact. Two marvelous songs, constructed in the style of early nineteenth-century ballads, are virtually throw-aways. Mr. Sondheim disciplines his music, insisting that it furnish power to the work as a whole and not function separately. Sometimes we wish he would let go a little; the "Green Finch" song, so lovely, is imprisoned in its own activity.

Mr. Prince has staged the unfolding story in a series of scenes, contrasting with each other, but sharing the central tone of comedy laid over grimness. Mr. Prince's effects are always powerful, and sometimes excessively so. The throat cuttings, for example, repeated half a dozen times, are simply too bloody. They are used on us like beatings.

Besides Mr. Cariou and Miss Lansbury, Victor Garber is most attractive as Anthony, Ken Jennings is strong and touching as Tobias, a hapless apprentice, and Jack Eric Williams is funny and sings beautifully as the villainous Beadle.

There is very little in *Sweeney Todd* that is not, in one way or other, a display of extraordinary talent. What keeps all its brilliance from coming together as a major work of art is a kind of confusion of purpose.

For one thing, Mr. Sondheim's and Mr. Prince's artistic force makes the Grand Guignol subject matter work excessively well. That is, what needs a certain disbelief to be tolerable—we have to be able to laugh at the crudity of the characters and their actions—is given too much artistic power. The music, beautiful as it is, succeeds, in a sense, in making an intensity that is unacceptable.

Furthermore, the effort to fuse this Grand Guignol with a Brechtian style of sardonic social commentary doesn't work. There is, in fact, no serious social message in *Sweeney*; and at the end, when the cast lines up on the stage and points to us, singing that there are Sweeneys all about, the point is unproven.

These are defects; vital ones; but they are the failures of an extraordinary, fascinating, and often ravishingly lovely effort.

. . . . . . . . . . . . . . . . . . . . . . . . . . .

**ABOVE:** From left, Jack Eric Williams, Len Cariou, and Angela Lansbury in *Sweeney Todd.*

**LEFT:** A scene from the original Broadway production of *Sweeney Todd*, 1978.

# REVIVAL

November 4, 2005

# Grand Guignol, Spare and Stark

By BEN BRANTLEY

Only a few days after Halloween—a holiday, the horror movies tell us, that brings out the beast in the criminally insane—the inmates have indeed taken over the asylum. Brace yourself. They're putting on one helluva show.

Sweet dreams, New York. The thrilling new revival of Stephen Sondheim and Hugh Wheeler's *Sweeney Todd: The Demon Barber of Fleet Street*, which opened last night at the Eugene O'Neill Theatre in a production starring Michael Cerveris and Patti LuPone, burrows into your thoughts with the poisoned seductiveness of a campfire storyteller who knows what really scares you. John Doyle, the show's ferociously inventive director and designer, has aimed his hypnotic interpretation of this 1979 musical at the masochistic child in everyone, the squirming tyke who wants to have his worst fears confirmed and dispelled in one breath.

First produced at the Watermill Theatre in Newbury, England, and subsequently in the West End in London, Mr. Doyle's interpretation (recast for New York) presents its Victorian-age story of gory revenge as a tale told by a madman about a world gone mad. Set in a bleak wooden box of a room that suggests an underfinanced psych ward in limbo, this show begins with a wheyfaced young man in a straitjacket, surrounded by people in

institutional white coats. He has the numbed look of someone who has seen the unspeakable. When he sings the show's opening words—"Attend the tale of Sweeney Todd"—you're going to attend, all right, whether you want to or not.

Surely no previous production of *Sweeney Todd* has had such a high quotient of truly unsettling horror or such a low quotient of conventional stage spectacle. Mr. Doyle, conditioned by the economic limitations of long years in regional theater, delivers what is, on one level, a skeletal *Sweeney*. This production features one set, 10 actors (excellent) and 10 musicians (also excellent). The actors and musicians, by the way, are the same people.

Yet this concentration of resources only tightens both narrative pull and emotional focus. The original Broadway *Sweeney*, directed by Harold Prince, was a big-picture masterpiece that placed the show's luridness in a distancing Dickensian social framework. Mr. Doyle's version, by contrast, draws you claustrophobically close. As they say at the entrance to spook houses, enter if you dare.

· · · · · · · · · · · · · · · · · · · · · · · ·

**RIGHT:** Michael Cerveris as the demon barber and Patti LuPone as Mrs. Lovett in the 2005 Broadway revival of *Sweeney Todd*.

# EVITA

By WALTER KERR

There's an eerily prophetic line close to the very opening of *Evita*, the Tim Rice–Andrew Lloyd Webber musical that chooses to sing about the brief, bizarre life of Eva Perón and her joint rule of Argentina with her dictator-husband, Juan. The evening opens with the announcement of her death at 33—we pick it up from the inside of a movie theater, as an ongoing western is suddenly replaced on the screen by the huge shadow of a man proclaiming the news—and then proceeds at once to the state funeral of a woman who was both hated and held to be sainted.

Che Guevara—complete with stogie, tam, fatigues and flowing mane—is our guide through the ceremonies. As the great movie screen glides up and away to rest on the back wall, where it will be used to relay real-life snapshots of Eva's worldly progress from back-stairs bedrooms to the top of the political heap, Che provides a mocking obbligato to the cries of mourning—cries that have the staccato ring of nails being driven into a coffin.

The lady's coffin is not yet closed, though. That will be done by Che himself, slapping the great lid shut and sending clouds of dust flying into the bleak, steelwork sky. He then sings the couplet that is going to prove both accurate and, to the entertainment, damaging: "As soon as the smoke from the funeral clears/ We're all gonna see she did nothing for years."

That is precisely the problem confronting director Harold Prince and the onetime authors of *Jesus Christ Superstar*. As they have charted out the enterprise, Evita is going to use a sleek-haired tango singer to make her way to the big city, she's going to dump him for a succession of more and more important lovers, she's going to snare the mighty man who's about to win Argentina's lethal game of musical chairs, she's going to pose as a friend of the poor while accumulating an impressive

supply of furs and diamond-studded gowns, she's going to be called a whore before she's through, and her body's due to waste away as cancer strikes her early.

Yet we almost never see any of these things happen dramatically onstage. We hear about them at second hand, mainly from the omnipresent Che who slips in and out among the dancers to tell us that dirty deeds are afoot. Whenever Che is briefly silent, we are getting the news from lyrics or recitative sung by top-hatted aristocrats, breathless messengers, almost anyone at hand. It is rather like reading endless footnotes from which the text has disappeared, and it puts us into the kind of emotional limbo we inhabit when we're just back from the dentist but the novocaine hasn't worn off yet.

To be fair, there are at least two passages in which we are really present at a key confrontation. The first occurs when Evita strides peremptorily into Perón's bedroom to dispossess the schoolgirl mistress in residence. "I've just unemployed you," she snaps to the youngster as she snatches her suitcase from beneath the bed and swiftly packs it. It's probably *because* two people have settled something face-to-face that we are so taken with the melodic plaint that follows ("Another Suitcase in Another Hall") as the dispossessed Jane Ohringer sits forlornly on that suitcase in a deserted street, wondering what cast-offs do next.

And, near the second act's end, there is a genuine personal clash between Evita and Perón, both pacing from one bedroom to another, she determined on being named Vice President, he bluntly pointing out that her glitter is gone and what's left will soon be ashes. If we ever begin, however remotely, to feel something for this no-holds-barred opportunist, it is as she crumples to the floor still insisting that half the power is hers. The contest between approaching death and a

stubborn will stirs a faint twinge in us, I think, because it's been acted out, fought harshly before our eyes.

Otherwise we are condemned to hearing what we want to know—*need* to know, if we're to offer any kind of response—relayed to us by a narrator. The use of Che Guevara for the purpose seems to me approximately as opportunist as Evita's own manipulations. Not because, factually, he wasn't there at the time, had nothing whatever to do with the Peróns. But because he is most often employed to make certain that we won't go developing a crush on Evita ourselves.

This last possibility seems a most unlikely one in any case, given what we do know about Eva Perón before entering the theater; it is at once accented by actress Patti LuPone's leering tongue, her firmly set jaw, and the ice water that plainly runs in her veins. (Miss LuPone sings the role well, and moves with a rattlesnake vitality.) But, just to make doubly sure, interlocutor Che (vigorously managed by Mandy Patinkin) is steadily available to sneer ("She's the New World madonna with the golden touch," "She didn't say much/ But she said it loud," and "You let down your people, Evita!").

In effect, this keeps us permanently outside the action, unable to decipher Evita's complexities for ourselves. We ask ourselves, in vain, how this dubious and remote heroine managed to get close enough to Perón to work her will on him, what it was she did to endear herself to a gullible population. Because vital scenes are simply absent, there are no conclusions, no judgments, we can arrive at on our own. They've all been handed down, hammered down, from the outset. We're not participants, we're recipients of postal cards (and photographs) from all over. Which is a chilly and left-handed way to write a character-musical.

The evening is not boring. Though the Rice-Webber score sometimes sounds as though Max Steiner had arranged it for Carmen Miranda, there are waltzes and polkas and threatening marches to keep us alert for tricky tempo-shifts; the lyrics, however, lack the odd and very human perceptions that often distinguished *Jesus Christ Superstar*. Bob Gunton is a more interesting Perón than you'd expect to find in such company, largely because he's a man of several minds, brutal enough privately but strangely wary about the insecurities of public life.

And director Prince has put his customary firm mark on the staging, making economical, highly efficient use of placards, banners, torches and bodies as he conducts the Peróns through their open-air rallies and ostentatiously glittering inaugurations. Evocative use is made, in collaboration with choreographer Larry Fuller, of squared-off blocks composed of slithering upper-crust figures and thumpingly booted army men eluding one another in counterpoint. And the thunder of the open-throated choruses at the Broadway is massive enough just possibly to be heard in Argentina. If your

curiosity stays alive at *Evita* in spite of all the undramatized hearsay that isn't going to satisfy it, it's due to the authoritative crackle of ringmaster Prince's whip. Listen, the whip says. You listen.

· · · · · · · · · · · · · · · · · · · · · · · · · ·

**ABOVE:** Patti LuPone as Evita Perón (center), and, to her right, Bob Gunton as Juan Perón and Mandy Patinkin as Che Guevera.

Those furry guys with tails were the ones who were advertised as "now and forever" kinds of creatures. But it was the story of the masked man with the mutilated face that wound up entering the statistic books as the longest-running musical. In any case, the title characters of *Cats* (which opened in 1982 and closed in 2000) and *The Phantom of the Opera* (which opened in 1987 and has yet to close) loomed over Broadway, brawny and seemingly inexhaustible, for forty-some years (and counting) between them. And both productions—mutants of pop crossed with opera and Broadway razzmatazz—were born in the laboratory of Andrew Lloyd Webber, whose colonial reign over the American musical theater began with *Evita* in 1979 and lasted well into the 1990s.

Webber's glory years coincided with the age of Frank Rich as the *Times* chief theater critic. Rich would turn out to be one of Lloyd Webber's most vigorous and articulate detractors, but he had some (mildly) approving words for the go-for-broke spectacle of the composer's shows. In reviewing *Cats*, a paean to feline style and resilience adapted from poems by T. S. Eliot, Rich wrote that the show transported audiences into a "fantasy world that could only exist in the theater and yet, these days, only rarely does." And when *Phantom* opened five years later, he said the show remade "La Belle Epoque in the image of our own Gilded Age." He also said that *Phantom* was hardly "a credible heir to the Rodgers and Hammerstein musicals" that haunted its composer's "creative aspirations."

That more or less sums up the British musical imports that dominated (at least at the box office) the excess-loving boom years of New York in the 1980s and early '90s. In addition to the Lloyd Webber shows, these included two London-bred extravaganzas from the French songwriting team of Alain Boubil and Claude-Michel Schonberg: *Les Misérables*, adapted from Victor Hugo's panoramic novel of revolution in France, and *Miss Saigon*, a retelling of the tragedy of *Madame Butterfly*, set during the Vietnam War. The sung-through scores were pretty, sure. But what about that descending helicopter (in *Miss Saigon*), or that falling chandelier (in *Phantom*)? Even with stars like Michael Crawford in *Phantom* and Jonathan Pryce in *Miss Saigon*, it was the scenery that people talked about.

More and more space in *Times* reviews was being devoted to scenic design, and amusement park rides and theme parks became commonplace metaphors. Such imagery would only increase when the Walt Disney Company invaded Broadway (and dislodged Lloyd Webber from his throne) in the 1990s with stage versions of their animated musical cartoons *Beauty and the Beast* (1993) and the sensationally successful *The Lion King* (1996). I reviewed the latter, and its pageantry, whipped up by the director Julie Taymor, wowed me as much as that of *Phantom* had impressed Rich. But our objections to both shows were also similar. "It's when *The Lion King* decides to fulfill its obligations as a traditional book musical," I wrote, "that it goes slack."

Though *The Lion King* featured a score by the pop chart–topper Elton John and electronically amplified oomph figured in the British-born musicals, it was still hard to argue that Broadway had caught up with the rock revolution begun decades earlier. True, the 1981 Motown-style *Dreamgirls* had Frank Rich declaring its director, Michael Bennett, the heir to Jerome Robbins as Broadway's greatest musical magician. A 1993 stage version of the Who's rock opera *Tommy* was described by Rich as "at long last the authentic rock musical that has eluded Broadway for two generations." (The *Times* rock critic, Jon Pareles, begged to differ.) And I certainly went over the moon for *Rent* (1996), a rock-flavored retelling of the opera *La Bohème* by the gifted young composer Jonathan Larson (who died shortly before it first opened Off Broadway).

Much of the charm of *Rent*, though, lay in its emotional intimacy. And by and large, the greatest creative heat seemed to be concentrated in introspective (and often smaller-scale) musicals that explored personal and cultural ambivalence. Many of them would begin life Off Broadway. Rich called William Finn's *Falsettos* (1992), a portrait of shifting sexual identity within one middle-class family, "a show in which the boundary separating Off Broadway and Broadway is obliterated." George C. Wolfe's *Bring in 'da Noise, Bring in 'da Funk*, which began life downtown at the Public Theater, translated the history of black Americans through the history of tap dancing and, in doing so, I wrote, spoke "to its audiences with an electricity and an immediacy that evoke the great American musicals of decades past."

But for depth of imagination in exploring the possibilities of the musical, there was still no one to match Stephen Sondheim, who ventured into territory as far flung as the perilous forests of classic fairy tales for *Into the Woods* (1987) and the atelier of the French painter Georges Seurat for *Sunday in the Park with George* (1984). The latter (which, for the record, began Off Broadway at Playwrights Horizons) won the Pulitzer Prize in 1985, and was, as a study of who and what makes art, "as much about itself and its creators," wrote Rich, "as it is about the universe beyond."

Another kind of self-exploration was happening at the same time, as Broadway began more and more to revisit, recycle and, on happy occasion, reinvent shows from its own past. If this indicated a general lack of innovation (and a surplus of desperation) among Broadway producers, every so often a revival would come along that seemed to belong even more to now than to then. When the 1975 musical *Chicago*, which presented American jurisprudence as vaudeville-style showbiz, returned to Broadway in 1996, it plugged into the sensibilities of an audience newly educated in the ways of spin and packaging in politics. Still, I wrote, "This production isn't smoke and mirrors. It's flesh and blood shaped by discipline and artistry into a parade of vital, pulsing talent." The original *Chicago* ran for two years. The current version of this tale of aging chorines who murder their way to celebrity (which has, appropriately, become a sort of halfway house for stars of all stripes seeking to revitalize their careers) is, as this book goes to press, still alive and kicking high.

**OPPOSITE:** Michael Crawford in the original Broadway production of *The Phantom of the Opera*, 1988.

December 21, 1981

# *Dreamgirls*

### By FRANK RICH

When Broadway history is being made, you can feel it. What you feel is a seismic emotional jolt that sends the audience, as one, right out of its wits. While such moments are uncommonly rare these days, I'm here to report that one popped up at the Imperial last night. Broadway history was made at the end of the first act of Michael Bennett's beautiful and heartbreaking new musical, *Dreamgirls*.

*Dreamgirls* is the story of a black singing group that rises from the ghetto to national fame and fortune during the 1960s. Like the Supremes, to which they bear more than a passing resemblance, the Dreams have their share of obstacles to overcome on the way up. At the end of Act I, the heroines are beginning to make it in Las Vegas, but there's some nasty business to be dealt with backstage. The act's hard-driving manager, Curtis (Ben Harney), has come into the Dreams' dressing room to inform Effie, who is both his lover and the group's best singer, that she is through.

Effie is through because the Dreams are at last escaping the showbiz ghetto of rhythm and blues to cross over into the promised and lucrative land of white pop. To take the final leap, the Dreams must change their image—to a new, more glamorous look and a "lighter" sound. Effie no longer fits: she's fat, and her singing is anything but light. And Curtis's bad news does not end there. Not only does he have a brand-new, svelte Dream in costume, ready to replace Effie on stage, but he also has chosen another Dream to replace Effie in his bed.

It's at this point that Jennifer Holliday, the actress who plays Effie, begs Curtis to let her stay, in a song titled "And I Am Telling You I'm Not Going." Miss Holliday is a young woman with a broad face and an ample body. Somewhere in that body—or everywhere—is a voice that, like Effie herself, won't take no for an answer. As Miss Holliday physically tries to restrain her lover from leaving, her heart pours out in a dark and gutsy blues;

then, without pause, her voice rises into a strangled cry.

Shortly after that, Curtis departs, and Miss Holliday just keeps riding wave after wave of painful music—clutching her stomach, keeling over, insisting that the scoundrel who has dumped her is "the best man I'll ever know." The song can end only when Mr. Bennett matches the performer's brilliance with a masterstroke of his own—and it's a good thing that Act I of *Dreamgirls* ends soon thereafter. If the curtain didn't fall, the audience would probably cheer Jennifer Holliday until dawn.

And, with all due respect to our new star, there's plenty more to cheer. If Miss Holliday's Act I solo is one of the most powerful theatrical coups to be found in a Broadway musical since Ethel Merman sang "Everything's Coming Up Roses" at the end of Act I of *Gypsy*, so *Dreamgirls* is the same kind of breakthrough for musical stagecraft that *Gypsy* was.

In *Gypsy*, the director-choreographer Jerome Robbins and his collaborators made the most persuasive case to date (1959) that a musical could be an organic entity—in which book, score and staging merged into a single, unflagging dramatic force. Mr. Bennett has long been Mr. Robbins's Broadway heir apparent, as he has demonstrated in two previous *Gypsy*-like backstage musicals, *Follies* (which he staged with Harold Prince) and *A Chorus Line*. But last night the torch was passed, firmly, unquestionably, once and for all. Working with an unusually gifted new composer, Henry Krieger, and a clever librettist, the playwright Tom Eyen—as well as with a wholly powerhouse cast and design team—Mr. Bennett has fashioned a show that strikes with the speed and heat of lightning.

He has done so in a most imaginative way. *Dreamgirls* is full of plot, and yet it has virtually no spoken scenes. It takes place in roughly 20 locations, from Harlem to Hollywood, but it has not one realistic set. It is

a show that seems to dance from beginning to end, yet in fact has next to no dance numbers.

How is this magic wrought? *Dreamgirls* is a musical with almost 40 numbers, and virtually everything, from record-contract negotiations to lovers' quarrels, is sung. More crucially, Mr. Krieger has created an individual musical voice for every major player and interweaves them all at will: in one cathartic backstage confrontation ("It's All Over"), the clashing of seven characters is realized entirely in musical terms.

What's more, the score's method is reinforced visually by Robin Wagner's set. Mr. Wagner has designed a few mobile, abstract scenic elements—aluminum towers and bridges—and keeps them moving to form an almost infinite number of configurations. Like the show's voices, the set pieces—gloriously abetted by Tharon Musser's lighting and Theoni V. Aldredge's costumes—keep coming together and falling apart to create explosive variations on a theme.

Linking everything together is Mr. Bennett. He keeps *Dreamgirls* in constant motion—in every conceivable direction—to perfect his special brand of cinematic stage effects (montage, dissolve, wipe). As if to acknowledge his historical debt to Mr. Robbins, he almost pointedly re-creates moments from *Gypsy* before soaring onward in his own original way.

Some of his images are chilling. In Act I, an exchange of payola money between two men blossoms into a surreal panorama of mass corruption that finally rises, like a vision out of hell, clear to the roof of the theater. Throughout the show, Mr. Bennett uses shadows and Klieg lights, background and foreground action, spotlighted figures and eerie silhouettes, to maintain the constant tension between the dark and bright sides of his dreamgirls' glittery dreams.

And in that tension is the emotional clout of the show. Like its predecessors among backstage musicals, *Dreamgirls* is about the price of success. Some of that price is familiar: broken love affairs, broken families, broken lives. But by telling the story of black entertainers who make it in white America, this musical's creators have dug into a bigger, more resonant drama of cultural assimilation. As the Dreams blunt the raw anger of their music to meet the homogenizing demands of the marketplace, we see the high toll of guilt

and self-hatred that is inflicted on those who sell their artistic souls to the highest bidder. If "dreams" is the most recurrent word in the show, then "freedom" is the second, for the Dreams escape their ghetto roots only to discover that they are far from free.

This upsetting theme is woven into the evening's very fabric. Mr. Krieger gives the Dreams songs that perfectly capture the rhythm-and-blues music of the '50s, and then replays them throughout the evening to dramatize (and satirize) the ever-changing, ever-more-emasculated refining of the Motown sound. (Indeed, the Dreams' signature number is used to clock their personal and esthetic progression much as "Let Me Entertain You" was used in *Gypsy*.) Mr. Eyen has supplied ironic, double-edge lyrics (notably in a song called "Cadillac Car"), and Harold Wheeler's subtle, understated orchestrations are sensitive to every delicate nuance of the Dreams' advance through recent pop-music history.

Perhaps inevitably the cast's two standouts are those who play characters who do not sell out and who suffer a more redemptive form of anguish: Miss Holliday's Effie and Cleavant Derricks, as a James Brown–like star whose career collapses as new musical fashions pass him by. Like Miss Holliday, Mr. Derricks is a charismatic singer, who conveys wounding, heartfelt innocence. When, in Act II, he rebels against his slick new Johnny Mathisesque image by reverting to his old, untamed Apollo shenanigans during a fancy engagement, he gives *Dreamgirls* one of its most crushing and yet heroic solo turns. But everyone is superb: Mr. Harney's Machiavellian manager, Sheryl Lee Ralph's Diana Rosslike lead Dream, Loretta Devine and Deborah Burrell as her backups, Obba Babatunde as a conflicted songwriter and Vondie Curtis-Hall as a too-honest agent.

Is *Dreamgirls* a great musical? Well, one could quarrel with a few lapses of clarity, some minor sags, the overpat and frantic plot resolutions of Act II. But Mr. Bennett and Miss Holliday have staked their claim to greatness. And if the rest of *Dreamgirls* isn't always quite up to their incredible level, I'm willing to suspend judgment until I've sampled the evidence another four or five times.

. . . . . . . . . . . . . . . . . . . . . . . . .

**ABOVE:** From center, Loretta Devine, Jennifer Holliday, Sheryl Lee Ralph, and Cleavant Derricks with members of the cast in *Dreamgirls*.

**RIGHT:** Jennifer Holliday, Sheryl Lee Ralph, and Loretta Devine in *Dreamgirls*.

May 30, 1982

# LITTLE SHOP OF HORRORS

By MEL GUSSOW

*Little Shop of Horrors*, at the WPA Theatre, drawn from a low-budget 1960 horror movie by Roger Corman, is a Faustian musical about a timid clerk who sells his soul to a man-eating cactus. Admittedly this is rather a rarefied idea for a musical comedy, but the evening is as entertaining as it is exotic. It is a show for horticulturists, horror-cultists, sci-fi fans and anyone with a taste for the outrageous.

The evening, with score by Alan Menken and book and lyrics by Howard Ashman, begins as a kind of New York slum version of *The Little Shop Around the Corner*, but before it has gone halfway round that sentimental corner, it has turned into *The Invasion of the Body Snatchers*.

The show's hero (Lee Wilkof) shyly pines for a waif (Ellen Greene), his fellow flower seller for a Skid Row flower shop (a nice floral design by Edward T. Gianfrancesco). He finds a way to her heart and to success with the discovery of a bizarre new plant. The plant is green and toothy—a cross between an avocado and a shark. Placed in the window, it quickly becomes a tourist attraction, which proves that the world will beat a path to your door if you invent a better flytrap.

Existing on a diet of human blood—in a pinch it tries rare roast beef from the deli— the plant grows larger and larger until it is a monstrous mutant. This is a singing Thing, a pistil-packing vampire. It is also a scene-stealer, finally hogging the entire stage and threatening the audience.

As the gardener of the supertuber, Mr. Wilkof has an affable, offhanded manner that allows him to get away with grotesque activities such as homicide, and Miss Greene is sweetly guileless as his self-sacrificing love. Franc Luz plays a villainous dentist with a swaggering air of self-mockery. There are engaging performances by Michael Vale as the well-meaning proprietor of the shop, and by a backup trio of urchins (Leilani Jones, Jennifer Leigh Warren and Sheila Kay Davis), who view the strange events with more amusement than alarm.

The score, played by a small combo led by the composer as pianist, is a spicy blend of rock, pop and Latin. The lyrics, a step down from the music, have an appropriate simplicity. Mr. Menken and Mr. Ashman collaborated on the musical version of Kurt Vonnegut's *God Bless You, Mr. Rosewater* (also at the WPA), and their new show shares some of the same cynical sensibility.

In *Little Shop of Horrors* there is even a late-blooming attempt at a message—or Flowergram—in the finale entitled "Don't Feed the Plants." One could approach the evening as a hothouse version of *Dr. Strangelove or How I Learned to Stop Worrying and Love the Plant*, but that would be taking it much too seriously. As intended, this is a fiendish musical creature feature.

. . . . . . . . . . . . . . . . . . . . . . . . . . . . . . . . . .

**RIGHT:** Audrey II and members of the cast in *Little Shop of Horrors*.

October 8, 1982

# CATS

By FRANK RICH

There's a reason why *Cats*, the British musical which opened at the Winter Garden last night, is likely to lurk around Broadway for a long time—and it may not be the one you expect.

It's not that this collection of anthropomorphic variety turns is a brilliant musical or that it powerfully stirs the emotions or that it has an idea in its head. Nor is the probable appeal of *Cats* a function of the publicity that has accompanied the show's every purr since it first stalked London 17 months ago. No, the reason why people will hunger to see *Cats* is far more simple and primal than that: it's a musical that transports the audience into a complete fantasy world that could only exist in the theater and yet, these days, only rarely does. Whatever the other failings and excesses, even banalities, of *Cats*, it believes in purely theatrical magic, and on that faith it unquestionably delivers.

The principal conjurers of the show's spell are the composer Andrew Lloyd Webber, the director Trevor Nunn and the designer John Napier. Their source material is T. S. Eliot's one volume of light verse, *Old Possum's Book of Practical Cats*. If the spirit of the Eliot poems is highly reminiscent of Edward Lear, the playful spirit of *Cats* is Lewis Carroll, refracted through showbiz. Mr. Nunn and Mr. Napier in particular are determined to take us to a topsy-turvy foreign universe from the moment we enter the theater, and they are often more extravagantly successful at that here than they were in the West End *Cats* or in their collaboration on *Nicholas Nickleby*.

Certainly the Winter Garden is unrecognizable to those who knew it when. To transform this house into a huge nocturnal junkyard for Eliot's flighty jellicle cats, Mr. Napier has obliterated the proscenium arch, lowered the ceiling and stage floor and filled every cranny of the place with a Red Grooms-esque collage of outsized rubbish (from old Red Seal records to squeezed-out toothpaste tubes) as seen from a cat's-eye perspective.

Well before the lights go down, one feels as if one has entered a mysterious spaceship on a journey through the stars to a cloud-streaked moon. And once the show begins in earnest, Mr. Napier keeps his Disneyland set popping until finally he and his equally gifted lighting designer, David Hersey, seem to take us through both the roof and back wall of the theater into an infinity beyond.

The cast completes the illusion. Luxuriantly outfitted in whiskers, electronically glowing eyes, mask-like makeup and every variety of feline costume—all designed by Mr. Napier as well—a top-notch troupe of American singer-dancers quickly sends its fur flying in dozens of distinctive ways. It's the highest achievement of Mr. Nunn and his associate director-choreographer, Gillian Lynne, that they use movement to give each cat its own personality even as they knit the entire company into a cohesive animal kingdom. (At other, less exalted times, Mr. Nunn shamelessly recycles *Nickleby* business, as when he has the cast construct a train—last time it was a coach—out of found objects.)

The songs—and *Cats* is all songs—give each cat his or her voice. If there is a point to Eliot's catcycle, it is simply that "cats are much like you and me." As his verses (here sometimes garbled by amplification) personify all manner of cat, so do the tuneful melodies to which Mr. Lloyd Webber has set them. The songs are often pastiche, but cleverly and appropriately so, and, as always with this composer, they have been orchestrated to maximum effect. Among many others, the eclectic musical sources include swing (for the busy Gumbie cat), rock (the insolent Rum Tum Tugger), Richard Rodgers–style Orientalism (a pack of Siamese) and Henry Mancini's detective-movie themes (Macavity, the Napoleon of crime).

But while the songs are usually sweet and well sung, *Cats* as a whole sometimes curls up and takes a catnap, particularly in Act I. The stasis is not attributable to the music or the energetic cast, but to the entire show's lack of spine. While a musical isn't obligated to tell a story, it must have another form of propulsion (usually dance) if it chooses to do without one. As it happens,

*Cats* does vaguely attempt a story, and it also aspires to become the first British dance musical in the Broadway tradition. In neither effort does it succeed.

If you blink, you'll miss the plot, which was inspired by some unpublished Eliot material. At the beginning the deity-cat, Old Deuteronomy (an owlishly ethereal Ken Page), announces that one cat will be selected by night's end to go to cat heaven— "the heaviside layer"—and be reborn. Sure enough, the only obvious candidate for redemption is chosen at the climax, and while the audience goes wild when the lucky winner finally ascends, it's because of Mr. Napier's dazzling *Close Encounters* spaceship, not because we care about the outcome of the whodunit or about the accompanying comic-book spiritualism.

As for Miss Lynne's profuse choreography, its quantity and exuberance do not add up to quality. Though all the cat clawings and slitherings are wonderfully conceived and executed, such gestures sit on top of a repetitive array of jazz and ballet cliches, rhythmically punctuated by somersaults and leaps.

It's fortunate for *Cats* that Miss Lynne is often carried by the production design and, especially, by her New York cast. At the risk of neglecting a few worthy names, let me single out such additional kitties as Anna McNeely's jolly Jennyanydots, Donna King's sinuous Bombalurina, Bonnie Simmons's tart Griddlebone, Reed Jones's railroad-crazed Skimbleshanks and Harry Groener's plaintive Munkustrap—the only real flaw in this large company is Terrence V. Mann's Rum Tum Tugger, who tries to imitate Mick Jagger's outlaw sexuality and misses by a wide mark.

By virtue of their songs, as well as their talent, there are two other performers who lend *Cats* the emotional pull it otherwise lacks. Stephen Hanan, singing Gus the Theater Cat to the show's most lilting melody, is a quivering bundle of nostalgia and dormant hamminess who touchingly springs back to life in an elaborate flashback sequence. To Betty Buckley falls the role of Grizabella the Glamour Cat and the task of singing "Memory," the Puccini-scented ballad whose lyrics were devised by Mr. Nunn from

great noncat Eliot poems, notably "Rhapsody on a Windy Night." Not only does Miss Buckley's coursing delivery rattle the rafters, but in her ratty, prostitute-like furs and mane she is a poignant figure of down-and-out catwomanhood.

One wishes that *Cats* always had so much feeling to go with its most inventive stagecraft. One wishes, too, that we weren't sporadically jolted from Eliot's otherworldly catland to the vulgar precincts of the video-game arcade by the overdone lightning flashes and by the mezzanine-level television monitors that broadcast the image of the off-stage orchestra conductor (the excellent Stanley Lebowsky). But maybe it's asking too much that this ambitious show lift the audience—or, for that matter, the modern musical—up to the sublime Heaviside layer. What *Cats* does do is take us into a theater overflowing with wondrous spectacle—and that's an enchanting place to be.

. . . . . . . . . . . . . . . . . . . . . . . .

Scenes from *Cats*. **OPPOSITE:** Ken Page and Betty Buckley. **ABOVE:** Members of the cast.

August 22, 1983

# *La Cage aux Folles*

By FRANK RICH

*La Cage aux Folles* is the first Broadway musical ever to give center stage to a homosexual love affair—but don't go expecting an earthquake. The show at the Palace is the schmaltziest, most old-fashioned major musical Broadway has seen since *Annie*, and it's likely to be just as popular with children of all ages. Were you hoping for a little more? I must confess that I was. The glitz, showmanship, good cheer and almost unflagging tunefulness of *La Cage aux Folles* are all highly enjoyable and welcome,

but, in its eagerness to please all comers, this musical is sometimes as shamelessly calculating as a candidate for public office.

Sometimes, but, happily, not always. There are more than a few startling occasions in this rapaciously busy extravaganza when the vast machinery comes to a halt— when David Mitchell's glorious pastel-hued scenic visions of St.-Tropez stop flying, when the transvestite dancing girls vanish, when the running gags about whips and wigs limp away. Suddenly, we find ourselves alone with

the evening's stars, George Hearn and Gene Barry, and they insist on providing the intimacy and candor that the evening otherwise avoids. You simply won't be able to get enough of these performers, or of the Jerry Herman songs that accompany their more tender self-expressions.

Mr. Hearn plays Albin, who, as Zaza, is the headline attraction at the nightclub that gives the musical its title. For 20 years, Albin has had a tranquil domestic life with Georges (Mr. Barry), the club's impresario. Albin is the more flamboyant of the pair. It is he who must dress up in drag every night to entertain the customers and who has the most to fear from growing old. What Mr. Hearn does with this role is stunning—a breakthrough, at last, for a fine, hard-working actor who last season alone paid his dues in two Broadway flops.

Whether in his female impersonations or in civilian guise, Mr. Hearn is neither campy nor macho here: he could be any run-of-the-mill nightclub entertainer in midlife crisis. But it is precisely his ordinariness that makes him so moving. When Mr. Hearn sits in front of his dressing-room mirror to sing plaintively of how he applies "a little more mascara" to make himself feel beautiful, we care much more about what the illusion of feminine glamour means to the otherwise humdrum Albin than we do about the rather routine illusion itself.

The charming Mr. Barry has nothing as showy to do, but his contribution is invaluable. He gets two sweet ballads, "Song on the Sand" and "Look Over There," that are unvarnished declarations of Georges's long-time devotion to Albin; though the lyrics can be soupy, Mr. Barry sings them with such modest simplicity and warmth that we never question their sincerity. Nor do we question Georges's self-loathing when, in a quivering and falsely merry voice, he sells out his lover for the sake of middle-class propriety.

If you add up all of the high points by Mr. Barry and Mr. Hearn—including a soaring arm-in-arm duet called "With You on My Arm"—you have the winning half of *La Cage aux Folles*. And in Mr. Herman, there is always a third partner in that achievement. We expect snappy, old-style Broadway melodies from the author of *Hello, Dolly!* and *Mame*—as well as the thrown-in Hit Song sung in a restaurant (here it's a dandy, a "Those Were the Days"–style item titled "The Best of Times")—but we don't expect passion. This time we get that passion, and it is Mr. Herman's score, jauntily conducted by Donald Pippin, that gives the charge to every genuine sentiment in the show.

When the stars aren't delivering those songs, *La Cage aux Folles* can be as synthetic and padded as the transvestites' cleavage. In sharp contrast to Mr. Herman, Harvey Fierstein, writer of the book, has misplaced his craftsmanship and bite on this outing;

he's exercised few of his options to bolster a property that was thin and coarse to begin with. The tiny plot of *La Cage* is dribbled out with painful lethargy in Act I, then resolved chaotically (and confusingly) for the final curtain. Worse, there is a homogenized, sit-com tone to the script, which suggests that Mr. Fierstein is pandering to what he apparently regards as a squeamish Broadway-musical audience.

But even when the authors are cautiously watering down their material, their splashy entertainment usually hums along in its unabashedly conventional way. Wait for those privileged occasions when Mr. Hearn, Mr. Barry and Mr. Herman summon up the full courage of the show's convictions, and you'll hear *La Cage aux Folles* stop humming and sing.

Scenes from *La Cage aux Folles*. **OPPOSITE:** George Hearn as Zaza. **ABOVE:** Gene Barry and George Hearn with members of the ensemble.

# REVIVAL

April 19, 2010

# SQUINT, AND THE WORLD IS BEAUTIFUL

By BEN BRANTLEY

Their plumage is wilting, their wigs are askew, and their bustiers keep slipping south to reveal unmistakably masculine chests. Yet the ladies of the chorus from *La Cage aux Folles* have never looked more appealing than they do in the warm, winning production that opened Sunday night at the Longacre Theatre.

Terry Johnson's inspired revival of Jerry Herman and Harvey Fierstein's musical, starring a happily mismatched Kelsey Grammer and Douglas Hodge (in a bravura Broadway debut), delivers the unexpected lesson that in theater, shabby can be not just chic but redemptive. This deliberately disheveled show, incubated at the tiny hit-spawning Menier Chocolate Factory in London, is a far cry from the high-gloss original production of 1983 or the glamorous, soulless revival that opened less than six years ago.

The Riviera nightclub of the title—run by Georges (Mr. Grammer) and the setting for a popular racy transvestite revue starring his partner, Albin (Mr. Hodge)—looks as if it could do with a coat of paint and perhaps a delousing. Georges, whose dapper evening jacket is definitely not bespoke, has a worn-down, worn-out appearance. And no matter how much rouge and mascara Albin applies, the dumpy, jowly chanteuse he becomes onstage will never resemble the screen siren of his mind's eye.

As for the Cagelles, the revue's scrappy six-member corps de ballet (pared down by half from their last Broadway incarnation),

let's just say that even the most myopic club patron isn't going to mistake them for real live girls. "We are what we are, and what we are is an illusion," they sing in gravelly chorus in their opening number. But the deception being peddled so adroitly here isn't one of mistaken sexual identity.

What makes this version work—transforming a less-than-great musical into greatly affecting entertainment—is its insistence on the saving graces of the characters' illusions about themselves and, by extension, the illusions of the production in which they appear. As presented here *La Cage* is (you should pardon the expression) a fairy tale, a sweet, corny story that asks us to take people (the good-hearted ones, anyway) at their own valuation.

Try to see it their way, the show suggests; squint hard, and life at this dump will appear, for a second, beautiful. The old-fashioned, feel-good musical (which *La Cage* defiantly is, for better or worse) has always demanded such leaps of faith from its audience. Mr. Johnson's interpretation coaxes a parallel between the willful make-believe happening onstage and our willingness to subscribe to it. The show's very plot, we come to realize, is the triumph of musical-theater logic over reality.

. . . . . . . . . . . . . . . . . . . . . . . . .

Scenes from the 2010 Broadway revival of *La Cage aux Folles*. **OPPOSITE, TOP:** Kelsey Grammer and Douglas Hodge. **OPPOSITE, BOTTOM:** Douglas Hodge. **ABOVE:** Douglas Hodge and Kelsey Grammer.

May 3, 1984

# SUNDAY IN THE PARK WITH GEORGE

By FRANK RICH

In his paintings of a century ago, Georges Seurat demanded that the world look at art in a shocking new way. In *Sunday in the Park with George*, their new show about Seurat, the songwriter Stephen Sondheim and the playwright-director James Lapine demand that an audience radically change its whole way of looking at the Broadway musical. Seurat, the authors remind us, never sold a painting; it's anyone's guess whether the public will be shocked or delighted by *Sunday in the Park*. What I do know is that Mr. Sondheim and Mr. Lapine have created an audacious, haunting and, in its own intensely personal way, touching work. Even when it fails—as it does on occasion—*Sunday in the Park* is setting the stage for even more sustained theatrical innovations yet to come.

If anything, the show snugly fitted into the Booth owes more to the Off Broadway avant-garde than it does to past groundbreaking musicals, Mr. Sondheim's included. *Sunday* is not a bridge to opera, like *Sweeney Todd*; nor is it in the tradition of the dance musicals of Jerome Robbins and Michael Bennett. There is, in fact, no dancing in *Sunday*, and while there's a book, there's little story. In creating a work about a pioneer of modernist art, Mr. Lapine and Mr. Sondheim have made a contemplative modernist musical that, true to form, is as much about itself and its creators as it is about the universe beyond.

The show's inspiration is Seurat's most famous canvas, *A Sunday Afternoon on the Island of La Grande Jatte*. That huge painting shows a crowd of bourgeois 19th-century Parisians relaxing in a park on their day off. But *La Grande Jatte* was also a manifesto by an artist in revolt against Impressionism. Atomizing color into thousands of dots, Seurat applied scientific visual principles to art. Seen from a distance, his pointillist

compositions reveal people and landscapes in natural harmony. Examined up close, the paintings become abstractions revealing the austerity and rigor of the artist's technique.

Seurat, here embodied commandingly by Mandy Patinkin, could well be a stand-in for Mr. Sondheim, who brings the same fierce, methodical intellectual precision to musical and verbal composition that the artist brought to his pictorial realm. In one number in *Sunday*, Seurat's work is dismissed by contemporaries as having "no passion, no life"—a critique frequently leveled at Mr. Sondheim. But unlike the last Sondheim show, *Merrily We Roll Along*, this one is usually not a whiny complaint about how hard it is to be a misunderstood, underappreciated genius. Instead of a showbiz figure's self-martyrdom, we get an artist's self-revelation.

In Act I, this is achieved by a demonstration of how Seurat might have created *La Grande Jatte*. In a fantastic set by Tony Straiges—an animated toy box complete with pop-ups—Mr. Patinkin's George gradually assembles bits and pieces of the painting, amending and banishing life-size portions of it before our eyes. In the process, Mr. Lapine and the congenitally puzzle-minded Mr. Sondheim provide their own ironic speculations about who the people in Seurat's picture might be. The most prominent among them is identified as the painter's mistress (named Dot, no less, and radiantly performed by Bernadette Peters). The others include such diverse types as boorish American tourists, a surly boatman and a class-conscious German servant.

Yet most of these people are little more than fleeting cameos. As is often the case in Sondheim musicals, we don't care about the characters—and here, more than ever, it's clear we're not meant to care. To Seurat, these people are just models for a meditative

composition that's not intended to tell any story: In his painting, the figures are silent and expressionless, and even Dot is but fodder for dots. Mr. Lapine and Mr. Sondheim tease us with their characters' various private lives—which are rife with betrayals—only to sever those stories abruptly the moment Seurat's painting has found its final shape. It's the authors' way of saying that they, too, regard their "characters" only as forms to be manipulated into a theatrical composition whose content is more visual and musical than dramatic.

As a result, when Seurat finishes *La Grande Jatte* at the end of Act I, we're moved not because a plot has been resolved but because a harmonic work of art has been born. As achieved on stage—replete with pointillist lighting by Richard Nelson and costumes by Patricia Zipprodt and Ann Hould-Ward—the "fixing" of the picture is an electrifying coup de theatre. Tellingly enough, the effect is accompanied by the first Sondheim song of the evening that allows the cast to sing in glorious harmony. The song's lyric, meanwhile, reminds us that the magical order of both the painting and this musical has transfigured—and transcended—the often ugly doings in "a small suburban park" on an "ordinary Sunday."

Act II, though muddled, is equally daring: The show jumps a full century to focus on a present-day American artist also named George (and again played by Mr. Patinkin). This protagonist is possibly a double for Mr. Sondheim at his most self-doubting. George makes large, multimedia conceptual sculptures that, like Broadway musicals, require collaborators, large budgets and compromises; his values are distorted by a trendy art world that, like show business, puts a premium on hype, fashion and the tyranny of the marketplace.

The fanciful time-travel conceits that link this George to Seurat are charming. Rather less successful is the authors' reversion to a compressed, conventional story about how the modern George overcomes his crisis of confidence to regenerate himself as a man and artist. When George finally learns how to "connect" with other people and rekindles his esthetic vision, his breakthrough is ordained by two pretty songs, "Children and Art" and "Move On," which seem as inorganic as the equivalent inspirational number ("Being Alive") that redeems the born-again protagonist in Mr. Sondheim's *Company*.

The show's most moving song is "Finishing the Hat"—which, like many of Mr. Sondheim's best, is about being disconnected. Explaining his emotional aloofness to Dot, Seurat sings how he watches "the rest of the world from a window" while he's obsessively making art. And if the maintenance of that solitary emotional distance means that Seurat's art (and, by implication, Mr. Sondheim's) is "cold," even arrogant, so be it. *Sunday* argues that the esthetic passion in the cerebrally ordered classicism of modern artists is easily as potent as the sentimental passion of romantic paintings or conventional musicals.

In keeping with his setting, Mr. Sondheim has written a lovely, wildly inventive score that sometimes remakes the modern French composers whose revolution in music paralleled the post-impressionists' in art. (A synthesizer is added for the modern second act.) The accompanying lyrics can be brilliantly funny. Mr. Sondheim exploits the homonyms "kneads" and "needs" to draw a razor-sharp boundary between sex and love; a song in which Seurat's painted figures break their immortal poses to complain about "sweating in a picture that was painted by a genius" is a tour de force. But there's often wisdom beneath the cleverness. When Seurat's aged mother laments a modern building that her son admires, the Eiffel Tower, Mr. Patinkin sings that "all things are beautiful" because "what the eye arranges is what is beautiful."

What Mr. Lapine, his designers and the special-effects wizard Bran Ferren have arranged is simply gorgeous, and the fine supporting players add vibrant colors to their palette. Mr. Patinkin is a crucible of

**ABOVE:** Mandy Patinkin as the Impressionist painter Georges Seurat.

intellectual fire—"he burns you with his eyes," says Dot, with reason—and the wonderful Miss Peters overflows with all the warmth and humor that George will never know.

Both at the show's beginning and end, the hero is embracing not a woman, but the empty white canvas that he really loves—for its "many possibilities." Look closely at that canvas—or at *Sunday in the Park* itself—and you'll get lost in a sea of floating dots. Stand back and you'll see that this evening's two theater artists, Mr. Sondheim and Mr. Lapine, have woven all those imaginative possibilities into a finished picture with a startling new glow.

**RIGHT:** Mandy Patinkin and cast members in a scene from the original Broadway production of *Sunday in the Park with George,* 1984.

March 13, 1987

# Les Misérables

By FRANK RICH

If anyone doubts that the contemporary musical theater can flex its atrophied muscles and yank an audience right out of its seats, he need look no further than the Act I finale of *Les Misérables*.

At that point in the gripping pop opera at the Broadway, the strands of narrative culled from Victor Hugo's novel of early-19th-century France intertwine in a huge undulating tapestry. The unjustly hounded fugitive Jean Valjean (Colm Wilkinson) is once more packing his bags for exile on the "never-ending road to Calvary," even as his eternal pursuer, the police inspector Javert (Terrence Mann), plots new malevolent schemes. The young lovers Marius and Cosette are exchanging tearful farewells while Marius's unrequited admirer, Eponine, mourns her own abandonment. And everywhere in the Paris of 1832 is the whisper of insurrection, as revolutionary students prepare to mount the barricade.

Were *Les Misérables* unfolding as a novel—or in one of its many film adaptations—these events would be relayed sequentially, or through literary or cinematic cross-cutting. But in the musical theater at its most resourceful, every action can occur on stage at once. Such is the thunderous coup that brings down the Act I curtain.

The opera-minded composer Claude-Michel Schonberg, having earlier handed each character a gorgeous theme, now brings them all into an accelerating burst of counterpoint titled "One Day More." The set designer John Napier and lighting designer David Hersey peel back layer after layer of shadow—and a layer of the floor as well—to create the illusion of a sprawling, multilayered Paris on the brink of upheaval. Most crucially, the directors Trevor Nunn and John Caird choreograph the paces of their players on a revolving stage so that spatial relationships mirror both human relationships and the pressing march of history.

The ensuing fusion of drama, music, character, design and movement is what links this English adaptation of a French show to the highest tradition of modern Broadway musical production. One can hardly watch the Act I finale without thinking of the star-crossed lovers and rival gangs preparing for the rumble in the "Tonight" quintet of *West Side Story*—or of the revolving-stage dispersal of Tevye's shtetl following the pogrom in *Fiddler on the Roof*. In *Les Misérables*, Mr. Nunn and Mr. Caird have wedded the sociohistorical bent, unashamed schmaltz and Jerome Robbins staging techniques from those two American classics with the distinctive directorial style they've developed on their own at the Royal Shakespeare Company. This production is the Nunn-Caird *Nicholas Nickleby* gone gloriously show biz—which is to say, with conviction, inspiration and taste.

The evening may not appeal to those enraptured by the 1,300-page edition of Hugo. The musical thinks nothing of condensing chapters of exposition or philosophical debate into a single quatrain or unambiguous confrontation; encyclopedic digressions and whole episodes are thrown out. Unlike *Nicholas Nickleby*, which slavishly attempted to regurgitate its entire source, *Les Misérables* chooses sweeping and hurtling motion over the savoring of minute details. That artistic decision, however arguable, is in keeping with the difference between Hugo and Dickens as writers, not to mention the distinction between musicals and plays as theatrical forms.

While facts and psychological nuances are lost and even the plot is often relegated to a program synopsis, the thematic spirit of the original is preserved. Sequence after sequence speaks of Hugo's compassion for society's outcasts and his faith in God's offer of redemption. When the poor Fantine is reduced to "making money in her sleep," her downtrodden fellow prostitutes are apotheosized in golden light as their predatory clients circle in menacing shadows. When the story's action moves from the provinces to Paris, two hulking wooden piles of domestic bric-a-brac converge to form an abstract representation of a mean slum, bordered on every side by the shuttered windows of a city coldly shunning its poor. In a subsequent and dazzling transition, the towers tilt to form an enormous barricade. Later still, the barricade twirls in mournful silence to become a charnel house—*Guernica* re-imagined as a Dada sculpture—crammed with the splayed corpses of a revolution that failed.

Except for that uprising's red flag, Mr. Napier's designs, all encased in a dark, beclouded prison of a proscenium, are drained of color. *Les Misérables* may be lavish, but its palette, like its noblest characters, is down-to-earth—dirty browns and cobblestone grays, streaked by Mr. Hersey with the smoky light that filters down to the bottom of the economic heap. The proletarian simplicity of the design's style masks an incredible amount of theatrical sophistication. In one three-dimensional zoom-lens effect, Valjean's resolution of a crisis of conscience is accompanied by the sudden materialization of the courtroom where the moral question raised in his song ("Who Am I?") must be answered in deed. *Les Misérables* eventually takes us from the stars where Inspector Javert sets his metaphysical perorations to the gurgling sewers inhabited by the parasitic innkeeper, Thenardier—and in one instance even simulates a character's suicidal fall through much of that height.

Mr. Schonberg's profligately melodious score, sumptuously orchestrated by John Cameron to straddle the eras of harpsichord and synthesizer, mixes madrigals with rock and evokes composers as diverse as Bizet (for the laborers) and Weill (for their exploiters). Motifs are recycled for ironic effect throughout, allowing the story's casualties to haunt the grief-stricken survivors long after their deaths. The resourceful lyrics—written by the one-time London drama critics Herbert Kretzmer and James Fenton, from the French of Alain Boublil and Jean-Marc Natel—can be as sentimental as Hugo in translation. Yet the libretto has been sharpened since London, and it is the edginess of the cleverest verses that prevents the Thenardiers' oom-pah-pah number, "Master of the House," from sliding into *Oliver!*

It's New York's good fortune that Mr. Wilkinson has traveled here with his commanding London performance as Valjean intact. An actor of pugilistic figure and dynamic voice, he is the heroic everyman the show demands at its heart—convincingly brawny, Christlike without being cloying, enraged by injustice, paternal with children. Mr. Wilkinson anchors the show from his first solo, in which he runs away from his identity as paroled prisoner 20601 with a vengeance that burns his will into the inky void around him. He is symbiotically matched by Mr. Mann's forceful Javert, who at first acts with his sneering lower lip but soon gains shading in the soliloquy that passionately describes the authoritarian moral code driving him to stalk the hero obsessively for 17 years.

Though uniformly gifted as singers, the American supporting cast does not act with the consistency of its West End predecessors. Randy Graff delivers Fantine's go-for-the-throat "I Dreamed a Dream" like a Broadway belter handed a show-stopper rather than a pathetic woman in ruins. David Bryant, as Marius, brings fervor to a touching hymn to dead comrades ("Empty Chairs at Empty Tables"), but not before he's proved a narcissistic romantic lead.

That *Les Misérables* easily overrides its lesser performers, candied romantic tableaux and early Act II languors is a testament to the ingenuity of the entire construction. This show isn't about individuals, or even the ensemble, so much as about how actors and music and staging meld with each other and with the soul of its source. The transfiguration is so complete that by evening's end, the company need simply march forward from the stage's black depths into a hazy orange dawn to summon up Hugo's unflagging faith in tomorrow's better world. The stirring sentiments belong to hallowed 19th-century literature, to be sure, but the fresh charge generated by this *Misérables* has everything to do with the electrifying showmanship of the 20th-century musical.

· · · · · · · · · · · · · · · · · · · · · · · · · ·

**OPPOSITE:** A scene from *Les Misérables*.

# THE PHANTOM OF THE OPERA

By FRANK RICH

It may be possible to have a terrible time at *The Phantom of the Opera*, but you'll have to work at it. Only a terminal prig would let the avalanche of pre-opening publicity poison his enjoyment of this show, which usually wants nothing more than to shower the audience with fantasy and fun, and which often succeeds, at any price.

It would be equally ludicrous, however—and an invitation to severe disappointment—to let the hype kindle the hope that *Phantom* is a credible heir to the Rodgers and Hammerstein musicals that haunt both Andrew Lloyd Webber's creative aspirations and the Majestic Theatre as persistently as the evening's title character does. What one finds instead is a characteristic Lloyd Webber project—long on pop professionalism and melody, impoverished of artistic personality and passion—that the director Harold Prince, the designer Maria Bjornson and the mesmerizing actor Michael Crawford have elevated quite literally to the roof. *The Phantom of the Opera* is as much a victory of dynamic stagecraft over musical kitsch as it is a triumph of merchandising *uber alles*.

As you've no doubt heard, *Phantom* is Mr. Lloyd Webber's first sustained effort at writing an old-fashioned romance between people instead of cats or trains. The putative lovers are the Paris Opera House phantom (Mr. Crawford) and a chorus singer named Christine Daae (Sarah Brightman). But Mr. Crawford's moving portrayal of the hero notwithstanding, the show's most persuasive love story is Mr. Prince's and Ms. Bjornson's unabashed crush on the theater itself, from footlights to dressing rooms, from flies to trap doors.

A gothic backstage melodrama, *Phantom* taps right into the obsessions of the designer and the director. At the Royal Shakespeare Company, Ms. Bjornson was a wizard of darkness, monochromatic palettes and mysterious grand staircases. Mr. Prince, a prince of darkness in his own right, is the master of the towering bridge (*Evita*), the labyrinthine inferno (*Sweeney Todd*) and the musical-within-the-musical (*Follies*). In *Phantom*, the creative personalities of these two artists merge with a literal lightning flash at the opening coup de theatre, in which the auditorium is transformed from gray decrepitude to the gold-and-crystal Second Empire glory of the Paris Opera House.

The physical production, Andrew Bridge's velvety lighting included, is a tour de force throughout—as extravagant of imagination as of budget. Ms. Bjornson drapes the stage with layers of Victorian theatrical curtains—heavily tasseled front curtains, fire curtains, backdrops of all antiquated styles—and then constantly shuffles their configurations so we may view the opera house's stage from the perspective of its audience, the performers or the wings. For an added lift, we visit the opera-house roof, with its cloud-swept view of a twinkling late-night Paris, and the subterreanean lake where the Phantom travels by gondola to a baroque secret lair that could pass for the lobby of Grauman's Chinese Theatre. The lake, awash in dry-ice fog and illuminated by dozens of candelabra, is a masterpiece of campy phallic Hollywood iconography—it's Liberace's vision of hell.

There are horror-movie special effects, too, each elegantly staged and unerringly paced by Mr. Prince. The imagery is so voluptuous that one can happily overlook the fact that the book (by the composer and Richard Stilgoe) contains only slightly more plot than *Cats*, with scant tension or suspense. This *Phantom*, more skeletal but not briefer than other adaptations of the 1911 Gaston Leroux novel, is simply

a beast-meets-beauty, loses-beauty story, attenuated by the digressions of disposable secondary characters (the liveliest being Judy Kaye's oft-humiliated diva) and by Mr. Lloyd Webber's unchecked penchant for forcing the show to cool its heels while he hawks his wares.

The stunts and set changes, the evening's histrionic peaks are Mr. Crawford's entrances—one of which is the slender excuse for Ms. Bjornson's most dazzling display of Technicolor splendor, the masked ball ("Masquerade") that opens Act II. Mr. Crawford's appearances are eagerly anticipated, not because he's really scary but because his acting gives *Phantom* most of what emotional heat it has. His face obscured by a half-mask—no minor impediment—Mr. Crawford uses a booming, expressive voice and sensuous hands to convey his desire for Christine. Those who visit the Majestic expecting only to applaud a chandelier—or who have 20-year-old impressions of Mr. Crawford as the lightweight screen juvenile of *The Knack* and *Hello, Dolly!*—will be stunned by the force of his Phantom.

It's deflating that the other constituents of the story's love triangle don't reciprocate his romantic or sexual energy. The icily attractive Ms. Brightman possesses a lush soprano by Broadway standards (at least as amplified), but reveals little competence as an actress. After months of playing *Phantom* in London, she still simulates fear and affection alike by screwing her face into bug-eyed, chipmunk-cheeked poses more appropriate to the Lon Chaney film version.

Thanks to the uniform strength of the voices—and the soaring, Robert Russell Bennett–style orchestrations—Mr. Lloyd Webber's music is given every chance to impress. There are some lovely tunes, arguably

his best yet, and, as always, they are recycled endlessly: if you don't leave the theater humming the songs, you've got a hearing disability. But the banal lyrics, by Charles Hart and Mr. Stilgoe, prevent the score's prettiest music from taking wing.

Yet for now, if not forever, Mr. Lloyd Webber is a genuine phenomenon—not an invention of the press or ticket scalpers—and *Phantom* is worth seeing not only for its punch as high-gloss entertainment but also as a fascinating key to what the phenomenon is about. Mr. Lloyd Webber's esthetic has never been more baldly stated than in this show, which favors the decorative trappings of art over the troublesome substance of culture and finds

more eroticism in rococo opulence and conspicuous consumption than in love or sex. Mr. Lloyd Webber is a creature, perhaps even a prisoner, of his time; with *The Phantom of the Opera*, he remakes La Belle Epoque in the image of our own Gilded Age. If by any chance this musical doesn't prove Mr. Lloyd Webber's most popular, it won't be his fault, but another sign that times are changing and that our boom era, like the opera house's chandelier, is poised to go bust.

**ABOVE:** Michael Crawford as the Paris Opera House phantom and Sarah Brightman as the chorus singer Christine.

**LEFT:** Sarah Brightman and Michael Crawford in the original Broadway production of *Phantom of the Opera*, 1988.

April 12, 1991

# Miss Saigon

### By FRANK RICH

There may never have been a musical that made more people angry before its Broadway debut than *Miss Saigon*.

Here is a show with something for everyone to resent—in principle, at least. Its imported stars, the English actor Jonathan Pryce and the Filipino actress Lea Salonga, are playing roles that neglected Asian-American performers feel are rightfully theirs. Its top ticket price of $100 is a new Broadway high, sprung by an English producer, if you please, on a recession-straitened American public. More incendiary still is the musical's content. A loose adaptation of *Madame Butterfly* transplanted to the Vietnam War by French authors, the *Les Misérables* team of Alain Boublil and Claude-Michel Schonberg, *Miss Saigon* insists on revisiting the most calamitous and morally dubious military adventure in American history and, through an unfortunate accident of timing, arrives in New York even as the jingoistic celebrations of a successful American war are going full blast.

So take your rage with you to the Broadway Theatre, where *Miss Saigon* opened last night, and hold on tight. Then see just how long you can cling to the anger when confronted by the work itself. For all that seems galling about *Miss Saigon*—and for all that is indeed simplistic, derivative and, at odd instances, laughable about it—this musical is a gripping entertainment of the old school (specifically, the Rodgers and Hammerstein East-meets-West school of *South Pacific* and *The King and I*). Among other pleasures, it offers lush melodies, spectacular performances by Mr. Pryce, Miss Salonga and the American actor Hinton Battle, and a good cry. Nor are its achievements divorced from its traumatic subject, as cynics might suspect. Without imparting one fresh or daring thought about the Vietnam War, the show still manages to

plunge the audience back into the quagmire of a generation ago, stirring up feelings of anguish and rage that run even deeper than the controversies that attended *Miss Saigon* before its curtain went up.

Challenged perhaps by the ill will that greeted their every move, the evening's creators, led by the director Nicholas Hytner, have given New York a far sharper version of *Miss Saigon* than the one originally staged in London. The much publicized (and inane) helicopter effect notwithstanding, this is the least spectacular and most intimate of the West End musicals. The most stirring

interludes feature two or three characters on an empty stage or in a bar girl's dingy hovel, and for once the production has been made leaner rather than fattened up for American consumption. If *Miss Saigon* is the most exciting of the so-called English musicals—and I feel it is, easily—that may be because it is the most American. It freely echoes Broadway classics, and some of its crucial personnel are Broadway hands: the co-lyricist Richard Maltby Jr., the choreographer Bob Avian, the orchestrator William D. Brohn.

Without two legendary American theatrical impresarios, David Belasco and

Harold Prince, there would in fact be no *Miss Saigon*. It was Belasco's turn-of-the-century dramatization of the *Madame Butterfly* story that inspired Puccini's opera, and it was Mr. Prince who, inspired by Brecht and the actor Joel Grey 25 years ago, created the demonic, symbolic Emcee of *Cabaret*, a character that is unofficially recycled on this occasion in a role called the Engineer and played by Mr. Pryce. These two influences are brilliantly fused here. Altered substantially but not beyond recognition, the basic *Butterfly* premise of an Asian woman who is seduced and abandoned by an American military man is affectingly rekindled in *Miss Saigon* by Mr. Schonberg's score and Miss Salonga's clarion, emotionally naked delivery of it. Whenever that tale flirts with bathos, along comes the leering, creepy Mr. Pryce to jolt the evening back into the hellish, last-night-of-the-world atmosphere that is as fitting for the fall of Saigon as it was for the Weimar Berlin of *Cabaret*.

The theatrical poles of *Miss Saigon* represented by its two stars are equally powerful. Miss Salonga, whose performance has grown enormously since crossing the Atlantic, has the audience all but worshiping her from her first appearance as Kim, an open-faced 17-year-old waif from the blasted Vietnamese countryside who is reduced to working as a prostitute in Saigon. As her romance with an American marine, Chris (Willy Falk), blossoms *South Pacific*–style in a progression of haunting saxophone-flecked ballads in Act I, the actress keeps sentimentality at bay by slowly revealing the steely determination beneath the gorgeous voice, radiant girlish features and virginal white gown.

Mr. Pryce, a great character actor whose nasty streak has been apparent since his memorable Broadway debut in Trevor Griffiths's *Comedians* 15 years ago, makes disingenuousness as electrifying as Miss Salonga's ingenuousness. The Engineer is a fixer, profiteer and survivor who can outlast Uncle Sam and Uncle Ho: a pimp, a sewer rat, a hustler of no fixed morality, sexuality, race, nationality or language. Wearing wide-lapelled jackets and bell-bottoms of garish color, he is the epitome of sleaze, forever swiveling his hips, flashing a sloppy tongue and fluttering his grasping fingers in the direction of someone's dollar bills or sex

organs. With his high-domed forehead and ghoulish eyes, Mr. Pryce is also a specter of doom, and he manages to turn a knee-jerk number indicting the greedy "American Dream" into a show-stopper with the sheer force of his own witty malice.

Of all the failings of modern British musicals, the most severe has been their creators' utter bewilderment about what happens between men and women emotionally, psychologically and sexually. *Miss Saigon* is not immune to this syndrome, either, and it shows up most embarrassingly in the lyrics characterizing Chris's stateside wife, who, despite a game portrayal by Liz Callaway, induces audience snickers and giggles in her big Act II solo. Chris himself is nearly as faceless, and Mr. Falk, a performer with a strong pop voice and a Ken doll's personality, does nothing to turn up the hero's heat.

However sanitizing the words and corny the drama of *Miss Saigon*, the real

impact of the musical goes well beyond any literal reading. America's abandonment of its own ideals and finally of Vietnam itself is there to be found in the wrenching story of a marine's desertion of a Vietnamese woman and her son. The evening's far-from-happy closing tableau—of spilled Vietnamese blood and an American soldier who bears at least some responsibility for the carnage—hardly whitewashes the United States' involvement in Southeast Asia. *Miss Saigon* is escapist entertainment in style and in the sense that finally it even makes one forget about all the hype and protests that greeted its arrival. But this musical is more than that, too, because the one thing it will not allow an American audience to escape is the lost war that, like its tragic heroine, even now defiantly refuses to be left behind.

. . . . . . . . . . . . . . . . . . . . . . . . . . . . . .

**OPPOSITE:** The helicopter scene from *Miss Saigon*.
**BELOW:** Lea Salonga as Kim.

# TOMMY

By FRANK RICH

The Broadway musical has never been the same since rock-and-roll stole its audience and threw it into an identity crisis. For three decades, from the moment *Meet the Beatles* usurped the supremacy of such Broadway pop as *Hello, Dolly!*, the commercial theater has desperately tried to win back the Young (without alienating their elders) by watering down rock music, simulating rock music and ripping off rock music. A result has been a few scattered hits over the years, typified by *Hair* and *Jesus Christ, Superstar*, most of which have tamed the rock-and-roll revolution rather than spread it throughout Times Square. Until now.

*Tommy*, the stunning new stage adaptation of the 1969 rock opera by the British group the Who, is at long last the authentic rock musical that has eluded Broadway for two generations. A collaboration of its original principal author, Pete Townshend, and the director, Des McAnuff, this show is not merely an entertainment juggernaut, riding at full tilt on the visual and musical highs of its legendary pinball iconography and irresistible tunes, but also a surprisingly moving resuscitation of the disturbing passions that made *Tommy* an emblem of its era. In the apocalyptic year of 1969, *Tommy* was the unwitting background music for the revelation of the My Lai massacre, the Chicago Seven trial, the Charles Manson murders. Those cataclysmic associations still reverberate within the piece, there to be tapped for the Who's generation, even as the show at the St. James is so theatrically fresh and emotionally raw that newcomers to *Tommy* will think it was born yesterday.

In a way, it was. Though the voices and pit band of this *Tommy* faithfully reproduce the 1969 double album, adding merely one song ("I Believe My Own Eyes"), a few snippets of dialogue and some extended passages of underscoring, the production bears no

resemblance to the Who's own concert performances of the opera (which culminated in an appearance at the Metropolitan Opera House in 1970) or to Ken Russell's pious, gag-infested 1975 film adaptation. Instead of merely performing the songs or exploiting them as cues for general riffs of dance and psychedelia, the evening's creators, who also include the choreographer Wayne Cilento and some extraordinary multi-media artists led by the brilliant set designer John Arnone, use their singing actors to flesh out the drama of *Tommy*. Better still, they excavate the fable's meaning until finally the opera's revised conclusion spreads catharsis like wildfire through the cheering house.

Both the story and its point are as simple as *Peter Pan*. The show's eponymous hero is a boy who is stricken deaf, dumb and blind at the age of 4 after watching his father return from a World War II prisoners' camp to shoot his mother's lover. Tommy's only form of communication proves to be his latent wizardry at pinball, a talent that soon turns him into a media sensation. As played by Michael Cerveris with the sleek white outfit, dark shades and narcissistic attitude of a rock star, the grown-up Tommy is nearly every modern child's revenge fantasy come true: the untouchable icon who gets the uncritical adulation from roaring crowds that his despised parents never gave him at home.

In this telling, Tommy is often played simultaneously by two child actors (representing him at ages 4 and 10) in addition to Mr. Cerveris. The isolated young Tommy's totemic, recurring cry of yearning—"See me, feel me, touch me, heal me"—flows repeatedly between inner child and grown man, giving piercing voice to the eternal childhood psychic aches of loneliness and lovelessness. It is this primal theme, expressed with devastating simplicity in Mr. Townshend's score and lyrics, that has made *Tommy* timeless,

outlasting the Who itself (which disbanded in 1982). Yet it is the evil of the authority figures the hero must overcome—a distant father (Jonathan Dokuchitz), a dismissive mother (Marcia Mitzman), a sexually abusive Uncle Ernie (Paul Kandel) and various fascistic thugs—that also makes *Tommy* a poster-simple political statement reflecting the stark rage of the Vietnam era.

As staged by Mr. McAnuff, that anger is present but the story is kept firmly rooted in its own time, from the '40s to the early '60s. The slide projections that drive the production design at first re-create in black-and-white the London of the Blitz, then spill into the vibrant Pop Art imagery of pinball machines, early Carnaby Street and Andy Warhol paintings before returning to black-and-white for televised crowd images that recall the early British rock explosion as witnessed on *The Ed Sullivan Show*. Mr. Cilento's compact dances similarly advance from wartime jitterbugging to the '50s sock-hopping of early rock-and-roll movies to evocations of the mod antics of *A Hard Day's Night* and its imitators in the '60s.

But the highly sophisticated theatrical style of this *Tommy*, which coalesces as a continuous wave of song, scenes, kaleidoscopic design and dance, owes everything to musical-theater innovations unknown until the mid-1970s. Mr. McAnuff, whose past Broadway works include the relatively stodgy *Big River* and *A Walk in the Woods*, shrewdly turns to examples set by such directors as Harold Prince, Michael Bennett and Robert Wilson. Here and there are echoes of the mock-documentary superstar sequences of *Evita* and *Dreamgirls*, in which abstract scaffolding and bridges suggest a show-biz firmament and a surging mob. From Mr. Wilson, whose theater experiments have sometimes involved autistic boys eerily resembling the fictive Tommy, Mr. McAnuff

and his designers take the notion of threading a few repeated images abstractly through the action: floating chairs, mirrors, the Union Jack, airplane propellers and disembodied Man Ray eyes, not to mention doors and windows reminiscent of '60s rock-album cover art and the hallucinogenic mythology such art canonized. (Sometimes the new incidental scoring takes some hints from Mr. Wilson's musical collaborator, Philip Glass.) These dreamy visual touchstones are constantly reshuffled and distorted throughout *Tommy* for subliminal effect, reaching their apotheosis in an inevitable (and superbly executed) set piece in which the entire theater becomes a gyrating pinball machine celebrating the rebellious hero's "amazing journey" to newfound freedom.

Even in that blowout sequence, *Tommy* eschews the heavy visual spectacle of recent West End rock operas (and Broadway musicals) to keep its effects lithe and to the point. Dominating the stage instead of being usurped by hardware, the performers can shine as well, from the dazzling Mr. Cerveris, who grows from melancholy youth to strutting pop belter, to Ms. Mitzman's powerfully sung mother, Mr. Kandel's sinister Uncle Ernie and the tireless ensemble, its youngest members included.

When the time comes for the entire company to advance on the audience to sing the soaring final incantation—"Listening to you I get the music/ Gazing at you I get the heat"—*Tommy* has done what rock-and-roll can do but almost never does in the theater: reawaken an audience's adolescent feelings of rebellion and allow them open-throated release. But reflecting the passage of time and Mr. Townshend's own mature age of 47,

this version takes a brave step further, concluding with a powerful tableau of reconciliation that lifts an audience of the 1990s out of its seats.

"Hope I die before I get old," sang the Who in "My Generation," its early hit single. A quarter-century or so later, Mr. Townshend hasn't got old so much as grown up, into a deeper view of humanity unthinkable in the late 1960s. Far from being another of Broadway's excursions into nostalgia, *Tommy* is the first musical in years to feel completely alive in its own moment. No wonder that for two hours it makes the world seem young.

**ABOVE:** Michael Cerveris (in white) in a scene from *Tommy*.

# Damping '60s Fire of *Tommy* for '90s Broadway

By JON PARELES

Broadway is grateful for the Who's *Tommy*, the staged rock opera that opened to generally admiring reviews on Thursday at the St. James Theatre and set a box-office record the next day. It has a thrilling score, eye-popping stage and visual effects, and a secure place in the memory of the baby-boomers every Broadway entrepreneur would love to draw.

*Tommy*, the hopeful buzz goes, will be the show that finally brings Broadway into the rock era, ending the generation gap that makes so many Broadway shows the province of tourists and the elderly. Its storytelling moves at the pace of MTV, with video screens providing instant "set" changes behind jump-cutting action onstage. Although a few dissenting voices have been raised (notably John Lahr's in *The New Yorker*), nearly everyone else seems to like it. Everyone, that is, except people who cared about *Tommy* in the first place.

Those sourpusses, with me among them, can hardly believe that the Broadway extravaganza had the chutzpah to bill itself as *The Who's Tommy*. The Who's *Tommy* was released in 1969 and performed around the world by the Who, and the band saw no reason to mess with a good thing as late as 1989, when the surviving members of the Who and supporting musicians performed the complete score in New York and Los Angeles. But the Who's *Tommy* isn't on Broadway. Despite the recycling of the songs, the show is Pete Townshend's and Des McAnuff's *Tommy*, rewritten by its original composer and the show's director. Their changes turn a blast of spiritual yearning, confusion and rebellion into a pat on the head for nesters and couch potatoes.

As might be expected, Broadway's *Tommy* subdues most of the music, trading Roger Daltrey's rock belting for conventional Broadway emoting and taming the Who's glorious power chords with unnecessary keyboard doodling. Songs chug where they should explode, although "I'm Free" does give the show a glimmer of real rock. Meanwhile, some dance numbers would be at home amid the already once-removed 1950s pastiche of

*Grease*, or in the granddaddy of rock musicals, the rock-hating *Bye Bye Birdie*. In one scene, Tommy's cohorts are dressed as Edwardian-style Mods; then they show up as the Mods' sworn enemies, leather-jacketed Rockers.

On Broadway, though, inauthenticity goes with the *Playbills*; no one, after all, expected *Oklahoma!* to offer pure country music or *The King and I* to present Siamese traditions. Broadway also dares not trouble the viewers; "Fiddle About," in which evil Uncle Ernie does nasty things to young Tommy, is a strictly hands-off affair. And the revised opera also inverts the story Townshend originally told, scrambling the Who's *Tommy* so thoroughly that only the sheer momentum of the original tunes (with their rewritten lyrics) can hold the ending together.

In the 1969 *Tommy*, the deaf, dumb and blind pinball wizard regains his senses, then becomes a star. The acclaim induces messianic pretensions, and he cracks. He promises a communal idyll (in "Welcome") but establishes a tyrannical cult, forcing would-be followers at "Tommy's Holiday Camp" to play sensory-deprivation pinball.

Tommy had more in common with David Koresh or Charles Manson than he does with the sympathetic character on Broadway. "I'm free," Tommy proclaimed, "I'm waiting for you to follow me." And in the original *Tommy*, as might be expected in the 1960s, his prospective followers rose up against him, declaring "We're Not Gonna Take It" and adding, "Don't want no religion." Tommy withdraws, back to his autistic refrain of "See me, feel me, touch me, heal me," and in an ambiguous last verse, he seems to be struck by revelations from a higher power: "Right behind you I see the millions/On you I see the glory."

Consciously or not, the original *Tommy* must have been Mr. Townshend's reaction to his own celebrity and the way it interlocked with the bewildering late-1960s combination of newfound independence and longing for direction. He even wrote a sequel to "We're Not Gonna Take It": "Won't Get Fooled Again," the Who's definitively angry, cynical response to promised changes. "Meet the new boss, same as the old boss."

On Broadway, *Tommy* seeks neither spiritual fulfillment nor political ferment; the revised goal is domestic comfort. The

cult-leader references have been excised: no "disciples" in "Pinball Wizard," no "messiahs pointed to the door" in "I'm Free." As the Broadway *Tommy* ends, Tommy rejects his stardom and goes back to his family's house. The followers, and the press, can't believe he's leaving them on their own. Although the vehemence of the song doesn't make much sense anymore, the music is so catchy that motivation hardly matters. In what the Broadway script now calls "We're Not Going to Take It," Tommy sings, "You don't have to claim a share of my pain/You're normal after all." And finally, he addresses his family as he sings, "Listening to you I get the music." Everything is settled, the nuclear family is safe, and there's no need for any higher aspiration than to be home again.

It's an appealing message for the intended audience, the boomers who can afford $65 for the best seats, with their hair shorter or vanishing, their responsibilities more local, their concerns with jobs and mortgages and children. Broadway's *Tommy* insists, "Those are the true miracles and you have them already," and the show's authors pretend there was never anything more to it than that. Dorothy has turned her back on the

wonders of Oz and prefers black-and-white Kansas. The *Pequod*, after bagging Moby-Dick, sails easily back to Nantucket.

The new *Tommy*, created with the 47-year-old Mr. Townshend's participation, may represent the older man's ideas of what's most important in adult life. He and Mr. McAnuff may also have fiddled about with *Tommy* after commercial calculations, deciding that a Broadway audience would like an ending with triumphant reconciliation rather than the prospect of struggle and uncertainty. Regardless, *Tommy* on Broadway doesn't mean that rock has prevailed on the Great White Way. Its whiz-bang staging may teach other Broadway musicals some new tricks, no matter what idiom they use for the tunes. But the new *Tommy*, like *Guys and Dolls*, is a nostalgia trip offering familiar music to an audience that grew up with it: business as usual built on a rock opera that once promised more.

Scenes from *Tommy*. **OPPOSITE:** Donnie Kehr, Anthony Barrile, and Christian Hoff. **ABOVE:** Jonathan Dokuchitz, Buddy Smith, and Marcia Mitzman.

# BEAUTY AND THE BEAST

By DAVID RICHARDS

As Broadway musicals go, *Beauty and the Beast* belongs right up there with the Empire State Building, F. A. O. Schwarz and the Circle Line boat tours. It is hardly a triumph of art, but it'll probably be a whale of a tourist attraction. It is Las Vegas without the sex, Mardi Gras without the booze and Madame Tussaud's without the waxy stares. You don't watch it, you gape at it, knowing that nothing in Dubuque comes close.

At an official cost of nearly $12 million—unofficial estimates run considerably higher—the Walt Disney Company has re-created on the stage of the Palace Theatre its 1991 blockbuster animated feature, right down to the ravenous wolves, the dancing spoons and the enchanted rose that sheds its petals as true love's hopes run low. Family audiences tired of prancing felines are apt to find this cause for celebration. Others may look upon the eye-boggling spectacle as further proof of the age-old theory that if you throw enough money at the American public, the American public will throw it right back.

The scenery by Stan Meyer—mostly in that ornate, slightly scary German Gothic style that passes for picturesque at Disney—is almost always on the move. No apparition, disappearance, thunderbolt, rainstorm or swirling fog bank is beyond the capabilities of the show's special-effects engineers. Any one of Ann Hould-Ward's costumes would be the envy of a Beaux Arts ball. And if you thought the chandelier crashing to the stage in *The Phantom of the Opera* was something, wait until the Beast (Terrence Mann), presumably dead, rises up from the castle floor, floats 10 feet or so into space, then starts to spin like a human propeller. Before the spinning is done and you've caught your breath, he has somehow shed all things beastly and become a dashing prince again. (Take that, Siegfried and Roy.)

The astonishments rarely cease. Yet strange as it may sound, that's the very

drawback of *Beauty and the Beast*. Nothing has been left to the imagination. Everything has been painstakingly and copiously illustrated. There is no room for dreaming, no quiet tucked-away moment that might encourage a poetic thought. For an evening that puts forth so much, *Beauty and the Beast* has amazingly little resonance. What you see is precisely what you get. In the end, the musical says far less about the redemptive power of love than it does about the boundless ingenuity of what is called Team Disney.

The movie's strength—at least from Broadway's perspective—is the Academy Award–winning score by Alan Menken and his partner, Howard Ashman, who died early in 1991, before work began on the stage version. Such songs as "Belle," "Be Our Guest" and "Gaston" are happily reminiscent of Lerner and Loewe, and the title number speaks stirringly of love, as few Broadway ballads do these days. To them, Mr. Menken, working with the lyricist Tim Rice, has added seven new numbers, partly to bring out the sensitive side of the Beast, partly to underscore Belle's fortitude. However, the production, directed by Robert Jess Roth, is reluctant to let a song be a song in its own way and time. Two kinds of delivery are recognized: the hard sell and the harder sell.

"Be Our Guest," the first-act show-stopper, knows no shame in that regard. Its lavishness is close to delirium, its giddiness beyond camp. If you are one of the six people in America who don't know the plot, a wicked witch has transformed the handsome prince into a cross between Quasimodo and a buffalo, and the staff of the castle is slowly turning into sundry household objects: teacup, feather duster and the like. When it looks as if Belle, the pensive town beauty, might break the curse by falling in love with the Beast, the housewares get pretty excited. Hence, the production number.

Before long, the spatula is cavorting with the fork, the rug is doing cartwheels and the dinner plates are parading down a grand staircase like arrogant showgirls angling for a sugar daddy. The choreographer, Matt West, is responsible for this interlude, although Busby Berkeley on magic mushrooms might have staged it. For its duration, at least, the extravaganza elevates *Beauty and the Beast* to a realm of hallucinogenic lunacy that surely goes against every sane and sober principle Disney stands for.

The actors resemble their cartoon counterparts as much as real actors could reasonably be expected to. In the case of Susan Egan, who plays Belle, a quintessential Disney heroine, being pretty, unspoiled and plucky (but never rude) is mostly what's required. Tom Bosley, as her eccentric inventor father, limits himself largely to a dazed and bumbling manner. The others, however, are variously done up as steaming teapot (Beth Fowler, giving the evening's warmest performance), grandfather clock (the amusingly Napoleonic Heath Lamberts), overstuffed armoire (the imperious Eleanor Glockner) and gold candelabrum (the rather-too-excitable Gary Beach). In place of hands, Mr. Beach has melted candles that function, periodically, as flame-throwers. This will appease all those little boys in the audience who would just as soon Belle got lost in the woods.

Much of the movie's charm stems from the way objects are made to look and behave like people. Reversing the anthropomorphic process, the musical prides itself on how cleverly people can be made into objects. Even Gaston (Burke Moses), the town Adonis, gives the impression that he is inflated with helium and destined for a place of honor in Macy's Thanksgiving Day Parade. He has piano keys for teeth, his pompadour rises off his forehead like a tidal wave and he preens like Arnold. Whenever

he socks his dopey sidekick, Lefou (Kenny Raskin), the sound technicians provide the sort of "pows" and "thwunks" that you normally hear when Popeye flattens Bluto. Lefou, naturally, goes sprawling halfway across the stage.

While the tale of *Beauty and the Beast* is not fraught with psychological complexities, Linda Woolverton's book expands her screenplay without noticeably deepening it. Only the primary emotions and the most elemental reactions stand a chance of holding their own against the bustle and blazing pyrotechnics, anyway. The miracle

of Mr. Mann's performance is not its epic monstrousness or the fury of his amplified roars. It's miraculous because somehow, despite the masses of matted fur, the padding and the protruding incisors, he actually manages to convey the delicacy of awakening love. (His eyes have a lot to do with it. Ringed with concentric circles of black, they can be ineffably sad.) Elsewhere, simple-mindedness prevails, cheerfully and unapologetically.

*Beauty and the Beast* is Disney's first official Broadway musical, with more, apparently, to come. Nobody should be

surprised that it brings to mind a theme-park entertainment raised to the power of 10. Although not machine-made, it is clearly the product of a company that prizes its winning formulas. Inspiration has less to do with it than tireless industry.

The result is a sightseer's delight, which isn't the same thing as a theatergoer's dream.

. . . . . . . . . . . . . . . . . . . . . . . . . . . . .

**ABOVE:** From left, Gary Beach, Terrence Mann, and Susan Egan in *Beauty and the Beast.*

May 10, 1994

# PASSION

By DAVID RICHARDS

For years, people have accused Stephen Sondheim of being all head and no heart. Whenever the subject of love arose, it seemed, he had difficulty hiding his skepticism. He could already see the bitter end in the rosy beginning, the inevitable disenchantment lurking under the transports of ardor. No one was cleverer at dissecting feelings. As for feeling feelings, well, presumably that just wasn't his forte.

In *Passion*, however, Mr. Sondheim has dropped his defenses. With the playwright and director James Lapine, he has written an unalloyed love story, one that wants to penetrate the heart's deepest mysteries. Ironically, he has come up with his most somber musical since *Sweeney Todd*. But was it supposed to be this somber? I think not.

The lovers—Giorgio, a dashing army captain in a remote garrison in 19th-century Italy, and Fosca, the sickly and physically ill-favored woman who literally throws herself at his feet—are unlike any who have appeared on a Broadway musical stage. While you could describe *Passion*, which opened last night at the Plymouth Theatre, as another Beauty and the Beast tale, there is this daring and radical difference: it's the beast (the woman) who remakes the beauty (the captain) with the unconditional force of her love.

Donna Murphy, dressed in olive drab, her face wan, her eyes feverish, is spellbinding as the wretched Fosca. Indeed, her performance is so painfully honest in its depiction of a desperate and lonely woman that there are moments when you simply have to look away. She is also more than a little scary in the role, as her need for the captain, who can barely abide her sight, grows into a voracious obsession. For much of the intermissionless evening, *Passion* dwells just this side of the macabre.

At a time when musicals are staking their reputations on extravagant scenery and head-turning special effects, you have to appreciate the composer's unremitt-ing intelligence, his willingness to work on an intimate scale (although the heart may be the largest landscape of all), and his refusal to back off from troublesome subjects. This is his fourth collaboration with Mr. Lapine (following *Sunday in the Park With George*, *Into the Woods* and the revised *Merrily We Roll Along*), and the pair have achieved an uncommonly graceful intertwining of dialogue and music.

The score contains some insinuating melodies (no titles are listed in the program) that appear to have been forged out of cries and whispers. You can hear madness in the ecstatic lilt. The sharp drum rolls that mark the soldiers' days also could be summoning distressed souls to order. Imagine *A Little Night Music* on a night the midsummer sun fails to shine and you'll have a sense of the unusual tone: romantic but with an edge.

Still, the boldness of the enterprise never quite pays off. The musical leads an audience right up to the moment of transcendence but is unable in the end to provide the lift that would elevate the material above the disturbing. In a lamentable season for original musicals, *Passion* is easily the worthiest. But its adult ambitions, more than its achievements, are what command admiration.

Admittedly, the show, which closely follows the 1981 Italian film *Passione d'Amore*, is bucking some strongly entrenched myths in popular entertainment. We've long been conditioned to expect love at first sight between attractive people, and love between unattractive people on the condition that they have pleasing personalities. We're unprepared for this kind of mismatch.

*Passion* begins in Milan with the traditionally sensual depiction of love—Giorgio (Jere Shea), naked in bed with Clara (Marin Mazzie), the luscious married woman who is his mistress—and then proceeds to chip steadily away at that image. What captain and mistress call "so much happiness" is only skin deep, however inviting that skin may be.

Transferred to the provincial outpost where Fosca dwells, hermitlike, among a regiment of coarse soldiers, Giorgio is confronted with something he has never experienced:

> *Love without reason, love without mercy,*
> *Love without pride or shame.*
> *Love unconcerned*
> *With being returned—*
> *No wisdom, no judgment*

> *No caution, no blame.*

The lyric is surely one of Mr. Sondheim's most direct and most personal. There is, you'll notice, no face-saving wordplay, none of the old corrosive irony. He wants us to believe that the love of Fosca, whole and unqualified, cracks Giorgio wide open. Wrapped up to the neck in dour gowns but exposing her profoundest emotions, she is more naked than Clara ever is on the sheets.

While Corneille would have understood the idea of a great and unyielding love forcing the object of its desires to surrender, it's not a notion the 20th century is comfortable with. Fosca, on occasion, seems to be engaging in emotional blackmail. And you can't discount Giorgio's ego either. Does he end up loving Fosca or does he love the love he's inspired in her? You will not walk away from *Passion* with a clear and exultant sense of things. The creators may want this to be an affirmative work, but the aftertaste is vaguely sour.

The production is very much dominated by Ms. Murphy, who has a lot of the Greek fury about her, albeit an ailing one. At the opposite end of the spectrum is Ms. Mazzie, glittery and golden, an alluring presence in swishing silks. As Giorgio, Mr. Shea must respond to them both, of course. From a superficial pretty boy, assured of his charms, he evolves into a sensitive man, shaken to his depths. It's a difficult transformation because he has to resist Fosca at every turn. With Mr. Lapine's guidance, Mr. Shea matures persuasively.

Gregg Edelman, as the colonel of the garrison and Fosca's cousin, and Tom Aldredge, as a grizzled doctor, serve primarily to advance the narrative, but they do so with gruff military efficiency.

In "Being Alive," the closing number from *Company*, the 1970 musical that established Mr. Sondheim as the most gifted composer and lyricist of his generation, Bobby, the eternal bachelor, pleads:

> *Somebody need me too much,*
> *Somebody know me too well,*
> *Somebody pull me up short*
> *And put me through hell and give me support*
> *For being alive.*

Nearly 25 years later, in *Passion*, Giorgio gets Bobby's wish. But he doesn't seem to know exactly what to make of it.

**OPPOSITE:** Clockwise from top left, Jere Shea, Marin Mazzie, and Donna Murphy in *Passion*.

February 14, 1996

# RENT

### By BEN BRANTLEY

The subject of the work is death at an early age. And in one of the dark dramatic coincidences theater occasionally springs on us, its 35-year-old author died only weeks before its opening. Yet no one who attends Jonathan Larson's *Rent*, the exhilarating, landmark rock opera at the New York Theatre Workshop, is likely to mistake it for a wake.

Indeed, this vigorous tale of a marginal band of artists in Manhattan's East Village, a contemporary answer to *La Bohème*, rushes forward on an electric current of emotion that is anything but morbid. Sparked by a young, intensely vibrant cast directed by Michael Greif and sustained by a glittering, inventive score, the work finds a transfixing brightness in characters living in the shadow of AIDS. Puccini's ravishingly melancholy work seemed, like many operas of its time, to romance death; Mr. Larson's spirited score and lyrics defy it.

*Rent* inevitably invites reflections on the incalculable loss of its composer, who died of an aortic aneurysm on Jan. 25, but it also shimmers with hope for the future of the American musical. Though this production still has its bumps, most visibly in its second act, Mr. Larson has proved that rock-era song styles can be integrated into a character-driven story for the stage with wildly affecting success. (Only the Broadway version of the Who's *Tommy* has supported that premise in recent years, and its characters were more icons than real people.)

Actually, while Mr. Larson plays wittily with references to Puccini's masterpiece, the excitement around *Rent* more directly recalls the impact made by a dark-horse musical Off Broadway in 1967: *Hair*. Like that meandering, genial portrait of draft-dodging hippies, this production gives a pulsing, unexpectedly catchy voice to one generation's confusion, angst and anarchic, pleasure-seeking vitality.

The setting has shifted east, from Washington Square to St. Mark's Place; the drug of choice is now heroin, not LSD; and the specter that gives its characters' lives a feverish, mordant edge isn't the Vietnam War but H.I.V.

And Mr. Larson has provided a story line and ambitious breadth of technique miles away from *Hair*, with its funky, loosely plotted patchwork of countercultural ditties and ballads. But both works, in a way, are generational anthems, not so much of protest, finally, but of youthful exuberance, even (or especially) when the youth in question is imperiled.

The denizens of Mr. Larson's bohemian landscape are directly descended from their Puccini prototypes but given a hip, topical spin. The poet Rodolfo becomes Roger (Adam Pascal), a songwriter who has shut down emotionally after the suicide of his girlfriend. The painter Marcello is now Mark (Anthony Rapp), a video artist who shares an abandoned industrial loft with Roger on Avenue B.

Mark has recently been thrown over by his lover, Maureen (Idina Menzel), the show's answer to Musetta and a performance artist who has left him for another woman, the lawyer Joanne (Fredi Walker). And Puccini's frail, tubercular Mimi sheds her passivity to be reincarnated as Mimi Marquez (Daphne Rubin-Vega), a tough stray kitten of a woman who dances in an S-and-M club.

The plot is a peppery hash of lover's quarrels and reconciliations, with a slightly labored subplot in which the men's landlord, Benjamin (Taye Diggs), a former confrere gone Yuppie, padlocks their building while trying to evict a colony of homeless people next door.

Obviously, poverty is less picturesque in Mr. Larson's world than in Puccini's. (The moon, in the most inspired touch in Paul Clay's gritty set, is only an oversize Japanese lantern.) This show's equivalent of the Latin Quarter cafe scene, with its jolly parade of children and vendors, is an angry Christmas Eve vignette set among bag people on St. Mark's Place. And this Mimi has cold hands because she needs a fix.

Moreover, Mimi, who is H.I.V.-positive, isn't the only candidate for an early death. Roger and his friends, Tom Collins (Jesse L. Martin), a self-styled computer age philosopher, and Angel (Wilson Jermaine Heredia), a transvestite sculptor, also carry the virus. Accordingly, the leitmotif of the show is the image of time evaporating; its credo, quite unabashedly, "Seize the day."

Mr. Larson gives refreshingly melodic life to these sentiments with a score of breathtaking eclecticism, lovingly and precisely interpreted by the production's excellent five-member band, led by Tim Weil.

The styles include not only electric rock but salsa, Motown, be-bop and reggae, with a firm nod to Stephen Sondheim and even a passing one to Burt Bacharach. There is also a disarmingly dexterous use of operatic, multi-voiced counterpoint and of duets that range from the exquisite (the candle-lit meeting of Roger and Mimi) to the two-fistedly comic (Musetta's waltz becomes "Tango: Maureen").

An alternately agile and baldly declarative lyricist with a tireless knack for all manner of rhymes, Mr. Larson, like his characters, is clearly a child of postmodernism. (This, after all, is a show that rhymes "curry vindaloo" with "Maya Angelou.") But he ultimately avoids the style of brittle, defensive irony, with everything framed in quotation marks, that has become the hallmark of downtown theater in recent years.

In fact, on one level, *Rent* is about breaking through the self-protective detachment, here embodied by both Roger and Mark, of a generation weaned on the archness of David Letterman and the blankness of Andy Warhol. Like such other recent works as Mr. Sondheim's *Passion* and Nicky Silver's *Raised in Captivity*, this show directly addresses the idea of being cut off from feelings by fear.

This is definitely not a problem for Mr. Larson. Indeed, one forgives the show's intermittent lapses into awkwardness or cliché because of its overwhelming emotional

sincerity. And when the whole ensemble stands at the edge of the stage, singing fervently about the ways of measuring borrowed time, the heart both breaks and soars.

It should also be pointed out that Mr. Greif lets his cast come to the edge of the stage to serenade the audience entirely too often. He is also guilty of staging that obscures crucial plot elements. And he and his choreographer, Marlies Yearby, don't make the most of the varied possibilities of the score. Only the heady, intricately rhymed "Vie Bohème" banquet number, which concludes the first act, and the erotically staged death of Angel really match the inventive sweep of the music.

The cast, however, is terrific, right down to the last ensemble member, and blessed with voices of remarkable flexibility and strength. The unflaggingly focused Mr. Rapp gives the show its energetic motor; the

golden-voiced Mr. Pascal its meditative soul and Ms. Rubin-Vega its affirmative sensuality. Mr. Martin, Ms. Walker, Mr. Heredia and Ms. Menzel are all performers of both wit and emotional conviction.

It is the latter trait that lifts *Rent* well above the synthetic, cleverly packaged herd of Broadway musical revivals and revues. Along with George C. Wolfe and Savion Glover's *Bring in 'da Noise, Bring in 'da Funk*, this show restores spontaneity and depth of feeling to a discipline that sorely needs them. People who complain about the demise of the American musical have simply been looking in the wrong places. Well done, Mr. Larson.

**BELOW:** From left, Daphne Rubin-Vega (in red parka), Taye Diggs (in red sweater), Anthony Rapp (in red sweater), Adam Pascal, and members of the cast in *Rent*.

March 17, 1996

# THE SEVEN-YEAR ODYSSEY THAT LED TO *RENT*

By ANTHONY TOMMASINI

Jonathan Larson's rock musical *Rent* was conceived seven years ago on a sticky summer night.

Mr. Larson was sitting in a dilapidated lawn chair on the roof of his ramshackle walk-up on the outskirts of Greenwich Village, talking with Billy Aronson, a young playwright he had recently met. They were drinking Mr. Larson's favorite thirst quencher: lemonade made from cheap concentrate and seltzer.

But the composer with the sad brown eyes and goofy grin was nursing frustration and hurt. His futuristic rock musical, *Superbia*, had been performed in a workshop at Playwrights Horizons. His music and lyrics had won high praise among some downtown theater people. But the show was too big, too negative; no producer was ready to take it on. Mr. Larson was getting fed up with waiting on tables at the Moondance Diner in SoHo and making demonstration tapes of himself performing his own songs in an endless effort to secure a backer.

Now the lanky, articulate Mr. Aronson was proposing an enticing concept for a show: a contemporary American musical version of Puccini's *Bohème*. An opera buff who could just afford standing-room tickets at the Metropolitan Opera, Mr. Aronson thought there were rich and ironic parallels between Puccini's lyrical tale of boisterous Left Bank bohemians in 1830s Paris and the struggles of young urban artists today.

Excited by the possibilities, Mr. Larson immediately envisioned a gritty, uplifting show that could be his breakthrough work—"*Hair* for the '90s," he unabashedly predicted. The time had come to reclaim Broadway from stagnation and empty spectacle, he said, "to bring musical theater to the MTV generation."

He didn't know *La Bohème* beyond a puppet version he had seen as a child. But he knew bohemian life. He was living it—from the grungy Greenwich Street apartment with a four-legged relic of a bathtub dominating the kitchen, to the dynamic street life of artists, immigrants, addicts and hippie holdouts in the neighborhood, to his circle of friends who shared clothes, money and sometimes lovers.

But more than that, like Puccini's characters, Mr. Larson had been shaken by friends who were dealing with a stigmatized fatal illness that especially preyed on the poor and the young. He wanted to set the play in the East Village, amid poverty, homelessness, spunky gay life, drag queens and punk. He wanted to "blast people out with a grisly, messy show," as he told Mr. Aronson.

It took seven years of arguments, workshops and worry, but that show, *Rent*, finally opened last month at New York Theatre Workshop to some of the most glowing reviews of the last decade. Immediately, the six-week run at the 150-seat East Village theater was extended through March 31 and sold out. A bidding war began for the right to produce the $240,000 show on Broadway. It culminated in the decision to reopen *Rent*, with a projected budget of more than $2 million, at the Nederlander Theatre on April 29. Tony Award nominations seem inevitable. Record deals are being discussed.

Like many musicals, the making of *Rent* involved determination, pluck and vision. But the authenticity and spirit that critics and audiences have responded to derive from Mr. Larson's personal odyssey. This is the story of a composer who almost realized his dream.

As everyone who follows the theater knows by now, Mr. Larson, 35, died of an aortic aneurysm on Jan. 25 as *Rent* was about to start previews. His roommate, Brian Carmody, coming back at 3 A.M. from a night of pub-hopping, found Mr. Larson's body on the kitchen floor. He had apparently started to boil some water, then collapsed. The flame was still on beneath the empty teakettle, its enamel peeling from the heat.

Mr. Larson's sudden death seemed bitterly tragic, coming on the brink of such recognition. "Jonathan wanted this so badly," said Michael Greif, the director of *Rent*. "He had worked his whole life for it."

No doubt what would have most gratified Mr. Larson about the critical reaction to *Rent* were the comments that it was indeed "the rock opera of the '90s," as it was immodestly billed. "Larson is certainly not the first composer to take aim at that elusive target," wrote the critic John Lahr in *The New Yorker*. "But he may be the first to have hit it." Writing in the *New York Times*, Ben Brantley called *Rent* an "exhilarating landmark rock opera" and praised its "glittering, inventive score."

Like many ambitious, creative people, Mr. Larson was contradictory. He was rattled by his lack of professional success but confident of his talent. (He once broke up with a woman because she said he could not write an authentic gospel song.) He came from a comfortable suburban home in Westchester; yet he seemed to relish his ragtag bohemian style of life. He expected musical theater to be literate, bracing and up to date. To Mr. Larson, a friend recalled at his memorial, "Stephen Sondheim was God; Jerry Herman was the devil."

Just hours before he died, Mr. Larson was interviewed by *The Times*—the only hint he would have of the media attention that was about to engulf his work. That night, he described the evolution of *Rent*. And as he talked of the struggle to create it, he emphasized one point: that the show was motivated by his need "to respond in some way" to his friends coping with AIDS, and to celebrate the lives of people who have died young.

Jonathan Larson is now one of them.

## The Early Years: First, a Songwriter

After Mr. Aronson entered the picture in 1989, he wrote partial lyrics for three songs that Mr. Larson set to music and later completed: the anthem title song; the pop takeoff "Santa Fe," and the love duet "I Should Tell You." They pooled money to hire singers for a demonstration tape and started playing it for potential producers.

"The response to the concept of an East Village *La Bohème* was great," Mr. Larson said. "Also to my music. The response to Billy's lyrics was not so hot."

This is not the way Mr. Aronson remembers it. "We just weren't sure how to go further together," Mr. Aronson said. "We had different styles: mine was more of an ironic, comic approach; his was direct and gutsy. So Jonathan asked if he could take the show over himself."

The parting was amicable. At the time, 1991, Mr. Larson wrote a formal letter to Mr. Aronson stating that "if any such miracle as a production ever happens," he would give him credit and compensation for the idea. Mr. Aronson is listed in the New York Theatre Workshop program under "original concept/additional lyrics."

Yet something beyond creative differences had prodded Mr. Larson to venture off on his own. During this period, three of his friends had died because of AIDS. His life had already been deeply touched by the illness through a childhood friend, Matthew O'Grady, a strapping blond Irish-American, as different from Mr. Larson as he could be. While Mr. Larson was working four days a week at the diner, hiding out in his cluttered apartment to compose music on an electric keyboard and cultivating his artist friends, Mr. O'Grady was becoming financially successful in the software business and cultivating his wardrobe. "My only creativity was putting together an outfit in the morning," Mr. O'Grady remembered.

But they remained devoted. "Jonathan was the first person in high school I told I was gay," Mr. O'Grady said. "He was such a support. I used to give him shopping bags of my old clothes. He only wore the black ones."

When Mr. O'Grady learned he was H.I.V.-positive 10 years ago, Mr. Larson was the first friend he talked with. "When I joined the support group Friends in Deed," Mr. O'Grady said, "Jonathan came with me to meetings and held my hand. He went through this with me."

For Mr. Larson, the experience found an outlet in a rock monologue he dedicated to Mr. O'Grady, *Tick, Tick…Boom!*, which he performed himself in 1990 at a workshop and later took to the Village Gate. In this intense, angry solo, a man wakes on his 30th birthday, downs some junk food and complains for 45 minutes about his frustrated ambitions, turning 30 in the tenuous 90's and much more. Toward the end, he sings of a friend who has just revealed he is H.I.V.-positive. That friend, of course, was Mr. O'Grady.

Creating this show dramatically altered the course and tone of *Rent*. For in *Tick, Tick…Boom!* Mr. Larson was able to vent his anger and move on. "*Rent* was an answer, in a way, to *Tick, Tick…Boom!*" said Edward Rosenstein, a documentary film maker who was one of Mr. Larson's closest friends.

"Somehow, Jonathan found the nerve to keep working in the diner, to be true to his art, to realize that life was to be lived a day at a time," Mr. Rosenstein said. "How could he kvetch about his struggles when friends were dying? The peacefulness and affirmation that everyone finds in *Rent*—that came to Jonathan only in the last five years."

## The Staged Reading:
## In Search of a Structure

By fall 1992, Mr. Larson had a completed draft. Biking one day across the East Village, he saw construction being done on the New York Theatre Workshop. He thought the space, across the street from the iconic La Mama theater, would be ideal for *Rent*. He tracked down the artistic director, James C. Nicola, and dropped off a demonstration tape and script. Excited by the material, Mr. Nicola offered to develop it.

"What drew Jonathan and me together in a philosophical place was the belief in how tragic it was that pop music and theater music had gotten a divorce," Mr. Nicola said. "I felt he was the first composer I had run into who had the possibility of doing something about it."

The next step was to present a staged reading to get a sense of the entire show. This happened in March 1993, and the problems were evident.

"We all thought the songs were great," Mr. Nicola said. There were gospel songs, rhythm and blues, hard rock, ballads and a grunge duet for Mimi, a strung-out dancer in an S&M club, and Roger, her punk-rocker boyfriend, both of whom are H.I.V.-positive. "But the main response was that the show was unclear and structurally out of balance," Mr. Nicola added. "In theatrical time, the first act took the longest; yet it was only one night in the story. The second act was much shorter, almost by half; but a whole year of the story took place. So there was an incredibly long setup, and a compressed wrap-up, but no center."

The problems began to be addressed when Mr. Greif, currently the artistic chief of the La Jolla Playhouse in California, was brought in by Mr. Nicola to direct. "Jonathan had firm ideas and he loved battling them out with us," Mr. Greif said of their work during that period. "But there was give and take. Probably only a third to a half of the material that existed at that time remains in the play today."

With Mr. Nicola's backing, Mr. Larson submitted the demonstration tape and script for consideration for a Richard Rodgers Studio Production Award. The jury chairman was Stephen Sondheim, who had seen and admired *Superbia* and had become a mentor to Mr. Larson. "He has been a huge supporter of my work for 12 years," Mr. Larson said during that last interview. "Whenever I have a problem, he is always there."

## The Workshop:
## Finally, a Look at It All

In January 1994, Mr. Larson won the $45,000 award, which financed a workshop presentation of *Rent* at the theater's brick-walled performance space that October. Finally, Mr. Larson's friends had a chance to see the show they had been hearing in bits and pieces for five years.

Jonathan Burkhart, another close friend of Mr. Larson's in the freelance film and television business, used to come home to find a song from *Rent* sung by the composer on his answering machine. But when he heard the entire show in the workshop, he was startled to discover that whole episodes and bits of dialogue had been lifted from their circle of friends.

"There's a lot of me and Jonathan in Roger and Mark," Mr. Burkhart said, referring to the bohemian roommates in *Rent*: Mark, the earnest video artist who has rebelled against his comfortable suburban roots; and Roger, the H.I.V.-infected punker and recovered addict who reacts to his illness by sitting alone at home trying to write his "one song, before I go."

"It's complicated," Mr. Burkhart said. "Like Roger, Jonathan was always staying at home, trying to write that one great song. In some ways I'm like Mark, always hiding behind my camera, never finding myself an in-depth project."

In the show, Mark's former girlfriend Maureen, a performance artist, has left him for a public-interest lawyer, Joanne, a large-and-in-charge black woman. "A while ago," Mr. Burkhart said, "Jonathan had a girlfriend who wound up getting involved with another woman; and more recently, the same thing happened to me."

Mr. O'Grady sees a reflection of himself and Mr. Larson in another scene—that of the support group for people with H.I.V. and their friends, modeled on the Friends in Deed meetings that he and Mr. Larson attended together. But in this scene there are undisguised portrayals of specific friends who have died. One of them, Gordon, interrupts the meeting to angrily challenge the "forget, regret" bromides.

The tolerant, playful moments in which the gay and straight characters of *Rent* support one another, the way the bohemians form a tense solidarity with the homeless—such themes reflect the struggling community life that Mr. Larson exulted in. Indeed, in the search for actors, Bernard Telsey, the show's casting director, wanted the *Rent* ensemble to look like "authentic East Village people." But, "I also wanted them to sing like Sondheim singers," Mr. Telsey said.

### The Countdown to Opening Night

Three nights before that final dress rehearsal, while watching a run-through of Act II, Mr. Larson complained of chest pains and asked to be taken to an emergency room. An EKG at Cabrini Medical Center revealed no heart irregularities, according to Mr. Burkhart. Two days later, still not feeling well, Mr. Larson went to the hospital—this time to St. Vincent's. Again he was sent home, Mr. Burkhart said.

The next night, the final dress rehearsal was plagued with technical problems. But the vitality came through and an invited audience whooped and

cheered. Afterward, Mr. Larson sat for his interview with *The Times*. The theater was crowded and noisy and the only quiet place was the cramped box office. Mr. Larson looked tired and a bit wistful, but not overtly nervous. He was cautiously optimistic about the future of *Rent* and his own prospects as a composer.

Two hours later he was dead.

The first preview was canceled. Instead, the cast, crew, Larson family members and friends gathered at the theater. Mr. Rosenstein said afterward of the *Rent* songs that were sung: "This was his funeral, and Jonathan had written his own score for it. Listen to this show; Jonathan has prepared us for his death."

On Feb. 3, the Minetta Lane Theatre was packed for a public memorial service. Mr. Larson's Adelphi friend Victoria Leacock arrived from abroad just in time to speak.

When she went home, she found a holiday card in her mail from Mr. Larson with two tickets to *Rent* and a message of consolation. The previous year they had lost two friends to AIDS. The note read: "Darling Vix, '96 will be our year. (No more funerals.)"

Three weeks later, Mr. Larson's father, his brother-in-law, Charles McCollum, and Ms. Leacock spent a gray, drizzly day visiting Broadway theaters at the behest of the show's producers. "It was the most miserable afternoon of our lives," Ms. Leacock said. "To be doing this without Jonathan."

Maybe *Rent* will jolt Broadway. Maybe it will be a living testimonial to Jonathan Larson, as his father hopes. "Bittersweet is the word that keeps coming up," he said. "But for us, it's a lot more bitter than sweet."

. . . . . . . . . . . . . . . . . . . . . . . . . . . . . . .

**ABOVE:** Jonathan Larson and Michel Greif.

April 26, 1996

# BRING IN 'DA NOISE, BRING IN 'DA FUNK

### By BEN BRANTLEY

It's a strange and mighty force that is connecting the audience and the performers at the Ambassador Theatre. People watching the show there seem to find themselves yelping, whooping and sobbing without even being

aware of it. And when the dancers onstage conclude a number with a jubilant roar, the audience roars right back.

This white-hot exchange of energy can sometimes be found at rock concerts, but rarely at a Broadway musical anymore. And that, improbably enough, is what is being described here.

Sing hallelujah! *Bring in 'da Noise, Bring in 'da Funk*, George C. Wolfe and Savion Glover's telling of black American history through tap dancing, is alive and flying higher than ever on Broadway.

Sometimes you're not fully aware of a vacuum until it has been filled. For years now, the Broadway musical slate has been dominated by revivals and pastiche operettas. Attending them was like visiting a pop museum: a perfectly pleasant experience, but underlined with a sense of detachment. They usually had very little to do with the world outside the theater.

Yet the best American musicals, of both stage and screen, have seldom been just slices of chipper escapism; they have also persistently struck, both directly and subliminally, chords of concerns with which their audiences would be very familiar.

Consider a list as varied as *West Side Story*, the Busby Berkeley movies of the Great Depression and the sentimental Rodgers and Hammerstein musicals of the 1940s and '50s. These all, in their ways, addressed the fears and anxieties of their times—about urban tensions, poverty, the losses of war and the disorientation of the succeeding boom years—then recast them in forms that found sense and affirmation through the rhythms of music and dance.

*Noise* restores that link. Though the show's historic sweep goes back to the earliest days of slavery, every scene throbs with a visceral sense of the contemporary. The pulse of conflict and exasperation you sense walking to the theater through Times Square—with the aggressive pace of its crowds, the nerve-jangling noises of jackhammers and the attention-getting cries of street performers—is the pulse that informs *Noise*. And while it may be the story of one race, the ways in which Mr. Glover, the show's star and choreographer, and Mr. Wolfe, its director, turn exasperation and anger into art belong to all audiences.

There is, accordingly, a fertile spirit of generosity about *Noise*. It is evident from its very first moments, in which Mr. Glover and his fellow dancers conduct a dialogue in tap. They are tossing a rhythm among themselves, like children with a ball, and they seem to pass it on to the show's narrators, the singer Ann Duquesnay and the actor Jeffrey Wright. And when the dancers directly face the house, it's as if they're throwing the ball to the audience. You actually feel that you've somehow joined in the dance.

This is enriched by the feeling that we're being let in on the creative process, on the shaping of the dance itself. Almost all the numbers trace an arc from tentativeness to full-blown, assured performances. This is most evident in Mr. Glover's splendid second-act solo, in which he demonstrates the techniques of legendary tap artists of the past and then synthesizes them into an exultant style of his own.

All the dancers—Baakari Wilder, Jimmy Tate, Vincent Bingham and Dule Hill—maintain the distinct, loose-jointed styles they displayed last fall, but they also seem to have grown in presence. Their movements project through the larger theater like lightning. Jared Crawford and Raymond King, the drummers who find symphonic music in plastic buckets and pots and pans, match the dancers in their contagious exuberance. It's as if they're all blissfully drunk on their own talent.

As for Mr. Glover, he appears more than ever to be today's answer to Fred Astaire, with the same prodigious inventiveness and a nimble elegance all his own. Like Astaire, he wears perfection with a shrug; everything he does feels utterly spontaneous, yet not at all accidental. A natural star whose charisma lies not in a fixed persona but a fluid mutability, he seems to be always reinventing himself before our eyes.

Mr. Wright is wonderful as a drawling, white-jacketed guide (with a Bobby Short voice, no less) to the Harlem Renaissance. And the commanding Ms. Duquesnay, who can change voices like a mockingbird, wickedly speaks the part of a Shirley Temple–ish child star (danced by Mr. Glover, with Mr. Wilder devastatingly on target as a Bill Robinson type) and does a bold impersonation of a bleary Billie Holiday selling her pain.

What these scenes are taking on, of course, is the manner in which black talent has been appropriated, tamed and marketed for the mainstream. The same feeling is suggested in the Harlem Renaissance and Hollywood dance sequences.

But none of these vignettes are merely derisive. Mr. Wolfe and his company know that even when the beat that the show celebrates seems submerged, it is always waiting to erupt again. And when it does, in its purest, most ecstatic form, the foundations of the Ambassador seem to shake in happy response.

Scenes from *Bring in 'da Noise, Bring in 'da Funk*.
**OPPOSITE, LEFT AND RIGHT:** Savion Glover.
**ABOVE:** Sarion Glover and his reflection.

LEFT: Samuel E.
Wright as Mufasa.

November 14, 1997

# The Lion King

By BEN BRANTLEY

Suddenly, you're 4 years old again, and you've been taken to the circus for the first time. You can only marvel at the exotic procession of animals before you: the giraffes and the elephants and the hippopotamuses and all those birds in balletic flight. Moreover, these are not the weary-looking beasts in plumes and spangles that usually plod their way through urban circuses but what might be described as their Platonic equivalents, creatures of air and light and even a touch of divinity.

Where are you, really, anyway? The location is supposed to be a theater on 42d Street, a thoroughfare that has never been thought of as a gateway to Eden. Yet somehow you have fallen into what appears to be a primal paradise. And even the exquisitely restored New Amsterdam Theatre, a former Ziegfeld palace, disappears before the spectacle within it.

Such is the transporting magic wrought by the opening 10 minutes of *The Lion King*, the director Julie Taymor's staged version of the Midas-touch cartoon movie that has generated millions for the Walt Disney Company. And the ways in which Ms. Taymor translates the film's opening musical number, "Circle of Life," where an animal kingdom of the African plains gathers to pay homage to its leonine ruler and his newly born heir, is filled with astonishment and promise.

For one thing, it is immediately clear that this production, which opened last night, is not going to follow the path pursued by Disney's first Broadway venture, *Beauty and the Beast*, a literal-minded exercise in turning its cinematic model into three dimensions. Ms. Taymor, a maverick artist known for her bold multicultural experiments with puppetry and ritualized theater, has her own distinctive vision, one that is miles away from standard Disney fare.

And while this *Lion King* holds fast to much of the film's basic plot and dialogue (the book is by Roger Allers and Irene Mecchi), Ms. Taymor has abandoned none of the singular, and often haunting, visual flourishes she brought to such surreal works as *Juan Darien*, which was revived at Lincoln Center last season, and *The Green Bird*.

There has been much jokey speculation about the artistic marriage of the corporate giant and the bohemian iconoclast, which has been discussed as though Donald Trump and Karen Finley had decided to set up housekeeping. But that rich first number, in which those life-size animal figures assume a transcendent, pulsing existence, seems to suggest that these strange bedfellows might indeed live in blissful harmony.

Unfortunately, it turns out that these glorious opening moments are only the honeymoon part of this fable of the coming of age of a lion with a father fixation. Throughout the show's 2 hours and 40 minutes (as against the 75-minute movie), there will be plenty of instances of breathtaking beauty and scenic ingenuity, realized through techniques ranging from shadow puppetry to Bunraku.

But in many ways, Ms. Taymor's vision, which is largely rooted in ritual forms of theater from Asia and Africa, collides with that of Disney, where visual spectacle is harnessed in the service of heartwarming storytelling. There were hopes that the Disney-Taymor collaboration might reflect what Katharine Hepburn reportedly said about Fred Astaire and Ginger Rogers: "He gives her class, and she gives him sex" (if you think of Ms. Taymor as Astaire and you substitute sentiment for sex).

But Ms. Taymor's strengths have never been in strongly sustained narratives or fully developed characters. It is the cosmic picture that she's after, a sense of the cycles of life and death, of rebirth and metamorphosis. Accordingly, many of the strongest scenes in this *Lion King* are edged in mortal darkness, including a lovely vignette in which lionesses stalk their prey.

Since the movie version had a fashionably eco-friendly aspect, with pointed reference to the delicate balance of nature, Ms. Taymor's animistic viewpoint is not entirely out of place here. But although many of the actors have charm and freshness, they are hampered to some extent by the masks and puppet effigies that turn them into animals. You will gasp again and again at the inventive visual majesty of this show, realized through the masks and puppets of Ms. Taymor and Michael Curry, scenic design by Richard Hudson, and Donald Holder's wonderful elemental lighting. But you may be harder pressed to muster the feelings of suspense and poignancy that the film, for all its preachiness, really did evoke.

The words and the jokes here are familiar from the movie. So are many of the mostly unexceptional songs, with music and lyrics by Elton John and Tim Rice, although this production includes additional music and lyrics (by Lebo M, Mark Mancina, Jay Rifkin, Hans Zimmer and Ms. Taymor) that incorporate a more authentic sense of tribal rhythms and call-and-response choruses.

There's an irresistible pull to this music, and when the performers take to the aisles, their puppet appendages in tow, the show takes on a celebratory carnival feeling that almost matches its opening. It's when *The Lion King* decides to fulfill its obligations as a traditional Broadway book musical that it goes slack.

Garth Fagan's choreography is, for the most part, on the clumsy side. A romantic ballet in which the grown Simba (Jason Raize) and his lioness girlfriend (Heather Headley) discover their attraction while other pairs of lovers float in the air above them still seems like a concept waiting to be worked out. And the rendering of the show's best-known number, "Hakuna Matata," a paean to the easy life, surprisingly lacks effervescence.

Still, *The Lion King* remains an important work in a way that *Beauty and the Beast* simply is not. Ms. Taymor has introduced a whole new vocabulary of images to the Broadway blockbuster, and you're unlikely to forget such sights as the face of Simba's dead father forming itself into an astral mask among the stars.

There will inevitably be longueurs for both adults and children who attend this show. But it offers a refreshing and more sophisticated alternative to the standard panoply of special effects that dominate most tourist-oriented shows today. Seen purely as a visual tapestry, there is simply nothing else like it.

**RIGHT:** Tsidii Le Loka in a scene from the original Broadway production of *The Lion King*, 1997.

# VII. A NEW CENTURY

Despite the enduring success and youth appeal of *Rent*, by the beginning of the twenty-first century it was clear that Broadway was never going to reclaim its status as America's hummable hit-maker-in-chief. So it decided to turn disk jockey. Jukebox musicals—shows that took their scores from back catalogues of pop music—became the dominant new species of the new century's first decade. Songs by the Beach Boys, Elvis Presley, Johnny Cash, Bob Dylan, John Lennon, Billy Joel, the Four Seasons and Green Day all became the basis of crowd-courting (but not, it often turned out, crowd-pleasing) musicals.

But the mother of all these shows—the one that made producers think that vinyl was the new gold—was *Mamma Mia!*, a British-born production that proved that people had not only really listened to but also remembered fondly the Swedish pop quartet ABBA. That group's hook-festooned disco hits from decades earlier were woven into a romantic plot with a literal-mindedness that seemed to show both how silly and how irresistible the very notion of the organic musical is.

It wasn't just old records that fueled Broadway's recycling business. Revivals of old—and not-so-old—musicals started showing up with what felt like the regularity of the black-and-white films in rotation on the Turner Classic Movies television channel. And whereas Hollywood once regularly raided Broadway's latest crops of musicals to turn them into movies, it was now Broadway that was transforming Hollywood films into musicals. *The Producers*, director Mel Brooks's smash-hit 2001 adaptation of his own 1968 movie, was to this genre what *Mamma Mia!* was to the jukebox show. And the critical and commercial success of screen-to-stage translations like *Hairspray* and *Billy Elliot* has guaranteed that the formula will continue to figure in Broadway's future.

You could hardly blame Charles Isherwood when, in his review of the Off Broadway production of *Spring Awakening* (2006), he asked, "When was the last time you felt a frisson of surprise and excitement at something that happened in a new musical?" But every now and then, a show like *Spring Awakening*—an insolent, rocking adaptation of Frank Wedekind's anguished nineteenth-century drama of adolescent sexuality turned toxic—would arrive smelling of fresh pheromones instead of mothballs. And it might even be pitched at theatergoers who weren't old enough to remember when the Four Seasons (or ABBA) were the monarchs of the airwaves.

*Avenue Q* (2003), a show that took its cues from the children's television program *Sesame Street,* used puppets and simple sing-along melodies to capture the angst of early adulthood for Generation Y-ers. It demonstrated, I wrote, that "ambivalence, indecision and low expectations can be the basis for a thoroughly infectious musical." Preadolescent girls who might once have stepped into theaters only to see *The Nutcracker* at Christmastime became repeat attendees of *Wicked* (2003), which transformed the witches from *The Wizards of Oz* into *Gossip Girls*–style broomstick riders for whom popularity was everything.

Subjects that would have been considered beyond the pale of musicals in the previous century were being boldly breached, with styles to match. In what was perhaps the unlikeliest hit of the decade, manic depression was channeled into propulsive, electronically amplified song in *Next to Normal* (2009). This tale of a suburban family under siege to a mother's mental illness was, I wrote, hardly a feel-good musical; it was, instead, "a feel-everything musical" that asked its audiences "to discover the liberation in knowing where it hurts." Even the songbook musical showed it could go rogue on occasion with *Fela!* (2010), which introduced Broadway (and many Americans) to the genre of Afrobeat in telling the strange-but-true history of the Nigerian pop star and revolutionary Fela Anikulapo Kuti.

And, for better or worse, musicals were a part of the mainstream American conversation in a way they hadn't been in years. Two shows that opened in 2011 made international headlines, though in their form and content, they could hardly have been more different. *Spider-Man: Turn Off the Dark* and *The Book of Mormon* both embodied what the American musical had become and where it might be going.

*Spider-Man*—which marked the return to Broadway of Julie Taymor (whose *Lion King* was still packing in audiences)—was the ultimate example of the Broadway musical as theme-park ride, with its masked superhero (played by an assortment of stuntmen) soaring over the audience to do battle with supervillains. The show was also the most expensive ever mounted, racking up costs of $65 million before it even opened, and quite possibly the most disaster-prone. Accounts of injuries sustained by cast members in previews became a ghoulish draw for theatergoers accustomed to the voyeuristic thrills of reality television. And if it seems unlikely that *Spider-Man* (which opened to some of the worst reviews of all time) will ever recoup its investment, people continue to go to it, still hoping perhaps that an actor will fall out of the sky.

*The Book of Mormon* was notorious even before it went into previews. Conceived by Trey Parker and Matt Stone, the creators of the iconoclastic *South Park* series, this musical was indeed inspired by the religious text of its title, but it seemed destined to be an equal-opportunity offender. But like *The Producers* ten years earlier (which had featured a show-stopper with high-kicking Storm Troopers called "Springtime for Hitler"), *The Book of Mormon* turned out to be one great big funny valentine to the classic Broadway musical, the kind that Rodgers and Hammerstein made famous. The real religion at the center of this show wasn't Mormonism, I wrote; it was the absurd, valiant and glorious "religion of the musical, which lends ecstatic shape and symmetry to a world that often feels overwhelmingly formless." And in 2011, audiences were lining up, once again, to hear the gospel.

**OPPOSITE:** Andrew Rannells and Josh Gad in the original Broadway production of *The Book of Mormon*, 2011.

April 20, 2001

# THE PRODUCERS

By BEN BRANTLEY

How do you single out highlights in a bonfire? Everybody who sees *The Producers*—and that should be as close to everybody as the St. James Theatre allows—is going to be hard-pressed to choose one favorite bit from the sublimely ridiculous spectacle that opened last night.

There is, for starters, that swanning song-and-dance man Adolf Hitler having his Judy Garland moment, lovingly seated in a spotlight at the edge of the stage. And of course there are those Nazi storm troopers making like the June Taylor Dancers, and all those sweet, oversexed little old ladies using their aluminum walkers to tap-dance.

But how about those glittering, swastika-wearing pigeons in cages that coo a fluttery backup to a demented Nazi on a roof in Greenwich Village? And what about Matthew Broderick bringing out the Fred Astaire in his nerdlike character and reminding us in the process that Fred Astaire really was kind of a nerd? And how about—yeah, how about—Nathan Lane, in his most delicious performance ever, re-enacting the entire show in a song that lasts about five minutes and feels like 30 seconds?

Oh, let's stop for breath, step back a second and admit that *The Producers*, the comic veteran Mel Brooks's stage adaptation of his own cult movie from 1968, is as full of gags, gadgets and gimmicks as an old vaude-villian's trunk. But the show, which has a book

by Mr. Brooks and Thomas Meehan with songs by Mr. Brooks (you heard me), is much more than the sum of its gorgeously silly parts.

It is, to put it simply, the real thing: a big Broadway book musical that is so ecstatically drunk on its powers to entertain that it leaves you delirious, too. Mr. Brooks, a Brooklyn boy who grew up in the age of Cole Porter and Busby Berkeley, is totally, giddily in love with the showbiz mythology he is sending up here.

With the inspired assistance of Susan Stroman, his director and choreographer, and the happiest cast in town, Mr. Brooks has put on a show that is a valentine to every show there is, good and bad, about putting on a show. And the expert production team—Robin Wagner (sets), William Ivey Long (costumes) and Peter Kaczorowski (lighting)—turns the stage into a bright, endlessly evocative dream-scape that skewers and celebrates the looks of great musicals from *Gypsy* to *Follies*.

Whether as an actor, film director or writer, Mr. Brooks has always worked from a manic imagination, in which jokes breed jokes that keep morphing into ever-more absurd mutant forms. Here, he channels the hyper-charged, free-associating style of the stand-up improviser into a remarkably polished riff on the kinds of entertainment he grew up with. The whole evening operates on a self-perpetuating, can-you-top-this energy, generating enough electricity to light up California for the next century.

For a production that makes a point of being tasteless, *The Producers* exudes a refreshing air of innocence. In fact, ardent fans of the film, which starred Zero Mostel and Gene Wilder, may feel it has been defanged. As a movie, *The Producers* was harsher and cruder in its satire, though you could also detect the sentimental streak that emerges more fully here. For the musical adaptation, Mr. Brooks is still biting the hand that feeds him, but at the same time he is kissing it quite sincerely.

If you grew up in the 1960s, you probably know the plot. Max Bialystock (Mr. Lane), an operatically desperate impresario of Broadway flops, meets Leopold Bloom (Mr. Broderick), a public accountant who is as repressed as Max is flamboyant. This unlikely couple cooks up what would seem to be a sure-fire scam, given Max's history: produce a play that is guaranteed to fail, selling more than 1,000 percent in investments, and then abscond with the backers' money.

Their choice as the worst of all possible plays? A paean to the Third Reich by one Franz Liebkind (Brad Oscar), a pigeon-keeping Nazi, called *Springtime for Hitler*. And for the worst of all possible directors? A theater queen to end all theater queens, the lavender-voiced Roger De Bris (Gary Beach), first seen in a ballgown and headdress that he worries makes him look like the Chrysler Building. (He's right.)

315

This is all more or less straight from the movie, as is Max's systematic trading of sexual favors for checks (made out to "Cash," which is remarked upon as an unusual title for a play) with scores of rich, lonely geriatric women. But Mr. Brooks, whose knack for musical pastiche was evident in the screwball production numbers in the movies *Blazing Saddles* and *High Anxiety*, here turns practically everything into an occasion for song and dance.

When Mr. Lane's Max, suggesting a cozy version of David Merrick (if such a phenomenon were possible), flings his opera cape around himself, we're goners. He is so clearly enamored of that self-dramatizing gesture, so absolutely thrilled to be strutting in a way that only Broadway musicals permit.

Tirelessly agile (great extensions, Mr. Lane), droll and exhibitionistic, with a clarinet speaking voice that segues naturally into song, this Max is the perfect agent for seducing timid little Leo into the unholy pleasures of showbiz. For that, finally, is what *The Producers* is about.

And what a pleasure it is to watch Mr. Broderick being seduced. This popular movie actor puts aside the boyish charm, for once, creating a slumped, adenoidal figure that suggests a male version of Peggy Cass's Agnes Gooch in *Auntie Mame*. It's a cartoon, you think at first; he won't be able to sustain it. But he does, somehow managing to make hunched introversion into an extroverted style. Leo remains a deadpan hysteric, even as he picks up a top hat and cane to lead a bevy of Amazonian chorines through a fantasy routine in which he sees his name in lights.

That scene is a homage to "Rose's Turn" in *Gypsy*. (Ethel Merman's name is invoked in the show, though hardly in vain.) In fact, *The Producers* is more packed with steals and references than a deconstructionist's college term paper. For Max's marathon courting of rich old ladies, Mr. Wagner has come up with a doily of a set that spoofs the Loveland fantasy sequence in *Follies*.

There's even a dancer-reflecting mirror à la *Chorus Line*, for the big Nazi numbers, which then turns into a crucial visual aid in Ms. Stroman's answer to Busby Berkeley–style formation dancing. And you can find gleefully over-the-top reworkings of the classic Ziegfeld beauty parades and the office as prison routines of *How to Succeed in Business Without Really Trying*.

In like manner, Mr. Brooks's bouncy, endearingly generic melodies (given robust flesh by Glen Kelly's arrangements) keep recalling songs you know you've heard before but can't quite place. The lyrics are charmingly straightforward, joke-laden and often obscene, although they never feel remotely offensive.

There should, in fact, be plenty in *The Producers* to offend all sorts of people. You could start with the characterization of the effete Roger De Bris and the Village People–like artistic crew overseen by his sinuously swishy assistant (Roger Bart), who of course becomes a victim of the old "walk this way" gag. And then there's Ulla (Cady Huffman), the ultimate sex machine of a Swedish secretary with the requisite unpronounceable name.

But in this production, shrill stereotypes are transformed into outsize comic archetypes, recalling the prelapsarian days of ethnic and sexual humor before political correctness. And that the jokes are often so hoary (an African-American policeman is, of course, "black Irish") only adds to the feeling of a buoyant comic free-for-all, an American answer to commedia dell'arte.

Mr. Bart, Ms. Huffman and Mr. Oscar (who does a German beer-garden number that crosses the Führer with Al Jolson) are all wonderfully enjoyable company. And Mr. Beach's Roger, who winds up filling in for the original Adolf (he breaks a leg, natch) on the opening night of *Springtime*, becomes every aging crooner who played the Palace rolled into one brilliantly mismatched package.

It seems inevitable that a show that keeps trying to top itself is eventually going to hit the ceiling. And after the *Springtime for Hitler* musical-within-the-musical sequence, which fulfills one's wildest expectations, *The Producers* can't really get any bigger, though it works hard at attempting it. But there are always the diverting presences of Mr. Lane and Mr. Broderick, who have the most dynamic stage chemistry since Natasha Richardson met Liam Neeson in *Anna Christie*.

Really, the only thing to lament about the arrival of *The Producers*, aside from the impossibility of getting tickets, is the extent to which it outdoes its competition. You want vaudeville-style fantasy sequences à la *Follies*? You want a 1950s-style musical courtship à la *Bells Are Ringing*? Or predatory transvestites à la *The Rocky Horror Show*?

*The Producers* has all of these things in forms that for pure spiritedness and polish trump every one of these current revivals. Mr. Brooks has taken what could have been overblown camp into a far warmer realm in which affection always outweighs irony. Who wants coolness, anyway, when you can have such blood-quickening heat?

· · · · · · · · · · · · · · · · · · · · · · · · · · · · · ·

Scenes from *The Producers*. **PAGE 307, TOP:** Matthew Broderick, Cady Huffman, and Nathan Lane. **PAGE 307, BOTTOM:** Nathan Lane and Matthew Broderick as Max Bialystock and Leopold Bloom.

**OPPOSITE, TOP:** Matthew Broderick and Cady Huffman. **OPPOSITE, BOTTOM:** Gary Beach, Matthew Broderick, and Nathan Lane. **BELOW:** Nathan Lane and Matthew Broderick.

**FOLLOWING SPREAD:** Matthew Broderick and Nathan Lane.

# Mamma Mia!

By BEN BRANTLEY

It is a widely known if seldom spoken truth that when the going gets tough, the tough want cupcakes. Preferably the spongy, cream-filled kind made by Hostess. Actually, instant pudding will do almost as well; so will peanut butter straight from the jar. As long as what's consumed is smooth, sticky and slightly synthetic-tasting, it should have the right calming effect, transporting the eater to a safe, happy yesterday that probably never existed.

Those in need of such solace—and who doesn't that include in New York these days?—will be glad to learn that a giant singing Hostess cupcake opened at the Winter Garden Theatre last night. It is called *Mamma Mia!*, and it may be the unlikeliest hit ever to win over cynical, sentiment-shy New Yorkers. That includes the Winter Garden's long-lived previous tenant, a show in which some scrappy cats sang poems by T. S. Eliot.

For if you take apart *Mamma Mia!* ingredient by ingredient, you can only wince. It has a sitcom script about generations in conflict that might as well be called *My Three Dads*. The matching acting, perky and itali-cized, often brings to mind the house style of *The Brady Bunch*.

The choreography is mostly stuff you could try, accident-free, in your own back-yard. And the score consists entirely of songs made famous in the disco era by the Swedish pop group ABBA, music that people seldom admit to having danced to, much less sung in their showers. Yet these elements have been combined, with alchemical magic, into the theatrical equivalent of comfort food.

*Mamma Mia!*, which opened (and con-tinues to run) in London more than two years ago, is bland, hokey, corny, stilted, self-con-scious and—let's not mince words—square. But in the hands of the director Phyllida Lloyd and her remarkably consistent crew and performers, these traits are turned into virtues, creating what is surely the canniest exercise in klutziness to hit Broadway.

Although drenched in an atmosphere of punchy spontaneity, *Mamma Mia!* is extremely artful in manufacturing its air of artlessness. The show's writer, Catherine Johnson, has devised a plot expressly to string together more than 20 ABBA songs, written by Benny Andersson and Bjorn Ulvaeus (some in collabo-ration with Stig Anderson), most of which are used with lyrics unaltered.

Let's get that plot out of the way: 20-year-old Sophie Sheridan (Tina Maddigan) is about to be married, and she wants her father to give her away. The problem is that, having peeked into her mother's diary from the year of Sophie's birth, she discovers that her father could be any one of three men.

So she summons them all to her wedding on the Greek island where Mom, a feisty, independent soul named Donna (Louise Pitre), runs a taverna. Mark Thompson's simple, flexible set is appropri-ately rendered in shades of blue and white designed to soothe, a bug-free island for escapists. Any touches of luridness are reserved for his costumes.

This story line, similar to that of the smirkier 1968 movie *Buona Sera, Mrs. Campbell*, winds up serving as a nifty peg-board for both that bouncy electronic music and the kind of contrasting of mother-versus-daughter values that is regular fare for the Lifetime channel. It also allows members of a graying disco generation to shake their booties once again.

In her youth, it happens, Mom headed a rock trio, Donna and the Dynamos. And among the wedding guests are, of course, the other members of that group: the chic, lean and thrice-married Tanya (Karen Mason) and the round, no-nonsense Rosie (Judy Kaye), a cookbook writer. How can they resist putting on their old costumes and singing their old songs?

This is not, for the record, your basic organic musical. Songs spring directly from the plot, but with a jolting, self-aware literal-mindedness. Don't even ask how "Chiquitita," a Spanish-flavored ballad, turns directly into a vehicle for Tanya and Rosie to cheer up the distraught Donna. Or how Donna lets a bitter confrontation segue straight into "The Winner Takes It All."

The full charms of this approach don't become evident until about 20 minutes into the show, when Donna accidentally encoun-ters Sam (David W. Keeley), a hunky archi-tect and one of the three potential fathers. (The others are played by Dean Nolen and Ken Marks.)

Donna, in work clothes with a drill in her hand, strikes a pose of shock, everyone else onstage freezes, and suddenly she's singing, with full-throated alarm, the title number, a spirited song of regretful attrac-tion. ("Mamma mia, here I go again/ My my, how can I resist you?") Every now and then, the members of a friendly chorus of Greek peasants pop their heads over the walls to echo her.

The effect, and I've never before seen it rendered so evocatively onstage, conjures up the way old Top 40 hits will insinuate them-selves into your mind at critical emotional moments, providing unsolicited soundtracks. Actually, *Mamma Mia!* often suggests a world in which everyone is the star of his or her own music video, the kind you can create at those small karaoke sound stages in amuse-ment parks.

Similarly, Anthony Van Laast's chore-ography, which includes a fantasy sequence in scuba gear, never looks studied, though of course it is. In the party numbers, you have the impression of the kind of synchronized exuberance that sometimes spontaneously settles onto a dance floor shared by the same people for a long time. It is also reas-suring to see an ensemble of so many varied body types. Again, the idea is that they could be you or me.

Since they are meant to be stand-ins for the audience, the performers emerge less as specific characters than as hearty arche-types. But they're agreeable company, and they agilely walk a fine line between sincer-ity and spoof. This is true even during, er, snappy dialogue like the following:

"I'm old enough to be your mother."

"You can call me Oedipus."

Ms. Pitre has a terrific pop belter's voice, and she's delightful when she's boogy-ing down with her chums, though you wish she could loosen up a bit for the heavy emo-tional scenes with her daughter and suitors past. Ms. Mason has vivid bite playing a vamp of a certain age. Ms. Maddigan is a lus-cious ingénue.

And Ms. Kaye comes close to creating a fully shaped character out of air. Her courtship bid to the adamantly single Bill (Mr. Marks), in which she sings "Take a Chance on Me," is the most charming number in the show.

Unbidden, the audience starts clapping along happily with that one. By that point, you've surely realized that whether you're conscious of it or not, you've been listening to ABBA music all your life. Mr. Andersson's and Mr. Ulvaeus's hook-driven, addictively tuneful melodies have been heard, in some

form, in many an elevator, dentist's office and supermarket aisle.

*Mamma Mia!* manipulates you, for sure, but it creates the feeling that you're somehow a part of the manipulative process. And while it may be widely described as a hoot by theatergoers embarrassed at having enjoyed it, it gives off a moist-eyed sincerity that is beyond camp.

The woman who accompanied me to *Mamma Mia!* wore hard-edged black and an air of weary skepticism. At one point, she hissed irritably at me, "I hate the '70s." That

was early, though. When the curtain calls came, she was openly weeping and laughing at herself for doing so.

- - - - - - - - - - - - - - - - - - - - - - - - - - - -

**ABOVE:** From left, Karen Mason, Louise Pitre, and Judy Kaye in *Mamma Mia!*

# HAIRSPRAY

By BEN BRANTLEY

If life were everything it should be—that is, if life were more like the endearing new musical called *Hairspray* that opened last night at the Neil Simon Theatre—your every waking thought would be footnoted by a chorus of backup singers of early '60s vintage. You know, the kind who always come up with helpful bons mots like "ow-oot" and "bop-be-ba, ba-ba-ba-ba," whether the lead singer's heart is breaking or quaking.

Consider the effect that such encouragement has on one Tracy Turnblad of Baltimore, as she walks to school through a landscape that includes a frolicsome gutter rat, the flasher who lives next door and that familiar old derelict with his portable bar stool. Those happy backup voices in her head, engraved by endless spinnings of vinyl in her bedroom, guarantee that her view of the streets is more than rosy: it's hot pink and filled with promises of romance, stardom and the righting of social inequalities.

And, oh, by the way, when Tracy (embodied with trustworthy sincerity by Marissa Jaret Winokur) requires some extra assistance, when she needs to help her agoraphobic mom cut loose and live a little, for example, a Supremes-like trio in dazzling red steps out of a poster and onto the sidewalks to deliver the message personally. Among the advice offered: "The future's got a million roads for you to choose/ But you'll walk a little taller in some high-heel shoes."

And there you have the dewy essence of *Hairspray*, which is adapted from John Waters's 1988 movie about rock 'n' roll and race relations and features a captivatingly humane Harvey Fierstein (of *Torch Song Trilogy*) in the role created by the drag goddess Divine. If you're not at all taken by the fantasy of the Supremes showing up to bestow a little Motown magic on your bedraggled, overworked mother, then you will probably be in the minority of theatergoers who will not find this musical irresistible.

Otherwise, you won't need Ecstasy or any other of those fashionable drugs said to generate warm, fuzzy and benevolent feelings. So what if it's more than a little pushy in its social preaching? Stocked with canny, deliriously tuneful songs by Marc Shaiman and Scott Wittman and directed by Jack O'Brien with a common touch that stops short of vulgarity, *Hairspray* is as sweet as a show can be without promoting tooth decay.

The buzz on *Hairspray*, which is centered on a television disc-jockey show in which white kids dance to black music, has been of the overblown variety that can wind up stinging its creators. It's been touted, for example, as the next *Producers*, the multi-Tony-winning Mel Brooks musical.

In truth, *Hairspray* doesn't have the same breathtaking confidence in its powers of invention. There are moments (rare ones) when it seems to lose its comic moorings to drift into repetition, and it definitely overdoes the self-help-style anthems of uplift.

But like *The Producers*, *Hairspray* succeeds in re-creating the pleasures of the old-fashioned musical comedy without seeming old-fashioned. Think of it, if you insist on such nomenclature, as a post-postmodern musical. It's a work that incorporates elements of arch satire, kitsch and camp—all those elements that ruled pop culture for the past several decades—but without the long-customary edges of jadedness and condescension.

Remember all that talk some months back about how the age of irony was over? That diagnosis turned out to be embarrassingly premature. But *Hairspray* offers winning evidence for the charms of an irony-free world, at least for a few hours.

Yes, it is inspired by a film by John Waters, a director whose name became a byword for midnight gross-out movie iconoclasm; yes, it does star a large man in drag (Mr. Fierstein); and yes the show's songs, its broad but witty book (by Mark O'Donnell and

Thomas Meehan) and its eye-tickling look (sets by David Rockwell, costumes by William Ivey Long) are chock full of knowing references to other musicals and pop artifacts.

Mr. Rockwell's delightful pop-up cartoon set, for example, makes allusions to that earlier teenage classic *Bye Bye Birdie!*

Yet for all that, *Hairspray* has none of the wink-wink, isn't-this-a-hoot sensibility that often characterizes pastiche musicals. Mr. O'Brien has made sure that none of his ensemble members—who include the freshest array of young singers and dancers since *Rent*—keep even an inch of distance from their material.

They inhabit their popsicle-colored world without a whit of self-consciousness, which means that even when they're being subversive, they glow like Andy Hardy. When a young man named Seaweed, played by Corey Reynolds, flicks opens a switchblade in a moment of crisis, it's with a Boy Scout spirit of resourcefulness instead of street menace. Hip they may be, with their high ratted hair and light-reflecting clothes. But these kids are too warm to be cool.

The same friendly tone is carried out on every level, but its backbone comes from its music. Mr. Shaiman, the show's composer and its co-lyricist with Mr. Wittman, isn't sending up the music of the age of *American Bandstand*. Nor is he simply replicating it. What he's doing instead is taking the infectious hooks and rhythms from period pop and R & B and translating them into the big, bouncy sound that Broadway demands.

Corny Collins (Clarke Thorell), the Dick Clark–like host of his *American Bandstand*–like show, calls his young dancers "the sugar and spice-est, nicest kids in town." So maybe within their ranks there are a couple of no-goodniks who would judge people by their dress size or the color of their skin. Basically, Corny's description fits the kids and show like a latex glove.

For *Hairspray* is, above all, Nice. This may be regarded as faint praise in New York, capital of Type A personalities. But Nice, in this instance, doesn't mean bland. Think of it spelled out in neon, perhaps in letters of purple and fuchsia. That's the kind of Nice that *Hairspray* is selling. And it feels awfully good to pretend, for as long as the cast keeps singing, that the world really is that way.

**RIGHT:** Marissa Jaret Winokur
as Tracy and Harvey Fierstein as
her mom in *Hairspray*.

October 25, 2002

# Movin' Out

By BEN BRANTLEY

When a young man kicks up his heels in the new Broadway show *Movin' Out*, which opened last night at the Richard Rodgers Theatre, the feeling isn't just fancy-free. True, Eddie, a strapping boy in his salad days, has every reason to be frisky. He is newly split from his fiancée, and there are plenty of delicious women just waiting to step out with him.

But when he jumps into the air, showing off (the ex happens to be nearby), his heels skew lopsidedly, as if some inner kink of uncertainty were warping his movements. The song he's strutting to is one of those pop tunes by Billy Joel that sound merely catchy at first, and then sad when you listen harder. You look at the leaping lad again and wonder a bit nervously if he might lose his balance.

This haunting little vignette, performed by the dazzling athletic dancer John Selya, is just a blip in the continuous flow that is *Movin' Out*, the choreographer Twyla Tharp's shimmering portrait of an American generation set to Mr. Joel's music. But the scene sums up the dynamic that keeps you engaged through what, baldly described, sounds like a snoozy series of clichés—the kinds of things regularly sung about, as a matter of fact, in Top 40 pop ballads of the 1970s.

Yet Ms. Tharp and her vivid team of dancers unearth the reasons certain clichés keep resonating and, more important, make them gleam as if they had just been minted.

In chronicling the stories of five blue-collar friends from their glory days in high school through the Vietnam War and its long hangover, *Movin' Out* vibrates with a riveting uneasiness. The show translates the subliminal anxiety you always feel watching dancers onstage—will they be able to stay in sync? will they slip? will they tumble?—into a study of characters who cannot find equilibrium. They are adolescents jolted out of their expected roles in life before they have had a chance to form their identities.

Everyone in *Movin' Out* ultimately does fall down, literally or otherwise. Of course, under the supervision of Ms. Tharp, who created such milestones in modern dance as *Deuce Coupe*, they do so with an aching grace.

Even at a time when the Broadway musical keeps stretching into new categories to find new audiences, *Movin' Out* fits no pigeonhole. Its closest parallel from recent memory is *Contact*, Susan Stroman's effervescent, self-described "dance play." And in using the work of a pop composer like Mr. Joel, *Movin' Out* brings to mind the jukebox musical smashes *Mamma Mia!* (with the songs of ABBA) and *We Will Rock You* (Queen).

Yet Ms. Tharp's production has little of the old-style showbiz wit and flourish that Ms. Stroman brought to her delightful trio of danced playlets. Nor does *Movin' Out* trade as obviously as *Mamma Mia!* does on what might be called the karaoke quotient: the pleasure in listening to familiar feel-good music that makes you want to sing along.

*Movin' Out*, for the record, has only one principal vocalist: the remarkably accomplished pianist and Billy Joel–soundalike Michael Cavanaugh, who performs on a platform above the dancers with an excellent 10-piece band. There's a self-contained polish about his singing that does not encourage theatergoers to join in. Up to the show's finale, you're unlikely to feel any overwhelming urge to tap your feet or shimmy your shoulders.

This is because Ms. Tharp has created numbers that, at their best, internalize the score. Each principal performer seems to have his or her own special dialogue with the songs; the dances become shaded personality sketches, expressing individual reactions to mass-marketed music.

It helps that the characters in the show, which is set in Mr. Joel's native Long Island, are just the sort of people who would grow up listening to and identifying with Billy Joel songs. They are less rebellious, less hip precursors to the New Jersey kids who would latch on to Bruce Springsteen.

Ms. Tharp honors the hopeful squareness of her characters' youths and the self-destructive, masochistic streak that runs through Mr. Joel's ballads of disappointment in adulthood. Throughout, she makes wonderfully elegant use of their uncool klutziness. You can imagine yourself becoming these characters in a way that the idealized sophistication of Astaire and Rogers, say, does not allow.

The show begins with a prologue, set to "It's Still Rock 'n' Roll to Me," in which the characters introduce themselves with the sort of exuberant, rough-edged poses common to teenagers, guys flexing their muscles and girls wriggling their hips. The dominant feeling is of people trying on attitudes that don't fit.

There are five fully defined characters: Eddie (Mr. Selya) and Brenda (Elizabeth Parkinson), the king and queen of the prom, who break up soon after the show begins (to the strains of "Scenes From an Italian Restaurant"); James (Benjamin G. Bowman) and Judy (Ashley Tuttle), whose love seems more durable; and Tony (Keith Roberts), part of a tight trio of friends with Eddie and James.

What follows has been examined to the point of weariness in films like *The Deer Hunter* and *Coming Home* and novels like *Machine Dreams*. The three men go to Vietnam as soldiers. Only two return, and all four survivors—the men and women—bear psychic wounds that will not stop festering.

That is pretty much it, folks, and yes, you've heard it before. But with a wide-ranging physical vocabulary that quotes everything from *Swan Lake* to Michael Jackson's moonwalk, Ms. Tharp uses this basic story in the way choreographers of storybook ballets used fairy tales like "Sleeping Beauty." The dancers' movements, especially those of the men, keep uncovering deeper emotional levels that are anything but simple.

**OPPOSITE:** John Selya (in the air) as Eddie with members of the cast.

325

A NEW CENTURY

August 1, 2003

# Avenue Q

By BEN BRANTLEY

In the savvy, sassy and eminently likable *Avenue Q*, which opened last night at the Golden Theater, an idealistic young man stares into the audience and sings, in a voice shiny with hope, "Something's coming, something good."

Feeling some nagging tug of déjà vu? It's entirely possible. Some 40 years ago, another idealistic young man on another Broadway stage sang exactly the same lyrics, and has continued to do so in innumerable revivals ever since.

But that was Tony, the starry-eyed hero of the breakthrough musical *West Side Story*. And Tony is not to be confused with Princeton, the starry-eyed hero of *Avenue Q*, which is a breakthrough musical of a very different stripe. After fervently anticipating the good things of the future, Tony went on to fall deeply and unconditionally in love, kill his girlfriend's brother and die violently, leaving an exceedingly pretty corpse, all within a matter of days.

Princeton, too, has stars in his eyes. But after he sings about "something coming," he falls kind of, sort of in love (or maybe not); gets lost looking for his purpose in life; lies around moping in his apartment while takeout food cartons pile up; and when last heard from, is still very much alive, though in a continuing state of what looks like terminal uncertainty. And, oh, did I mention? He has two heads. That's literally. Figuratively, he has a lot more.

Ah, what a difference half a century makes when it comes to leading men in American musicals. Tony, originally played by Larry Kert, belonged to an era in theater when sung emotions were big, clean and uncompromising. If you felt pretty, then Miss America could just resign; if you loved somebody, then the whole planet Earth turned into a star.

In *Avenue Q*, first staged last spring Off Broadway at the Vineyard Theatre, Princeton is embodied by both an oversize hand puppet and John Tartaglia, the always

visible actor who manipulates Princeton and provides his voice. And he is very clearly part of a generation whose members find question marks creeping into every sentence they utter.

Unlike the self-destructive, street-smart adolescents in *West Side Story*, who always seemed about to explode whenever they sang or danced, the overschooled college graduates (some furry, some fleshy) of *Avenue Q* look as if they might deflate as they work their way through bouncy ditties about failure, sex and the general pettiness of life.

The role models for Princeton and his sometime girlfriend, Kate Monster (Stephanie D'Abruzzo), and their underemployed chums are not the misunderstood rebels portrayed by James Dean and Marlon Brando, but the gentle, instructive and fallible cloth creatures of *Sesame Street*.

This does not mean that the denizens of Avenue Q, an imaginary outpost of disenfranchised young New Yorkers, don't have the verve to rule a Broadway stage. Their creators, the songwriting team of Robert Lopez and Jeff Marx, demonstrate that ambivalence, indecision and low expectations can be the basis for a thoroughly infectious musical.

If the plot line sometimes seems to sag and wander in the manner of its aimless characters (and its lopsided first act does go on too long), the individual performances and songs are never less than sharply focused and completely committed to the moment.

Even more than *Rent*, the only other show on Broadway pitched directly to theatergoers over 12 and under 40, *Avenue Q* shimmeringly reflects the sensibility of that demographic segment so coveted by television advertisers. For Broadway producers, who count every head in their audiences that isn't gray as a bonus, *Avenue Q* qualifies as a serious blessing.

Like the more abrasive and ambitious *Jerry Springer: The Opera*, currently onstage

in London, *Avenue Q* dares to co-opt television, the theater's longtime adversary. This show, which has a book by Jeff Whitty and is directed by Jason Moore, addresses Americans who were weaned on the small screen, and specifically on the educational antics of friendly anthropomorphic teachers like Big Bird and Cookie Monster.

Mr. Lopez and Mr. Marx know that the songs you hear as a child are unlikely to leave your head entirely, and that whether you like it or not, such tunes and rhymes are likely to keep popping up as frames of reference for situations that on the surface could hardly seem less appropriate.

That's the delicious central conceit that infuses every element of *Avenue Q*, from its bright but gritty *Sesame* streetscape of a set (designed by Anna Louizos, and deftly scaled up for Broadway) to its archly educational animated segments, which parse words and phrases like "commitment" and "one-night stand" on video screens on either side of the stage.

But it is in its songs and performances that *Avenue Q* plays most piquantly on the contrasts between the world according to children's television and the reality of adult life. The nature of the twinkly songs, unfailingly tuneful and disgustingly irresistible, can be deduced from their titles: "Everyone's a Little Bit Racist," "Schadenfreude," "The Internet Is for Porn" and "You Can Be as Loud as the Hell You Want (When You're Makin' Love)."

To deliver such numbers with any distancing sarcasm would be fatal. And even when their heads are flipping back and forth rhythmically like windshield wipers, the cast members (many of whom have worked in children's television) do not patronize their own perkiness. Irony is a conditioned reflex for these characters, and it doesn't get in the way of their basic sincerity.

ABOVE: From left, Ann Harada, Natalie Venetia Belcon, John Tartaglia, Jennifer Barnhart, and Jordan Gelber in *Avenue Q*.

June 8, 2004

# AVENUE Q *TONY COUP IS BUZZ OF BROADWAY*

By JESSE McKINLEY

When *Avenue Q* won the Tony Award for best musical on Sunday night, just how big a surprise was it? Well, even the technicians inside Radio City Music Hall apparently thought that another show, the popular hit *Wicked*, was going to win.

In the moments after the announcement that *Avenue Q* had won, two giant video screens inside the hall read, "Best Musical: Wicked."

Embarrassed Tony officials said the mistake was a result of a "technical glitch," but you could hardly blame them for it. For weeks *Wicked* had been considered a prohibitive favorite to win the award, the evening's top prize.

The show, after all, had all the elements of a winner: box office success, respectable reviews, a spring 2005 national tour. Instead, industry analysts found themselves trying to explain how *Avenue Q*, a modest musical with singing puppets playing in a small Broadway theater, had pulled off what many in the business were calling one of the biggest upsets in Tony history. (Unfortunately for Tony organizers, if preliminary television ratings are to be believed, very few viewers got in on the drama.)

There even seemed to be a sense of shock inside the producing office for *Avenue Q*, where some were nursing hangovers yesterday from a long night celebrating the show's three victories, which included awards for best score (the show's music and lyrics) and best book (its dialogue and structure).

"I was absolutely prepared to win best score and have a great party and say job well done," said Jeffrey Seller, one of the show's lead producers. "Then after we won for best book, I said, 'I think we might win the big one.'"

The consensus around Broadway was that the show had run a clever campaign to woo voters, including full-page newspaper advertisements and a pizza party for out-of-town voters. (The Tonys are voted on by 735 theater professionals and journalists nationwide, of whom perhaps 80 to 90 reside outside the New York area.) The producers sent out hundreds of promotional CDs, with a new song, "Rod's Dilemma," written especially for the Tony race, about a puppet voting in an election.

The campaign, which one production member estimated cost about $300,000, also leaned heavily on political imagery: promotional buttons were handed out at the theater, and the box office was decorated to resemble a campaign headquarters.

"We were definitely running behind, so we wanted to remind people that we were a viable choice," said Drew Hodges, the creative director of SpotCo, the advertising company that devised the ads. "And we wanted to keep everything in the tone of the show, which is irreverent and contemporary."

The motto of the Q campaign, "Vote Your Heart," seemed to many to be remarkably blunt. The message: vote for the little guy instead of *Wicked*, which, with a $14 million budget and weekly sales of more than $1 million, had been given, fairly or not, an air of blockbuster invincibility. By comparison *Avenue Q*, playing in the 796-seat Golden Theatre, generally grosses about $400,000 a week but has a much lower running cost.

Mr. Seller, who made a fortune producing *Rent* on Broadway, said the campaign was merely trying to remind voters of *Avenue Q*, which transferred from a small Off Broadway house, the Vineyard Theatre on Union Square, to Broadway last summer.

"I think we were able to get people thinking about *Avenue Q* again," he said. "We felt if we could get them to think about it again and see it again, we'll have a shot."

Other theories and explanations were also being floated, including that perhaps voters had decided *Wicked*, with an advance of more than $20 million, did not need the victory as much as *Avenue Q*.

The result also seemed to give rest, for the moment at least, to the notion that the road voters and their allies—a bloc of approximately 150 votes—somehow control the Tony outcome. *Wicked*, after all, which starts a tour next March, is expected to be a much bigger earner than *Avenue Q*, which is a quirkier (read less mainstream) show and won't hit the road till fall 2005.

For his part, David Stone, the lead producer of *Wicked*, said he never believed that his show was a slam-dunk to win best musical. "We were never as certain about the outcome as the pundits were," he said, offering congratulations to *Avenue Q*.

Mr. Stone added that his show, playing the 1,773-seat Gershwin Theatre, had added an eight-week block of tickets yesterday and subsequently sold more than $1 million in tickets by noon, presumably on the strength of its televised production number. "We're going to be here for a long time," he said.

*Avenue Q*, meanwhile, was also having a record day at the box office, bringing in an estimated $500,000 in sales by 2 p.m. The show recouped its $3.5 million investment in April.

Scenes from *Avenue Q*. **OPPOSITE, TOP:** Princeton (puppet), John Tartaglia, and members of the cast. **OPPOSITE, BOTTOM:** Kate Monster (puppet), Stephanie D'Abruzzo, Princeton, and John Tartaglia.

October 31, 2003

# WICKED

By BEN BRANTLEY

She's flying! She's actually flying!

No, not that winged monkey who levitates over the audience. And not the slinky babe with green skin on the broom, though she definitely has her sky-scraping moments. No, the one I'm talking about is that improbably small woman in the white dress, the one who doesn't even need that floating mechanical bubble she uses for transportation.

That's Kristin Chenoweth, who is currently giving jaw-dropping demonstrations of the science of show-biz aeronautics in *Wicked*, the Technicolorized sermon of a musical that opened last night at the Gershwin Theatre. Playing Glinda the Good Witch in this equally arch and earnest show, a revisionist look at *The Wizard of Oz*, Ms. Chenoweth must put across jokes and sight gags that could make angels fall.

Never for a second, though, does she threaten to crash to earth. Even lying down, Ms. Chenoweth—who performed similar magic in *You're a Good Man, Charlie Brown* four years ago (and won a Tony)—remains airborne, proving that in the perilous skies of Broadway, nothing can top undiluted star power as aviation fuel.

Be grateful, very grateful, that Ms. Chenoweth, who spent a brief exile in the land of sitcoms, has returned to the stage with none of the routinized glibness associated with weekly television. She provides the essential helium in a bloated production that might otherwise spend close to three hours flapping its oversized wings without taking off.

Lightness of touch is not the salient characteristic of this politically indignant deconstruction of L. Frank Baum's *Oz* tales. Built on songs by Stephen Schwartz (*Pippin*) and a book by Winnie Holzman (adapted from Gregory Maguire's novel of the same title), the show is steeped in talent.

There is, for starters, Idina Menzel, the vulpine vocal powerhouse who created the role of the omnisexual Maureen in *Rent* and who here brings her larynx of steel to the role of Glinda's dearest rival, Elphaba, a.k.a the Wicked Witch of the West. (Wicked, by the way, turns out to be a morally relative word, but let's not open that can of semantics.)

The director of *Wicked* is the understandably in-demand Joe Mantello (*Take Me Out, Frankie and Johnny in the Clair de Lune*). The top-flight designers include Eugene Lee (sets), Susan Hilferty (costumes) and Kenneth Posner (lighting). And the overstuffed cast roster features both gold-standard veterans (Joel Grey, Carole Shelley) and bright rising talents (Norbert Leo Butz, Christopher Fitzgerald).

Yet it's hard to avoid the impression that whenever Ms. Chenoweth leaves the stage, *Wicked* loses its wit, while its swirling pop-eretta score sheds any glimmer of originality. There are visual and verbal jokes aplenty throughout this thorned re-creation of Baum's enchanted land, where Glinda and Elphaba get to know each other long before a little brat named Dorothy shows up. But more often than not, the humor brings to mind a slightly sweaty young college professor with a social conscience, hoping to win over his students by acting funky and cracking wise.

The story, as in Mr. Maguire's novel, is a tale of two witches: the superficial, self-adoring, cosmetically perfect Glinda and the restless, dissastified, highly intelligent Elphaba, who, having grown up with green skin in a white wizard's world, smarts from the stigma of looking different.

The contrast between the young women, who wind up as reluctant roommates at sorcery school, is used to examine a society that values surface over substance, the illusion of doing good over the genuinely noble act. It goes without saying that you don't have to squint to find parallels with a certain contemporary Western nation in which artful presidential photo ops win more votes than legislative change.

Take, for example, this declaration from the Wizard of Oz himself (Mr. Grey), who (as per Baum) is really an American migrant in Emerald City: "When I first got here, there was discord and discontent. And where I come from, everyone knows: The best way to bring folks together is to give

them a really good enemy."

And remember those winged monkeys that were so scary in the 1939 movie version? In *Wicked*, the Wizard plans to use them as spies to "report on subversive animal activity." Animals, by the way, once had the power of speech in the land of Oz, but they are fast falling victim to a persecution campaign that would transform them into, well, animals.

There's a similarly political backstory for many of the major elements of the original *Oz* tale, including the transformation of Dorothy's famous sidekicks, the Scarecrow, the Tin Man and the Cowardly Lion. But the show's central focus is Elphaba, who soon discovers an affinity for the oppressed of Oz.

That's how Elphaba, the brightest student at Shiz University (which deliberately summons images of the Hogwarts school from the Harry Potter books), becomes a rebel with a broomstick. And how *Wicked* at moments bizarrely comes to read as an allegory of those privileged student dissidents from the 1960s and '70s who traded beer blasts for Molotov cocktails. (Think *Weathermen! The Musical*.)

That's one side, anyway, of the lopsided equation that is *Wicked*. The other side involves the ambivalent, ever-shifting relationship between Elphaba and Glinda, in which the adversarial women learn from each other and which recalls sobfests about female friendships like the movie *Beaches*. (You keep expecting Glinda to start singing, "Did you ever know you were my hero, Elphaba?")

As a parable of fascism and freedom, *Wicked* so overplays its hand that it seriously dilutes its power to disturb. Much of the impact of Baum's original novel, like that of so many fantasy stories, came from haunting, symbolic figures that readers interpret on their own terms. Though there have been numerous literary analyses of Baum's *Oz* as a coded case for populism and agrarian reform, the book never feels like a tract.

*Wicked*, on the other hand, wears its political heart as if it were a slogan button. This is true not only of the dialogue, but also of Mr. Schwartz's generically impassioned songs, which have that to-the-barricades

**OPPOSITE:** Idina Menzel as Elphaba, a.k.a. the Wicked Witch of the West, in *Wicked*.

sound of the ominously underscored anthems of *Les Misérables*. Though the talk is festooned with cutely mangled words ("swankified," "thrillified," "gratitution") that bring to mind the language of Smurfs, there's a rock-hard lecture beneath the preciousness. Mr. Mantello reconciles the gap between form and content only in Ms. Chenoweth's performance.

The show comes closest to realizing its dark, admonitory vision in Mr. Lee's sets. An ingeniously arranged technoscape of wheels and cogs, overseen by the wondrous metal dragon that rests atop the proscenium, this Oz suggests a lite version of the futurist city of Fritz Lang's *Metropolis*. And Ms. Hilferty has supplied costumes that transform the ensemble members into something like the creepy, mutating figures in Bosch paintings.

They are not an especially frolicsome bunch by Broadway musical standards. And the choreographer Wayne Cilento's "musical staging" registers as a series of spasmodic, disconnected poses that suggest that the dehumanization of the Ozians is already well under way.

Yet at the same time, *Wicked* just wants to have fun, and most of the cast members are hard pressed to find a balance between grinning ebullience and scowling satire. (It makes you appreciate the sharply honed double edge of *Urinetown*.) Ms. Shelley, as the school's sinister headmistress, stays in high gargoyle gear throughout. As the craven, scheming Wizard, Mr. Grey struggles valiantly against his natural impulse to make the audience like him (and loses).

Michelle Federer, as Elphaba's wheelchair-bound sister, embodies a clunky psychological subtext with surprising grace. Mr. Fitzgerald's Puckish charm gets lost in the role of a nerdy Munchkin. And the quirky brilliance of Mr. Butz (*Thou Shalt Not*), who plays a pampered prince pursued by both leading witches, is drowned in standard-issue camouflage that recalls every hunky hero of the Disney musicals on Broadway. He even has to sing a throbbing *Aida*-style (that is, Elton John–style) duet with Ms. Menzel.

Despite the green skin, Elphaba is a bizarrely colorless role, all furrowed-brow sincerity and expansive power ballads. Ms. Menzel miraculously finds the commanding presence in the plainness of her part, and

she opens up her voice in flashy ways that should be required study for all future contestants on *American Idol*.

But even such committed intensity is no match for Ms. Chenoweth's variety. Though this petite, even-featured blonde would seem to have a set and familiar persona, it's amazing how she keeps metamorphosing before your eyes and ears.

Her voice shifting between operetta-ish trills and Broadway brass, her posture melting between prom-queen vampiness and martial arts moves, she evokes everyone from Jeanette MacDonald to Cameron Diaz, from Mary Martin to Madonna. And her precisely graded vocal and physical inflections turn even predictable one-liners into something so startling that you have to laugh.

Her vividness creates a balance problem, since *Wicked* is nominally Elphaba's story. Surely the show's creators didn't mean for audiences to root so ardently for a terminally superficial party girl, even before her political rehabilitation.

But, ah, when you have an actress who can so skillfully sell and send up her character, turning social vices into show-stopping virtues, how can you resist? What Ms. Chenoweth manages to do with the lyrics of a song of self-admiration called "Popular" is a master class in musical phrasing.

I was so blissed out whenever Glinda was onstage that I never felt I was wasting time at *Wicked*. I just kept smiling in anticipation of her return when she wasn't around.

The talented Ms. Menzel will no doubt dazzle audience members whose musical tastes run to soft-rock stations. But for aficionados of the American musical, it's Ms. Chenoweth who's the real thing, melding decades of performing traditions into something shiny and new. *Wicked* does not, alas, speak hopefully for the future of the Broadway musical. Ms. Chenoweth, on the other hand, definitely does.

**RIGHT:** Kristen Chenoweth as Glinda the Good Witch in *Wicked*.

# MONTY PYTHON'S SPAMALOT

By BEN BRANTLEY

The meeting of the Broadway chapter of the Monty Python fan club officially came to order—or to be exact, came to disorder—last night at the Shubert Theatre with the opening of *Monty Python's Spamalot*, a resplendently silly new musical.

Favorite routines first created by that surreal British comedy team for the 1975 movie *Monty Python and the Holy Grail* were performed with an attention to detail found among obsessive history buffs who re-enact Civil War battles on weekends. Python songs were sung with the giggly glee of naughty Boy Scouts around a campfire. And festive decorations were provided in the form of medieval cartoon costumes and scenery helpfully described in the show as "very expensive."

It seems safe to say that such a good time is being had by so many people (including the cast) at the Shubert Theatre that this fitful, eager celebration of inanity will find a large and lucrative audience among those who value the virtues of shrewd idiocy, artful tackiness and wide-eyed impiety. That includes most school-age children as well as grown-ups who feel they are never more themselves than when they are in touch with the nerdy, nose-thumbing 12-year-olds who reside within.

*Spamalot*, which is directed (improbably enough) by that venerable master of slickness Mike Nichols, is the latest entry in the expanding Broadway genre of scrapbook musical theater. Such ventures, which include flesh-and-blood versions of Disney cartoons and jukebox karaoke shows like *Mamma Mia!*, reconstruct elements from much-loved cultural phenomena with wide fan bases. Only rarely do these productions match, much less surpass, the appeal of what inspired them. Generally, they simply serve as colorful aides-mémoire for the pop group, television show or movie to which they pay tribute. Within this category, *Spamalot* ranks high, right up there with (try not to wince,

Pythonites) the sweetly moronic *Mamma Mia!*, which repackages the disco hits of ABBA into a comfy singalong frolic.

This means it is possible for theatergoers who are not Python devotees to enjoy themselves at *Spamalot*, which has a book and lyrics by Eric Idle (an original Python) and music by John Du Prez and Mr. Idle. It would seem unchivalrous not to share in at least some of the pleasure that is being experienced by a cast that includes Tim Curry, Hank Azaria, David Hyde Pierce and a toothsome devourer of scenery named Sara Ramirez.

Still, the uninitiated may be bewildered when laughs arrive even before a scene gets under way. The mere appearance of a figure in a certain costume (say, a headpiece with ram's horns) or the utterance of a single word (i.e., "ni") is enough to provoke anticipatory guffaws among the cognoscenti. Punch lines come to seem almost irrelevant.

*Monty Python and the Holy Grail* was the first film feature from a troupe that revolutionized sketch comedy. First seen on British television in 1969 with the series *Monty Python's Flying Circus*, this group of Oxbridge-erudite young Brits (John Cleese, Graham Chapman, Terry Jones, Michael Palin and Mr. Idle) and one American soul mate (Terry Gilliam) combined the anarchy of the Marx Brothers with a rarefied British spirit of absurdity and a straight-faced irreverence regarding all sacred cows. *The Holy Grail* stayed true to the formula of the Python television series, channeling the troupe's vision of a disjointed world of colliding sensibilities and cultural references into a retelling of the myth of King Arthur and his Knights of the Round Table.

Much of the joy of *The Holy Grail* lies in its imaginative use of its low budget, turning limited locations and homemade props into a comment on the bogusness of cinematic authenticity. And the cast peerlessly delivered its fatuous material with unconditional sincerity.

The moviemaker's self-consciousness that infused *The Holy Grail* has been reconceived in theatrical terms for *Spamalot*. (Tim Hatley's deliriously artificial sets and costumes bring to mind a collaboration between a cynical Las Vegas resort designer and a stoned class committee for a junior-senior prom.) So the fractured tale of the quest of King Arthur (Mr. Curry) and his ditsy knights for the Holy Grail has been woven into another quest: that of bringing the king and his entourage to the enchanted land called Broadway.

This expressed goal makes *Spamalot* a two-tiered operation. On the one hand there is the dutiful acting out of the movie's most famous set pieces (the killer-rabbit scene, the bring-out-your-dead scene, the taunting Frenchman scene, etc.). On the other hand, and (surprisingly) it's the friskier hand, the show spoofs classic song-and-dance extravaganzas, suggesting what the satiric revue *Forbidden Broadway* might be like if it had an $11 million budget.

The vignettes lifted straight from the movie have an ersatz quality, in the way of secondhand jokes that are funnier in their original context. Broadway performance demands an exaggeration that doesn't always jibe with the unblinking earnestness of the Python style. (The interpolated song "Always Look on the Bright Side of Life" loses the shock appeal it had when it was first sung, by a chorus of men nailed to crucifixes, in another Python movie, *Life of Brian*.)

Do these disparate elements hang together in any truly compelling way? Not really. That *Spamalot* is the best new musical to open on Broadway this season is inarguable, but that's not saying much. The show is amusing, agreeable, forgettable—a better-than-usual embodiment of the musical for theatergoers who just want to be reminded now and then of a few of their favorite things.

**ABOVE:** In front, from left, David Hyde Pierce, Hank Azaria, Tim Curry, Steve Rosen, and Christopher Sieber in *Spamalot*.

337

May 3, 2005

# THE 25TH ANNUAL PUTNAM COUNTY SPELLING BEE

By CHARLES ISHERWOOD

In the long, exhausting reality show formerly known as life, which cannot be traversed with the aid of TiVo, there are peaks and there are valleys. Qualifying as traditional high points are weddings and children's birthdays, career triumphs, the day you bought those jeans that actually flatter. Adolescence, in its entirety, is generally considered prime valley material.

Certainly, the middle-school days must be dark for the six young misfits testing their wits in *The 25th Annual Putnam County Spelling Bee*, the effortlessly endearing new musical that opened on Broadway at Circle in the Square last night after a successful run Off Broadway at the Second Stage Theatre.

William Barfee is saddled with a chronic sinus condition, a last name that invites pointed mispronunciation (it's

supposed to rhyme with parfait, thank you), and a deluded belief that he looks O.K. in shorts. Marcy Park suffers from secret dismay at her own outrageous capability. Who really wants to speak six languages if you can't meet a boy in any of them? Then there's Logainne Schwartzandgrubenierre, perhaps the most abjectly afflicted: pigtails at an inappropriately advanced age, a mortifying lisp and two gay dads to boot.

And yet a taste of life's glory is not outside the reach of even these miniature eccentrics and their equally odd competitors: mousy Olive Ostrovsky, the permanently flushed Leaf Coneybear and Chip Tolentino, the Boy Scout who has just earned his badge for raging hormones. A trophy from a spelling bee may not carry the social cachet of the homecoming queen's tiara, but small

victories are the best most of us can hope for in life, right?

In any case, it's the more private but enduring triumphs—the connection finally made with a member of the opposite sex, the discovery of previously unknown pockets of self-esteem—that are really being celebrated in *Spelling Bee*, which itself has graduated with honors from the local competition to the divisional championships. The happy news for this happy-making little show is that the move to larger quarters has dissipated none of its quirky charm.

In fact, the musical has managed to make lemonade from one of Broadway's most lemony spaces. The dreary basement lobby of the Circle in the Square always has, come to think of it, resembled the cinderblock nightmare of a prefab junior high slapped together in the 1960s. Plastering it with peppy posters promoting the French club, and plaques commemorating the mock achievements of the show's creative team, the set designer Beowulf Boritt invests an antiseptic space with cheesy warmth. (Little James Lapine, now a big-shot Broadway director, got the Dewey Decimal Award from the Putnam Librarians Association.) The theater itself, with its rows of steeply raked seats arrayed like bleachers on three sides, has been cleverly transformed into a mock gymnasium, with a basketball court stenciled on a scuffed wooden floor.

Like much else about this lovingly hand-stitched musical, the atmospheric décor should be cute to the point of cloying, but somehow it isn't. Likewise, the recruitment of audience volunteers of all ages to join in the competition still inspires delighted chuckles and palpable suspense, not squirms of irritation. At the reviewed performance, when the last surviving civilian, a shy-looking tyke with shaggy hair, skipped a syllable or two in

his last word, the audience slumped and sighed in unison.

Most crucially, the affectionate performances of the six actors burdened with the daunting challenge of inhabiting young souls have not been stretched into grotesque shape by the move to a large theater. Space doesn't permit me to celebrate them individually, as I probably should. But focus on any one of these talented performers, anxiously looking on as a competitor faces down a polysyllabic curveball, and you'll see the twitchy behavior of a real youngster, not actors self-consciously aping youthful mannerisms. Lisa Howard and Jay Reiss, meanwhile, who play the perky but unbending administrators of the bee, are no less skilled at finding the honorable qualities in more mature geekdom.

William Finn's score sounds plumper and more rewarding than it did Off Broadway. If it occasionally suggests a Saturday morning television cartoon set to music by Stephen Sondheim, that's not inappropriate. And Mr. Finn's more wistful songs provide a

nice sprinkling of sugar to complement the sass in Rachel Sheinkin's zinger-filled book. Ms. Sheinkin sets off a new comic firecracker every time a contestant furrows a brow and asks to hear a word used in a sentence, in accordance with the rigid bee rules: "Sally's mother told her it was her cystitis that made her special."

As befits a detail-oriented past master of the Dewey Decimal System, in refitting *Spelling Bee* for a larger theater, Mr. Lapine has sharpened all the musical's elements without betraying its appealing modesty. *Spelling Bee* is not extravagant in its aims, but it lives up to its goals in a way that the season's bigger, glitzier and more ambitious musicals mostly don't. Gold stars all around!

Scenes from *The 25th Annual Putnam County Spelling Bee*. **OPPOSITE:** From left, Deborah S. Craig, Jose Llana, Sarah Saltzberg, Jesse Tyler Ferguson, Dan Fogler, and Celia Keenan-Bolger. **BELOW:** From left, Jose Llana, Celia Keenan-Bolger, Lisa Howard, Deborah S. Craig (obscured), Dan Fogler, Jesse Tyler Ferguson, Jay Reiss, Sarah Saltzberg, and Derrick Baskin.

# Jersey Boys

By BEN BRANTLEY

A rush of vertigo, pleasurable but a little scary, descends around the middle of the second act of *Jersey Boys*, the shrink-wrapped musical biography of the pop group the Four Seasons, which opened last night at the August Wilson Theatre. This dizziness arrives during the kind of big showbiz moment (category: The Comeback) that anyone familiar with backstage back stories knows all too well.

Our superstar hero—in this case, the singer Frankie Valli, played by a genuine star-in-the-making named John Lloyd Young—has already scrambled from the mean streets of his youth to the heights of Top 40 glory and started the long, scraping slide downward. But there's this one song, see, that he knows can push him back into the big time, and no one will play it on the radio. So he takes his song straight to the people, and by golly, when he's finished performing it, the crowd goes wild. I'm talking about the real, mostly middle-aged crowd at the August Wilson Theatre, who seem to have forgotten what year it is or how old they are or, most important, that John Lloyd Young is not Frankie Valli.

That song, by the way, is "Can't Take My Eyes Off of You," an after-shave–soaked lounge ballad that was a hit in 1967 and is not a personal favorite of mine. But that's not the point. Nor is the point that Mr. Young—who has been doing a swell imitation of Mr. Valli's trademark nasal crooning throughout this *Behind the Music*–style concoction, directed with more efficiency than originality by Des McAnuff—has again delivered a spot-on evocation of a voice that continues to dominate golden oldie stations.

No, the real thrill, at least for those who want something more than recycled chart toppers and a story line poured from a can, is that Mr. Young has crossed the line from exact impersonation into something more compelling. It's that sort of melting from perfect wax effigy into imperfect flesh that Philip Seymour Hoffman achieves in the title role of the current movie *Capote*.

Inhaling the cheers of the crowd, Mr. Young as Mr. Valli glistens with that mix of tears and sweat, of humility and omnipotence, that signal that a hungry performer's need for approval has been more than met. And everything that has led up to that curtain call feels, for just a second, as real and vivid as the sting of your hands clapping together.

It would be, to borrow a phrase from the aforementioned song, just too good to be true that the rest of *Jersey Boys* should achieve this level of conviction. Shaped by the scriptwriters Marshall Brickman and Rick Elice as a cross between *Dreamgirls* (the Motown heartbreak-of-success musical) and Martin Scorsese's *Goodfellas* (the Mafia kneecap-break-of-success movie), the plot follows a much-traveled stretch of highway with few illuminating detours.

But in a year in which one pop-songbook show after another has thudded and died, *Jersey Boys* passes as silver instead of as the chrome-plated jukebox that it is. Unlike the recent Broadway flops *Good Vibrations* (the Beach Boys show), *All Shook Up* (the Elvis show) and *Lennon* (you figure it out), *Jersey Boys* has the advantage of featuring singers that actually sound like the singers they are portraying and a technology-enhanced band that approximates the original sound of their music.

The show's straightforward biographical approach is a relief after the hagiography of *Lennon* and the clunky fantasy story lines, inspired by the perversely inimitable *Mamma Mia!* (the ABBA show), of *Good Vibrations* and *All Shook Up*. Mr. Brickman (who collaborated with Woody Allen on the screenplays for *Annie Hall* and *Manhattan*) and Mr. Elice provide some likably sassy dialogue as they chart the evolution of their main characters from street kids in the urban wastelands of New Jersey to pop gods enshrined in the Rock and Roll Hall of Fame.

Mr. McAnuff, who won a Tony for repackaging rock for Broadway in *The Who's Tommy* in 1993, lends clarity and crispness to a shifting narrative that lets the different Seasons tell their own sides of their story. They are, in addition to Mr. Valli, Tommy DeVito (Christian Hoff), the group's bad-boy organizer; Bob Gaudio (Daniel Reichard), the genius songwriter; and Nick Massi (J. Robert Spencer), the self-described Ringo (as in Starr) of the bunch. If none of these actors matches the white-hot sincerity of Mr. Young, they are all appealing. And no one overdoes his allotted shtick.

But while *Jersey Boys* is based on fact, it rarely leaps over the clichés of a regulation grit-to-glamour blueprint. But ultimately what's demanded by the baby-boomer theatergoers that *Jersey Boys* seems destined to attract is a mimetically precise rendering of songs like "Big Girls Don't Cry," "Rag Doll" and "Walk Like a Man," composed by Mr. Gaudio with lyrics by Bob Crewe (portrayed here as a gay diva of a record producer by Peter Gregus). Because the show uses mood-setting standards by other artists in its first quarter, you can feel the audience getting restless, waiting for "the real thing."

But once the Four Seasons classics are rolled out, every other pair of shoulders in the house starts a-twitchin'. With their three-part-harmony behind Mr. Valli's hearty falsetto, the group's songs remain exasperatingly infectious. And as choreographed by Sergio Trujillo, Messrs. Young, Hoff, Reichard and Spencer come as close to simulating the originals as any pop impersonators on Broadway since *Beatlemania*.

The chief source of fresh air, though, is Mr. Young, who mutates from hopeful teenaged schlemiel to regretful falling idol with a spontaneity that never fades. When this Frankie Valli sings, you sense him channeling all the messy, happy, angry feelings of his life without straying from the required official voice. Like Mr. Valli, Mr. Young has a quirky authenticity that can't be faked or learned. His intense belief in his character shimmers like sunlight amid the fluorescence of *Jersey Boys*.

Scenes from *Jersey Boys*. **OPPOSITE, TOP:** From left, Daniel Reichard, John Lloyd Young, Christian Hoff, and J. Robert Spence. **OPPOSITE, BOTTOM:** John Lloyd Young as Frankie Valli (second from the left) with fellow Jersey boys.

December 11, 2006

# *SPRING AWAKENING*

By CHARLES ISHERWOOD

Think of the Broadway musical, its past, present or future, and any number of phrases may spring to mind, depending on your affection for this embattled but persistent form of popular entertainment.

The great American art form. Karaoke nightmare. Bring the kids, leave the I.Q. at home. Another op'nin, another revival.

Probably nobody thinks: pure sex.

That might just change. A straight shot of eroticism steamed open last night at the Eugene O'Neill Theatre under the innocuous name of *Spring Awakening*, and Broadway, with its often puerile sophistication and its sterile romanticism, may never be the same.

In *Spring Awakening*, with a ravishing rock score by the playwright Steven Sater and the singer-songwriter Duncan Sheik, flesh makes only a single, charged appearance. And for all its frankness about the quest for carnal knowledge, it is blessedly free of the sniggering vulgarity that infects too many depictions of sexuality onstage and on screen.

But in exploring the tortured inner lives of a handful of adolescents in 19th-century Germany, this brave new musical, haunting and electrifying by turns, restores the mystery, the thrill and quite a bit of the terror to that shattering transformation that stirs in all our souls sometime around the age of 13, well before most of us have the intellectual apparatus in place to analyze its impact. *Spring Awakening* makes sex strange again, no mean feat in our mechanically prurient age, in which celebrity sex videos are traded on the Internet like baseball cards.

Wait a minute. Nineteenth-century Germany? Was sex even invented back then? Officially no. When the Frank Wedekind play on which the musical is firmly based was self-published by the author in 1891, Freud's *Interpretation of Dreams* was still almost a decade away, and the subject of adolescent sexuality was so controversial that it was 15 years before the

play was produced, even in a heavily censored form.

The smartest decision made by the creators of this adaptation was to retain the original setting in provincial Germany, to resist a facile attempt at updating the material. It wouldn't have worked. The painful public silence on the subject of sex that warps the characters' minds and in some cases destroys their lives would make no sense in a contemporary context. But the yawning gap between the force of desire and the possibilities for its release is not exactly an antique phenomenon.

Adolescents today may not have to sheath their hormones in itchy woolen uniforms, but the emotional essence of the story still transmits an ache that few will fail to recognize. *Spring Awakening* lingers almost painfully on those passages in youth when the discovery of sex temporarily disorders everything: relationships to family, friends and the piano teacher; the feel of your body; even the fabric of the world itself, which suddenly seems to shimmer before you like a mirage, alive with danger and promise.

This agonizing state may not sound like something you want to return to, but *Spring Awakening* has been created with such care and craft that the voyage back is a deeply rewarding one. Michael Mayer's seamless direction works hand in hand with the inventive but unshowy choreography of Bill T. Jones to give potent physical expression to the turbulent impulses of adolescents living splintered lives. Outwardly, in narrative scenes written by Mr. Sater in a formal language appropriate to the era, they are obedient schoolchildren kept on short leashes by their stern parents and watchful teachers. But under their girlish frocks and constricting uniforms, the souls of incipient rock stars squirm and throb, bursting forth whenever a riff from a guitar signals the unquenchable force of their flourishing ids.

*Spring Awakening* has changed in small ways and improved in large ones since it opened last summer Off Broadway at the Atlantic Theater Company. It has moved further away from the Wedekind play, but only scholars are likely to care that a key plot turn, a sex scene with the central female character, the pubescent Wendla Bergman (Lea Michele), has been thoroughly softened from confused ambiguity into a consensual act.

Stephen Spinella and Christine Estabrook now play the roles of various adults, from sympathetic to snarlingly repressive. If their Boris-and-Natasha act as a pair of conniving schoolmasters is a little overripe, they are effective as the less villainous members of the parental class.

The set designer, Christine Jones, steadfastly re-creates the atmosphere of the Atlantic Theater, once a church, which gave an aptly transgressive perfume to the proceedings. Kevin Adams's gorgeous lighting has now become a key player in the mix, giving visual punctuation to the transitions between rock-concert romping and storytelling.

Most significant, the performances of the actors in the central roles of the anguished teenagers—Ms. Michele as the inquisitive Wendla; John Gallagher Jr. as Moritz Stiefel, the goof in mortal fear of failing grades and the mysterious blue legs that haunt his dreams; and Jonathan Groff as the free-thinking heartthrob Melchior Gabor—have become deeper and sharper.

Mr. Gallagher's lean face twists into a tortured exclamation point beneath the frenzied shock of hair that seems to symbolize Moritz's inner confusion. Failing at school and at life, Moritz hollers forth his frustration with an affecting scrape in his voice, in driving songs that ride on cutting electric guitar riffs and often explode into communal rants that fill the stage with schoolboys burning off energy in physical

abandon. (The supporting performances have improved too, with Jonathan B. Wright's gay seducer Hanschen now stealing all of his scenes with a delicious air of weary loucheness.)

Moritz turns to his friend Melchior for illumination on the subject of those disturbing nocturnal images that keep getting in the way of his Latin lessons, but Melchior's informal textbook only sends his friend's imagination careering down new erotic paths. Meanwhile Melchior's fertile mind has followed his hormones down the road to freedom, and he's ready to question every tenet of the social contract, and embrace every "ism" he can find, from social- to nihil-.

Imbued by Mr. Groff with a nice mix of ardency and thoughtfulness, Melchior most of all aches to embrace Wendla, whose own yearnings sometimes take disturbing form. Strangely excited by a schoolmate's confession that her father beats her, she begs Melchior to take a wooden switch to her.

As that daring sequence suggests, Mr. Sater, who wrote the book and lyrics, remains faithful to the play's awareness that the discovery of sex can carry in its heady wake both salvation and destruction, particularly when it is coupled with ignorance. Mr. Sheik's music, spare in its simple orchestrations, lush in the lapping reach of its seductive choruses, embodies the shadowy air of longing that infuses the show, the excitement shading into

fear, the joy that comes with a chaser of despair. The singing throughout is impassioned and affecting, giving powerful voice to the blend of melancholy and hope in the songs.

For the characters' confusions are ultimately not sexual but existential too. Sex is a central expression of life's mystery, and a metaphor for it too. But the awakening really taking place in *Spring Awakening* is to something larger than the insistent needs of the flesh. Mr. Sater and Mr. Sheik's angst-riddled teenagers are growing into a new awareness of "the bitch of living" itself. And the beauty of living too.

. . . . . . . . . . . . . . . . . . . . . . . . . . . . .

**ABOVE:** John Gallagher Jr., Jonathan Groff, and Lea Michele in *Spring Awakening.*

November 13, 2008

# Billy Elliot

By BEN BRANTLEY

Your inner dancer is calling. Its voice, sweet but tough and insistent, pulses in every molecule of the new Broadway musical *Billy Elliot*, demanding that you wake up sleeping fantasies of slipping on tap or ballet shoes and soaring across a stage. Few people may have the gift of this show's title character, a coal miner's son in northern England who discovers he was born to pirouette. But the seductive, smashingly realized premise of *Billy Elliot*, which opened Thursday night at the Imperial Theatre, is that everybody has the urge. And in exploring that urge among the population of a down-at-heels coal town suffering through the British miners' strike of the mid-1980s, this show both artfully anatomizes and brazenly exploits the most fundamental and enduring appeal of musicals themselves.

It's been more than three years since *Billy Elliot*, directed by Stephen Daldry and featuring a score by Elton John, first sent critics and audiences into a mass swoon in London, where it continues to play. The delay in bringing the show to Broadway hinted at fears that it might not sit comfortably on American soil.

Adapted by Lee Hall from his screenplay for the affectionately remembered 2000 movie of the same title (also directed by Mr. Daldry), *Billy Elliot* is told in thick working-class accents and an argot that, even in London, necessitated putting a glossary in the program. What's more, the show traffics in a particularly British brand of bitter treacle, wallowing in the glory of the bravely defeated and the pathos of small, trapped lives.

But the timing of the production's arrival here, with the United States newly chastened by severe financial woes and fears, gives it a resonance it might not have had in 2005, when big spenders ruled with complacency. *Billy Elliot* is a hard-times musical. And as the culture of the Great Depression made clear, in times of economic darkness there can be blessed relief in dreams of tripping the light.

Much of the power of *Billy Elliot* as an honest tear-jerker lies in its ability to give equal weight to the sweet dreams of terpsichorean flight and the sourness of a dream-denying reality, with the two elements locked in a vital and unending dialogue. This isn't wholesale escapism à la Busby Berkeley or *Mamma Mia!* In tone, it's closer to the song-dotted working-class films of Terence Davies or, on television, Dennis Potter's *Pennies from Heaven*.

This production never lets us forget the elemental tug of war between Billy's longing to dance and the forces pulling him away from it. Mr. Daldry and his prodigiously inventive team make sure that the conflict is carried through on every level, from Peter Darling's inspired scene-melding choreography, which gives a new spin to the idea of the integrated musical, to Ian MacNeil's fluidly moving sets and Rick Fisher's shadow-casting lighting. And it's telling that Mr. John's songs (with lyrics by Mr. Hall) are as infused with the energy of anger as of joy.

The plot, which sticks close to that of Mr. Hall's screenplay, doesn't even try to avoid the clichés common to tales of talented, odds-beating backwater youth. Billy is, natch, a motherless boy with a loving but unlettered father (a touching Gregory Jbara) and an adorably addled grandmother, played by the estimable Carole Shelley. Billy is portrayed by three young teenagers, Trent Kowalik, Kiril Kulish and, in the performance I saw, the excellent David Alvarez. (No public schedule is available for which Billy performs on which night.)

There's the inevitable inspirational teacher, a Mrs. Wilkinson (the sublime Haydn Gwynne, who created the role in London), who sees a spark of greatness in the lad. There's the time-honored progression from resistance—here by a rough, masculine culture suspicious of all things arty

(embodied by Billy's brother, played by Santino Fontana, and his father)—to acceptance, when the whole town bands together to help send the boy to London for his big audition. There are even, heaven help us, visitations by the fond ghost of Billy's mother (Leah Hocking).

Yet Mr. Daldry and company turn tripe into triumph by making us understand the depth of the appeal of its classic show-business fairy tale, not only to us but also to the people whose dreary daily existences touch on Billy's. The evidence of this appeal is abundant in *Billy Elliot*, most obviously in the motley ballet classes presided over by the wryly disparaging Mrs. Wilkinson and a Christmas frolic at the miners' hall where everybody dresses up as their favorite villainess, Margaret Thatcher. But it's not just the amateur performers who feel the ineffable pull of song and dance.

Billy's grandma shucks her shabby housecoat to reveal a sparkling dress and summons a spectral chorus of partners past as she recalls the respite from an unhappy marriage provided by nights of dancing with her alcoholic husband. Mrs. Wilkinson's grubby rehearsal pianist (Thommie Retter) strips out of his civvies to become a gyrating disco boy for a number called "Born to Boogie."

And Billy's best friend, Michael (Frank Dolce, who alternates with David Bologna), reveals the thrill of dressing up in his sister's clothes and making like Sophie Tucker in the show-stopping "Expressing Yourself." (The everyday metamorphosis-ready costumes are by Nicky Gillibrand.)

That number—and an electric outcry of frustration called "Angry Dance"—come closest to what one might expect from a venerable pop-chart topper like Mr. John. But much of his work here, far more restrained than his more mawkish scores for Disney musicals, is in a folksier vein, drawn from north country ballads and protest songs. And undercurrents

of anxiety, wistfulness and melancholy run through the most tuneful pieces.

This show makes sure that we always keep in mind the grittiness and despair of the society that produced Billy, so that the poetry of his dancing seems all the more startling and inexplicable. Mr. Darling's surreal blending of Mrs. Wilkinson's dance class with a clash between miners and police is one of the freshest, most exciting uses of narrative dance I've seen in years. And until the finale (which is a tad over-done), he rations his big, knock-'em-dead sequences. *Billy Elliot*, you see, isn't a dance show; it's about why people need dance.

The performances, for the most part, are broader than they were in London, with more mugging and heart-tugging stickiness. But the two most essential portrayals—that of Ms. Gwynne and Mr. Alvarez—were spot-on the night I saw the show. Hard-shelled and all too wary of the limits of her life, Ms. Gwynne's Mrs. Wilkinson perfectly embodies the tricky balance of sweet and salty the show requires.

And Mr. Alvarez, a natural lyrical dancer, exudes just the right air of con-viction and perplexity. This Billy can't articulate his need for dance, but he under-stands the potency and worth of his emo-tions. You always feel his ambivalence and, in the final scenes, his confounded sense of the privilege—and guilt—in enter-ing another realm.

For everyone else in the play, like most of us in the audience, the transcendence of dance is something to be sampled, falteringly and only occasionally, rather than lived. Billy's grandmother sings of her youthful nights on the dance floor: "It was bliss for an hour or so/But then they called time to go/ And in the morning we were sober."

*Billy Elliot* never doubts that it's the sobriety that endures in life. Which makes those intoxicating, fleet-footed flashes of art, where leaden bodies fly and discord turns into harmony, all the more to be cherished.

. . . . . . . . . . . . . . . . . . . . . . . . . . . . .

**ABOVE:** David Alvarez in the title role.

April 16, 2009

# NEXT TO NORMAL

By BEN BRANTLEY

No show on Broadway right now makes as direct a grab for the heart—or wrings it as thoroughly—as *Next to Normal* does. This brave, breathtaking musical, which opened Wednesday night at the Booth Theatre, focuses squarely on the pain that cripples the members of a suburban family, and never for a minute does it let you escape the anguish at the core of their lives.

*Next to Normal* does not, in other words, qualify as your standard feel-good musical. Instead this portrait of a manic-depressive mother and the people she loves and damages is something much more: a feel-everything musical, which asks you, with operatic force, to discover the liberation in knowing where it hurts.

Such emotional rigor is a point of honor for *Next to Normal*, sensitively directed by Michael Greif and featuring a surging tidal score by Tom Kitt, with a book and lyrics by Brian Yorkey. With an astounding central performance from Alice Ripley as Diana Goodman, a housewife with bipolar disorder, this production assesses the losses that occur when wounded people are anesthetized—and not just by the battery of pharmaceutical and medical treatments to which Diana is subjected, but by recreational drugs, alcohol and that good old American virtue, denial with a smile.

That theme was also at the center of the production that opened Off Broadway last year (at the Second Stage Theatre) under the same title and with most of the same cast, technical team and music. Yet the differences between *Next to Normal* then and now are substantial enough to inspire hope for all imbalanced shows in need of rehabilitation.

The earlier version had the same convictions but had yet to find the courage of them. A self-protective archness kept diluting its intensity, as though the darkness might go down more easily if the show were perceived as social satire, a riff on the nasty shadows cast behind white picket fences.

One bizarrely chipper sequence found Diana having a consumerist breakdown in a Costco store. Fantasies involving her husband and doctors exuded an exaggerated flippancy. And the electric-shock therapy sequence that ended the first act had the crowd-courting campiness of a vintage shock-rock band playing a big arena. Even Ms. Ripley, fine as she was, sometimes seemed to be performing with a bright, conspiratorial wink.

It was as if the creative team felt that its audiences wouldn't stay with it unless they were allowed to take an irony break from time to time. But the comic exaggerations and distortions had the opposite effect. Pull back from *Next to Normal*, and you start to see that its plot isn't so different from

those of dysfunctional-family movies of the week about healing and forgiveness. As for the what-lurks-within-the-rec-room aspect, there has been a surfeit of such exposés—in film, television and literature—since *American Beauty* took the Oscar a decade ago.

But the creators of *Next to Normal* realized they had something of authentic and original value beneath the formulaic flourishes. For the retooled version, first seen at the Arena Stage in Washington in November, they made the decision to toughen up and to cast off the last traces of cuteness. This meant never releasing the audience from the captivity of its characters' minds. That decision has transformed a small, stumbling musical curiosity into a work of muscular grace and power.

The plot is exactly the same. And I'm reluctant to describe it in detail, since the show staggers its revelations about what triggered Diana's illness and its impact on the other members of her family: her

husband, Dan (J. Robert Spencer, in the role originated by Brian d'Arcy James) and her children, Natalie (Jennifer Damiano) and Gabe (Aaron Tveit). Besides, simply to describe what occurs—which is mostly reflection and recrimination with a few visits to doctors—doesn't do justice to the excitement this show generates. And I'm sure medical and psychiatric experts would take issue with some of the details of Diana's condition.

But as one of her two doctors (both suavely played by Louis Hobson) says, there is no neat description or explanation for what she suffers from. And *Next to Normal* gives full weight to the confusion and ambivalence that afflict not only Diana but also everyone around her, including Natalie's new boyfriend, a sweet stoner named Henry (Adam Chanler-Berat, who is both credible and eminently likable).

Mr. Yorkey's lyrics are more likely to take the form of questions than answers. Mr. Kitt's score—while sustaining the electric

momentum of a rock opera—keeps shifting shapes, from dainty music-box lyricism to twanging country-western heartbreak, suggesting a restless, questing spectrum of moods. (The songs are propelled by the same rock 'n' roll jaggedness and vitality that animated Duncan Sheik's score for *Spring Awakening*, another musical about love and pain.)

Even the outsize, fractured projections of a house and (later) a face—bringing to mind the comic-strip pointillism of Roy Lichtenstein—on Mark Wendland's tiered industrial set feel newly appropriate. (Kevin Adams is the lighting designer.) This show is less about connecting the dots than about life as a state of fragmentation.

The notion that personality is fragile, always on the edge of decomposition, is exquisitely reflected in Ms. Damiano's astringent, poignant Natalie, a girl who lives in fear both of being invisible to her mother and turning into her. As for the mom that

everyone loves and loathes, Ms. Ripley is giving what promises to be the musical performance of the season. Her achingly exposed-seeming face and sweet, rawness-tinged voice capture every glimmer in Diana's kaleidoscope of feelings. Anger, yearning, sorrow, guilt and the memory of what must have been love seem to coexist in every note she sings.

None of these are particularly comfortable emotions. In combination they're a dangerous cocktail. But to experience them vicariously through Ms. Ripley is to tingle with the gratitude of being able to feel them all. Diana is right when she sings that "you don't have to be happy at all to be happy you're alive." Nor do musicals have to bubble with cheer to transport an audience as this one does.

Scenes from *Next to Normal*. **OPPOSITE:** Aaron Tveit, Alice Ripley, and J. Robert Spencer. **ABOVE:** Louis Hobson and Alice Ripley.

November 24, 2009

# *Fela!*

By BEN BRANTLEY

There should be dancing in the streets. When you leave the Eugene O'Neill Theatre after a performance of *Fela!*, it comes as a shock that the people on the sidewalks are merely walking. Why aren't they gyrating, swaying, vibrating, in thrall to the force field that you have been living in so ecstatically for the past couple of hours?

The hot (and seriously cool) energy that comes from the musical gospel preached by the title character of *Fela!*, which opened on Monday night, feels as if it could stretch easily to the borders of Manhattan and then across a river or two. Anyone who worried that Bill T. Jones's singular, sensational show might lose its mojo in transferring to Broadway can relax.

True, this kinetic portrait of Fela Anikulapo Kuti, a Nigerian revolutionary of song, has taken on some starry producers—including Shawn Carter (Jay-Z) and Will and Jada Pinkett Smith—and shed 15 or 20 minutes since it was staged Off Broadway last year. But it has also acquired greater focus, clarity and intensity. In a season dominated by musical retreads and revivals, *Fela!*, which stars the excellent Sahr Ngaujah and Kevin Mambo (alternating in the title role), throbs with a stirring newness that is not to be confused with novelty.

For there has never been anything on Broadway like this production, which traces the life of Fela Kuti (1938–97) through the prism of the Shrine, the Lagos nightclub where Fela (pronounced FAY-lah) reigned not only as a performer of his incendiary songs (which make up most of the score) but also as the self-proclaimed president of his own autonomous republic.

As brought to the stage by Mr. Jones—the show's venturesome choreographer, director and, with Jim Lewis, its book writer—*Fela!* doesn't so much tell a story as soak an audience to and through the skin with the musical style and sensibility practiced by its leading man. That style is Afrobeat, an amalgam of diverse cultural elements that will be parsed and reassembled during the show by its performers and the wonderful Antibalas, an Afrobeat band out of Brooklyn.

Irresistible music is always more than its individual parts, though. The sum of them here captures the spirit of rebellion—against repression, inhibition and conformity—that dwells within all of us, but which most of us have repressed by early middle age. It has been surfacing in wave after wave of jazz, funk and rock 'n' roll since the 1920s. And it has been translated into smooth Broadway-ese over the years, in shows about restless youth like *Hair*, *West Side Story* and even *Bye Bye Birdie*, all currently in revival.

The form that spirit took in popular music in Nigeria in the 1970s, though, was more visceral and more far-reaching than anything Broadway gave birth to. That was when Fela was at the height of his popularity as a recording star and political agitator who understandably frightened the Nigerian military dictatorship. It wasn't just what Fela said about a country broken by corruption and oppression. It was how his music said it.

The astonishment of *Fela!* is that it transmits the force of this musical language in ways that let us feel what it came out of and how it traveled through a population. When you arrive at the theater, just look at the stage—transformed into an eye-awakening, graffiti-decorated shrine by Marina Draghici (who also did the celebratory costumes)—and you'll see the source of that pulse: it's in the bodacious, mini-skirted hips that can be tantalizingly glimpsed swaying in and out from the stage's wings.

As choreographed by Mr. Jones, an eminence of contemporary dance who won a Tony for his work on *Spring Awakening*, *Fela!* leads with its hips. Its star, who makes his entrance through the aisles amid a human locomotive of shoulder-rolling men, identifies that pelvic motion as "nyansh," what you hear—and feel—in the bass.

Nyansh is Afrobeat's foundation, over which are layered elements explained in a number called "B.I.D. (Breaking It Down)," which traces the musical education of Fela from his youth in Lagos (where highlife jazz dominated) to his student days in London (where he listened to John Coltrane and Frank Sinatra). Somewhere along the way, the sounds of Chano Pozo and James Brown entered his aural landscape, and Fela heard a synthesis that he believed would change not only his life but all of Africa.

The show covers a lot of biographical territory, ranging through the United States as well as Africa, though with far less strain than in its Off Broadway incarnation. Set in the Shrine on the eve of Fela's planned departure from Nigeria, months after a violent government raid on his compound that left many of his followers wounded and his beloved mother dead, the production shifts between past and present via an assortment of sophisticated theatrical tools (including magical lighting by Robert Wierzel and video design by Peter Nigrini, with top-grade wrap-around sound by Robert Kaplowitz).

But it's the music and the movement that tell us most about the man and his world. *Fela!* never stops dancing, and Mr. Jones uses his ravishing ensemble to evoke everything from joyous sensuality to the kind of governmental oppression that turns people into zombies. Both actors portraying the pot-smoking, sax-tooting Fela lead their

ensemble, which winds up including us, with charismatic authority.

Mr. Ngaujah, who originated the role and now appears in it five times a week, has an insolent, instinctive majesty that feels utterly organic, as if it's been conjured by the music itself. Mr. Mambo wears his pain, his rage and his humor closer to the surface; he's a slightly less compelling musical presence, but a more lucid storyteller.

As commanding as both these men are—and as spirited as the male dancers (including the brilliant, sui-generis tap artist Gelan Lambert) are—it's the women who ultimately rule this universe. Saycon Sengbloh shimmers as the seductress who introduces Fela to Marx and the American black-power movement.

And Lillias White plays Funmilayo, the government-baiting feminist who was Fela's mother and whose ancestral spirit haunts her son. As anyone who saw her in *The Life* knows, Ms. White's voice can penetrate the heavens, so it seems perfectly plausible that Funmilayo could become the goddess that Fela visits in the afterlife, in the show's most elaborately conceived and fantastical sequence.

But the heart, soul and pelvis of *Fela!* are located most completely in the phalanx of female dancers (I counted nine, but they feel legion) who stand in for the 27 women Fela married. Fela called these beauties his queens, and they are hardly your traditional chorus line.

Imperial and exquisitely self-contained, these women never sell themselves with the smiling avidity you're used to from Broadway dancers. They don't need to. Their concentrated magnetism draws you right to their sides, whether they're parading among the audience or wriggling onstage.

By the end of this transporting production, you feel you have been dancing with the stars. And I mean astral bodies, not dime-a-dozen celebrities.

. . . . . . . . . . . . . . . . . . . . . . . . . .

**OPPOSITE:** A scene from *Fela!* **ABOVE:** Sahr Ngaujah as Fela Anikulapo Kuti.

April 21, 2010

# AMERICAN IDIOT

By CHARLES ISHERWOOD

Rage and love, those consuming emotions felt with a particularly acute pang in youth, all but burn up the stage in *American Idiot*, the thrillingly raucous and gorgeously wrought Broadway musical adapted from the blockbuster pop-punk album by Green Day.

Pop on Broadway, sure. But punk? Yes, indeed, and served straight up, with each sneering lyric and snarling riff in place. A stately old pile steps from the tourist-clogged Times Square might seem a strange place for the music of Green Day, and for theater this blunt, bold and aggressive in its attitude. Not to mention loud. But from the moment the curtain rises on a panorama of baleful youngsters at the venerable St. James Theatre, where the show opened on Tuesday night, it's clear that these kids are going to make themselves at home, even if it means tearing up the place in the process.

Which they do, figuratively speaking. *American Idiot*, directed by Michael Mayer and performed with galvanizing intensity by a terrific cast, detonates a fierce aesthetic charge in this ho-hum Broadway season. A pulsating portrait of wasted youth that invokes all the standard genre conventions— bring on the sex, drugs and rock 'n' roll, please!—only to transcend them through the power of its music and the artistry of its execution, the show is as invigorating and ultimately as moving as anything I've seen on Broadway this season. Or maybe for a few seasons past.

Burning with rage and love, and knowing how and when to express them, are two different things, of course. The young men we meet in the first minutes of *American Idiot* are too callow and sullen and restless— too young, basically—to channel their emotions constructively. The show opens with a glorious 20-minute temper tantrum kicked off by the title song.

"Don't want to be an American idiot!" shouts one of the gang. The song's signature electric guitar riff slashes through the air, echoing the testy challenge of the cry. A sharp eight-piece band, led by the conductor Carmel Dean, is arrayed around the stage, providing a sonic frame for the action. The simple but spectacular set, designed by Christine Jones, suggests an epically scaled dive club, its looming walls papered in punk posters and pimpled by television screens, on which frenzied video collages flicker throughout the show. (They're the witty work of Darrel Maloney.)

Who's the American idiot being referred to? Well, as that curtain slowly rose, we heard the familiar voice of George W. Bush break through a haze of television chatter: "Either you are with us, or with the terrorists." That kind of talk could bring out the heedless rebel in any kid, particularly one who is already feeling itchy at the lack of prospects in his dreary suburban burg.

But while *American Idiot* is nominally a portrait of youthful malaise of a particular era—the album dates from 2004, the mid-point of the Bush years, and the show is set in "the recent past"—its depiction of the crisis of post-adolescence is essentially timeless. Teenagers eager for their lives to begin, desperate to slough off their old selves and escape boredom through pure sensation, will probably always be making the same kinds of mistakes, taking the same wrong turns on the road to self-discovery.

*American Idiot* is a true rock opera, almost exclusively using the music of Green Day and the lyrics of its kohl-eyed frontman, Billie Joe Armstrong, to tell its story. (The score comprises the whole of the title album as well as several songs from the band's most recent release, *21st Century Breakdown*.) The book, by Mr. Armstrong and Mr. Mayer, consists only of a series of brief, snarky

dispatches sent home by the central character, Johnny, played with squirmy intensity by the immensely gifted John Gallagher Jr. (*Spring Awakening*, *Rabbit Hole*).

"I held up my local convenience store to get a bus ticket," Johnny says with a smirk as he and a pal head out of town.

"Actually I stole the money from my mom's dresser."

Beat.

"Actually she lent me the cash."

Such is the sheepish fate of a would-be rebel today. But at least Johnny and his buddy Tunny (Stark Sands) do manage to escape deadly suburbia for the lively city, bringing along just their guitars and the anomie and apathy that are the bread and butter of teenage attitudinizing the world over.

The friend they meant to bring along, Will (Michael Esper), was forced to stay home when he discovered that his girlfriend (Mary Faber) was pregnant. Lost and lonely, and far from ready for the responsibilities of fatherhood, he sinks into the couch, beer in one hand and bong in the other, as his friends set off for adventure.

Beneath the swagger of indifference, of course, are anxiety, fear and insecurity. The boys discover that while a fractious 21st-century America may not offer any easy paths to fulfillment, the deeper problem is that they don't know how to believe in themselves.

Line by line, a skeptic could fault Mr. Armstrong's lyrics for their occasional glibness or grandiosity. That's to be expected, too: rock music exploits heightened emotion and truisms that can fit neatly into a memorable chorus. The songs are precisely as articulate—and inarticulate—as the characters are, reflecting the moment in youth when many of us feel that pop music has more to say about us than we have to say

for ourselves. (And, really, have you ever worked your way through a canonical Italian opera libretto, line by line?)

In any case the music is thrilling: charged with urgency, rich in memorable melody and propulsive rhythms that sometimes evolve midsong. The orchestrations by Tom Kitt (the composer of *Next to Normal*) move from lean and mean to lush, befitting the tone of each number. Even if

you are unfamiliar with Green Day's music, you are more likely to emerge from this show humming one of the guitar riffs than you are to find a tune from *The Addams Family* tickling your memory.

But the emotional charge that the show generates is as memorable as the music. *American Idiot* jolts you right back to the dizzying roller coaster of young adulthood, that turbulent time when ecstasy and

misery almost seem interchangeable states, flip sides of the coin of exaltation. It captures with a piercing intensity that moment in life when everything seems possible, and nothing seems worth doing, or maybe it's the other way around.

**ABOVE:** John Gallagher Jr. and Tony Vincent in *American Idiot.*

February 5, 2011

# *Spider-Man* Isn't Just the Talk of Broadway, It's the Punch Line

By PATRICK HEALY

Joan Rivers gave a suggestion to the director Julie Taymor the other night: "Hire a stunt person to fall on someone every three or four weeks—that'll keep audiences showing up."

Like talk show hosts, magazine editors, entertainment bloggers, other comics, even an animation studio in Taiwan, Ms. Rivers is getting a lot of mileage out of the new Broadway show *Spider-Man: Turn Off the Dark*.

She was there backstage at the Foxwoods Theatre on Wednesday, schmoozing with the cast and Ms. Taymor, who is directing the show, to develop more material for her stand-up act, which lately has begun with a moment of silence for "those Americans risking their lives daily—in *Spider-Man* the musical," a reference to the four performers who have been injured working on the show.

*Spider-Man* has not even officially opened yet. The date has been delayed five times to fix myriad problems, with Sunday afternoon being preview performance No. 66 and the opening planned for Monday night being pushed back five more weeks to March 15. But this $65 million musical has become a national object of pop culture fascination—more so, perhaps, than any show in Broadway history.

Last month, *Spider-Man* became the first Broadway show since *The Producers* to land on the cover of *The New Yorker*; the cartoon, by Barry Blitt, who also did *The Producers* cover in 2001, showed several injured Spider-Men in a hospital ward.

"For our cover we always ask ourselves, would our one million readers know what we were making reference to?" said Francoise Mouly, art editor of *The New Yorker*. "But in no time at all, *Spider-Man* has gotten enough notoriety that we knew the cover would make people laugh. Even the show's producers laughed; they've been hounding us to buy copies of the artwork."

If most theater artists and producers are intensely protective of their shows, those at *Spider-Man* have a peculiar financial interest in being mocked. The musical, which marries a hugely popular comic book brand with music by Bono and the Edge of U2, is grossing about $1.3 million a week in ticket sales, the most of any Broadway show except the blockbuster *Wicked*, despite relatively little advertising and no major reviews yet.

By all accounts, including from inside *Spider-Man*, the show is a hot seller week to week—rather than building a huge eight-figure advance commensurate with its $65 million cost, which would suggest staying power. And that popularity has been fueled by the echo chamber of jokes, dinner party chatter and media attention among the fashionable and their hangers-on surrounding this technically ambitious show.

For all that, of course, there are some adults and children who simply have an attachment to Spider-Man, who want to see people swing from webs, or who think that the show might make for enjoyable live theater.

The injuries to the four performers generated the bulk of the publicity for the show this winter, including the departure of one of its stars, Natalie Mendoza, who sustained a concussion while backstage and left the production in late December after signing a confidentiality agreement and being paid an undisclosed amount.

But if the axiom that all publicity is good publicity has benefited the musical, what happens to *Spider-Man* when the publicity dies down?

A crucial question for *Spider-Man* is this: If tourists and parents with children head to the musical so they can have bragging rights at dinner parties or on the playground, will that translate into their friends going to see the show—once the laughs have died down—and will they themselves go back a second time or more, as many *Wicked* fans do? Some veteran theater producers say no.

"The $65 million price tag and the circus-like atmosphere of people getting injured or the show having technical problems, all of that is creating interest in the short term," said Elizabeth I. McCann, who has been producing on Broadway since the mid-1970s and has won multiple Tony Awards, mostly for plays. "But at some point, I think, people are going to say that the emperor has no clothes where the so-called musical spectacle of *Spider-Man* is concerned, and the adult audience will start to lose interest."

The musical's producers are trying to head off such a possibility by welcoming another set of tastemakers—celebrities—some of whom are friends of Bono and the Edge. Jon Bon Jovi, David Bowie, Kevin and Nick Jonas, Julian Lennon, Sean Penn and Jerry Seinfeld are among those who have seen the show. Kevin Jonas tweeted afterward: "Just saw spiderman on broadway so awesome! Everyone go see it." Ms. Taymor and Bono, who are both close to Ms. Winfrey, cooperated with her on a long article in *O: The Oprah Magazine*.

Ms. Taymor has juggled giving interviews and greeting celebrity visitors like Ms. Rivers while continuing to make changes to the show, but she said that she had largely blocked out the cultural noise surrounding *Spider-Man*.

"I took off my Google alerts on the show a while ago because a lot of the jokes and comments out there are negative, and I thought it's too hard to work under this kind of vitriol," she said in an interview.

On Wednesday night, Ms. Taymor looked queasy after Ms. Rivers suggested dropping performers from the rafters for thrills. (Ms. Rivers also suggested selling umbrellalike helmets to make more money.)

"Of course, someone's told you that before," Ms. Rivers said.

"No," Ms. Taymor said, before walking away, "you're the first."

. . . . . . . . . . . . . . . . . . . . . . . .

**OPPOSITE:** Spider-Man flies through the air.

June 14, 2011

# SPIDER-MAN: TURN OFF THE DARK

## 1 RADIOACTIVE BITE, 8 LEGS AND 183 PREVIEWS

By BEN BRANTLEY

There is something to be said for those dangerous flying objects—excuse me, I mean actors—that keep whizzing around the Foxwoods Theatre, where the mega-expensive musical *Spider-Man: Turn Off the Dark* has entered the latest chapter of its fraught and anxious existence. After all, if you're worried that somebody might fall on top of you from a great height, the odds are that you won't nod off.

Those adrenaline-raising acrobatics are a necessary part of the lumpy package that is *Spider-Man*, which had its long-delayed official opening on Tuesday night, after 180-some preview performances. First seen and deplored by critics several months ago—when impatient journalists (including me) broke the media embargo for reviews as the show's opening date kept sliding into a misty future—this singing comic book is no longer the ungodly, indecipherable mess it was in February. It's just a bore.

So is this ascent from jaw-dropping badness to mere mediocrity a step upward? Well, until last weekend, when I caught a performance of this show's latest incarnation, I would have recommended *Spider-Man* only to carrion-feasting theater vultures. Now, if I knew a less-than-precocious child of 10 or so, and had several hundred dollars to throw away, I would consider taking him or her to the new and improved *Spider-Man*.

The first time I saw the show, it was like watching the *Hindenburg* burn and crash. This time *Spider-Man*—which was originally conceived by the (since departed) visionary director Julie Taymor with the rock musicians Bono and the Edge (of U2)—stirred foggy, not unpleasant childhood memories of second-tier sci-fi TV in the 1960s, with blatantly artificial sets and actors in unconvincing alien masks.

*Spider-Man* may be the only Broadway show of the past half-century to make international headlines regularly, often with the adjective "troubled" attached to its title. So I'm assuming you already know at least a bit of its long and tortuous history of revision, cancellation, indecision and injury (from production-related accidents), and of its true star.

That would be Ms. Taymor (who retains an "original direction by" credit), who in the 1990s was hailed as the new Ziegfeld after reinventing a Disney animated film, *The Lion King*, as a classy, mass-appeal Broadway blockbuster. The prospect of her hooking up with Spidey, the nerdy-cool Marvel Comics crime fighter, seemed like a swell opportunity for another lucrative melding of pageantry, puppetry and culture high and low.

Those elements were certainly in abundance in the *Spider-Man* I saw several months ago. That production, which featured a script by Ms. Taymor and Glen Berger, placed its young superhero in a broader meta-context of Greek mythology and American Pop art, with a "geek chorus" of commentators and a classical goddess named Arachne as the morally ambiguous mentor of Spidey and his awkward alter ego, Peter Parker.

Unfortunately, traditional niceties like a comprehensible plot and characters got lost in the stew. After critics let loose with howls of derision, *Spider-Man* took a three-week performance hiatus to reassemble itself, with tools that included audience focus groups. Exit Ms. Taymor. (Bono, the Edge and Mr. Berger stayed put.)

Enter Philip William McKinley—a director whose credits include several versions of Ringling Brothers and Barnum & Bailey's *Greatest Show on Earth*—and Roberto Aguirre-Sacasa, a writer of both plays and comic books. Now if you check out the directory of paid theater listings in *The New York Times*, you'll see that the title *Spider-Man* is prefaced by the promising (if slightly desperate-sounding) words: "REIMAGINED! New Story! New Music!"

This is not false advertising. *Spider-Man* now bears only a scant resemblance to the muddled fever dream that was. It is instead not unlike one of those perky, tongue-in-cheek genre-spoof musicals (*Dames at Sea*, *Little Shop of Horrors*) that used to sprout like mushrooms in Greenwich Village, with witty cutout scenery and dialogue bristling with arch quotation marks.

Well, that is, if you could imagine such a show being stripped of its irony and supersized by a diabolical mad scientist with an enlarging ray. Though *Spider-Man* has shed its geek chorus and scaled down the role of Arachne (T. V. Carpio), it retains the most spectacular-looking centerpieces from the Taymor version. (George Tsypin is the set designer.) They include a vertiginous vision of Manhattan as seen from the top of the Chrysler Building, judiciously repositioned for plot purposes.

But they do seem out of proportion to what has become a straightforward children's entertainment with a mildly suspenseful story, two-dimensional characters, unapologetically bad jokes and the kind of melodious rock tunes that those under 12 might be familiar with from listening to their parents' salad-day favorites of the 1980s and '90s.

Scenes from *Spider-Man: Turn Off the Dark*.
**OPPOSITE, TOP:** Patrich Page (center) and members of the cast. **OPPOSITE, BOTTOM:** Patrich Page (in video), Reeve Carney (far right), and members of the cast.

March 24, 2011

# The Book of Mormon

By BEN BRANTLEY

This is to all the doubters and deniers out there, the ones who say that heaven on Broadway does not exist, that it's only some myth our ancestors dreamed up. I am here to report that a newborn, old-fashioned, pleasure-giving musical has arrived at the Eugene O'Neill Theatre, the kind our grandparents told us left them walking on air if not on water. So hie thee hence, nonbelievers (and believers too), to *The Book of Mormon*, and feast upon its sweetness.

Now you should probably know that this collaboration between the creators of television's *South Park* (Trey Parker and Matt Stone) and the composer of *Avenue Q* (Robert Lopez) is also blasphemous, scurrilous and more foul-mouthed than David Mamet on a blue streak. But trust me when I tell you that its heart is as pure as that of a Rodgers and Hammerstein show.

That's right, the same Rodgers and Hammerstein who wrote the beloved *Sound of Music* and *King and I*, two works specifically (and deliciously) referenced here. Like those wholesome, tuneful shows, *The Book of Mormon* is about naïve but plucky educators set down in an unfamiliar world, who find their feet, affirm their values and learn as much as they teach.

Of course different times call for different contexts. So instead of sending a widowed British governess to a royal court in 19th-century Siam or a nun in training to an Austrian chateau, *The Book of Mormon* transports two dewy missionaries from Salt Lake City to 21st-century Uganda.

And rather than dealing with tyrannical, charismatic men with way too many children, our heroes (enjoyably embodied by Josh Gad and Andrew Rannells) must confront a one-eyed, genocidal warlord with an unprintable name. And a defeated, defensive group of villagers, riddled with AIDS, who have a few choice words for the God who let them wind up this way. And local folks like the guy who keeps announcing that he has maggots in his scrotum. That's enough to test the faith of even the most optimistic gospel spreaders (not to mention songwriters).

Yet in setting these dark elements to sunny melodies, *The Book of Mormon* achieves something like a miracle. It both makes fun of and ardently embraces the all-American art form of the inspirational book musical. No Broadway show has so successfully had it both ways since Mel Brooks adapted his film *The Producers* for the stage a decade ago. Directed by Casey Nicholaw and Mr. Parker, with choreography by Mr. Nicholaw, *The Book of Mormon* has its tasty cake (from an old family recipe) and eats it with sardonic relish.

If you know *South Park*, the 14-year-old animated sitcom about four naturally impious young lads, then you will know that Mr. Parker and Mr. Stone take a schoolboy's delight in throwing spitballs at things sacred, including most major religions. But you also may have gathered that these men take equal pleasure in the transcendent, cathartic goofiness of song-and-dance numbers. (As students they collaborated on the low-budget film *Cannibal! The Musical*, and their 1999 feature-length film, *South Park: Bigger, Longer & Uncut*, is one of the best movie musicals of recent years.)

As the composer of *Avenue Q*—which took public television–style teaching songs out of the kindergarten and put them into post-collegiate urban life—Mr. Lopez helped bring to Broadway young adults who had grown up on *Sesame Street*. And Mr. Nicholaw has demonstrated an affinity for savvy, high-energy musical pastiche with his work on shows like *Spamalot* and *The Drowsy Chaperone*.

Now, as a team, Messrs. Stone, Parker, Lopez and Nicholaw have created the ideal production for both the post–*Avenue Q* kids—the ones who wallow in the show tunes of *Glee* without shame and appear on YouTube lip-syncing to cast albums—and their older, less hip relatives. *The Book of Mormon* is utterly fluent in the language of musical entertainment from vaudeville to anthem-laden poperettas like *Les Misérables* and beyond. And it uses this vocabulary with a mixture of reverence and ridicule in which, I would say, reverence has the upper hand.

Which brings us, inevitably, to the issue of sacrilege. This show makes specific use of the teachings of the Mormon Church and especially of the ecclesiastical history from which the play takes its title. Church founders like Joseph Smith and Brigham Young appear in illustrative sequences, as does Jesus and an angel named Moroni. When delivered in musical-comedy style, these vignettes float into the high altitudes of absurdity.

But a major point of *The Book of Mormon* is that when looked at from a certain angle, all the forms of mythology and ritual that allow us to walk through the shadows of daily life and death are, on some level, absurd; that's what makes them so valiant and glorious. And by the way, that includes the religion of the musical, which lends ecstatic shape and symmetry to a world that often feels overwhelmingly formless.

All the folks involved in *Mormon* prove themselves worthy, dues-paying members of the church of Broadway. Whether evoking Salt Lake City–style spic-and-span-ness or squalid poverty in a drought-plagued village, Scott Pask's sets and Ann Roth's costumes have exactly the right heightened brightness, which stops short of the cartoonish. And as sung and danced, the production numbers have the pep and shimmer of yesteryear's showstoppers.

Set to eminently hummable melodies, Mr. Nicholaw's superb choreography (his best to date) manages to evoke the tap orgies of Busby Berkeley, the zoological pageantry of *The Lion King*, the calisthenic boogieing of latter-day Broadway and even Martha Graham–style Americana. These numbers are witty, ridiculous, impeccably executed, genuinely stirring and—contrary to expectation—free of snark or satirical malice.

Nearly all of them are surprising, and I don't want to give away much. But allow me to single out my personal favorites. "Turn It Off" is a hilarious chorus-line piece about repression, performed by the (all-male Mormon) missionaries and destined to make a star of its lead singer and dancer, Rory O'Malley (whose character is repressed in

his own special way). And then—oh, bliss—there's "Joseph Smith American Moses," a spirited, innocently obscenity-laden reworking of Jerome Robbins's "Small House of Uncle Thomas" sequence from *The King and I*.

The book is not quite on the level of the production numbers. (Isn't that always the way with musicals?) The fractious bromance between Elder Price (Mr. Rannells), a human Ken doll, and Elder Cunningham (Mr. Gad), a portly, hysteria-prone slob, will seem standard issue to anyone who has attended buddy comedy flicks since, oh, the 1980s. Mr. Gad's character, in the mold of Jack Black and Zach Galifianakis, is a variation on a screen type you can't get away from these days.

But Mr. Gad remains likable and funny (especially doing Bono in a number called "I Am Africa"), while Mr. Rannells makes brilliant use of his character's narcissism,

which isn't so far from the impulse that animates musical stage stars. As Nabulungi, the smart, dewy village girl who dreams of Salt Lake City, the sweet but savvy Nikki M. James gives a lovely, funny performance, never winking at her character's earnestness. And for combining polish, enthusiasm and individuality, the ensemble is the best in a musical since Susan Stroman's team for *The Producers*.

In a number that perfectly captures the essence of this happily paradoxical show, Mr. Rannells's character beards the den of the evil warlord (Brian Tyree Henry) and, much like Julie Andrews in *The Sound of Music*, sings radiantly of his faith and hope and determination. The warlord isn't buying any of it, and the priceless contrast between attitudes here is the difference between the world of musicals and the world of real life.

*The Book of Mormon* thoroughly understands this difference. This makes all the sweeter its celebration of the privilege, for just a couple of hours, of living inside that improbable paradise called a musical comedy.

. . . . . . . . . . . . . . . . . . . . . . . . . . . . . . .

**ABOVE:** Rema Webb, Andrew Rannells, and Josh Gad in *The Book of Mormon*.

LEFT: Andrew Rannells and Josh Gad (in white)
with members of the cast in a scene from *The Book
of Mormon*.

# CREDITS

The publisher, editors, and author wish especially to thank the following, without whose generosity and expertise this book would look much the poorer: Sara Krulwich, who created theater photography as an art and a specialty at the *New York Times*, and Phyllis Collazo, Heidi Giovine, William P. O'Donnell, Mary Hardiman, and Vin Alabiso, also at the *New York Times*; Ron Mandelbaum, Derek Davidson, and the staff of Photofest; Martha Swope, whose images are an institutional memory of Broadway during an astonishing five decades; David Leopold of the Al Hirschfeld Foundation; Harriet Culver, Van Bucher, and Eva Tucholka of Culver Pictures; and Joan Marcus.

© Bettmann/CORBIS: 2, 27, 58; Alfred Eisenstaedt/Time & Life Pictures/Getty Images: 95 (bottom left); Allan Grant/Time Life Pictures/Getty Images: 151; Archive Photos/Getty Images: 168; Bill Ray/Life Magazine/Time & Life Pictures/Getty Images: 236; Billy Rose Theatre Division, The New York Public Library for the Performing Arts: 11 (bottom left); 81. Clive Barda/ArenaPAL: 288–89; Clive Barda/*The New York Times*: 266; Courtesy of Rodgers & Hammerstein: An Imagem Company: 90, 91; Culver Pictures: 22, 23, 24, 34–35, 39, 45; Eileen Darby Images, Inc.: 149; Eileen Darby/Time & Life Pictures/Getty Images: 113 (top and bottom right), 114–15; Eileen Darby/Time Life Pictures/Getty Images: 105; Florence Vandamm/Museum of the City of New York/Vandamm Collection/Getty Images: 141; Frank Driggs Collection/Getty Images: 20; Friedman-Abeles: 160, 161, 170, 171, 172; George Karger/Pix Inc./Time Life Pictures/Getty Images: 88, 89, 98–99; Gjon Mili/Time Life Pictures/Getty Images: 96; Henry Groskinsky/Time Life Pictures/Getty Images: 42; Hulton Archive/Getty Images: 29, 49; Jerome Robbins Dance Division, The New York Public Library for the Performing Arts, Astor, Lenox, and Tilden Foundations: 11 (top left); Joan Marcus: 284, 291, 308, 310–11; John Dominis/Time Life Pictures/Getty Images: 194, 195; Mark Kauffman/Time Life Pictures/Getty Images: 199; Martha Swope © Billy Rose Theatre Division, The New York Public Library for the Performing Arts: 134, 238–39, 240, 241, 242, 243, 260–61, 264, 269, 270–71, 276, 277, 281, 282–83; Museum of the City of New York/Archive Photos/Getty Images: 140 (bottom); Museum of the City of New York/Getty Images: 54, 71, 92, 113 (bottom left); Museum of the City of New York/Vandamm Collection/Getty Images: 140

(top); Music Division, The New York Public Library for the Performing Arts, Astor, Lenox, and Tilden Foundations: 21, 25, 26, 31; Peter Stackpole/Time Life Pictures/Getty Images: 152; Photofest: 6–7, 12, 13, 14, 28, 32–33, 36, 38, 40–41, 46, 47, 48, 50, 51, 52–53, 60, 61, 63, 64, 65, 67, 68–69, 70, 72, 75, 76–77, 78–79, 80, 82, 84, 85, 95 (bottom right), 100, 101, 102–3, 106, 107, 108–9, 111, 116–17, 118, 119, 120, 121, 123, 125, 128, 133, 136, 137, 138–39, 142, 143, 144, 145, 148, 154, 155, 156–57, 158–59, 162, 163, 164, 165, 166–67, 173, 175, 178, 179, 180, 182, 183, 184, 188, 190, 191, 197, 198, 201, 202, 203, 204–5, 206, 209, 210, 211, 212, 213, 214–15, 223, 224, 227, 229, 230–31, 235, 237, 244, 248–49, 250, 254, 256–57, 259, 272–73, 274, 275, 287, 293, 294, 295, 297, 299; Popperfoto/Getty Images: 30; Ralph Morse/Pix Inc./Time Life Pictures/Getty Images: 93; Ralph Morse/Time Life Pictures/Getty Images: 122, 219; Ray Fisher/Time Life Pictures/Getty Images: 174; Sara Krulwich/*The New York Times*: 8–9, 15, 73, 126, 127, 146, 147, 176, 177, 186, 187, 216, 217, 220, 221, 233, 253, 262–63, 278, 279, 290, 301, 302, 305, 306–7, 312, 315, 316, 317, 318–19, 321, 322, 324, 327, 328, 331, 332–33, 335, 336–37, 338, 339, 340, 343, 345, 346, 347, 348, 349, 351, 353, 354, 357, 358–59; Sasha/Getty Images: 56, 57; *The New York Times*: 16, 87, 135, 193, 247; Topical Press Agency/Getty Images: 37; Vandamm Studio © Billy Rose Theatre Division, The New York Public Library for the Performing Arts: 66, 83, 95 (top); Vincent Laforet/*The New York Times*: 130; White Studio © Billy Rose Theatre Division, The New York Public Library for the Performing Arts: 11 (right).

## AL HIRSCHFELD

Al Hirschfeld's drawings stand as one of the most innovative efforts in establishing the visual language of modern art through caricature in the twentieth century. A self-described "characterist," Hirschfeld's signature work, defined by a linear calligraphic style, appeared in virtually every major publication of the last nine decades, including almost every other week in the *New York Times* for seventy five years. The illustrations listed below appear in *Broadway Musicals: From the Pages of the New York Times*. The dates in which they were published in the *Times* are noted.

*Lady in the Dark* with Gertrude Lawrence, Danny Kaye, and Victor Mature, February 23, 1941; *On the Town* with Betty Comden, Adolph Green, Chris Alexander, Nancy Walker, John Battles, and Sono

Osato, December 24, 1944; Ethel Merman in *Annie Get Your Gun*, April 21, 1946; *South Pacific* with Myron McCormick, Mary Martin, and Ezio Pinza, April 3, 1949; *Gentlemen Prefer Blondes* with Carol Channing, Jack McCauley, Eric Brotherson, George S. Irving, and Yvonne Adair, December 4, 1949; Douglas Deane, Tom Pedi, Stubby Kaye, Johnny Silver, Robert Alda, Sam Levene, B. S. Pully, Vivian Blaine, Pat Rooney Sr., and Isabel Bigley in *Guys and Dolls*, November 19, 1950: 132; *Peter Pan* with Mary Martin, Cyril Ritchard, Richard Wyatt, and Don Lurio, October 17, 1954; *Damn Yankees* with Gwen Verdon, Ray Walston, and Stephen Douglass, May 5, 1955; *The Music Man* with Robert Preston, David Burns, Helen Raymond, Pert Kelton, and Barbara Cook, December 15, 1957; *How to Succeed in Business without Really Trying* with Virginia Martin, Rudy Vallee, Robert Morse, and Bonnie Scott, October 8, 1961; Barbra Streisand in *Funny Girl*, March 22, 1964; The cast of *Hair*, April 14, 1968; *Follies* with Alexis Smith, Fifi D'Orsay, Ethel Shutta, Dorothy Collins, Mary McCarty, and Yvonne De Carlo, April 4, 1971; *Chicago* with Chita Rivera, Jerry Orbach, and Gwen Verdon, June 8, 1975; *Sweeney Todd* with Sarah Rice, Victor Garber, Joaquin Romaguera, Len Cariou, Angela Lansbury, Jack Eric Williams, and Edmund Lyndeck, February 25, 1979; *Rent* with Daphne Rubin-Vega, Taye Diggs, Fredi Walker, Adam Pascal, Wilson Jermaine Heredia, Anthony Rapp, Idina Menzel, and Jesse L. Martin, April 28, 1996; and Mel Brooks oversees *The Producers* with Nathan Lane, Matthew Broderick, Brad Oscar, Gary Beach, and Cady Huffman, April 15, 2001.

© The Al Hirschfeld Foundation. www.AlHirschfeldFoundation.org. Al Hirschfeld is represented by the Margo Feiden Galleries Ltd., New York.

# INDEX

**ON THE CASE:** A scene from the original Broadway production of *The King and I*, 1951.

**PAGE 2:** Robert Alda helps Isabel Bigley put her name in lights on the billing for *Guys and Dolls*, 46th Street Theatre marquee, New York, 1951.

**PAGES 6–7:** The Majestic Theatre, New York, c. 1949.

**PAGES 8–9:** A scene from the Broadway production of *The Producers*, 2001.

Editors' Note: Many of the reviews and feature articles in this book originally appeared in a longer version.

Project Manager: Eric Himmel
Editors: Susan Homer and Caitlin Kenney
Designer: Sarah Gifford
Production Manager: Ankur Ghosh

Library of Congress Cataloging-in-Publication Data
Broadway musicals / Ben Brantley.
    pages cm
 ISBN 978-1-4197-0337-9
1.  Musicals—New York (State)—New York—History and criticism.
2.  Musical theater—New York (State)—New York—Reviews. I.
Brantley, Ben, writer of added commentary. II. New York times.
 ML1711.8.N3N62 2012
 792.6'45097471—dc23

            2012006411

Printed and bound in China
10 9 8 7 6 5 4 3 2 1

Abrams books are available at special discounts when purchased in quantity for premiums and promotions as well as fundraising or educational use. Special editions can also be created to specification. For details, contact specialsales@abramsbooks.com or the address below.

THE ART OF BOOKS SINCE 1949
115 West 18th Street
New York, NY 10011
www.abramsbooks.com